# Theory and Methods in Political Science

### Edited by
### David Marsh
### and
### Gerry Stoker

First published in Great Britain 1995 by
**MACMILLAN PRESS LTD**
Houndmills, Basingstoke, Hampshire RG21 6XS
and London
Companies and representatives
throughout the world

A catalogue record for this book is available from the British
Library.

ISBN 0–333–61460–7 hardcover
ISBN 0–333–61461–5 paperback

 First published in the United States of America 1997 by
**ST. MARTIN'S PRESS, INC.,**
Scholarly and Reference Division,
175 Fifth Avenue, New York, N.Y. 10010

ISBN 0–312–12761–8 (cloth)
ISBN 0–312–12762–6 (paper)

This book is printed on paper suitable for recycling and made from fully
managed and sustained forest sources.

10   9   8   7   6
05   04   03   02   01   00

Printed and bound in Great Britain by Creative Print and Design (Wales), Ebbw Vale

# Contents

## PART 2   METHODOLOGICAL QUESTIONS

# List of Tables and Figures

## ■ Tables

## ■ Figures

# Notes on the Contributors

**Jenny Chapman** is Senior Lecturer in Politics at the University of Strathclyde. Her main interests are in feminism, empirical research and the post-Communist politics of Central Europe. Her book *Politics, Feminism and the Reformation of Gender* combined the first two interests in a comparative study of political recruitment and feminist strategies for fundamental change. She is engaged at present in a comparative empirical study of the hopes, expectations and political values of young people in Scotland and Central Europe.

**Fiona Devine** is Lecturer in Sociology at the University of Manchester. She is the author of *Affluent Workers Revisited* (1992) and is currently writing a book on social class in America and Britain, to be published in 1996.

**Mark Evans** is Lecturer in Politics at the University of York. He is the author of *Charter 88: A Successful Challenge to the British Political Tradition?* (1995) and his recent publications include articles on constitutional doctrine and revisionism in Britain.

**Daryl Glaser** obtained an M.A. in Sociology from the University of the Witwatersrand and a Ph.D. in politics from the University of Manchester. He lectures at the University of Strathclyde. He has published a number of articles on South African politics, and is currently working on a book on the subject. His principal area of research and writing is democratic theory.

**Colin Hay** is Lecturer and Research Officer in the Department of Sociology at Lancaster University. He has published widely in political sociology, social and political theory, and the theory of the state. He is currently completing an introduction to state theory, *Re-Stating Social and Political Change* (1995); and a co-edited book (with Bob Jessop) *Beyond the State? Recent Developments in State Theory* (1995).

**David Howarth** has completed a Ph.D. on the construction of black identity in South Africa in the Ideology and Discourse Theory Programme, Department of Government, University of Essex.

**Tom Mackie** is Senior Lecturer in Government at Strathclyde University. He is the co-author of the *International Almanac of Electoral History* and the *Europe Votes* series. His main research interests are in the fields of political parties and elections and he is currently researching parties and elections in post-Communist Eastern Europe and contemporary Italy.

**David Marsh** is Professor of Politics at the University of Strathclyde. He has published a large number of books and articles including recently *The New Politics of British Trade Unionism* (1992). He has edited four collections including (with R. A. W. Rhodes) *Policy Networks in British Politics* (1992).

**W. L. Miller** is Edward Caird Professor in Politics at the University of Glasgow. He has directed a series of surveys in Scotland, Britain, Central Europe and the successor states to the former Soviet Union, interviewing local and national politicians as well as members of the general public.

**R. A. W. Rhodes** is Professor of Politics at the University of Newcastle. He is the author of many books and articles, including *Public Administration and Policy Analysis* (1979); *Control and Power in Central–Local Relations* (1981); *The National World of Local Government* (1986); and *Beyond Westminster and Whitehall* (1988). He has been editor of *Public Administration* since 1986. Recently he has published four edited collections including (with David Marsh) *Implementing Thatcherite Policies: Audit of an Era* (1992).

**David Sanders** is Professor in the Department of Government of the University of Essex. He is the author of a large number of books and articles on international relations, methodology and British politics, including: *Losing an Empire, Finding a Role: British Foreign Policy Since 1945* (1990). He is joint editor of the *British Journal of Political Science*.

**Martin Smith** is Lecturer in Politics at the University of Sheffield. He has written widely on British politics, agricultural policy, comparative public policy and pluralism. His books include *Pressure, Power and Policy* (1993) and *Contemporary British Conservatism* (1995), the latter edited jointly with Steve Ludlam.

**Gerry Stoker** is Professor of Politics at the University of Strathclyde. He is the author of a large number of books and articles in the fields of local governance and urban politics including: *The Politics of Local Goverment* (1991); (edited, with John Stewart) *Local Government in the 1990s* (1995); (edited, with D. Judge and H. Wolman) *Theories of Urban Politics* (1995).

**George Taylor** is Director of the Centre for the Study of Public Policy at the University of Galway. He is the author of a number of articles on state theory, public policy and the British coal industry. He has just completed a book on the *Politics of Privatising British Coal*.

**Hugh Ward** is a Senior Lecturer in the Department of Government at the University of Essex. His recent research has focused on applications of rational choice theory to global environmental problems, democratic stability, and the fairness of electoral systems. He is currently working with David Marsh on the application of rational choice theory and evolutionary explanation to the theory of the state.

# Introduction
## Gerry Stoker

The purpose of this book is to examine the scope, content and methods of the discipline of political science and provide a guide to its key theoretical debates. To this end Part 1 of the book identifies various approaches to the study of politics; Part 2 reviews core methodological questions addressed by political scientists; and Part 3 looks at competing theories of the state and political power.

The decision to develop the book was motivated by three factors. First, political scientists have not been, in general, sufficiently reflective about the nature and scope of their discipline. They just do it rather than talk about it. Such an approach is in many ways healthy. However, the case for setting out explicitly the core features of political science has become increasingly compelling as the outside world increasingly demands evaluations of both its teaching and research.

The aim of this book is to provide an overview and systematic assessment of the main theoretical and methodological issues involved in the study of politics in a form accessible to students but also thought provoking for teachers and researchers. As most of the contributors are British, the focus of the book is on the literature and debates which have been particularly influential in the United Kingdom. Many of the illustrations or applications of arguments inevitably make reference to British experience. Yet this is not an insular book. We trust that readers from a range of countries will find the book attractive in offering a perspective on political science that is broader than that offered in many American texts. Our book provides a striking testament to the cosmopolitanism of British political science and the breadth of its international engagement with a wide range of perspectives and debates.

A second motivation for the book flows from the cosmopolitan character of our understanding of political science. Recognition of the huge growth in research and publication under the umbrella of political science makes the case for a guide to its variety and complexity. The American Political Science Association (APSA) founded in 1903 had in the 1990s close to 13 000 members from the United States of America and 70 other countries (APSA, 1994). The European Consortium for Political

Research started out with eight participants in its network in 1970 and by the mid-1990s there were about 200 participating institutions. The Political Studies Association of the United Kingdom was founded in 1950 with about 100 members. In the mid-1990s its membership stood at over 1100.

Decades of growth have seen political scientists adopt more diversified approaches and define more specialised fields of investigation than ever before. In mid-1960s W. J. M. Mackenzie wrote his 400 + page review of the academic study of politics and its development during the 1950s and 1960s *Politics and Social Science* in one sabbatical term. The book is broad in its scope and impressive in the range of literature reviewed. Mackenzie (1967) notes the break from the traditional study of institutions towards a more diverse discipline informed by behavioural studies and quantitative techniques. He goes on to review the contribution of Marxism, systems theory, game theory and the economic approach to the study of politics, as well as introducing insights from social biology and social physiology. It is impossible to imagine any single individual writing such a book in the mid-1990s, especially in such a short period of time! Today even to keep up with the literature in two or three sub-fields is a challenge for most ordinary mortals. In this context this book aims to offer a guide to developments in the discipline and the range of new and fascinating directions in the study of politics which will be an aid to students, researchers and academic practitioners alike.

A third motivation for the book was a view that the time was ripe for an assessment of recent developments in the study of politics as well as an examination of how the discipline should develop in the future. What emerges from the chapters in this book is how much core approaches such as institutional analysis or behaviouralism have adapted and changed in the light of critical comment and reflection by practitioners. Equally innovations in methods can be observed. Theories of the state and power also show much shifting of ground and argument on the part of the various traditions.

An adequate assessment of the various aspects of the discipline of political science requires a judgement to be made on the current state of the debate rather than an easy dismissal of a range of simplistic 'Aunt Sallys'. Behaviouralists in the 1990s do not take the view that the facts speak for themselves. Institutionalists do not view the formal and legal features of organisations as determining their character. Pluralists do not think that power is distributed equally in society. By providing an up-to-date account of various positions and arguments within political science this book can provide the basis for a sophisticated assessment.

In this Introduction we set ourselves a number of tasks: the first is to clarify and defend our understanding of the nature of political science; the second is to introduce the various approaches to political science identified in the book; the third takes up the issue of methodological challenges; and the final task is to outline the purposes of theory in political science.

# ■ What is political science?

The British have always been a bit uneasy about using the term 'political science'. The London School of Economics (LSE) was opened in London in 1895 as a school of economics and political science. However, British universities throughout the twentieth century have veered away from this nomenclature, preferring to use titles such as government, politics, political theory and institutions, or politics and international relations. The UK has a Political *Studies* Association rather in contrast to the American Political *Science* Association. The coyness about using the term 'science' undoubtedly reflects the special status claimed by natural scientists for their discipline and the disdain for the social *sciences* occasionally expressed by leading politicians. The most infamous illustration of the low esteem that some politicians have for the social sciences is the late Sir Keith Joseph's insistence that the United Kingdom's Social Science Research Council, the leading official funder of research, be renamed the Economic and Social Research Council (ESRC).

The choice of the title for this book – *Theory and Methods in Political Science* – is deliberate. It expresses a commitment to recapturing the term 'science' to describe all organised academic disciplines. The word 'science' is 'derived from the Latin *scientia* meaning simply knowledge acquired by study' (Potter *et al.*, 1981, p. 7). Following Mackenzie (1967, p. 17) we refer to political science to indicate 'simply that there exists an academic tradition of the study of politics, a discipline communicated from teacher to pupil, by speech and writing'. The discipline does not copy the methods of the natural sciences because they would not be appropriate. It offers 'organised knowledge' and demands of its practitioners certain intellectual disciplines in debate.

Above all, the discipline of political science rests its claim on the tenet that all knowledge is public and subject to challenge. There are no hidden truths and no purveyors of truth that can never be wrong. Political science demands from its practitioners that they produce arguments and evidence that will convince others.

> Emotional attachments, personal hunches and intuitive understanding do not adequately justify knowledge claims . . . Logical coherence and adequate evidence are the most widely accepted criteria by which we judge claims to knowledge (Zuckerman, 1991, p. 3).

Political science demands logical coherence. This implies precise and clear definitions of key concepts and justified derivations. Arguments should be constructed in a way that avoids inconsistencies and vagueness. Political science also demands a commitment to assessing whether the evidence assembled to support a proposition is adequate to the task. As will become clear, different approaches within political science emphasise different types of evidence, but none denies the *need* for evidence. Even in the case of political theory, arguments are often grounded in textual analysis, or normative principles are illustrated in practice.

Having provided a claim to the title 'science', the reader might think that task of this section is almost complete. Unfortunately this is not the case. If 'science' is a loaded word, then so too is 'political'. As Heywood (1994, p. 16) comments:

> Most academic study starts with a discussion of what the subject itself is about, usually provoked by asking a question such as 'What is Physics?', 'What is History?' or 'What is Economics?'. Such discussions have the virtue of letting students know what they are in for: what they are about to study and what issues and topics are going to be raised. Unfortunately for the student of politics, however, the question 'What is Politics?' is more likely to generate confusion than bring comfort or reassurance. The problem with politics is that debate, controversy and disagreement lie at its very heart, and the definition of 'the political' is no exception.

The expansion of political science has been accompanied by demands to widen the scope of its study. The chapters reviewing approaches to the study of political science in Part 1 of this book offer progressively wider definitions of what is 'political'. In Britain, traditional institutional studies which directed attention towards parliament and the Civil Service were challenged from the 1950s onwards to widen their scope in order to analyse elections, the mass public political parties and pressure groups. Political scientists adopting a behavioural approach can claim much of the credit for this expansion in the coverage of political science. As Gamble (1990, p. 412) comments:

> What behavioural methods have . . . done . . . is to advance the study of mass political behaviour and widen the definition of things political. The breach in the wall made by behaviouralism has been followed by other broader methodological approaches.

The 1970s and 1980s saw pressure to widen the definition of political still further. Dearlove and Saunders (1984) argue for a political science that pays attention to the non-democratic aspects of politics and places politics within the context of the social and economic environment. The demand was for a political science that took into account a wider range of institutions and related the analysis of politics to the concerns of other disciplines, especially economics and sociology.

Feminist writers took the argument a further step forward. Politics cannot be confined to a narrowly-defined range of public issues such as the economy or foreign affairs. Writing from a feminist perspective, Jenny Chapman argues in Chapter 5 that 'Politics is about *all* decisions that shape our lives, not only those made in a restricted arena conventionally defined as "politics'.' Private matters can become public matters. As Heller (1991, pp. 340-1) argues, 'The "political" becomes actually political if men and women so desire that it should be discussed, contested, decided in the public domain . . . No-one and nothing is excluded in principle.' In most Western democracies, for example, the negative experiences of some women in relation to male violence in the home is no longer seen as a private issue but rather as a matter for political discussion and action in the public arena.

Political science in the 1990s sees the political in a much broader way. As Gamble puts it:

> The political has come to be defined . . . to embrace other areas of social life such as gender, race and class. Politics has come to be understood as an aspect of all social relations, rather than an activity centred on the institutions of government. (Gamble, 1990, p. 412)

Leftwich (1984) argues that to confirm the drift away from a focus on the institutions of government the academic discipline of politics should adopt a process definition of politics. Politics, he argues, should be defined not in terms of an arena or set of institutions in which certain activities take place, but rather in terms of a generalised process within human societies.

> Politics is not a separate realm of public life and activity. On the contrary, politics comprises all the activities of co-operation and conflict, within and between societies, whereby the human species goes about organising the use, production and distribution of human, natural and other resources in the course of the production and reproduction of its biological and social life. (Leftwich, 1984, pp. 64-5)

Politics occurs throughout society: from family groups to the state, and from the voluntary association to the multinational corporation. Politics involves conflict and co-operation and reflects and indeed influences the structure of society.

Politics is a collective activity. As Anderson (1977, p. vii) comments:

> In essence, we act politically whenever we make decisions on behalf of other people and not for ourselves alone. Politics means planning and organising common projects, setting rules and standards that define the relationships of people to one another, and allocating resources among rival human needs and purposes.

It is easy to accept the claim that political activity of this form might be observed in the family, voluntary organisation and multinational corporations as well as in political parties and government.

Leftwich (1984, pp. 83-4) concludes that broadening the definition of politics demands a shift away from the identification of political science with the study of government and public affairs, to a focus on 'the politics of everyday life'. Students should be encouraged to study more systematically 'all groups and institutions they may be familiar with or interested in, whether it be in their families, clubs, departments, colleges, offices and factories'. By seeking 'to expand the study and understanding of politics in human societies' Leftwich's aim is to 'help prevent the discipline of Politics from withering, stagnating or becoming irrelevant'.

There is much of value in Leftwich's argument, but it would be a mistake for political science to go down the route he proposes towards an undifferentiated 'study of the politics of everyday life'. Politics is an aspect of all social relations, but as political scientists we should recognise that its practice in some arenas is more relevant and challenging. In particular politics has a special character in the arena of public affairs and government in relation to the making and determination of allocations or decisions through institutions which claim a legitimate authority. It is a collective, binding and justified activity whose special character makes a strong claim to be at the core of political science (see Crick, 1993).

In more abstract terms, we need a combination of both an arena and a process definition of the subject matter of political science. As a process of conflict and co-operation over the resources necessary to the production and reproduction of our lives, politics is an ubiquitous activity. Yet the discipline of politics should give special consideration to how that process is resolved in the act of government – in particular how issues reach and leave the governmental agenda and how, within that arena, issues are discussed, contested and decided.

The special character of government becomes clearer once it is seen as part of the modern state. Governments seek to provide orderly rule and they do so in a variety of different ways and institutional forms in the context of the powerful and extensive entity of the modern state. As Heywood (1994, p. 37) comments:

> The state is best thought of not just as a set of institutions but as a particular kind of political association, specifically one that establishes sovereign jurisdiction within defined territorial boundaries . . . The state commands supreme power in that it stands above all other associations and groups in society; its laws demand the compliance of all those who live within the territory.

The state, in the abstract, stands apart from civil society, but through the processes of politics and the practice of government the state and civil society have a complex, controversial and disputed relationship. It is precisely because of the centrality of the state to political science that in the final part of this book we examine a number of rival theories of the state.

Much political activity is managed at the interface of state and society. Not all politics, however, results in compromise and consensus. Sometimes the conflict is so sharp that violence, civil war and revolution become political instruments. In these circumstances the relatively orderly pursuit of politics gives way to more chaotic and more brutal forms. All forms of politics should be within the scope of political science. When studying constitutional, humdrum politics its latent potential to take more violent and dramatic forms should not be forgotten.

To summarise the view of political science that informs this book: by science we mean the organised production of knowledge that demands of its practitioners certain intellectual disciplines, in particular, logical coherence and adequate evidence. Politics is a wide spread activity which occurs in all arenas where human beings are engaged in the production and reproduction of their lives. It can involve conflict and co-operation, leading to the raising and resolution of issues through collective decision-making. Political science is an academic discipline which seeks systematically to describe, analyse and explain collective decision-making and the values and perspectives that underlie it. However, political science should pay particular attention to the collective arena constituted by the operation of government in the modern state because of the particular form of extensive and compulsory authority embodied within its activities. It should also recognise that if 'normal' politics breaks down, political activity can take a variety of more violent and brutal forms.

#  The diversity of approaches to political science

From what has been argued so far, it should be clear that political science is not 'a hard and fast area of study whose character and scope we have to take for granted, or assume to be unchanging or permanent' (Leftwich 1984, p. 4). The discipline of political science, to put it bluntly, is defined by those who do it. It should not come as a surprise to any reader that if there is some dispute and disagreement among practitioners about what political science is there is also a dispute about how to do it. Zuckerman (1991, p. 13) refers to the 'cacophonous sound of political science'. He goes on to note that political scientists 'display deep conflicts over appropriate assumptions, foci and methods of analysis, and they offer hypotheses and theories that directly contradict one another. They frequently describe the same phenomenon but offer very different analyses of it. They may even observe the world in different ways'. Political science is characterised by a diversity of approaches.

In Part 1 of this book, six 'approaches' to political science are identified. Other people have used the term 'schools' (Leftwich, 1984, p. 5; Zuckerman, 1991, ch. 3). 'Approaches' is our choice because the term 'schools' creates an exaggerated sense of cohesion and order within the various sub-divisions of political science. The approaches that we identify do, however, guide practitioners towards different ways of doing political science. They answer questions about the core subject matter to be addressed; the mode by which evidence should be obtained; the nature of the theoretical enterprise that should be undertaken; and offer diverse underlying assumptions about the nature and dynamics of politics. Some of the key characteristics of our six approaches to political science are presented in Table 1, accompanied by an assessment of their status within the discipline.

The choice of six approaches can be explained in terms of the evolution of the discipline. Normative theory and institutional studies are the 'twin pillars' of traditional political science (Held and Leftwich, 1984, p. 147) and despite 'reports of their death' remain central to the discipline. The first approach – normative theory – has an extremely long lineage within the study of politics. It is widely perceived to have suffered a decline in the 1950s and 1960s but to have bounced back since the 1970s. Writing in 1990, Miller concludes: 'There has been an upsurge of interest in the subject and confidence in its practitioners. Its standing within the political studies community as a whole seems also to have increased (p. 421).

Normative political theory is concerned with the discovery and application of moral notions in the sphere of political relations and practice. As Daryl Glaser shows in Chapter 1, doubts about this branch of the discipline devoted to the examination of what 'ought to be' have been expressed in several quarters. In broad terms, some have questioned the value of such debate and seen it as a pointless exercise producing tautological propositions that are true by definition but not in any wider sense. Others have questioned whether human agents are capable of moral choices. Yet political scientists have responded to these challenges to re-establish the claim strongly that normative theory can offer a rigorous and developed way of addressing the options open to human beings.

The study of political institutions is concerned with the rules, procedures and formal organisations of the political system and their impact on political practice. Historically, the strength of the institutional approach in political science reflects the influence of law, philosophy and historical studies in its development as an autonomous field of study. Much of the work of traditional institutional studies has rightly been subject to criticism for the weakness of its methods, the anti-theoretical, descriptive nature of its product, and an underlying prescriptive perspective based on an idealised conception of the virtues of liberal democratic government. Yet, as R. A. W. Rhodes argues in Chapter 2, the institutional approach has not disappeared as a result of these criticisms, but rather its substantive focus on the core institutions of the state and its reformulation in a variety of ways has ensured its continued centrality to the discipline of political science.

Behavioural and rational choice theory constitute more recent but well-established approaches within the discipline of political science. Indeed, in the USA the behavioural approach is dominant within the discipline. Its impact in Britain and continental Europe has been substantial but it remains one of many approaches. Behaviouralism concentrates on explaining political behaviour at the individual and aggregate level. In the 1950s and 1960s, behaviouralists were often highly critical of the traditional twin pillars of political science. Institutional studies were seen as being descriptive and lacking in rigour, and their focus on institutions less relevant than a focus on behaviour. The rules and regulations of institutions tell us what people should do, but as political scientists we should be interested in the way they in fact behave, in practice. Behaviouralists also made great play of the need to separate facts from values. Normative political theory was seen as being concerned with values and as such considered to be a rather pointless activity, an expression of various opinions but an approach incapable of providing evidence to resolve matters of dispute. The behaviouralists of the 1950s and 1960s expressed a preference for theory derived from 'the facts' and therefore beyond dispute. Their claim was to offer a new 'scientific' approach to the study of politics through the production of a series of laws or generalisations.

As David Sanders points out in Chapter 3, under criticism and challenge behaviouralism has backed away from some of the claims of its early advocates. In particular, the simplistic understanding of the facts/values distinction has been abandoned. Behaviouralists now acknowledge that facts do not speak for themselves but only make sense in the context of a framework of investigation. Ideas about what is important and the way things work structure all observations. Theory and fact are not independent of one another. Further claims to value-free analysis have been played down. The pluralist assumptions behind much earlier behaviouralist work is recognised. The claim to be able to derive 'scientific' laws and generalisations has also been watered down. Modern behaviouralism is more sophisticated in its approach and modest in its claims. Yet behaviouralism remains a strong force within political science. It distinctive character is provided by its focus on individual behaviour and a concern to generate causal and falsifiable theory. As Sanders suggests the pivotal behavioural question is: How would you know if your analysis was incorrect?

Rational choice theory has also established a strong following since the mid-1950s. The underlying assumption is that political behaviour can be understood as the result of choices made by self-interested individuals. Rational choice studies have sought to illuminate issues throughout the field of political science, from electoral competition to bureaucratic behaviour. A variety of rational choice literatures have been established, including game theory, social choice theory and public choice theory. The latter particularly has a strong, normative, anti-state, New Right thrust to many of its arguments. As Hugh Ward demonstrates in Chapter 4 the

**Table 1** *Approaches to political science*

| | *Subject matter* | *Methodological orientation* | *Nature of theory* | *Perspective on state and politics* | *Status within discipline* |
|---|---|---|---|---|---|
| Normative theory | The discovery and application of moral notions in the sphere of political relations and practice. | Deductive. Analytical. | Normative. Evaluative. Prescriptive. | Dominant liberal paradigm but no overarching perspective. | Strong tradition. If approach can meet positivist, relativist and determinist challenges, has a central role in addressing options open to human beings in rigorous and informed way. |
| Institutional studies | Rules, procedures and formal organisation of the political system and their impact on political practice. | Inductive. Relativist. Qualitative but not in all cases. | Normative. Prescriptive. Evaluative. Empirical. | In traditional phase promoted liberal democratic model of government and conservative attitudes to reform. In modern variant explicitly multitheoretical. | Abandoning of traditional political perspective and increasing methodological sophistication is giving approach a continuing role. Strong future role premised on recognition of the centrality of the state to politics. |
| Behavioural analysis | Explanation of political behaviour at the individual and aggregate level. | Tends to use aggregate data and quantitative analysis. In modern form recognition given to role of theory in generating hypotheses. Insists that central purpose of enquiry is to explain what is observed. Positivist undertones. | Empirical. Causal. Capable of generating falsifiable predictions. | Early claims of value free theory abandoned. In modern variant explicitly multitheoretical. | Early excessive claims of behaviouralists giving way to more modest and sophisticated analysis. Central commitment to idea of causality and empirical falsifiable theory building gives distinctive flavour and strength. |

| | | | | | |
|---|---|---|---|---|---|
| Rational choice theory | Social and political choices made by rational, self-interested individuals. | Deductive reasoning, leading to predictions and empirical theory. Positivist undertones. | Empirical. Predictive. Prescriptive. | Dominant but not inherent New Right paradigm. In modern variant explicitly multitheoretical. | Established as an approach which provides a useful way of investigating the conditions for collective choice. Needs to develop further capacity to deal with complex and uncertain decision-making conditions and non-egoistic motivations. |
| Feminism | The impact of and challenge to patriarchy. | Relativist, favouring qualitatve methods. Some attacks on quantitative methods and calls for an alternative feminist methodology. A fruitless and unnecessary search. | Normative. Prescriptive. Evaluative. Empirical. | Seeks to feminise debate and broaden definition of the political. | Recognised perspective and has had limited impact. Potential is substantial if it avoids the excesses of post-modernism. |
| Discourse analysis | How discourses – structures of meaning – make possible certain action. How these discourses are produced, function and change. | Relativist: dissolves distinction between realm of ideas and realm of real objects by viewing all objects and practices as meaningful only as part of a particular discourse. | Empirical. | Gives a primacy to politics, given that all practices are ultimately the product of political forces in conflict seeking to impose their ideas. Tendency towards elitist or marxist interpretations. | On the fringes of political science: high level of abstraction and generality in explanations a difficulty. Key contribution is focus on the structuring of social meaning as a political act. |

rational choice approach has been subject to a number of criticisms. He proposes that, if the approach is to develop, it needs to be both more modest in its claims, and more adventurous. The nature of human beings – their psychological complexity and frequent irrationality – suggests there are limits to the approach. Yet because individuals do make efforts at rational decision-making relative to their goals, considerable scope for the approach exists. Rational choice theory needs to develop further a capacity to examine choice-making under conditions of limited information and uncertainty. Scope for non-egoistic and moral motivations should be given. It should also be emphasised that the New Right premises associated with the public choice variant are not inherent in the approach. The rational choice approach has drawn (and should continue to draw) on a range of theoretical traditions. Its status is as a useful element in the 'tool kit' of political scientists.

The final pairing in terms of our identification of approaches to political science – feminism and discourse analysis – provide an important challenge to more established approaches. While both approaches can claim antecedents in the evolution of the discipline they have only come to the fore from the 1970s onwards.

The impact of feminism has in some respects been considerable. It has stimulated much rethinking in the more established elements of political science. Orthodox perspectives in normative theory and in the empirical studies of institutionalists and behaviouralists have been challenged and forced into a recognition of previous gender-blindness. Feminism has been instrumental in widening the scope (and understanding the nature) of political science, yet, as Jenny Chapman argues in Chapter 5, it still remains on the margins of the discipline. This partly reflects the 'dynamic conservatism' of mainstream political science which has displayed a capacity to incorporate elements of the feminist critique while retaining much of its original orientation. It also reflects the failure of some advocates of the feminist perspective to provide a sharp, empirical cutting edge to their work. The potential contribution of feminism to political science, however, remains considerable.

Discourse analysis has had less impact than has feminism. It offers an important link with post-modernism for political science because it sees the structuring of social meaning as the central political act. Discourse studies examine the way systems of meaning or 'discourses' shape the way people understand their position and their political activity. According to this approach, the production, functioning and changing of 'discourses' should be a focus of study because it provides a powerful tool for understanding the dynamics and character of politics in complex societies. Few political scientists would dispute the validity of such claims or deny the importance of language, symbols and the structuring of political debates. What remains unclear, however, is how far discourse analysis, which often operates at a high level of generality and abstraction, can tackle such concerns effectively. David Howarth in Chapter 6 provides a relatively optimistic assessment of the potential for discourse analysis.

This section has identified six approaches to political science. Some may be surprised by the omission of Marxism from the list. The contribution of Marxist thinking is considered at various points in the book, most notably in Chapter 13 with respect to Marxist theories of the state. We are sympathetic to the line of argument which suggests that Marxism has been instrumental in encouraging the broadening of the scope of political science discussed earlier (Berki, 1986) as the relationship of politics to wider economic and social forces is a central theme of Marxist writers. It is difficult, however, to include Marxism as a distinctive approach within political science because the thrust of its argument is to challenge the existence of political science as a separate discipline. As Callinicos (1984) argues, the historical materialism of Marxism demands a holistic approach cutting across disciplinary boundaries. Marxism disqualifies itself 'from being merely another approach to the study of politics' and 'makes claims that are obviously incompatible with the notion of an autonomous discipline of Politics' (Callinicos, 1984, p. 124). This is not to deny that the work of political scientists has been influenced by Marxist thought, and indeed many would accept the challenge laid down by Marxism to relate developments in politics to developments within the social totality. Marxist analysis of society plainly has implications for the study of politics, but it is inappropriate to include it as a separate approach to the subject.

# ■ Methodological issues and challenges

The six approaches to political science we identify are associated with particular ways of producing knowledge; that is, they have a certain methodological orientation. In the study of political science it is important to be aware of the methodological choices that are available. The challenge involves more than coping with the demands raised by a range of research techniques, although this is a considerable task in itself. The issue of methods brings into focus questions of broader philosophical concern. How can we know the social world? What counts as an adequate explanation of a social phenomenon? Part 2 of the book explores both the practical/technical and broader philosophical challenges confronting political science.

In debating the production of knowledge, political scientists use terms that may not be familiar to all readers; these terms are used as shorthand for describing complex understandings of the social world. An *ontological position* refers to a view about the nature of social existence and social beings. An *epistemology* expresses a view about how we know what we know and in particular about what constitutes an adequate explanation of a political event or process. Different broad ontological and epistemological positions inform different methodological orientations or preferences. The various approaches to political science that we have identified tend to prefer and find valuable different ways of knowing the world.

Several concepts are particularly worth introducing at this stage because they are used in chapters throughout the book; these concepts express different attitudes towards knowing the world. They are distinctive positions within a wide spectrum of opinion. *Positivists* hold that it is possible to know the world through experience and observation; the truth or otherwise of a statement can be determined through systematic empirical observation. Positivist political science would examine the available data and claim to produce general and sustainable propositions about political behaviour. *Critical realists* primarily see knowledge as having some universal character. Individuals act in a world that is not of their own choosing and their actions often produce unintended structural effects. Yet the ability of individuals to understand the structure of the social world is seen as being severely limited. The role of the political observer is to explain events with reference to the actions of individuals and organisations in a structural context. The observer of this political world can claim a particularly insightful vantage point from which to offer an explanation. *Relativists*, in contrast, repudiate the idea that objective, universal and timeless knowledge is possible: criteria for judging truth are relative to time, place and culture. For extreme relativists, to understand a political event would require the construction of an overall picture based on each individual conception of the events. A less extreme position suggests that the role of the observer is to tease out the broad patterns of meaning attached to an event by different groups within society.

Another common distinction to be made relates to how the observer forms his or her theories. The *deductive method* emphasises the value of drawing conclusions from first principles through a process of conceptual analysis and reflection. The *inductive method*, on the other hand, draws its conclusions by empirical observation and the search for patterns and generalisations.

The six approaches to political science identified in this book have certain 'gut' preferences (see Dunleavy and O'Leary, 1987, p. 336) for particular styles of explanation and methodological orientation (see Table 1 above). For example, *discourse analysis* holds the strongest relativist position, while *behaviouralists* come closest to the positivist position. Institutionalists and behaviouralists have traditionally preferred a more inductive style of explanation, in contrast to the more deductive style of rational choice theory and, of course, normative theory.

It is important to emphasise the extent to which all the approaches reviewed here do not wish to be trapped into extreme positions with respect to their broad methodological orientations. If the relativist position is pushed to the extreme it would 'culminate in total uncertainty or unwillingness to adhere to any principle or position' (Goodwin, 1992, p. 13). As Fiona Devine argues, in order to avoid the relativist trap most social scientists are keen to identify some criteria for evaluating competing theories (see Chapter 7). Equally, few political scientists would defend the position that 'the facts speak for themselves'. Thus Howarth, in Chapter 6, in discussing discourse analysis insists that there are criteria for evaluating competing theories but that these criteria can only be established within certain discourses. Sanders in Chapter 3 distances modern behaviouralists from an extreme positivist position and concedes that all empirical observations are coloured by the theoretical framework of the observer. Rational choice theorists favour a deductive style of theory building but then subject their theories to test and revision in the light of discoveries made through empirical observation. Equally, the inductive style of traditional institutional studies, which at times meant that the analysis never got beyond detailed description, has given way to a concern to develop multitheoretical frameworks which can then be subjected to empirical testing.

Dividing lines among approaches to political science can also be drawn on the basis of a preference for qualitative or quantitative methods. Devine in Chapter 7 provides a review of qualitative methods ranging from participant observation to interviewing. W. L. Miller, in Chapter 8, examines those quantitative methods used by political scientists to collect and analyse data. In broad terms, qualitative methods are most often preferred by institutional, feminist and discourse approaches. Quantitative approaches are most strongly associated with behaviouralist work and rational choice theory. Such preferences reflect significant differences in both the focus of study and the methodological orientation. Behaviouralists, given their concern with aggregate individual behaviour and with the falsifiability of theoretical statements generally, find quantitative methods more suitable. Equally, many feminists, given a concern with understanding people as conscious and social 'beings', are drawn to use qualitative research methods. Yet in principle, as Chapman argues in Chapter 5, feminist analysis is compatible with the use of quantitative methods. Equally, quantitative work on election studies can be complemented and challenged by work undertaken using qualitative techniques, as Devine demonstrates in Chapter 7. Indeed, her general conclusion about the qualitative/quantitative divide is difficult to disagree with; methods should be chosen according to research goals and the option of combining quantitative and qualitative analysis should not be overlooked.

We have dealt with some of the methodological challenges explored in this book. There are, however, at least two other challenges which the political scientist cannot ignore. In Chapter 9 the difficulties and uncertainties of comparative analysis are examined. For all humans and animals, let alone political scientists, comparison is an essential tool of discovery. As Mackenzie (1967, p. 310) argues, 'Search or trial and error are either random or they involve comparison . . . one cannot not compare. One way in which one learns about a situation, whether to explain it or to act on it, is by abstraction into elements and matching elements.' Comparison forms an essential element in the learning strategies of political scientists. It can take a variety of forms. For example comparisons could be made within a single state or on a cross-national basis. Working in a comparative framework raises a number of difficult conceptual and research challenges. As Tom Mackie and David Marsh argue in Chapter 9, comparison provides a powerful, if problematic, tool for political scientists.

The discussion of methodological questions in Part 2 is concluded in Chapter 10 by Colin Hay's review and commentary on the structure/agency debate. A dilemma faced across the whole of the social sciences is to what extent explanation should be couched in terms of the autonomous actions of individuals or seen as a product of the context or structure in which the individual operates and over which they have no control. Hay reviews various positions in the structure/agency debate. His own position provides a good illustration of a critical realist methodological orientation. The chapter concludes that it is essential for political scientists to be aware of the models of structure and agency which underlie their attempts to account for political change.

# ▪ The role of theory in political science

The six approaches to political science that we have identified generate a substantial range and variety of theory. In this final section of the introduction we clarify the question of what is meant by theory and argue for a recognition of its diversity of form as well as content. The discussion then moves on to introduce a major issue of theoretical dispute and controversy within political science – the nature of the state. Part 3 of the book is devoted to a review of state theory, and as such, illustrates how debate and argument are taken forward within the discipline of political science. In broad terms it illustrates how political science is done.

The fundamental purpose of theory is somehow to explain, comprehend and interpret 'reality'. Indeed, it is possible to go further and argue that without theory of some sort it is impossible to understand 'reality'. As Zuckerman (1991, p. 118) argues, 'without thinking we cannot perceive – much less describe or explain – the world "out there" . . . . Political Science, like any discipline of knowledge, cannot proceed by observations alone'. Without some idea of what is important, we cannot cut into the seamless web of our world. Theory, in crude terms, helps us to see the wood for the trees. Good theories select out certain factors as the most important or relevant if one is interested in providing an explanation of an event. Without such a sifting process no effective observation can take place. The observer would be buried under a pile of detail and be unable to weigh the influence of different factors in explaining an event. Theories are of value precisely because they structure all observations.

Theory provides a number of valuable functions in the quest to understand the way the social world works. First, it 'foregrounds' certain aspects of the world and provides a guide as to what to investigate. It enables us to see the world and focus on particular aspects of reality. Second, it acts as a useful 'filing system', a framework within which to place observations of reality. Third, theory enables patterns of ideas to develop. Theories are usually stated in a relatively abstract way, which condenses and systematises experience, allowing us to 'make some coherent sense of multiple bits of information' (Dunleavy and O'Leary, 1987, p. 343). A good theory not only meets some observational tests but also has a logical coherence and a depth. It links together, in a complex whole, a set of ideas and hypotheses. Finally, theory facilitates debate, exchange and learning within political science. Theoretical statements enable the identification of common ground as well as divergence and discrepancies between contrasting patterns of ideas.

The practice of theorising takes a variety of forms within political science (see Judge *et al.*, 1995). An initial distinction can be made between normative and empirical theories. *Normative Theories* are theories about how the world ought to be; the theorist posits a desired set of conditions and argues why it is preferred. Normative theory is concerned with 'the bearing or promoting of norms, in the sense of values' (Goodwin, 1992, p. 12). Closely related, are two types of theory that try to link values to 'facts'. *Prescriptive Theories* are instrumental: they are concerned with the best means of achieving a desired condition. *Evaluative theory* assesses a given condition by reference to a set of concepts and values.

The *Descriptive–Empirical* approach constitutes the other broad camp in theory-making. It is concerned with building an explanation based on the 'facts'. In a narrow sense, empirical theory is concerned with establishing causal relationships – what factors (independent variables) account for the phenomenon to be explained (dependent variable). In its strictest form the *causal theory* should be framed in such a way as to be capable of empirical falsification. A related variant of empirical theory operates on a deductive rather than an inductive basis. *Predictive* theorising starts with a set of premises and deduces conclusions about behaviour from these premises. While the assumptions underlying the theory may not be valid or verifiable empirically, it is argued that they lead to accurate predictions (explanations) about behaviour.

In a broader sense, empirical theory is about providing an understanding of reality. Theory in this sense can take the form of *models or conceptual frameworks*. Models are representations or stylised, simplified pictures of reality. They identify important components of a system but do not posit relationships among variables. Conceptual frameworks or perspectives provide a broad language and a form of reference in which reality can be examined. They go further than a model in providing interpretations of relationships between variables. Conceptual frameworks achieve a greater depth and breadth in their attempts to explain reality.

Again as Table 1 above illustrates, the six approaches to political science identified here favour the production of some types of theory over others. Normative theorists obviously concentrate on normative theory and its sub-sets. Institutional studies and feminist analysis are the most catholic in their tastes, offering all varieties with the general exception of predictive theory. A concern with predictive capability is characteristic of rational choice theory. Behaviouralists favour the generation of causal, falsifiable empirical theory. The broader style of empirical theorising is favoured by the other four approaches, excluding that is, normative theory.

The forms taken by theory in political science are diverse and so, not surprisingly, is the content. This point is illustrated in Part 3 of this book where we focus on theories of state. The choice of this theoretical field reflects a recognition, identified earlier, of the centrality of the state and its particular role within the political system that makes it an unavoidable and appropriate focus of study within political science. Another related reason for a focus upon theories of the state is because of the overarching and organising role they have played within political science over the past three decades. As Dunleavy (1987) argues theories of the state have emerged as a central linking element in contemporary political science and have helped to generate a substantial body of theory – guided research in a diverse range of fields within the discipline.

Chapters 11–13, by Martin Smith, Mark Evans and George Taylor respectively, review respectively pluralist, elitist and Marxist theories of the state. All show considerable diversity within perspectives and a process of change and development as the perspectives have reacted to internal debate and external criticism. Indeed, in Chapter 14 David Marsh argues that there is evidence of considerable convergence between the three positions, although significant differences remain. The separate dynamic development of traditions, the mutual colonisation of theoretical territory, and continual process of adaptation which can be observed in the case of the unfolding theories of the state is characteristic of the way much political science works.

# ■ PART 1 ■

# APPROACHES TO POLITICAL SCIENCE

# ■ *Chapter 1* ■

# Normative Theory
## Daryl Glaser

Normative political theory involves, in the words of Isaiah Berlin, 'the discovery, or application, of moral notions in the sphere of political relations'. It is, viewed in these rather narrow terms, a branch of moral philosophy, concerned with the foundational or basic moral questions that affect political life (Berlin, 1984, p. 120). The remit of the term can, however, be defined more broadly, to cover all political theorising of a prescriptive or recommendatory kind: that is to say, all theory-making concerned with what 'ought to be', as opposed to 'what is', in political life. Normative political thought finds expression in abstract moral reasoning but also in more detailed discussion of institutions and policies. If in philosophical mode it seeks out – or constructs – guiding moral precepts, in its more concrete applications political theory investigates the implications of moral precepts for actual political practice.

Normative theory has a long lineage, going back in the West at least to Ancient Greece and in the East to, among other sources, Confucian and Hindu philosophy. Since politics is about 'attending to the general arrangements of a set of people whom chance or choice have brought together' (Oakeshott, 1984, p. 219), normative theorising may appear to be, on the face of it, entirely natural: a way of bringing scholarly attention to the process of 'attending' to our 'arrangements'. Yet the idea of a distinctive field of theoretical activity devoted exclusively to what 'ought to be' has not met with universal acceptance in academic circles. Some critics have denied that human agents exercise meaningful moral choice; others have doubted that moral propositions can be meaningful or derived logically from facts about the world. A few have denigrated moral thought as such.

Despite such criticism, normative theory remains a living and vital branch of political studies. Indeed, it has benefited from a considerable revival of interest since the early 1970s, thanks in part to the influence of writers such as John Rawls and Robert Nozick. Its resuscitation follows a long period of retrenchment brought on by the critique from logical positivism in the 1930s and behaviourism subsequently (see Chapter 3). If for some time now these latter schools have been on the defensive, normative political theorists have displayed increasing confidence. None the less, normative theory faces challenges from new directions, as I will show.

In discussing the discipline of normative political theory I will focus largely on developments since the 1970s, although mention will be made, where appropriate, of antecedent thinkers and schools of thought.

# ■ The key methods and questions

Normative political theory is a way of talking about social institutions, especially those bound up with the exercise of public power, and about the relationship of individuals to those institutions. It scrutinises the justifications given for existing political arrangements and the justifiability of possible alternative arrangements.

Its practitioners employ a variety of *methods*. Three are typical. Normative theorists are concerned first and foremost with the *internal consistency* of moral arguments. In measuring this they bring to bear styles of argumentation drawn from, among other sources, formal logic and analytic philosophy. Second, they draw on *social science disciplines* such as social anthropology and history in order to check the correctness of the empirical premises of arguments, or to expose problems in moral arguments not immediately revealed by abstract reasoning. Finally, normative theorists measure the conclusions of their arguments against their own moral *intuitions*. Their arguments may expose the weakness of common-sense intuitions, but equally a conclusion that is strongly counter-intuitive may signal a weakness in the reasoning that generated it. Normative theorists will differ in the relative weight they attach to these three elements of abstract logic, social-scientific and historical evidence, and intuition.

The key *substantive* questions of political theory since the early 1970s can be arranged, very roughly, into two sets. The first centres on the existence and purpose of those public institutions we call the *state*. Are there moral grounds for a state? If so, for what sort? When should we feel obliged to obey its laws? When, by contrast, is civil disobedience justified?

A second set of substantive questions is concerned with issues of *distributive justice* and its implications for freedom or *liberty*. What is the relative moral importance of freedom and equality? Are there moral grounds for public policies designed to realise some conception of substantive social equality? Would such policies respect the autonomy and liberty of individuals and prove compatible with pluralism?

Later in this chapter I shall examine the way normative theorists have debated the role of the state in distributing goods – a topic which addresses substantive questions from both of these sets.

Political theorists discussing substantive questions are typically drawn to more basic, or *foundational*, issues of moral philosophy. Is there a rationally discernible objective basis to morality? If there is, in what might it consist? Alternatively, is morality a human artefact, the product of convention or community tradition? And why do the answers we give matter for political theory?

It is these foundational questions of moral philosophy that must be engaged first of all. Under the next heading I will examine the competing views that writers have adopted in relation to them. I will then go on to consider the views of those who doubt that moral philosophy is possible at all.

# ▋ The major positions in normative political theory

Since its 1970s revival, normative theory has developed in a variety of directions. Some of its practitioners have restated the bases of older positions; others (notably the feminists among them) have sought out novel terrain (on the latter, see Chapter 5 in this book and Pateman, 1989). While not exhausting the field, three broad approaches to normative political theory dominated the debates of the 1970s and subsequently, each drawing on writings of earlier decades and centuries. They are *utilitarianism, deontological liberalism* and *communitarianism*. I shall consider utilitarianism first.

## ☐ *Utilitarianism*

Utilitarianism is a political and moral philosophy associated famously with the radical nineteenth-century social reformer, Jeremy Bentham. Like many subsequent utilitarians, Bentham was suspicious of principles of political action founded on abstract or speculative claims about our natural rights and duties. Bentham appealed instead to what he understood to be basic facts about human nature disclosed by empirical observation. Human beings, he claimed, were motivated by a desire to achieve happiness and to avoid pain. Accordingly, Bentham thought, the *morally* correct political decisions were those which sought the greatest happiness of the greatest number in society. This happiness could be quantified in the form of utility – 'that property in any object whereby it tends to produce benefit, advantage, pleasure, good or happiness' – and the object of policy-makers should be to maximise aggregate social utility (Plant, 1993, p. 143; Bentham, 1967).

Bentham did not seek to prescribe the courses of action which would maximise happiness. The definition of what counts as utility would, in the end, be left to members of society. Each individual should define his or her own good, and in social decision-making the (subjectively defined) interests of each individual should enter equally into the overall 'calculus' of utility.

Utilitarianism in this classic form has suffered sustained criticism. The idea that pleasures and pains can be quantified, and that the otherwise incommensurable wants of diverse individuals can be compared impersonally, is widely considered to be implausible. Many critics have worried about the implications for individual or minority rights of a doctrine that conceives social utility in aggregate terms and refuses the constraints on social action which might be supplied by a theory of rights. Their anxiety is heightened by utilitarianism's reliance on the (expressed) preferences of individuals when some preferences may be highly anti-social (racist, for example). The injunction to seek the greatest happiness of the greatest number may sanction social engineering or a welfare-orientated technocracy sanctioned by majority consent. Alternatively, its model of the utility-maximising individual could sanction crude free-market apologetics, with the public choice theory of the New Right as its natural successor (see Chapter 4). Cultural elitists and religious thinkers fear that the equating of all wants amounts to a downgrading of the higher things of life, such as good art or divinely ordained truths revealed in the scriptures.

One trenchant early critic of Bentham's utilitarianism was John Stuart Mill. Mill eschewed a crudely quantitative utilitarianism in favour of one that accommodated qualitative judgements – allowing, for example, that certain kinds of intellectual or aesthetic experiences might be superior to others equally desired. Mill also argued for a utilitarianism that protected certain basic or vital interests of all individuals as a matter of right. Rights themselves contribute to general utility by 'making safe the very groundwork of our existence' (cited in Plant, 1993, p. 165), though whether Mill treats rights as being inviolable in the face of competing imperatives of a utilitarian kind is not completely clear. Mill noted that rights will at times come into conflict with other *rights* and that where they do, only calculations of relative utility can indicate which should prevail. Mill's arguments mark a departure from 'act-utilitarianism', according to which each act should be judged separately for its happiness-maximising consequences, to 'rule-utilitarianism', which would preserve whole systems of constraining rules because of the benefits they bring to society as a whole (Mill, 1978).

A number of writers since Mill have joined the effort to restate utilitarianism in more acceptable or more persuasive terms. Some have sought a greater subtlety or sophistication for their precepts, others have modified them substantially. While in part the foil of recent debates, utilitarianism has continued to be developed in its own right under a variety of labels – consequentialism, teleological ethics, proportionalism – and today presents a considerably more elusive target of attack than did its nineteenth century predecessor. Readers wishing to follow the more recent development of utilitarian thinking or debates around utilitarianism might usefully begin with A. Sen and B. Williams' collection *Utilitarianism and Beyond* or Raymond Plant's *Modern Political Thought* (Sen and Williams, 1982; Plant, 1993, ch. 4).

## ☐ *Deontological liberalism*

It is largely in *opposition* to this utilitarian legacy that political theorising revived in the 1970s. Or rather, it took off in opposition to teleological ethics of all kinds. By teleological ethics I mean here moralities that judge the worth of human conduct according to whether it fulfills a particular purpose or realises a particular end or *telos*. Though it does not specify the content of human happiness, utilitarianism is clearly teleological in this sense; but so, for example, is the Aristotelian idea that (male and non-slave) human beings fulfil their rational natures by participating as citizens in the common life of a community. A number of important thinkers writing in the 1970s – such as John Rawls, Robert Nozick, Ronald Dworkin and Alan Gewirth – insisted that teleological ethics transposed to political life was insufficient or even hazardous for human freedom, for two reasons already alluded to.

First, these writers argued, utilitarianism does not take account of the plurality of individual ends – either because it specifies one possible kind of purpose (the maximisation of happiness or utility) as being higher than others, or because it judges human good or welfare from the aggregate vantage point of society as a whole (or of its 'greatest number'), failing to consider each individual separately. Second, teleological ethics gives priority to the ends over the means which might be used to achieve them. In particular, it refuses to allow that the pursuit of aggregate social goals should be constrained by inviolable *rights* enjoyed by each individual.

Whilst, as mentioned above, utilitarians have attempted to address such complaints, their critics maintain that the defence of rights under utilitarianism is always contingent and insecure. Utilitarianism has underpinned much liberal thought, but a number of its critics have declared that liberalism requires a more convincing philosophical grounding (see especially Rawls, 1972).

The writers who made these arguments have come to be known as *deontological* or *Kantian* liberals (Sandel, 1984; Plant, 1993). They contrast deontology (the ethics of right or duty) favourably with teleology (the ethics of ends); and the principal reference point for a deontological ethics is Immanuel Kant. Kant was opposed to any conception of politics that might sacrifice individuals to a higher purpose. Individuals were, for him, ends and not means, and as such they were inviolable. Kantian liberals believe that individuals should be free to define and pursue their own ends, rather than having the ends of others imposed upon them.

If the deontologists have a pluralistic view of human ends, they are not relativists: certain constraints must be placed upon human behaviour, and these should take the form of rights, duties or entitlements that attach to individuals and which cannot be overridden. Individuals are free and autonomous beings, but they should not be free to violate the freedom and autonomy of others. They may pursue separate 'goods', but they must proceed within a framework of commonly agreed or universally respected 'rights'; and where the right and the good conflict, right should prevail.

Liberals insist that *collective* social action too must respect individual rights, which all deontological liberals insist includes a strong right to liberty. At the same time, liberals are distinguished from anarchists by acceptance that a public body of some kind is needed to guarantee rights and to make them effective. Even determinedly free market liberals recognise that in order to fulfill its most essential functions, the public body in question – the state – must subject individuals to laws that regulate their behaviour or make demands on their private resources (for example, through taxation). The role of the state becomes more controversial among deontological liberals who suggest that it seeks to satisfy welfare as well as libertarian rights. At this point a whole host of problems arise. What precisely is the state required, or entitled, to do? Should it simply maintain law and order, or intervene to redistribute wealth? Is there such a thing as a right to a certain minimum of welfare? If individual rights against the state are inviolable, what exactly are those rights?

Those arguing for universal human rights court more than just academic controversy. They are speaking to a world marked by the decline of universalistic projects such as socialism and liberalism; growing national, religious and territorial fragmentation; and by the advance of an identity politics amongst women and ethnic minorities. In such a world the ground for cross-cultural agreement about universal rights often seems tenuous. Of course, defenders of universal rights will insist that the current multiplication of inter-community conflicts only underlines the need to find some universally agreed yardsticks for adjudicating contending ethnic and cultural claims. That, indeed, is my own view. But there are important currents of normative theory whose exponents doubt that such a universal vantage point is either possible or desirable. Some feminists argue that the supposedly universal vantage point of liberal normative theory is in fact a male one: impersonal, abstract, rational and public, in contrast to the empathetic, practical and localised way in which women more comfortably address human disputes (Brown, 1993). Here I shall focus on another approach critical of deontology, that loosely referred to as *communitarian* (Sandel, 1984; Plant, 1993; Bellamy, 1993).

# ☐ *Communitarianism*

Communitarians begin with a critique of the liberal concept of the individual self. The liberal self is, as Michael Sandel puts it, 'unencumbered' – able to adopt a vantage point outside the community of which it is part, and to define and redefine its aims and commitments without reference to inherited traditions or shared goals. It is endowed with rights and duties specified in purely abstract and universal terms that discount the claims and obligations arising from our own personal and social ties. Communitarians believe that the individuated self of liberalism is dominant only where communal ties have become eroded and individuals find themselves alienated and adrift, though even here communal life or tradition is the necessary reference point of individual dissent. Normatively they consider such individualism undesirable, a symptom of something wrong. They prefer to speak of a 'situated' self – one that is embedded in a community and defined by the attachments and shared self-understandings which frame community life. It is from our community – whether it is a village or sub-culture or movement or ethnic group – that we derive the specific rights and obligations that make up our 'moral particularity'. At the same time we are necessarily 'implicated in the purposes and ends' of our community (Taylor, 1975; McIntyre, 1981; Sandel, 1984a, pp. 5–6; 1984b, pp. 171–4).

A conception of rights and duties as particular to communities, and of purposes as shared by them, conflicts sharply with the deontological liberal commitment to universal rights and individually particular ends. Communitarians are suspicious of the way deontologists insist that right (universal principles of justice) must constrain, or set boundaries on, pursuit of the collective good. The deontological liberals argue that since we cannot fully understand other people's ends, any societal pursuit of a higher social end will impose itself on the self-understandings of individuals who make up society. Sandel, on the other hand, insists that the shared life of a community can reduce this mutual opacity, allowing certain common self-understandings to emerge among people and, with these, goals which are genuinely common and not imposed. In Sandel's eyes, liberals devalue the good by leaving its definition open to the calculations of self-interested individuals. In a community, by contrast, there exists the prospect that all might work towards a morally worthy common good (Sandel, 1984).

If communitarians are suspicious of rights-based liberalism, they do not unite behind any common political alternative. Writers from a wide variety of ideological backgrounds have sought recourse in communitarian positions. They include the conservative writer Michael Oakeshott, attracted by communitarianism's defence of particularity and tradition against universalistic rationalism; and civic republicans such as Hannah Arendt and Michael Sandel, drawn to the prospect of a participatory public life. Today they attract a new strand of political thinkers wishing to recreate a sense of communal obligation between people on the ashes of what they perceive as the failed individualism of both the New Right and the New Left (see, for example, Etzioni, 1993).

If communitarianism proceeds from a critique of liberalism, it is itself vulnerable to the objection that it offers insufficient safeguards to individual liberty or protection against traditionalist or majoritarian tyranny. Some strands of communitarian thought connect with conservative notions of organic community in which moral conformity is stressed at the cost of individual dissent. Other strands allow for the possibility of a participatory or democratic community but, liberty defenders might argue, leave the individual vulnerable to a heteronomous majoritarian will. The vision of democracy by consensus which some radical communitarians advance as an alternative to majoritarianism is arguably impractical in a world of culturally individuated people, or one in which scarcity and conflicts of interest are ineradicable. The attempt to operate the rules of 'unitary democracy' in a diverse community moreover threatens to marginalise the (often distinctive) interests of those who are less effective participators (Mansbridge, 1980).

The more liberty-sympathetic or democratic-minded communitarians might reply that they envisage participation in, or identification with, only *some* kinds of community, and that widespread individual dissociation from common life is a symptom of the fact that a community no longer exists. The question for such communitarians is not whether individual dissent should be suppressed – it should not be – but how a community might be created that all can feel (undissentingly) a part of. Given that cohesive communities have become increasingly rare, and that they are difficult to recreate in today's mobile, globally interdependent world, this reply arguably leaves communitarianism in a condition of either pessimism or impotent utopianism. More important, seen from a liberty-protective standpoint, such an argument offers no good reason for downgrading individual rights. The guarantee of those rights could be considered necessary not only in the long period which must precede the successful recreation of communal life but, if experience of authoritarianism in some past communal experiments is anything to go by (see here, for example, Goodwin and Taylor, 1982), in any kind of commune we can hope realistically to create in the future.

Nevertheless, communitarianism does offer some powerful arguments. It makes us conscious of the way our inherited tradition shapes the way we reason morally, so that even in opposition to it we may find ourselves having to engage its language (for example, by referring to its customary or constitutional provisions protecting dissent). It reminds us that we are born with moral obligations as a community that we can only disown by sounding insensitive to those to whom our predecessors incurred moral debts (think here of Germans born after 1945 and the special responsibility they might have in fighting Fascism or racism). Communitarianism shows us further how some moral obligations we incur are to the people immediately around us, be they our family, friends or community, and that abstract moral language works better in public life than in the more informal and mutually empathetic life of, say, a group of acquaintances. In the latter's company it may often be more appropriate to act out of love or personal loyalty, in a spirit of protective paternalism or in ways that draw on intimate knowledge, rather than according to the impersonal and undifferentiating principles favoured by deontologists. Finally, the communitarian ideal of social solidarity addresses a genuine deficiency of our atomised modern life and is probably shared by many who defend individual rights.

# ■ The main objections to normative theory

The range of positions recovered or generated in the political theorising since the 1970s is, it is clear, very wide. The disagreements internal to political theory between utilitarians, deontologists, communitarians and others (as well as within these camps) sometimes run very deep. However, it may also be helpful to consider the views of some of those who doubt that the enterprise of normative theory is possible at all. In what follows I shall consider three broad types of external criticism of normative theory: *logical positivism*, *relativism* and *determinism*.

## □ *Logical positivism*

Logical positivism is a school of analytic philosophy inspired in part by the early writings of Ludwig Wittgenstein, in particular his *Tractatus Logico-Philosophicus* (1921). The *Tractatus* is a study of the logic of language: of what makes it meaningful or gives it the capacity to communicate truth. The elemental units of language which give it that power are, he concludes, names: for only names refer directly to the world outside language. Their meaning is not mediated by other propositions of language: they have external objects *as* their meaning. Conversely, only propositions which refer to external objects can be true. The sole exceptions here are tautological propositions, which are always true by definition, and contradictory propositions, which are always false, again by definition.

Wittgenstein did not himself specify the nature of the objects to which true propositions refer, but other logical positivists have insisted that they should be material objects or direct sense experiences. If that is so then normative theory is, as R. Plant puts it, 'in deep trouble', for its component parts – words like liberty and justice – do not refer to objects of a material or sensually-experienced kind. Wittgenstein himself considered the propositions of ethics, aesthetics, religion and metaphysics to be 'nonsense', and held that philosophy should confine itself to the factual or descriptive language of natural science (Wittgenstein, 1961; Plant, 1993).

This pretty much set the tone for subsequent condemnations of 'metaphysics' by the two schools of political studies which logical positivism certified as capable of telling objective truths about the world: behaviourial political science and the linguistic analysis of political concepts. Both behaviourists and linguistic analysts insisted on separating factually or logically true propositions from 'values', which in their view issued from emotions, sentiments and attitudes (see Chapter 3). Their writings suggested that normative theory was about subjective values and could never aspire to the status of a hard intellectual or scientific discipline.

How have normative theorists responded to such charges? One response has been to concede that moral propositions are not facts or logically derivable from facts, but to insist that this does no serious damage to the prospects of a rigorous normative theory. In the first place, normative theory can make *use* of 'facts' or, at any rate, of the evidence and arguments which come from the descriptive disciplines of social science. The nature of reality 'as it is' – in so far as we can know or understand it – is not immaterial to normative theorists. It has been cited in arguments about, for example, the universality or particularity of human traits and needs.

While it cannot derive values from facts, normative theory can disclose the logical relationships implicit in a particular moral discourse. Since the members of a moral community rarely subject their everyday language to rigorous examination, normative theorists do perform a special kind of service here, often to exacting standards.

A more ambitious response from normative theory insists that moral truths *can* be shown to have objective foundations. Alan Gewirth argues that rights to freedom and well-being can be deduced by strict logic from certain basic or generic requirements of human action (Gewirth, 1978). John Rawls seeks a moral argument which if not 'factual' is nevertheless not a product of particular values either. Rawls believes he can find this in the procedural device of the 'original position', where he tries to imagine the principles of justice that would be chosen by founders of a new order who have no prior knowledge of their natural endowments, social resources, status and so on – people who are forced to devise principles neutral enough to cover *any* prospective member of the future society, since *they* could be any one of those members (Rawls, 1972).

My own inclination is to doubt that values can be derived in a strictly logical way from facts, or that they can be factual themselves. Even if

Gewirth can demonstrate a strict logical link between a human right to freedom and well-being and certain facts about the requirements of human action, it is not clear what that would prove, since a person not sharing Gewirth's methodology could deny that rational consistency carries moral salience, or that the rational consistency of a moral proposition with a fact makes it a fact. Similarly, Rawls' brilliant idea of the original position is best seen, as Ronald Dworkin would have it, as a device whose choice in the first place reflects an antecedent moral commitment to equal concern and respect for human beings (Dworkin, 1977). Factual argumentation is salient to normative theory, but normative theory is not a variant of it.

## □ *Relativism*

Moral relativists, the second group of critics I wish to consider, might argue that if morals cannot be derived from facts then they are indeed, in the final instance, purely relative. And if they are purely relative – if no one value position can be described as better than another – then there is no point in normative theory as such. If moral claims are fiercely contested, yet at the same time matters of opinion rather than fact, how might one ever adjudicate them?

Communitarians answer that particular moralities may still have a role where transcendent ones are forgone: certain things may still be morally right *within* a particular community and its language game, even where they are not universally right or wrong. Pure moral relativism would require that every individual be an island: but the nature of language is that we are not, and that moral and other meanings are intersubjectively constituted. *Ipso facto*, there is still a place for morality in the world, and indeed for normative theorists who set out to explicate in a coherent and deep way what it is that a community's own cultural language entails in moral terms.

This answer will not quite do. Moral argument in today's world does not take place in hermetically sealed language games. Language games encounter each other when countries go to war, when they give each other economic or military aid, when they trade or pay debts, when they join common organisations and subscribe to common charters. If there is not as such a coherent global moral community, it is none the less clear that moral languages overlap, cross-cut, mix, engage with each other and shift in response to external pressures.

A communitarian might argue that if such fluid interaction heightens the possibility of a collision of moral language games, it requires all the more urgently that each be accorded equal respect, the better to avoid conflict or imposition. But this kind of reasoning seems plausible only up to a point. In some situations it may legitimate oppression within moral communities or abolish all agreed criteria of conflict resolution between them, thus confounding the aims of a communitarian pluralism. The pure celebration of moral and cultural differences will not help if another community's language game allows that your own territory be seized, or that one of your citizens be sentenced to death by a foreign power, or that their pollution should rain down on your forests and fields. There is at least a case, one might argue, for seeking cross-communal clarity about the criteria that might reasonably be used to adjudicate the competing claims of moral communities sharing spaces or resources.

What, in any case, *is* a moral community? It is difficult to see, say, a nation state as one, when most entities the size of a nation state will be certain to harbour differences of moral perception. Groups or individual dissidents in one nation state may feel oppressed by their own rulers and appeal to other nation states for help. Individuals may form group allegiances that cut across national boundaries. Again it is difficult to see an ethnic group or a sex as a moral community in the bounded sense. Perhaps only a genuinely voluntary association of consenting adults can be that. But even *it* participates in a wider moral universe when it interacts with others outside that association.

The strongest reply from normative theory to moral relativism is that there are certain basic precepts recognised as being morally right by at least some people across virtually all boundaries of moral community. The wrongness of torture is not a 'fact', but recognition of it has a beach-head wherever someone is being tortured, unless that person genuinely consents to being tortured. In other words, there are community-transcending moral language games that are also, in this sense, universal ones. The claim here is not that any given precept can be shown to have been present in all societies at all times, nor that all widely accepted precepts are just. It is simply that the cultural relativity of moral language does not itself serve as a plausible defence of an outrage in a world where we all speak to each other about morals, still less where we all claim to have signed up to some common moral rules. If moral discourse cuts accross cultural boundaries the argument against universalising moral theory from the standpoint of multiple language games loses much of its force.

## ☐ Determinism

A final argument against normative theory comes from determinism. There are bodies of theory which appear, at least on a certain reading, to deny that human beings exercise the powers of agency that are a precondition of moral choosing. There is no sense in judging a course of action to be morally blameworthy if those who carried it out had no real choice but to do so. Someone who is forced at gunpoint to kill another is generally not considered to be as culpable as someone who carefully plans and premediates a murder. Are there senses in which all of us are deprived of morally relevant choices, or in which our choices are at any rate more limited than normative theory supposes?

Several types of determinism can be distinguished. Some might regard the individual agent as determined, or at least very strongly constrained and pressured, by external forces beyond his or her control. Individuals might be subject to hidden structures or to unfolding historical processes driven by internal and impersonal logic. Forces or relationships associated with economic life are commonly attributed a more or less determining role in currents of both Marxism and liberalism; other determinists might stress national traditions or ecological constraints; and still others, supernatural forces. A second kind of determinism might hold that we are determined by forces inside ourselves beyond our control, such as our subconscious, or our genetic inheritance. It might even be said that there is no consciousness outside of brain processes, and so therefore no moral command centre not itself reducible to the firing of distinctive coalitions of pre-wired neurons. So in what sense are we free to make moral choices? Is there, indeed, a 'we' to do the choosing?

There are many components to the determinist case, and not all can be addressed here. I shall consider just two of the questions it raises. The first is whether the advocate of a determinist position is himself or herself amoral. A Marxist of determinist bent may still consider capitalism to be unjust and socialism just (Geras, 1985). A Freudian convinced of the power of the subconscious may still consider it desirable that a patient be shown the way to greater mental health. In these senses they may still make normative judgements; they may, indeed, have begun their research in order to solve a moral or normative 'problem', such as the existence of capitalism or neurosis. Moreover, value positions often lurk behind – or seek justification in – ostensibly value-free claims about ineluctable causal connections between phenomena such as, to cite one example, human nature and greed. Of course the presence of value assumptions in a scholarly enterprise does not show that its conclusions are false – but we should be alert to those values none the less, since they give us a deeper understanding of the strengths, weaknesses and larger significance of an intellectual project.

The second question is whether moral reasoning, as an intellectual activity, is judged to have a role in determining historical or personal outcomes. This is the really important question for the prospects of normative theory. There may be forces that constrain us, but do they leave us with important choices? In the making of those choices, can we be influenced by arguments about the rightness or wrongness of courses of action? Alternatively, can those who shape the behavioural sanctions and incentives that regulate us be so influenced? If the answers to these questions are 'yes', then normative theory has a 'role'.

Two things can be said here for normative theory, both of a tentative kind. The first is that it would be very difficult to demonstrate that we are *never* left with important and morally salient forms of choosing: even the previously mentioned person at gunpoint has *some* choice (between killing and being killed) and there are many situations in life where the range of choice available to us is much larger than in that scenario. Many writing in supposedly determinist currents (like Marxism) would readily concede a place to human agency within variously understood contexts of structural constraint (see Chapters 13 and 14).

If we *do* exercise meaningful choice, it seems at least plausible that moral language can influence the choices we make. Moral discourse is a part of our cultural environment, a part of the way cultures are communicated and reproduced. Of course we encounter moral language in many forms, and that part of it presented to us in theoretically explicit ways is just one of them. None the less, rigorous moral talk may count for something, especially among certain kinds of opinion-forming elites, such as educators, legal theorists and political thinkers. It will be most influential in legalistic cultures or cultures which esteem scholarship. Where participants in moral conversation are self-doubting, uncertain about an issue, or on a particular matter are disinterested, moral theory may help clarify their views, give expression to their inarticulate feelings or persuade them to modify views inconsistent with other things they believe.

This section has defended normative theory against the claims of positivism, relativism and determinism. The case for normative theory implicit in it may now be summarised more positively. Normative theory offers a medium for giving logically rigorous and factually informed consideration to human moral options in those areas where human beings have moral options – that is to say, where they exercise something we can recognise as free moral agency. Areas of moral choice may sometimes be considerable, and within their boundaries moral theory can make a difference. There is, of course, no guarantee that the difference it makes will be for the better, or that the approaches generated by normative theory will be 'good' ones (they will in any case be many). Engagement with normative theory nevertheless proceeds from the hope that moral actors who debate their options in an an open and self-conscious way will, on the whole, do fewer of the things most of us would consider bad than those who proceed unreflectively or suppress moral debate.

# ■ Normative theory applied: justice and liberty

One important area of application of normative theory is justice, or the distribution of goods. Here normative theorists have reached into the heart of – and arguably have influenced – one of the most persistent and hard-fought controversies in post-1930s Western political life: how far should the state intervene to structure or pattern the distribution of goods in society? It is a debate which has raged against the background of the growth, (and, since the mid-1970s, the economic and legitimation crises) of the 'welfare state'.

One camp in this debate may be called, very roughly, *social democratic*: the camp which argues or implies that there are moral grounds for the state to engage in forms of social provision or redistribution of goods. Since such actions involve coercive transfers of resources from some citizens to others, how might they be justified in societies that claim to respect individual autonomy and liberty? Several answers are possible.

A defence of the welfare state might be made on the utilitarian ground that it ensures the greatest happiness for the greatest number; for example, because those who have few goods gain a greater utility from obtaining at least some, or because welfare economics raises general welfare by boosting aggregate demand (Plant, 1993, ch. 4). The deontological objection to such arguments is that they subordinate individual rights to a single concept of welfare. At the same time they leave welfare itself on an insecure footing. So what strategies are open to social-democratic deontological liberals?

The strategy made famous by John Rawls is that of the 'original position'. As I noted earlier, Rawls asks us to imagine the founders of a state who have no advance knowledge of their talents or prospects or social ranking in the new order. From behind this 'veil of ignorance' they must select the principles of justice that will govern the distribution of primary social goods such as well-being and liberty. Rawls believes they will choose two principles: a First Principle of equal liberty, which enjoys special priority, and a Second Principle, which permits only those inequalities in the distribution of goods that benefit the least advantaged. Though inviolable, the principles chosen allow for a plurality of ends in the distribution of all but primary goods. Moreover, they are in theory compatible with a wide variety of socioeconomic systems, from capitalism to democratic socialism (Rawls, 1972; Daniels, 1975).

A second deontological strategy finds warrant for intervention in the market in a foundational principle that is categorical and needs no justification. This is the approach of Ronald Dworkin, for whom the basic principle in question is equal concern and respect for human beings (Dworkin, 1977). Dworkin asks what it means for a government to treat its citizens equally. He notes (using American nomenclature here) that conservatives and liberals will come up with different answers. He then sets out to explicate the liberal answer. He believes such a government will take equally seriously the different ends and preferences of its citizens. It cannot do this by distributing goods centrally according to uniform criteria, and so must allow the workings of a market. However, it is not only preferences that are differentiated: so are people's talents, levels of inherited wealth and special needs. In a free market these will translate into inequalities of outcome which liberals cannot defend. The liberal will therefore seek to reform the market, and will probably turn to a mixed economic regime – 'either redistributive capitalism or limited socialism' (Dworkin, 1984, p. 69).

A third possible justification of state provision would follow from a theory of basic and universal human needs. The problem here, of course, is that there is little agreement (say, across cultures) about what constitute the 'primary goods' of human beings. I have already alluded to Alan Gewirth's answer. Whatever the diversity of ends that humans might choose, certain basic requirements must be met – the generic requirements of voluntary and purposive action – before they can even begin to act as moral agents. These requirements include both freedom and well-being. To these there is a universal right. The right to well-being cannot, however, be satisfied limitlessly without contravening the right to freedom. As with Dworkin, Gewirth comes out in favour of a meliorative 'supportive state' rather than either the free market or full substantive egalitarianism (Gewirth, 1978).

A fourth approach is communitarian. Michael Walzer, in his *Spheres of Justice*, argues that proper distributive criteria vary not only between cultures and communities but also between different 'spheres of justice' such as security and welfare, money and commodities, office, hard work, free time, education, love and divine grace. He argues for a 'complex equality' designed to ensure that the distributive criteria salient to one sphere do not impinge on other spheres where different criteria are appropriate. In a market society this may mean giving special attention to preventing those who legitimately have a certain amount of money from using it to, say, buy people, or office, or honour, or exemption from military service: commodities money should not be permitted to buy. In the sphere of security and welfare there must be a more or less extensive system of communal provision in recognition of need and membership of a community: but since definitions of need and basic goods vary, there can be no universal individual *right* to any particular set of goods beyond the right to life and basic subsistence. Beyond these the appropriate policies of redistribution will flow from shared community understanding and shifting political determination (Walzer, 1985).

All these positions allow that redistributions can be morally legitimate. It is this conclusion which *libertarians* regard as an infringement of basic liberties and as supplying ultimately a licence for totalitarianism. Libertarians may be of Left or Right, but it is those of the Right – the free marketeers – that have mounted the more influential challenge to social democratic or welfarist ideas. Free market libertarians range in turn from outright anarchists who refuse any kind of state authority (such as Murray Rothbard) to those who justify a minimal state (such as Robert Nozick). Here I shall be concerned with libertarian objections to one specific aspect of the state's role: its interventions to provide social goods and redistribute wealth.

Why do libertarians consider such interventions a threat to basic rights and freedoms? It is helpful here to introduce a basic distinction, famously discussed by Isaiah Berlin, between 'negative' freedom, defined in terms of the absence of coercive constraints on action; and 'positive' freedom, defined as the power to achieve desired ends or to achieve self-mastery. Berlin believes that only the former is properly counted as freedom. Policies to enable individuals to achieve their ends may be justifiable, even where they involve coercion of others – this would be so in the case of helping the poor via taxation – but they should not be considered as increasing freedom (Berlin, 1984).

Free market libertarians concur in a definition of liberty purely in negative terms. They are extremely reluctant to see any part of this liberty traded off for some other social good. Coercive state social intervention by definition abridges individual negative liberty. Such abridgement is, according to libertarians, both morally unjustifiable and deleterious to social welfare.

This is the argument of, for example, F. A. von Hayek. Hayek believes that the only possible basis of social freedom and economic success is the self-directing individual. Individuals should have equal access to negative liberty, secured through the rule of impersonal laws and regulations that allow them to pursue their own ends within the law. State distribution of income or wealth violates not only liberty but also equality. It requires that the state determine rules of distribution (based, for example, on need or desert) which discriminate against some individuals and in favour of others. These rules cannot be devised on uncontroversial criteria and are inevitably arbitrary in their effects.

Nor can state distribution be justified as a corrective to social injustice. To argue that a given distribution of goods is unjust is to imply that it constitutes a deliberately intended outcome for which redress might be sought. Injustice can only result from the malign intentions of particular individuals. In a free market society, distributions are the result of the unintended consequences of countless voluntary transactions. There is thus no party from which redress might legitimately be exacted.

Hayek also argues that state economic and social intervention produces failure. He dislikes the assumption that complex human societies can be planned rationally, arguing that this fails to register the limits of human knowledge. Spontaneously-evolved institutions resulting from the unintended effects of voluntary transactions among large numbers of people are, he argues, more likely to be successful than institutions deliberately designed by a supposedly omniscient centre. For Hayek, free market policies are thus not only more just but are also less harmful to social welfare, including that of the poor (Hayek, 1960; Plant, 1993, ch. 3).

Robert Nozick develops his own distinctive libertarian position. He disagrees with anarchist arguments against a state, favouring instead a minimal state that restricts itself to maintaining law and order. He rejects all other kinds of intervention on the grounds that they violate individual autonomy as conceived by Kant: instead of treating individuals as ends in themselves, they use some individuals without their consent for some supposedly higher purpose, such as the achievement of a particular distribution of goods. Nozick develops a particular theory of property ownership that he terms 'historical'. He argues that if a person's holdings came to him or her by a just process of aquisition or transfer, no government could justly transfer a part of those holdings to another without consent. The pursuit of a 'patterned' distribution of goods at a particular time violates historically-inherited entitlements to property.

This, of course, raises the question of how just entitlements to holdings are acquired in the first place. Here Nozick uses a Lockean argument: we acquire entitlements by mixing our own labour – which we own – with unowned resources. Provided this primary aquisition does not worsen the situation of others at that time, it is just. All inequalities resulting from the subsequent use and free exchange of holdings is just so long as the initial appropriation of resources is just (Nozick, 1974; Paul, 1981).

There is no space here to debate the merits of these various libertarian and social democratic arguments. A brief concluding comment can, however, be made. None of the above arguments is uncontested. Each raises a host of problems. In my view those posed by the libertarian arguments are more acute. It can be argued that Hayek overstates the extent to which given distributions of goods constitute an unforeseen outcome; it may be that inegalitarian outcomes are the predictable result of a certain kind of exchange system, and that the participants in its exchanges are aware of these external consequences of their private transactions. Arguably, Nozick cannot demonstrate why 'labour mixing' should carry the moral weight that it does, nor why all voluntary exchanges of justly acquired property are just, even where, say, those exchanges are structurally unequal. The argument that free markets bring the greater benefits to the poor carries moral weight, but of a utilitarian kind, and still awaits historical verification.

Arguments about the right to goods may be problematic in their own ways, but I think the social democratic (and leftwards) camp shows that there are strong moral arguments for redistribution. Those who accept a Dworkian premise – that human beings deserve to be treated with equal concern and respect – cannot treat as morally neutral the inegalitarian results of economic systems (such as the market) that are products of history and convention rather than of natural or purely spontaneous human activity. And writers such as Gewirth do demonstrate something incontrovertible: that to be a freely choosing agent we must have both liberty and well-being. More than that can be said: to be active participants in politics, and thus collectively self-determining, we may need access to politically relevant resources on a roughly equal basis. Substantive (if rough) equality may be a precondition of equal political agency.

# ■ Evaluating normative theory

The big issues facing normative theory can be 'summarised' in many ways. I shall content myself with identifying what I consider to be its two central questions. One is whether normative theory is possible at all. I have laid out a few of the arguments *against* – positivist, relativist and determinist – and suggested that none finally establishes its case. Contrary to the claims of its critics, I argued, normative theory can offer a rigorous and informed way of addressing options open to human beings in those spheres of life in which they can exercise free moral agency.

The second major question is internal to normative theory. Which decisions about human goods should be left to individuals privately, or political communities collectively, to determine according to their preferences, and which should be either constrained or guided by fundamental principles?

It is unhelpful to divide participants in normative political debates into relativists on the one hand and those claiming to have identified objective moral principles on the other. The utilitarians, deontologists and communitarians all seek their fixed points, and all would leave certain important matters to individual, democratic or community decision.

The classic utilitarians find their point of fixity in the assumption of a rational, utility-maximising individual, in the scientistic hope that it might be possible empirically to measure and compare preferences, and in the principle of utility itself. On the question of the actual content of utility they are, however, relativists of a sort. The Benthamites at least are relativist also in so far that they would not constrain the individual's free choice of ends by unassailable natural right claims. The deontologists find their fixed point in a variety of starting points – God, human nature or social contracts – and in the principle of fundamental, trans-historical claims of right and justice. On the other hand, they are content to leave the choice of ends to individuals themselves, viewing principles of right and justice in part as the necessary groundwork for this free choosing. Finaly, communitarians tie moral obligation to community, eschewing the individualistic relativism of the other two camps; at the same time they allow for an inter-community relativism, denying the universal moral vantage point of the 'unencumbered self'.

In my own view, these three camps all offer important arguments. Benthamite utilitarianism itself seems largely to be spurious. However, the idea that the moral worth of human conduct can be established without any reference to the benefits and harms it brings seems perverse, and it is doubtful that even a hardened deontologist would wish to claim that it can be. The morally relevant harms and benefits in question may be those that follow from observing certain rules rather than individual actions; they may accrue to individuals over some longer term or in ways that are difficult to specify in narrowly practical terms. Deontologists, who argue for the recognition of rights, or for something prior to rights, such as equal concern and respect for human beings, must have in mind the thought that violating these rights and precepts will bring harm. If observing them brought nothing but centuries of historically-proven misery, even deontologists would think twice about advocating them.

Nevertheless, the deontological tradition itself generates arguments which no utilitarian, consequentialist or proportionalist can ignore comfortably. It is all very well to talk of harms and benefits, but can these simply be weighed up so that wherever aggregate totals of benefit outweigh harms, a course of action can be considered proper? Again, it is intuitively sensible to take account of consequences, but what kinds of consequence count as acceptable? If a policy brings benefit to many but intolerable harm to a few, is it therefore to be judged as being morally acceptable? Here, only a hardened utilitarian could say that it can be.

Deontology stipulates criteria which any just outcome must satisfy. It appeals to the conviction that individuals cannot be treated unfairly, or as means to ends, or be deprived of liberty and well-being. The weighing of harms and benefits of public policies will not, even where each agent's preference counts for one, automatically respect this conviction. Paradoxically, deontology might disclose where ruder calculations of cost and benefit become acceptable: where fundamental rights are not at stake, perhaps, or where they conflict. Because it often makes 'foundationalist' assumptions about human nature or need, deontology will also be more open to the possibility that some rights exist which are not disclosed by our immediate subjective preferences, and that their protection is a precondition to pursuing our individually or democratically chosen ends.

The main problem with communitarianism is that it is reluctant to accept that individual rights might be appealed to against community morality, or to recognise that community moralities meet each other in a globalised moral village. Though endorsing a pluralism *of* moral communities, it lacks a principle of individual rights in which to anchor a normative commitment to pluralism *within* (all) moral communities. Of the three traditions, however, communitarianism is the only one to remind us that important areas of decision-making are not of the public kind to which abstract rules can easily be applied; and that in public life itself, collective democratic decision-making and participation themselves properly decide a lot of what we are entitled, or obliged, to do.

# ■ Further reading

Plant (1993) offers a good introduction to the concerns of normative theory while also pursuing some definite arguments of his own. Sandel's edited collection (Sandel, 1984), offers a good overview of the first ten years or so of the debate. The classic texts of the Anglo-American discussion since the early 1970s have been Rawls (1972), Nozick (1974) both for deontological liberalism; and Walzer (1985) in the case of communitarianism. Hare (1982) offers a notable statement of a kind of utilitarianism, as does John Harsanyi in his 'Morality and the Theory of Rational Behaviour', reprinted in Sen and Williams (1982), useful and mostly critical. For some noteworthy examples of more recent approaches in normative political theory, see Rorty (1989), which presents a 'pragmatist' perspective; Bauman (1993), which offers a post-modern account; Pateman (1989), for a feminist critique of normative political theory; Rawls (1993), which presents a modification of his earlier universalist positions; and Etzioni (1993), a well-timed restatement of an increasingly fashionable communitarianism.

# ■ Chapter 2 ■

# The Institutional Approach
## R. A. W. Rhodes

The institutional approach was the dominant tradition of political analysis in both Britain and USA but little has been written about what it is. Our forebears in political science were not preoccupied with methodology. Not for them the lengthy digression on how to do it. They just described, for example, the government of France, starting with the French Constitution. The focus on institutions was a matter of common sense, an obvious starting point for studying a country and therefore there was no need to justify it. The assumptions and practices in the study of political institutions were taken for granted.

As practitioners of the institutional approach were 'almost entirely silent about all of their suppositions' (Eckstein, 1979, p. 2), this chapter constructs the missing framework from their works. There is no great tome setting out the principles and practices of institutional analysis. For example, Manheim and Rich's (1991, pp. 352 and 358) textbook on research methods in political science devotes one paragraph to describing the approach and lists two items for further reading (see also Johnson and Joslyn, 1991). Similarly, nowhere in the seven volumes of the *Handbook of Political Science* is there a chapter defining or defending the study of political institutions, although Volume 5 is devoted to specific institutions and processes (Greenstein and Polsby, 1975). The first section of this chapter defines the study of political institutions, distinguishing between the institutional approach as a subject matter, as a method, and as theory. The second section describes and assesses the major criticisms of the approach. The third section identifies three present-day approaches to the study of political institutions: constitutional studies, public administration and the new institutionalism. Finally, in the concluding section I assess the limits of the approach and its continuing usefulness.

This chapter is not a detective story and I will not keep the reader guessing about its plot. There are four themes. First, I argue that the study of political institutions is a core subject in the discipline of political science and, while being associated with the 'classics' or traditional political science, it remains relevant. Second, I want to show that the study of political institutions is part of the tool kit of every political scientist. Third, the institutional approach will only thrive if located in an explicit theoretical context, preferably a multi-theoretical context where it is used to explore competing hypotheses drawn from several theories. Finally, the approach must draw on the plurality of methods in the social sciences, not just the tools of the trade of the historian and lawyer.

# ■ Defining the institutional approach

## ☐ *Subject matter*

The study of political institutions is central to the identity of the discipline of political science. Eckstein (1963, pp. 10–11) points out that 'political science emerged . . . as a separate autonomous field of study divorced from philosophy, political economy, and even sociology [which] may have created a tendency to emphasise the study of formal–legal arrangements'. If there is any subject matter at all that political scientists can claim exclusively for their own, a subject matter that does not require acquisition of the analytical tools of sister fields and that sustains their claim to autonomous existence, it is, of course, formal–legal political structure.

The preoccupation with institutions was as great in the UK. Thus Graham Wallas (1948 [1908], p. 14) bemoaned the fact that 'all students of politics analyse institutions and avoid the analysis of man'. In short, institutions were, and remain, one of the pillars of the discipline of politics (see, for example, Butler, 1958, pp. 11–12; Leftwich, 1984, p. 16; Mackenzie, 1967, p. 62; Ridley, 1975, p. 18).

## ☐ *Method*

If the subject matter of the institutional approach is obvious, then as Oakeshott comments, 'there has been an ominous silence about the manner in which this study is to be conducted' (1967, p. 302). The traditional or classic institutional method is *descriptive–inductive, formal–legal* and *historical–comparative*.

## ☐ Descriptive–inductive

The descriptive approach, also known as 'contemporary history' (Butler, 1958, p. 48), employs the techniques of the historian and explores specific events, eras, people and institutions, generating:

studies which systematically describe and analyse phenomena that have occurred in the past and which explain contemporary political phenomena with reference to past events. The emphasis is on explanation and understanding, not on formulating laws. (Kavanagh, 1991, p. 482)

It is too crude to say that history investigates the particular while political science looks for the general, but there is a large grain of truth in this distinction. Also, history is extolled as 'the great teacher of wisdom':

The study of history does more than furnish the facts and enable us to make or test generalisations. It enlarges the horizon, improves the perspective; and it builds up an attitude towards events that may be termed the historical sense. We become aware of a relationship between apparently isolated events. We appreciate . . . that the roots of the present lie buried deep in the past, and . . . that history is past politics and politics is present history. (Sait, 1938, p. 49)

Because political institutions are 'like coral reefs' which have been 'erected without conscious design', and grow by 'slow accretions', the historical approach is essential (Sait, 1938, p. 16); on the limits to contemporary history and historical case studies, see Blondel, 1976, pp. 68–72; and Cowling, 1963, pp. 20–38).

The hallmark of the descriptive–inductive approach is 'hyperfactualism'. In other words, 'observation was to come first; the fact stood paramount' (Landau, 1979, p. 133). The great virtue of institutions was that:

they appeared as real. They were concrete; they could be pointed to, observed, touched. They could be examined for their operations . . . And . . . what could be more logical, more natural, than to turn to the *concreteness* of institutions, the *facts* of their existence, the character of their *actions* and the *exercise* of their power. (Landau, 1979, p. 181; see also Easton, 1971, pp. 66–78; and Johnson, 1975, p. 279)

The approach is inductive because we draw inferences from repeated observations. The key points are that the study of political institutions displays a preference for 'letting the facts speak for themselves' matched only by its distaste for theory, especially modern social and political theory, which was seen as 'secondary – even dangerous' (Landau, 1979, p. 133; and, for an example, see Browning in Wilson, 1989, pp. i and ii).

## ☐ Formal–legal

Eckstein (1979, p. 2) defines this method succinctly:

Formal–legal inquiry involves two emphases. One is the study of public law: hence the term *legal*. The other involves the study of formal governmental organisations: hence *formal*. These emphases coalesce . . . in the study of public laws that concern formal governmental organisations – in the study of 'constitutional' structure. [Emphasis as in original.]

The term 'constitution' often refers to the 'documentary constitution . . . and a historical account of the growth of written constitutions' (Wolf-Philips, 1972, p. 9) but this use is too narrow. Herman Finer, possibly the doyen of the institutional approach (see below), defines a constitution as 'the system of fundamental political institutions' (Finer, 1932, p. 181). In other words, the formal–legal approach covers the study of written constitutional documents but extends far beyond them.

Mackenzie (1967, p. 278) notes that 'before 1914 it would have been inconceivable that one could discuss political systems without also discussing legal systems'. The tradition might lack 'vitality' in Britain but it 'survives' in France, Germany and Italy (see also Ridley, 1975, p. 15). Formal–legal studies were not as dominant in Britain because of the 'baleful shadow' of Dicey, who produced 'a cripplingly restricted view of public law' which was an important cause of the late development of public law in Britain (Drewry, 1995, p. 45). However, although the study of public law never occupied as central a position in political science in Britain as on the Continent, none the less it remained an essential ingredient in the analysis of constitutions and formal organisations (for a survey of the current state of public law in Britain, see Drewry, 1995).

## ☐ Historical–comparative

The study of political institutions is also comparative. As Woodrow Wilson (Wilson, 1899, p. xxxiv) argues:

> our own institutions can be understood and appreciated only by those who know other systems of government . . . By the use of a thorough comparative and historical method . . . a general clarification of views may be obtained. (For a modern illustration, see Ridley, 1975, pp. 7 and 102).

The finest exponent of the historical–comparative approach is Herman Finer (Finer, 1932; see also Chapman, 1959; Wheare, 1946, 1951). In sharp contrast to many of his contemporaries, Finer did not adopt a country-by-country approach, but compared institution with institution across countries. He locates his institutional analysis within both a theory of the state (ch. 1) and the economic and historical context (ch. 2 and 3). Finer claims that his approach is scientific, 'explaining objectively the why and wherefore of things'. He surveys the main political institutions 'not only in their legal form, but in their operation' (Finer, 1932, p. viii), and as they evolved stage by stage (Finer, 1954, p. 4). But why did he focus on political institutions? For Finer, 'the essence of the state is in its monopoly of coercive power, declared and enforced as the only legitimate monopoly' (1954, p. 10, but see 1932, pp. 20–2 and to show that his conception of the state was not unique, see also Sait, 1938, ch. 5; and Wilson, 1899, p. 572).

Political institutions are 'instrumentalities': 'The State is a human grouping in which rules a certain power-relationship between its individual and associated constituents. This power-relationship is embodied in political institutions. (Finer, 1932, p. 181).

Then and only then does he begin to compare the political institutions of the USA, Britain, France and Germany. His analysis covers the elements of state organisation, including democracy, separation of powers, constitutions, central–local territorial relations, and federalism. Finally, he turns to 'the principal parts of modern political machinery, namely, the Electorate, the Parties, Parliament, the Cabinet, the Chief of State, the Civil Service and the Judiciary' (Finer, 1932, p. 949). Finer's approach is not narrow and formal. It is grounded in a theory of the state and explores both the evolution of the institutions and their operation. The critics of the institutional approach do not do justice to Finer's 'powerful', 'unsurpassed' analysis (Finer, S. E., 1987, p. 234).

# ☐ *Theory*

The institutional approach makes statements about the causes and consequences of political institutions and it espouses the political values of liberal democracy.

# ☐ Causal statements

As Eckstein (1979, p. 3) notes the formal–legal approach provides both a general theoretical framework and prescriptive explanations. First, its proponents treat legal rules and procedures as the basic independent variable, and the functioning and fate of democracies as the dependent variable. For example, Duverger (1959) criticises electoral laws on proportional representation because they fragment party systems and undermine representative democracy.

Second, rules prescribe behaviour; that is, behaviour occurs because of a particular rule. For example, local authorities in the UK limit increases in the council tax because they know that the government can impose a legal ceiling, or cap. The influence of rules and procedures on political behaviour lies at the heart of the case for the study of political institutions.

A recent example of the institutional approach in Britain is Nevil Johnson, who argues (Johnson, 1973, pp. xi–xii) that political institutions: 'have a certain autonomy as determinants of political behaviour and activity'; 'express . . . ideas about political authority . . . and embody a continuing approach to resolving the issues which arise in the relations between citizen and government'; and 'show a great capacity for survival' so 'the procedural norms which they embody may continue to be influential'. However, this view of institutions as a cause of political actions is too narrow. There is also an important normative argument.

## ☐ Political values

Although hyperfactualism is a characteristic of the study of political institutions, one of the great benefits claimed for the approach is that 'it provides an opportunity for reintegrating the empirical study of politics with the analysis of political values (Johnson, 1975, p. 280; see also Ridley, 1975, p. 19). Johnson's (1975, pp. 276–7) rationale for study of political institutions draws on the political philosophy of Michael Oakeshott:

> political institutions express particular choices about how political relationships ought to be shaped; they are in the nature of continuing injunctions to members of a society that they should try to conduct themselves in specific ways when engaged in the pursuit of political ends. This is to define political institutions as necessarily containing a normative element.

And the normative elements, or values, most commonly espoused are those of liberal democracy, referred to in Britain as 'the Westminster model'.

The Westminster model has several defining features about which there is limited agreement. The relevant characteristics include: disciplined, programmatic majority party government; institutionalised opposition; a neutral career Civil Service; and Cabinet government. However, Wilson (1994, p. 193) argues that the defining characteristic is 'the unity of the legislature and executive secured through a disciplined political party'. This model was exported to Commonwealth countries on independence but its sway also extended to the USA with proposals from the American Political Science Association to introduce a more disciplined, and more responsible, party system (APSA, 1950). Most important, the model was a defining characteristic of 'the British School' of political science (Gamble, 1990, p. 407), also known as the Whig tradition (see Birch, 1964). Thus, as Gamble (1990, pp. 408–9) comments, there was:

> a widespread consensus on the character and the merits of British political institutions. The leading practitioners of political science were convinced that change needed to be evolutionary and gradual and there were strict limits to what could be achieved through political action. Study of the past revealed both the achievements of English political institutions and the difficulty of improving upon them without endangering their survival. What was celebrated was the practical wisdom embodied in England's constitutional arrangements, a quality demonstrated by the continuity of British institutions which was in sharp contrast to the interruptions and disorders common elsewhere.

The concern with preserving tradition and the case for evolutionary change persists to this day (see, for example, Johnson, 1980).

So, the institutional approach is: a subject matter covering the rules, procedures and formal organisations of government, which employs the tools of the lawyer and the historian to explain the constraints on both political behaviour and democratic effectiveness, and fostering liberal democracy, especially the Westminster model of representative democracy. Clearly, not everybody who employs the institutional method subscribes to every point noted above, but enough recur to justify this characterisation.

# ■ The critics

The study of political institutions has numerous critics, many of whom substitute vigour for accuracy. David Easton (Easton, 1971 [1953]) was the most influential critic of the traditional study of politics, shaping the attitudes of a generation of US behavioural political scientists. Easton's main aim was to develop a systematic conceptual framework which would identify the significant political variables and their relationships to each other. Given his theoretical ambitions, he found the study of political institutions wanting on two grounds. First, the analysis of law and institutions could not explain policy or power because it did not cover all the relevant variables (Easton, 1971, ch. 6). Second, 'hyperfactualism', or 'reverence for the fact' (p. 75), meant that political scientists suffered from 'theoretical malnutrition' (p. 77), neglecting 'the general framework within which these facts could acquire meaning' (p. 89).

Other behaviouralist critics verged on intemperate. Thus, Macridis (1963, pp. 47–8) claims that comparative government was 'excessively formalistic in its approach to political institutions'; did not have 'a sophisticated awareness of the informal arrangements of society and of their role in the formation of decisions and the exercise of power'; was 'insensitive to the non-political determinants of political behaviour'; was 'descriptive rather than problem-solving, or analytic in its method'; was insensitive to hypotheses and their verification; and, therefore, was unable to formulate a comparative 'political theory of dynamics'. In short, the study of political institutions was not behaviouralism. It was 'state-centred' when the fashion of the day dictated that political science should adopt a 'society-centred perspective' (Nordlinger, 1981, p. 1).

The criticisms also extend to methods; behaviouralism proselytised for positivist research methods and quantification. Thus, Macridis (1963, p. 49) advocates research which elaborates a tentative classificatory scheme; conceptualises a problem-orientated approach; formulates a hypothesis or a set of hypotheses; and tests hypotheses by empirical data to eliminate the untenable and formulate new ones. This new science of politics had little truck with the methods of history or law. Thus, historical methods are inadequate because they focus on the unique and cannot explain systematically the structure and behaviour of governments. Legal analysis is inadequate because of the gap between the formal statements of the law and the practice of government (see, for example, Blondel, 1976, pp. 20–5, 68–72 and 127–8). Because the study of political institutions had an outmoded organising perspective and employed methods which offended the canons of the 'new science', its position as one of the twin pillars of political science was under challenge (see, for example, Dearlove, 1989, pp. 522–3).

There are some obvious problems with these criticisms. First, the critics erect a straw man; for example, Macridis's criticisms are simply wrong when applied to Herman Finer, who contextualises institutions, explores the relationship between formal requirements and informal behaviour, and seeks to explain cross-national institutional differences and their consequences for democracy. Perhaps the main complaint is that Finer uses an unfashionable approach with an outmoded argot.

The second, and most common, mistake is to turn, often justifiable, criticisms of methods into a general condemnation of the focus on institutions. There are limits to historical and legal methods but, equally, behaviouralism and its methods have their long-standing critics. (See, for example, Bernstein, 1979, Parts 1 and 2; and for a critique by an institutionalist, see, Johnson, 1989, ch. 4.) Logically it is possible to study institutions using scientific methods.

Third, the theoretical criticisms are often misplaced. For example, the 'British School' is an 'organising perspective (Gamble, 1990a, p. 405). It is not a causal theory in the behavioural sense (see pp. 17–18 above). An organising perspective provides a map of the subject and signposts to its central questions. For example, this perspective could stress the historical understanding of political institutions as the expression of human purpose and ideas (Greenleaf, 1983; Johnson 1975; Oakeshott, 1967). Critics of the study of political institutions often concentrate their fire on the associated organising perspective, which is neither testable nor refutable, and logically separable from the study of institutions.

Fourth, there is not necessarily any connection between the institutional approach and particular values or prescriptions for reform. The Whitehall model is less alluring in the post-colonial era, but the study of political institutions remains as important a part of political science as ever. It also has a new practical rationale as the emerging democracies of Eastern Europe write their constitutions and redesign their institutional arrangements (see, for example, Elster, 1993).

Finally, critics link the study of political institutions with its founders and dismiss the approach because it is not 'at the cutting edge' of the discipline. Questions of short-term fashion aside, the study of institutions remains a central pillar of British political science (see Gamble, 1990a, pp. 419–20; Hayward, 1986, p. 14). Continuity is as much a feature of British political science as it is of British politics, a parallel which should not be written off as mere coincidence.

Some criticisms are justified: institutionalists all too often do not spell out either their organising perspective or their causal theory, and do not explore the limits of their preferred approach. It may be true that:

> Some early or classical approaches to politics . . . have overstated the formal nature of . . . regular procedures and given insufficient weight to the less formal processes which themselves become institutionalised through repetition or duration over time.

However,

> It does not . . . follow that we can, or should, dispense with a concept that pinpoints regular processes or mechanisms for channelling certain activities, meeting certain recurrent challenges and contingencies and settling disagreements on and about the allocation of values – or indeed determining what the values are which will be allocated in a given territory in a specific era. (Bogdanor, 1987, p. 291)

By distinguishing between subject, method and theory, it is much easier to identify which bits of the approach to keep and which to discard. The focus on institutions and the methods of the historian and the lawyer remain relevant; the reforms of the Westminster model less so. Implicit assumptions must give way to an explicit theory within which to locate the study of institutions.

# ■ Varieties of institutionalism

The most striking feature about the study of political institutions in Britain is not, however, the continuity of the tradition I have just documented, but its fragmentation into several new approaches. This section reviews briefly three types of institutional analysis: *constitutional studies*, *public administration*, and the *'new institutionalism'*.

# ☐ *Constitutional studies*

The key characteristic of constitutional studies is that it remains the home of both the formal–legal approach and liberal–democratic reformism. Also, despite the often-recorded death of traditional institutionalism, this sub-field has remained productive since the 1970s. The traditional approach may no longer dominate but it is difficult to understand how Dearlove (1989, p. 531) can talk of the decline of constitutional studies when his own footnotes list a dozen books. Gamble (1990a, p. 416) concludes that 'writing on all aspects of the constitution has flourished in Britain in the last 20 years' and even a selective bibliography of constitutional studies would be long (see, for example, Harden, 1992; Lewis and Harden, 1986; Jowell and Oliver, 1989; Marshall, 1984; Norton, 1982, 1991a, 1991b; and Oliver, 1991).

If this large literature can be summarised in one paragraph, then its dominant characteristic is reforming the constitution. Commentators describe changes in British politics, compare practice to constitutional conventions, and conclude that the executive is too powerful, with few checks on its ability to enact policy; and that there is too little legal protection of civil liberties. The call is for a new constitutional settlement and a Bill of Rights, and it comes from all points on the political spectrum (compare, for example, Barnett *et al.*, 1993, with Mount, 1993). Dawn Oliver (1991) provides a more balanced assessment of the changing constitution. Her central thesis is that 'the accountability of government, its effectiveness and the status of citizenship are closely interrelated' and present arrangements are 'defective . . . in securing these three essentials of good government' (Oliver, 1991, p. 202). She does not argue for a particular reform package but considers the pros and cons of the several proposals for reform advocated by such groups as Charter 88; for example, freedom of information; a Bill of Rights. Her objective is stimulate 'a wider consciousness of the defects of the system as it operates at present and an appreciation of the complexities of the process of reform' (p. 215). Most commentators in this vein are considerably less cautious (see, for example, Lewis and Harden, 1986; and for more examples and a critique, see Norton, 1991b).

Constitutional studies remain, therefore, a prime example of formal–legal methods in the study of political institutions, and vulnerable to the conventional critique of the institutional approach. There are two responses to the standard criticism that formal–legal methods are guilty of formalism or focusing on rules and procedures to the neglect of behaviour.

First, Johnson (1975, p. 276) claims that institutional analysis does not take such a restrictive view; it does analyse institutions in action. More importantly, he sees institutions as expressions of political purpose and, therefore, institutional analysis must explore 'the manner in which the life of institutions expresses (or fails to express) the intentions implicit in the norms, procedures or rules which determine the character of the institutions themselves' (Johnson, 1975, p. 277). So, a purely formal analysis would be 'misconceived'.

Second, constitutional studies should be seen as 'a point of explanatory departure' (Dearlove, 1989, p. 538) within a broader theoretical framework for studying the state. Modern political theory provides several such frameworks, ranging from pluralism with its liking for hypotheses and refutation to hermeneutics and the structure-agency problem. I argue only for the general point that, to avoid formalism, it is essential to locate constitutional studies within a broader perspective or theory.

# ☐ Public administration

Public administration is a major sub-field within political science. Definitions invariably include such phrases as the study of 'the institutional arrangements for the provision of public services' (Hood, 1987, p. 504) or 'the study of public bureaucracies' (Rhodes, 1979, p. 7). Without doubt, its key characteristic is the study of institutions, to the point where its critics complain about the 'descriptive', 'formal' nature of the subject (Dunleavy, 1982, p. 215). Thus, William Robson (1975, p. 195) describes the dominant approach as 'institutional. It concentrated attention on the authorities engaged in public administration, analysed their history, structure, functions, powers and relationships. It enquired how they worked and the degree of effectiveness they achieved.' However, traditional public administration, just like traditional political studies, had to confront its behavioural challenge in the 1960s (although behaviouralism did not supplant traditional approaches; see, for example, Drewry and Butcher, 1988; Jones and Stewart, 1983).

Organisation theory is a firmly-established part of the intellectual history of public administration and, from the 1950s onwards, it developed many schools of thought (for a brief survey, see, Henry, 1986). The 'classics' include Max Weber and the study of bureaucracy, and Frederick Winslow Taylor and scientific management. However, this stress on formal structure was criticised strongly by proponents of the human relations approach who emphasised the importance of informal organisation, especially group behaviour in the workplace. After the Second World War, the emphasis shifted to the study of organisational decision-making and to organisations as systems interacting with a larger environment. After that, approaches multiplied and it is impossible to summarise them here (see Hood, 1990; Rhodes, 1991).

The key characteristic of organisation theory is that it always kept its concern with formal organisation. Early theorists debated the relative

,‗‗‗‗ce of formal organisation (for example, the rules of a bureaucracy) versus informal organisation (or the behaviour of individual
employees). Contingency theorists explored the 'fit' between an organisation's structure and its environment, arguing there was no best way to
organise either a business or a public bureaucracy (see, for example,
Greenwood *et al.*, 1980). Policy network theories adopt a 'state-centric'
approach to public policy making, studying 'behaviour within institutional
contexts' (Gamble, 1990a, p. 417). Thus, policy emerges from the
interaction between government organisations (especially central government departments or agencies) and a network of other organisations
(especially professional and economic interests). Policy networks is an
institutionalist approach (see Marsh and Rhodes, 1992b).

Outside public administration, organisation theory had little impact on
political science, in part because it 'sublimated politics' (Wolin, 1960,
p. 423) to narrow questions of efficiency and ignored political institutions
for 'trivial organisations' (Perrow, 1986, p. 172, but for a notable
exception, see Allison, 1971). In other words, as for constitutional studies,
organisation theory needs a broader organising perspective or theory; a
point often made by its own critics (for a resumé of the several debates, see
Donaldson, 1985). None the less, public administration remained a safe
reservation for the institutional approach in both its traditional and
organisation theory guises.

## ☐ *The 'new institutionalism'*

According to March and Olsen (1984, p. 734) traditional political
institutions 'have receded in importance from the position they held in
the earlier theories of political scientists'. They criticise contemporary
political science because, for example; it is *contextual*, or sociocentric,
emphasising the social context of political behaviour and downgrading the
importance of the state as an independent cause (p. 735); *reductionist*,
explaining politics as the outcome of individual actions (pp. 735–6); and
*utilitarian*, explaining individual actions as motivated by rational self-
interest (pp. 736–7). In contrast, the new institutionalism 'insists on a more
autonomous role for political institutions'. Thus:

> The bureaucratic agency, the legislative committee, and the appellate court are
> arenas for contending social forces, but they are also collections of standard
> operating procedures and structures that define and defend interests. They are
> political actors in their own right. (p. 738)

For the reader of this chapter, the assertion that 'the organisation of
political life makes a difference' (p. 747) prompts the question: 'What is
new about the new institutionalism?' The answer of several critics is 'not a

lot' (see, for example, Almond, 1988; and Jordan, 1990) and the claims of, for example, Olsen (1988, p. 32)) are modest. Thus, he suggests that behavioural models of decision making are possible sources of theoretical ideas; and 'Hopefully, a new institutionalism will also move the study of politics closer to political theory, history and law – without returning to the old tradition of historical-descriptive, legalistic institutionalism.'

Hall (1986, pp. 19–20) also wants to compose an historical–institutional explanation: 'that is capable of explaining historical continuities and cross-national variations in policy' (see also Bulmer, 1994). He defines institutions as 'formal rules, compliance procedures and standard operating practices that structure relationships between individuals in various units of the polity and the economy'. But, he claims that his approach differs from earlier forms of institutionalism because his definition of institutions covers not only 'the constitution and formal political practices' but also 'less formal organisational networks'. Hall's approach prompts the conclusion that the 'new' institutionalism is the meeting of history and organisation theory to study political institutions. If these individual ingredients are as old as the hills, then the mixture is novel (although not new; see Chandler, 1969).

It is difficult to disagree with Jordan's assessment (1990, pp. 482, 484) that the new institutionalism attracted so much attention because the label marked 'a disposition to oppose the political science mainstream' and reflected 'the shift of ground by some of those interested in the state'. Indeed, the study of institutions could be new only to the advocates of American behaviouralism or European state theory who had deliberately downgraded its importance. It had always remained part of the political science mainstream.

# Conclusions: redefining the institutional approach

It is tempting to conclude that the study of political institutions is not so much theory or method as *topic*. To do so would be to undervalue the importance of political institutions for understanding both government and the discipline of politics. I now summarise the central arguments of this chapter before assessing the limits to the various approaches to the study of political institutions by returning to my original headings of subject, theory and method.

The institutional approach is one of the central pillars of the discipline of politics. It focuses on the rules, procedures and formal organisations of government. Its methods are institutional–descriptive, formal–legal, and historical–comparative. It employs the techniques of the historian and the lawyer. It seeks to explain the relationship between structure and democracy and the ways in which rules, procedures and formal organisation succeed or fail in constraining political behaviour.

The institutional approach remains a defining characteristic of the British School of politics. Also, constitutional studies, public administration and the new institutionalism all took institutions as the starting point for their analysis. Thus, the institutional approach is widely practised, often with a slightly apologetic air because it is a subject in search of a rationale. This rationale lies in a multitheoretic approach employing a plurality of research methods.

## ☐ *Subject*

For a modern audience, it is worth saying again that the study of political institutions is a core subject for the discipline of politics in the late twentieth century. It does not matter that much research is along traditional descriptive lines, for the simple reason that we know so little about the most important political institutions such as central government departments or the executive. Butler (1958, p. 108) comments, 'There are many operations of national and local government that have never been described – or never described adequately. There are no areas that have been so comprehensively treated that they could not profitably be restudied from a fresh angle.' With only minor reservations, that assessment still applies to the study of British government (Rhodes, 1995).

Even more important, the subject is central to the 'integrity of political science' (as argued in the Introduction to this book). To repeat, 'the state system *exists*. Political science, as science or as discipline or profession, must recognise its institutional matrix or pay a price in irrelevance and futility' (Waldo, 1975, p. 7, [emphasis as in original]; see also Blondel, 1976, ch. 7). There is, therefore, noteworthy agreement between mainstream political science and its state theory critics about the centrality of political institutions to the discipline of politics. But, and it is an important qualification, political institutions form only part of the explanation whatever the theory under scrutiny.

## ☐ *Theory*

In criticising the institutional approach for its distrust of theory I have not argued for any one organising perspective or theory. The discipline of politics is too eclectic to justify such theoretical imperialism on my part. What I am saying is that political scientists ought to be explicit about the intellectual baggage they bring to the choice of problem and the analysis of it. We must cast off the implicit assumptions of the traditional approach to political institutions and replace them with explicit perspectives or theories. I prefer multitheoretic research that assesses competing hypotheses drawn from the several modern political theories (on which, see Dunleavy and O'Leary, 1987). More important, however, is a critical stance towards any theory. No theory is ever true, it is only more or less instructive. You can learn from the critical assessment of one theory; you can learn more from a comparative critical assessment of several theories when they are brought to bear on a single topic. The study of political institutions will benefit greatly from such multi-theoretic research.

# ☐ *Method*

By long association, the institutional approach employs the skills of the historian and the lawyer. Even the new institutionalists claim to have rediscovered the value of an historical approach. Drewry's (1995) call for closer links between politics and public law continues to rehabilitate the traditional approach to the study of institutions. So far, so useful, but it is not far enough. The return to history and law perpetuates a false antithesis between the institutional approach and behavioural methods. Behaviouralists as false prophets of the new science of politics are one thing, but behaviouralism as methodological pluralism is another. The behavioural revolution brought much greater methodological sophistication to the study of politics and the study of political institutions can draw on the full range of methods, not just on history and law.

Two examples of such methods will illustrate the point. First quantification and statistical analysis are as useful for the analysis of institutions as for the political behaviour of individuals. The sources, and narrative techniques, of the historian are the most common way of describing the roles of British Cabinet Ministers. However, it is possible to use statistical techniques. For example, it is easy to count how much time ministers spend on their several activities, including the frequency of their appearances in Parliament. This information can be analysed by department or ministerial tenure to see if ministers who have been in post for many years spend less time in Parliament than newly-appointed ministers (see, for example, Dunleavy *et al.*, 1990). Statistical analysis is not a rival to the institutional approach: they complement each other.

Second, although case studies are the stock-in-trade of the historian and criticised for focusing on the particular and the unique, they can compare and generalise. As I have argued elsewhere (Rhodes, 1994, pp. 182–4), the comparative case method allows valid generalisations provided that there is a theoretical statement against which to compare the case studies. If there are several case studies, carried out to a standard design, with each case compared to the initial theory in turn, it is possible to make analytical, not statistical, generalisations. It is even possible to generalise based on a single case study – the heuristic case method – if the case study sets out explicitly to test a theoretical proposition (see also Eckstein, 1975; and Yin, 1984). To exploit fully the potential of the case method, the institutional approach must shake off its distrust of theory while retaining 'thick descriptions'.

The discipline of political science is prone to fads and fashions. One senior colleague commented, 'You only need to sit still, it all comes "round again".' It may well do, but not in an identical form. There is a future for the institutional approach but not as it existed in its classic form. The distaste for theory, the exclusive reliance on history and law, the reformism of the Westminster model must all go if the approach is to thrive. The issue cannot be posed as if virtue always lies with the historians and all we have to do is to wait for the behaviouralists to see the error of their ways. What we have to do is to learn lessons from behaviouralism. Methodological pluralism and the multitheoretic approach reinvent the institutional approach, they do not restate it in its classic form. And, just as important, a defensible institutional approach provides the discipline of political science with a clear sense of identity. Eckstein (1979) is a critic of formal–legal study. None the less, he sees it as a 'science of the state' which should 'not be confused with political science' (p. 1). Here lies a crucial contrast with the central argument of this chapter: this *staatswissenschaft* is not distinct from political science – it is its heart.

# ■ Further reading

For such a diffuse topic, it is difficult to identify the 'key' texts. On 'classic' institutionalism there is no alternative to Finer, 1954 (the one-volume abridged version). For a more recent statement of 'classic' institutionalism, see Johnson, 1975. On present-day variants, there is no one source covering all species of institutionalism. On constitutional studies, see Oliver, 1991. On organisation theory, see Perrow, 1986. On policy networks, see Marsh and Rhodes, 1992b. On institutional economics, see Jackson, 1982 and North, 1986. On the 'new institutionalism', see March and Olsen, 1984 (reprinted in 1989, ch. 1). On modern theories of the state, see Dunleavy and O'Leary, 1987. Finally, on the methods of the historian, see Kavanagh, 1991; and Barzun and Graff, 1992; on case studies, see Rhodes, 1994; and on the relevance of legal studies to politics, see Drewry, 1995.

# ■ Chapter 3 ■

# Behavioural Analysis
## David Sanders

The behavioural approach to social and political analysis concentrates on a single, deceptively simple, question: Why do people behave in the way they do? What differentiates behaviouralists from other social scientists is their insistence (a) that *observable* behaviour, whether it is at the level of the individual or the social aggregate, should be the focus of analysis; and (b) that any explanation of that behaviour should be susceptible to empirical testing.

Scholars working in the behavioural tradition have investigated a wide range of substantive problems. Behaviouralists have extensively analysed the reasons that underlie the main form of mass political participation in democratic countries: voting (for example, Heath *et al.*, 1994). They have also examined the origins of participation in other, more unconventional, forms of political activity such as demonstrations, strikes and even riots (e.g. Barnes and Kaase, 1979). At the elite level, behaviouralists have analysed leadership behaviour, placing particular emphasis on the connections between the way in which leaders view the world (their attitudes and values) and the particular actions that they take (for example, Allison, 1971; King, 1985; Sanders, 1990; Dunleavy *et al.*, 1993). In terms of social aggregates, behavioural analysis has examined the actions of interest groups (for example, Grant and Marsh, 1979; Wilson, 1990) and political parties (for example, Budge and Fairlie, 1983; Budge and Laver, 1992). At the international level, behavioural analysis has also focused on the actions of nation states (for example, Rosenau, 1969), as well as on the behaviour of non-state actors such as multinational corporations, international terrorist groups and supranational organisations such as the EU (for example, Keohane, 1984; Baldwin, 1993). In all these diverse contexts, the central questions that behaviouralists seek to answer are simple: What do the actors involved actually do? How can we best explain why they do it?

These are obviously not the only questions that can be asked about individual and social actors. Behaviouralists simply believe that they are the most important ones.

This chapter is divided into four sections. The first provides a brief outline of the origins of behaviouralism and summarises the core analytic assertions that underpin it; the second section reviews the main criticisms that, with varying degrees of justification, have been levelled at the behavioural approach; the third part describes one major study – Gurr's analysis of political violence – which illustrates some of the more positive features of behavioural analysis; and the final section considers the influence that behaviouralism continues to exert on contemporary political researchers.

# ■ The rise of the behavioural movement and its core characteristics

The behavioural movement, which assumed an important position in the social sciences in the 1950s and 1960s, had its philosophical origins in the writings of Auguste Comte (Comte, 1974) in the nineteenth century and in the logical positivism of the 'Vienna Circle' in the 1920s. Positivism, which was popularised in Britain by Alfred Ayer and in Germany by Carl Hempel, asserted that analytic statements made about the physical or social world fell into one of three categories. First, such statements could be useful tautologies: they could be purely definitional statements that assigned a specific meaning to a particular phenomenon or concept. For example, we might define families living on less than one-third of the average weekly wage as 'living below the poverty line'. Second, statements could be empirical, that is to say, they could be tested against observation in order to see if they were true or false. Third, statements that fell into neither of the first two categories were devoid of analytic meaning. For the positivists, in short, meaningful analysis could proceed only on the basis of useful tautologies and empirical statements: metaphysics, theology, aesthetics and even ethics merely introduced meaningless obfuscation into the process of enquiry.

It would not be correct, of course, to assume that behaviouralism accepted all the philosophical precepts of positivism. Even as behaviouralism was gaining increasingly wide acceptance among social scientists in the 1950s, positivism itself was being subjected to ferocious philosophical criticism – not least on the grounds that it was unclear whether positivism's assertion that there were only three types of statement was itself tautological, empirical or meaningless. This said, behaviouralism's view of the nature of empirical theory and of explanation were strongly influenced by the positivist tradition. Although there are many definitions of these two critical terms, most behaviouralists would probably accept something along the lines of the following:

(a) An *empirical theory* is a set of interconnected abstract statements, consisting of assumptions, definitions and empirically-testable hypotheses, which purports to describe and explain the occurence of a given phenomenon or set of phenomena.
(b) An *explanation* is a causal account of the occurrence of some phenomenon or set of phenomena. An explanation of a particular (class of) event(s) consists in the specification of the minimum non-tautological set of antecedent necessary and sufficient conditions required for its (their) occurrence.

The importance of these definitions of theory and explanation lies in the implications that they have for theory evaluation. For positivists, the crucial question that should always be asked about any purportedly explanatory theory is: "How would we know if this theory were incorrect?" Behaviouralism's endorsement of the central importance of this question is precisely what demonstrates its intellectual debt to positivism. For both positivists and behaviouralists, there are three main ways in which explanatory theories can be evaluated. First, a 'good' theory must be internally consistent: it must not make statements such that both the presence and the absence of a given set of antecedent conditions are deemed to 'cause' the occurence of the phenomenon that is purportedly being explained. Second, a 'good' theory relating to a specific class of phenomena should, as far as possible, be consistent with other theories that seek to explain related phenomena. Third, and crucially, genuinely explanatory theories must be capable of generating empirical predictions that can be tested against observation. The only meaningful way of deciding between competing theories (which might appear to be equally plausible in other respects) is by empirical testing. This testing can be conducted either at the level of the individual social actor or at the level of the social aggregate – whichever is appropriate given the nature of the theory that is being tested.

It is this emphasis on empirical observation and testing that produces the two characteristic features of the behavioural approach to social enquiry. The first – and least contentious – of these is behaviouralism's commitment to the systematic use of all the relevant empirical evidence rather than a limited set of illustrative supporting examples. This commitment simply means that, when a particular theoretical statement is being investigated, the researcher must not limit her/himself to a consideration of only those observed cases that provide 'anecdotal' support for the theoretical claims that are being made. Rather, the researcher must consider *all* the cases – or at least a representative sample of them – that are encompassed by the theoretical statement that is being evaluated.

It is in this context that the use and development of statistical techniques is justified by behaviouralists – as a vehicle for analysing large amounts of 'relevant empirical evidence'. It should be emphasised in the strongest possible terms, however, that behaviouralism is *not* synonymous either with quantification or with the downgrading of qualitative research. Certainly, behavioural researchers have frequently used quantitative techniques as heuristic devices for handling evidence. There is nothing intrinsic in behaviouralism's epistemological position, however, that requires quantification. On the contrary, quantitative and qualitative forms of empirical analysis are equally acceptable to behavioural researchers. What matters for them is not whether evidence is qualitative or quantitative but (a) that it is used to evaluate theoretical propositions; and (b) that it is employed sytematically rather than illustratively.

The second characteristic feature of behavioural analysis is slightly more subtle in its implications – but no less important. It is simply that scientific theories and/or explanations must in principle be capable of being falsified. Note here that the reference is to 'scientific' rather than simply to 'empirical' or 'explanatory' theories. This usage reflects behaviouralism's commitment to Karl Popper's revision of 'traditional' positivism in which he (a) substituted the principle of falsifiability for that of verification; and (b) simultaneously identified the falsifiability criterion as the line of demarcation between 'scientific' and 'pseudo-scientific' enquiry (Popper, 1959).

In order fully to appreciate the import of this statement, a brief digression is necessary. We need to consider precisely what is meant by a theory or an explanation being 'falsifiable'. Consider the familiar statement that Popper himself used as an example: 'All swans are white'. Suppose that we observe a black swan. What does this tell us about the statement? One interpretation is that observing the black swan shows the statement to be empirically false: the statement was in principle *capable* of being falsified and it *has* been falsified. But there is another way of interpreting the statement in the light of a black swan being observed. The statement says that all swans are white: it follows that the black swan that we have observed cannot be a swan because it is not white: the statement, therefore, is not 'false'.

Can both of these interpretations be correct? The answer is that they can. Each interpretation makes a different set of assumptions about the definition of a swan. The first assumes that a swan is a large bird with a long neck that looks very pretty when it paddles through water; it says nothing of the bird's colour. In these circumstances, the definitions of 'swan' and 'colour' are *independent*: there is no overlap between them. In other words, it is *possible* to observe something that has all the characteristics of a swan regardless of its colour – we have observed a black swan; and, therefore, the initial statement must have been false. The second interpretation assumes that a swan is a large bird with a long neck that looks very pretty when it paddles through water *and that it is also white*. In other words, this second interpretation assumes that whiteness is part of the *definition* of being a swan. In these circumstances, when a black 'swan' is observed it cannot be a swan, because part of the definition of it being a swan is that it is white.

What is clear from this discussion is that the status of the statement depends upon whether or not its constituent terms are independently defined. With the first interpretation, the terms "swan" and "white" *are* independently defined. As a result, the statement is an empirical or falsifiable one: it is possible to test it against the world of observation. With the second interpretation, however, the terms "swan" and "white" are *not* independently defined. As a result, the statement is (partially) tautological: it is simply an untestable assertion that one of the defining features of a swan is that it is white.

This problem of interpretation is common in the social sciences. Consider the following statement. 'In general elections people vote against the incumbent government if they are dissatisfied with its performance.' Without further information, we cannot tell whether this is a testable empirical statement or merely a definitional tautology. The statement can, in fact, be interpreted in two completely different ways. First, we can interpret the statement in purely tautological terms. Looking at a particular election, we could say (a) that every voter who voted for the government *must* have been satisfied with its performance (otherwise s/he would not have voted for it); and (b) that every voter who did not vote for the government could not have been satisfied with its performance (otherwise s/he would have voted for it). With this interpretation, we can always 'believe' in the statement but we have not *demonstrated* that it is empirically correct; we have treated it purely as a tautology. The second interpretation is to regard the statement as an empirical one – but this is possible only if we provide a definition of dissatisfaction with the government that is independent of the act of voting. If we were to devise some independent way of measuring dissatisfaction, then we would obviously be able to test our initial statement against any available empirical evidence. We *might* find that all those who voted for the government were satisfied with its performance and that all those who voted against it were dissatisfied – in which case we would have corroborated the statement. Crucially, however, by providing independent definitions of 'voting' and of 'dissatisfaction' we create the possibility that the statement might be empirically incorrect: we render the statement *falsifiable* – even though we might hope that it will not be *falsified*.

Having distinguished between falsifiable and non-falsifiable statements, Popper goes on to suggest that theories can only be regarded as 'scientific' if they generate empirical predictions that are capable of being falsified. Theories which do not generate such predictions are merely sophisticated tautologies which explain nothing – no matter how elegant and elaborate they might appear. Many behaviouralists are unconcerned as to whether or not their research should be described as 'scientific'. Crucially, however, they are unequivocally committed to the principle of falsifiability. While behaviouralists do not deny that there are other ways of evaluating the adequacy of a particular theory, they none the less insist that a genuinely explanatory theory must engender falsifiable propositions of the form 'If A, then B; if not A, then not B'; and it must specify causal antecedents that are defined independently of the phenomenon that is supposedly being explained.

All this is not to suggest, however, that behaviouralists believe that all aspects of their theories must be capable of being falsified. As Lakatos (1971) has argued, most theories in the physical and social sciences contain a non-falsifiable set of 'core' propositions. These core propositions often take the form of highly abstract assumptions that are not susceptible to empirical testing. The non-falsifiability of the 'core' propositions, however, does not necessarily mean that the theory itself is non-falsifiable. Provided that a series of testable predictions, which can be examined in the light of empirical observation, can be derived logically from the 'core', then the theory as a whole can be regarded as falsifiable: it does represent something more than sophisticated tautology; it does provide the analyst with an opportunity to specify the conditions under which s/he would know that the theory was 'incorrect'.

Behaviouralists, then, emphasise the twin notions that theories should (a) seek to explain something; and (b) be capable, in principle, of being tested against the world of observation. For behaviouralists, non-falsifiable theories are not really theories at all. They are merely elaborate fantasies – of varying degrees of complexity – that scholars can choose to believe or disbelieve as they wish. For behaviouralists, theory evaluation must proceed beyond merely examining a theory in order to assess its internal consistency and the nature of the 'puzzles' that it seems to resolve: theory evaluation must also involve subjecting theoretical propositions to empirical test.

# ■ Criticisms of the behavioural approach

As with any other general approach in the social sciences, behaviouralism has been the target of a number of important criticisms. These criticisms can be grouped under three broad headings, and each will be examined in turn below.

# Objections to the positivist claim that statements which are neither definitions (useful tautologies) nor empirical are meaningless

It was noted earlier that behaviouralism has its philosophical roots in positivism. It would appear to follow that any weaknesses inherent in positivism must also therefore be inherent in behaviouralism. Among the many criticisms that have been levelled at positivism, perhaps the most important is the simple proposition that the large class of statements that positivism labels as 'meaningless' in fact contains many ideas that can add very significantly to our understanding of social behaviour and the human condition. In strict positivist terms, there can be no role for normative theory – for the investigation of what ought to be – because normative discourses are not restricted to definitional and empirical statements. Similarly, there can be no role for aesthetic or moral arguments, for the same reason. And there can be no role for the sort of hermeneutic analysis that seeks to understand social behaviour through deep introspection about the nature of human perceptions, thought processes and motivations. If positivism seeks to exclude these forms of reflection, the argument runs, it must be in error.

The extent to which positivists genuinely ever did deny the value of non-empirical analysis need not concern us here. It is important to point out, however, that most contemporary researchers who continue to work in the behaviouralist tradition would almost certainly reject the notion that there can be no role for normative theory, aesthetics or hermeneutics in political and social analysis. They would argue, instead, that these approaches yield a different form of knowledge or understanding – not that they are 'meaningless'. In essence, modern behaviouralists acknowledge freely this particular criticism of positivism. They deflect it from themselves by recognising that other, potentially useful, forms of knowledge can be acquired by scholars working in other intellectual traditions. Modern behaviouralists – 'post-behaviouralists' – simply prefer to subject their own theoretical claims to empirical test. They also suspect that scholars working in non-empirical traditions are never able to provide a satisfactory answer to the crucial question: 'How would you know if you were wrong?'

# The tendency towards mindless empiricism

One of the claims of the early positivists was that theoretical under-standing could be obtained only through a process of enquiry that began with theory-free observation of 'all the facts up to now' and which then derived law-like generalisations inductively from the empirical regularities that were observed. Later positivists, notably Carl Hempel and Popper, strongly rejected this 'narrow inductivist' view of the nature of scientific enquiry, arguing that enquiry could only proceed if the researcher's efforts to observe 'relevant facts' were guided either by clear theoretical expectations or, at a minimum, by some kind of explanatory 'hunch'. Hempel (1966, pp. 11–12) is worth quoting at length in this context:

> [A narrow inductivist investigation] . . . could never get off the ground. Even its first [fact gathering] phase could never be carried out, for a collection of *all* the facts would have to await the end of the world, so to speak; and even *all the facts up to now* cannot be collected since there are an infinite number and variety of them. Are we to examine, for example, all the grains of sand in all the deserts and on all the beaches, and are we to record their shapes, their weights, their chemical composition, their distances from each other, their constantly changing temperature, and their equally changing distance from the centre of the moon? Are we to record the the floating thoughts that cross our minds in the tedious process? The shapes of the clouds overhead, the changing color of the sky? The construction and the trade name of our writing equipment? Our own life histories and those of our fellow investigators? All these, and untold other things, are, after all, among 'all the facts up to now'.

In spite of positivism's moves away from inductivism, there can be no doubt that, between the early 1950s and the mid-1970s, a number of scholars working within the behavioural tradition did still appear to be committed to an inductivist approach to research. It would be unnecessarily invidious to isolate particular examples of this tendency. It is none the less fair to say that, during this period, many behaviouralists acted as if law-like scientific generalisations could be constructed purely by identifying the statistical regularities evident in large quantities of empirical data. This emphasis on data and the concommitant downgrading of a priori theoretical reasoning in turn produced two undesirable tendencies in behavioural research.

The first of these was a tendency to emphasise what can be easily measured rather than what might be theoretically important. This sort of criticism is always easy to make, in the sense that one person's triviality may be another's profundity. None the less, the tendency to play down the potential importance of phenomena that are intrisincally difficult to measure has always been a matter of concern to both critics and advocates of behavioural research. This has been especially true in relation to the analysis of electoral behaviour. Since the explosion of behavioural research in the 1950s, voting studies have concentrated primarily on electors' social profiles, partisan identifications, ideological positions, policy preferences and economic perceptions. Complex models have been devised – and tested empirically – which show the relative importance, and causal ordering, of different aspect of these various phenomena in the determination of the vote. (See, for example, Sarlvik and Crewe, 1983; Heath *et al.*, 1985, 1991).

Yet, despite the considerable contribution that behavioural analysis has made to our understanding of a voter's decision calculus, it has often been argued that, somehow, an important part of what it means to vote – as well as part of the calculus itself – may have been omitted from behavioural analyses. There has perhaps been insufficient attention paid to inconsistencies and contradictions in voters' political perceptions and to the possibility not only that many voters change their political preferences frequently, but also that their preferences vary, quite genuinely, with the social context in which they are expressed. There are other areas – relating to the way in which individuals reflect, to a greater or lesser degree, upon themselves – where behavioural electoral research has simply not dared to tread. What sort of person do I think I am? What aspirations and expectations do I have about my future life? What sort of life do I think I am capable of leading or should lead? How do I relate my notions of personal morality to the moral stances of the major political parties? The answers to questions such as these *may* have no bearing on the way in which political preferences are formed and transformed. Within the behavioural frame of reference, however, it is very hard to envisage how the responses to such questions – given the difficulty of measuring those responses systematically – could ever be incorporated into formal analysis. As a result, they are largely excluded from the analytic frame.

A second, and related, undesirable feature of behavioural research that arises from its overly empirical focus has been a tendency to concentrate on readily observed phenomena – such as voting – rather than the more subtle, and perhaps deeper, structural forces that promote stability and change in social and political systems. One obvious concept that has been neglected by behavioural research in this context is that of *interests*. The notion of interests has played an important part in a wide variety of social and political theories ranging from Marx, Max Weber and Vilfredo Pareto in the domestic field to Hans Morgenthau and E. H. Carr in the field of international relations. In all these contexts, social actors – whether they are individuals, groups of individuals or even nation states – are seen as pursuing strategies that are aimed at maximising their 'interests'. Yet, as scholars working in the behavioural tradition have found repeatedly, it is extraordinarily difficult to observe the 'interests' of a particular individual, group or state directly. In consequence, behavioural research has tended to shy away from the theoretical and empirical analysis of interests – preferring to leave the field clear for scholars working in other, non-empirical traditions.

# ☐ *The assumed independence of theory and* ☐ *observation*

The early behaviouralists proclaimed their approach to social enquiry as being both 'scientific' and 'value-free'. They claimed not to be seeking to justify any particular ethical or political stance. Rather, they sought simply to uncover 'the facts' through impartial observation and to offer politically-neutral theories that would explain them in the most parsimonious way. As the passage from Hempel quoted earlier shows, the degree of inductivism thus implied – in which 'explanatory theory' emerges only after all the relevant facts have been surveyed impartially – was always impossible. Some sort of initial theoretical understanding is necessary before the researcher can decide what it is that should be observed:

> Modern behaviouralists – along with researchers working in other intellectual traditions – roundly reject the notion that theory and observation are independent. On the contrary, most post-behaviouralists would now accept the *relativist* view that what is observed is in part a consequence of the theoretical position that the analyst adopts in the first place.

Modern behaviouralists, however, are distinguishable from hard-line relativists. It is one thing to allow that observations are coloured by theory; it is quite another to conclude that this means that one set of theories and observations are as good as another. For modern behaviouralists, the ultimate test of a good theory is still whether or not it is consistent with observation – with the available empirical evidence. Modern behaviouralists are perfectly prepared to accept that different theoretical positions are likely to elicit different descriptions of 'reality' – that they are likely to produce different 'observations'. They insist, however, that whatever 'observations' are implied by a particular theoretical perspective, those observations must be used in order to conduct a systematic empirical test of the theory that is being posited.

Finally, it is worth noting that behaviouralists are sometimes criticised – with some justification – for failing to comprehend the 'big picture' of social and political transformation. That is to say, by emphasising the description and explanation of observable individual and group behaviour, behaviouralists underestimate the importance of 'more profound' social and political changes that might be taking place. For example, theorists who debate the ways in which 'the state' evolves under conditions of advanced capitalism (for example, Adorno, 1976; Habermas, 1976; Jessop, 1990) tend to deride behavioural analysis as being concerned merely with superficialities and with failing to offer a theory (or explanation) of significant social or political change. Behaviouralists respond by pointing out that broad-ranging social theories that purport to analyse significant social change must be based on some sort of empirical observation. If a writer wishes to argue, for example, that 'the capitalist state' is in 'crisis', then s/he must be able to specify what the observable referents of the crisis actually are: if there is a 'crisis', (some) people must be taking certain sorts of action or must be thinking certain things that enable the analyst to 'know' that a 'crisis' exists. Similarly, if some new form of social relationship is emerging (perhaps as a result of new patterns of economic production) then that new form of relationship must have some empirical referent or referents, otherwise, how can the analyst 'know' that the new form is indeed occuring? Behaviouralists are entirely prepared to recognise that broad-ranging social and political theories are both possible and desirable. They merely insist that, if such theories are to be credible, they cannot be couched indefinitively at so high a level of abstraction as to render them incapable of being tested empirically. For behaviouralists, social and political theories are supposed to describe and explain that which can be observed – whether it involves stasis or change. Theories of social change only start to be interesting to behaviouralists when they (a) specify the empirical referents that are used in order to make the judgement that profound change is indeed taking place; and (b) provide the empirical evidence which shows that these referents are indeed changing in the specified direction. Behaviouralism is entirely neutral as to what the 'referents' in any theory should be – this is the domain of the social theorist her/himself. To behaviouralists, however, a social 'theory' without clear empirical referents is nothing more than mere assertion.

# ■ The strengths of the behavioural approach

While it is clear from the foregoing discussion that the behavioural approach can be subjected to serious criticism, it would be very wrong to infer that all examples of behavioural research are flawed. On the contrary, behavioural research at its best can make a considerable theoretical and empirical contribution to the understanding and explanation of social behaviour.

The strengths of the behavioural approach derive primarily from its advocates' determination to pursue forms of analysis that are *capable of replication*. Scholars working in the behavioural tradition are always concerned to establish that other researchers who make similar sets of assumptions as them and examine the same evidence would draw broadly similar conclusions. This need to ensure that research findings are capable of replication necessarily means that behaviouralists are obliged to be very clear in their specification of: (a) what it is that they are trying to explain; (b) the precise theoretical explanation that is being advanced; and (c) the way in which they are using empirical evidence in order to evaluate that theoretical explanation. The need for clarity of exposition in turn means that behaviouralists rarely enter into that most sterile area of academic debate: 'What did writer $X$ mean when s/he argued $Y$?' For behaviouralists, unless $X$ makes it clear what s/he means in the first place, then $X$'s work is clearly not capable of being replicated and argument $Y$ is therefore likely to be treated with suspicion in any case.

The strengths of 'good' behavioural analysis can be illustrated by reference to Ted Gurr's classic study of the causes of political violence or, as he terms it, 'civil strife' (Gurr, 1968a, 1968b). The core of Gurr's analysis is extraordinarily simple. His basic thesis, which draws strongly on research undertaken in the psychological field, is that people resort to political violence because they are 'relatively deprived'. This proposition can be expressed as a simple causal diagram:

Relative deprivation (RD)   $\longrightarrow$   Civil strife

where *civil strife* involves participation in riots, acts of guerrilla warfare, assassinations and physical ·assaults on political opponents; *relative deprivation* (RD) is the gap between 'value expectations' and 'perceived value capabilities'; *value expectations* are the income, wealth, status, quality of life and political rights that individuals think they *ought* to obtain; and *perceived value capabilities* are the income, wealth and so on that individuals believe they *will* obtain. In Gurr's terms, therefore, an individual is relatively deprived to the extent that there is a gap between her/his expectations and perceived capabilities. His basic hypothesis is that, other things being equal, the more relatively deprived an individual is, the greater will be her/his propensity to participate in violent political activity. A corollary to this individual-level proposition is that social aggregates (for example, cities, regions or countries) characterised by high levels of relative deprivation will experience higher levels of civil strife than comparable social aggregates where RD is lower.

Because Gurr's analysis makes theoretical statements about the relationship between RD and political violence at both the individual and the aggregate level, his thesis can, in principle, be tested at both of these levels. At the individual level, the test would involve examining information on a representative sample of people in one or more countries. The simple empirical question to be investigated would be: 'Are the relatively deprived individuals also the ones who engage in acts of political violence?' If this relationship held perfectly and if (say) 1000 people had been interviewed, findings similar to those shown in Table 3.1 would be anticipated. At the aggregate level, the test would involve examining, say, all the countries in the world over a specified time period. The equivalent empirical question would be: 'Are the countries with high levels of RD also the ones which experience high levels of civil strife?' Again, if the relationship held perfectly, empirical findings something like those shown in Table 3.2 would be anticipated.

**Table 3.1**    *Hypothetical cross tabulation of the individual-level relationship between political violence and relative deprivation*

|  | Not politically violent | Politically violent | Total |
|---|---|---|---|
| Not relatively deprived | 950 | 0 | 950 |
| Relatively deprived | 0 | 50 | 50 |
| Total | 950 | 50 | 1000 |

Note:   Assumes 1000 hypothetical individuals.

**Table 3.2**    *Hypothetical cross tabulation of the aggregate-level relationship between political violence and relative deprivation*

|  | Countries with low political violence | Countries with high political violence | Total |
|---|---|---|---|
| Countries with low relative deprivation | 100 | 0 | 150 |
| Countries with high relative deprivation | 0 | 50 | 50 |
| Total | 150 | 50 | 150 |

*Note*: Assumes 150 hypothetical countries.

Because of the lack of suitable cross-national survey data for testing his thesis at the individual level, Gurr opts to test out his ideas at the aggregate level. To complicate matters, however, Gurr recognises that there are likely to be *other* phenomena – apart from RD – which might affect the levels of civil strife experienced in different countries: these 'other phenomena' also need to be incorporated into the empirical test of the model if the 'true' effects of RD are to be estimated. Accordingly, as Figure 3.1 shows, Gurr's main model also seeks to take account of the effects of the strength and durability of existing political insitutions ('institutionalisation' and 'legitimacy'); the 'coercive potential' of the state; any geographical and sociopolitical conditions that might be conducive to the successful prosecution of guerrilla warfare ('social – structural facilitation'); and each country's experience of 'past strife'. Gurr also distinguishes between relative deprivation that results from *recent* changes in economic and/or political conditions ('short-term deprivation') and relative deprivation that derives from *longer-term* deficiencies ('persisting deprivation'). On the basis of a set of theoretical arguments that need not concern us here, Gurr hypothesises the causal ordering of effects to be as shown in Figure 3.1.

**Figure 3.1**   *Basic theoretical model tested by Gurr in his aggregate cross-national analysis of civil strife*

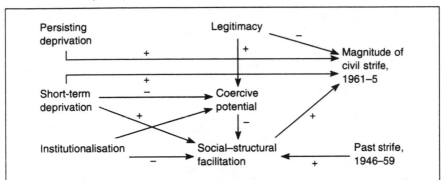

*Notes*:   A plus sign (+) indicates an hypothesised positive effect; a minus sign (−), indicates an hypothesised negative effect.
*Source*:   Ted Robert Gurr, 'A Causal Model of Civil Strife', *American Political Science Review*, 62 (1968), pp. 1104–24.

Before Gurr can test his theoretical ideas, however, he is obliged to *operationalise* the model outlined in Figure 3.1. Operationalisation is the process of translating an abstract verbal theory into a form that can be tested empirically – in this case, Gurr needs to obtain a score for each of the 112 countries included in his analysis. Operationalisation is necessary for the obvious reason that theories typically are couched in an abstract language (in this case, 'persisting deprivation', 'short-term deprivation', 'institutionalisation', 'social – structural facilitation' and so on) that does not always correspond directly to the world of observation. For each concept that the model defines, a set of empirical referents or *indicators* is required. Each of these indicators needs to be measured clearly and unambiguously so that every country analysed can be assigned a comparable 'score' for each concept. The specific indicators that Gurr employs for each of the concepts shown in Figure 3.1 are described in Table 3.3. An important part of his theoretical analysis – which cannot be reviewed here because of its length – consists in providing a set of arguments that link each concept to its operational indicators. However, since the concepts cannot themselves be directly measured, there is no formal, empirical, way of assessing the adequacy of these arguments: other scholars simply have to make their own judgements as to how plausible each of them is. The strength (or otherwise) of the arguments that are advanced at this stage of any enquiry determine the adequacy of the particular operationalisation that is provided. It is worth noting that almost all behavioural studies can be criticised – with varying degrees of justification – on the grounds that the operational indicators selected do not effectively measure the theoretical concepts to which they refer.

**Table 3.3**   *Main theoretical concepts and empirical indicators employed in Gurr's aggregate cross-national analysis of civil strife*

| *Concept* | *Indicator/operational measure* |
|---|---|
| **1. Persisting deprivation** | |
| • Economic discrimination | Percentage of population excluded from higher economic positions |
| • Political discrimination | Percentage of population excluded from the political elite |
| • Potential separatism | Percentage of population belonging to historically separatist regional or ethnic groupings |
| • Dependence on foreign capital | Percentage of GDP that accrues to foreign suppliers of goods or capital |
| • Lack of educational opportunity | Percentage of children not enrolled at primary or secondary school |
| **2. Short-term deprivation** | |
| • Short-term trade pattern | Whether or not the country's trade volume increased 1957–60 compared with 1950–57 |
| • Inflation | Whether inflation increased or decreased from 1958–61 to 1960–3 |
| • Growth rate | Whether GNP growth rate went up or down in 1960–63 compared with 1950–60 |
| • New restrictions imposed on political participation | 6-point scale of repressive government action; e.g<br>1 = harassment of a splinter party;<br>3 = banning of minor party; and<br>6 = dissolution of all parties |
| **3. Coercive potential** | Size of internal security forces as a percentage of the population, weighted by a 'loyalty' score |
| **4. Insitutionalisation** | Composite of:<br>• percentage of workforce unionised<br>• central government expenditure as a percentage of GDP<br>• duration of existing party system |
| **5. Legitimacy** | Composite of:<br>• whether or not political institutions were derived indigenously<br>• length of time since last major reform of domestic political institutions |
| **6. Social–structural facilitation** | Composite of:<br>• index of inaccessability of terrain<br>• degree of external support for insurgents<br>• size of Communist Party |
| **7. Magnitude of civil strife** | Composite index embracing incidence of demonstrations, political strikes, riots, local rebellions, assassinations, coups, mutinies plots, purges, widespread revolts, 1960–65. |

To those unfamiliar with computer-based techniques, the most difficult – indeed impenetrable – part of Gurr's work is undoubtedly his statistical analysis. For the purposes of the present exposition, there is no need to dwell on his statistical manipulations. It is sufficient to note (a) that Gurr's main purpose is to establish how much of the country-by-country variation in levels of civil strife can be explained by his measures of relative deprivation; and (b) that the multivariate statistical methodologies that he employs are well suited to this task. Gurr concludes that approximately a quarter of the cross-national variation in civil strife can be explained by varying levels of relative deprivation; that some of the remaining variation can be explained by other variables included in his model; and that just over a third of the variation remains 'unexplained'. In other words, what Gurr is able to show empirically is that there is some support for his initial hypothesis about the role of deprivation in the genesis of political violence. At the same time, however, his analysis also shows that other factors – some of which he is unable to specify – also exert important effects on the levels of political violence that different countries experience.

If this seems a rather timid conclusion, then so be it. Gurr begins his study with a single 'unicausal' explanation of civil strife. He then specifies an aggregate-level model that enables him to test his theoretical claims against the available empirical evidence. He concludes that the model derives some support from what is observed – that RD does indeed influence civil strife – but that there must be other factors at work which also cause people to resort to political violence. The implication of his empirical testing of his model is that further theoretical work is required – theorising which in turn requires a further round of empirical evaluation (Gurr, 1970). In all this, Gurr is engaging in a process of *retroduction* (Hanson, 1958). That is to say, his research involves a continuous interplay between theory and empirical testing – in which theory acts as a guide to empirical observation, operationalisation and testing and in which empirical findings are subsequently used to modify, revise and refine theory. Crucially, however, because Gurr's research follows behaviouralist precepts, it is always possible for the dispassionate observer to know exactly what it is that he is arguing and to know exactly what evidence he is using to substantiate his theoretical claims. In the often vague and confused world of social science theorising and research – in which some writers seem almost deliberately to deploy obfuscation as a means of pre-empting criticism – these are qualities to be cherished and nurtured. Gurr's analysis might be easy to criticise – particularly in terms of the operational indicators that are employed as surrogates for his major concepts. But, like all good behaviouralists, Gurr at least presents a clearly-expressed target for would-be critics. For behaviouralists, it is better to be clear and (possibly) wrong than to be so impenetrable that other writers are obliged to debate the 'meaning' of what has been written.

**Conclusion: the behavioural legacy in the 1990s**

Among behaviouralists working in the mid – 1990s, it is widely accepted that theoretical analysis must almost always be the starting point for serious empirical enquiry. This is not to say that theories cannot be modified, enhanced or rejected on the basis of empirical observation. Rather, theory acts as a vehicle for distancing the analyst from the potentially overwhelming detail of what can be directly observed, so that abstract deductions can be made about the connections between different phenomena. In addition, theory not only generates testable hypotheses but also provides guidelines and signposts as to the sort of empirical evidence that should be gathered in the first place. In short, theory plays an indispensable role in post-behavioural empirical analysis. Many post-behaviouralists would go even further than this in the direction of epistemological relativism. It often used to be argued that there was an 'objective' social reality 'out there' in the world of observation waiting to be discovered by 'scientific' analysis. This view is by no means so widely held in contemporary post-behavioural circles. Not only do post-behaviouralists accept that theory must play a central role in social analysis, they also recognise the possibility that different theoretical perspectives might generate different observations. Obviously, this possibility renders the task of subjecting rival theories to empirical testing rather more complicated. According to post-behaviouralists, however, it does not render the task any less necessary. Whatever observations a theory may engender, if it is to be considered a truly explanatory theory, it must generate falsifiable predictions that are not contradicted by the available empirical evidence. There is no reason why each theory should not be evaluated on its own observational terms. But unless a theory *can* be evaluated – that is, tested empirically – on its own observational terms, post-behaviouralists are not prepared to grant it the status of explanatory theory in the first place.

For behaviouralists and their modern post-behavioural counterparts, the main purpose of social scientific enquiry is to explain behaviour at individual and aggregate levels. The central question that behaviouralists ask is: 'Why do individuals, institutional actors and nation states behave the way they do?' Embedded in the behaviouralist notion of explanation is the idea of causality. Although behaviouralists are aware that causality may be as much a reflection of the way we think about the world as it is of 'reality', they none the less insist that unless a theory makes some sort of causal statement it cannot be deemed to explain anything. They also insist that, if an explanation is to be believed, it must make empirically falsifiable predictions that can be tested against observation. While it is never possible definitively to establish that a particular causal relationship exists, it is possible to determine how far a particular set of empirical observations is consistent with a specific proposition that links different phenomena together. For behaviouralists, in short, believable explanatory theories must be capable of receiving, and *must* receive, empirical support. Post-behaviouralists argue, with considerable justification, that nearly all social researchers who work with empirical materials subscribe broadly to this view. In this sense, the legacy of behaviouralism among empirical researchers is enormous. In many respects, we are all post-behaviouralists now.

# ■ Further reading

The list which follows provides an outline of texts that both employ and offer critiques of the behavioural approach to social explanation. The best introduction to the philosophy of science in general, and to behaviouralism's place within it, is Chalmers (1985). For various critiques and related ideas, see Winch (1958), Rudner (1966) and Thomas (1979). On positivism and 'scientific' approaches to social explanation more generally, see Kuhn (1970), Hempel (1965, 1966), Hanson (1958), Halfpenny (1982) and Chalmers (1990). On the philosophical origins of behaviouralism, see Carnap (1936, 1950), Schlick (1974) and Ayer (1971). For a useful explanation of some of the terms used in these studies, see Lacey (1976). For justifications of quantitative approaches to the analysis of empirical evidence in the social sciences, see Blalock (1964, 1969, 1970, 1972) and King (1989). For a recent summary of the ways in which qualitative data can be employed within the 'behavioural-scientific' approach, see King *et al.* (1994).

# Chapter 4

# Rational Choice Theory
## Hugh Ward

Since the 1950s rational choice theory has come to have an extremely important role in political science. Anthony Downs (1957; compare Downs 1991) was the pioneer in the application of rational choice theory to electoral behaviour and party competition. The individual votes for the party which, if it got into office, is expected to yield the highest utility. Parties are assumed to be motivated solely by the desire for office, competing for votes by changing their policy platforms. The empirical study of the effect of the state of the economy on electoral outcomes which started in Britain and the USA in the early 1970s (for a discussion, see Lewis-Beck, 1990, ch. 2) is in line of descent from Downs' work, although pocket book voting is only one possible expression of self-interest. Downs' work revolutionised electoral studies, although we shall below see how controversial the approach has been.

Why do so many of us continue to act in ways which harm the environment even though we know what we are doing is harmful? A plausible explanation is that we feel changing our own ways will have little or no impact on the overall problem; but there are major financial and other costs associated with living differently. The result is a failure of collective action in which rational self-interest leads to everyone being worse off (Hardin, 1969). Mancur Olson (1965) formalised this sort of argument, showing that self interested individuals would not always take part in collective action to further a shared goal. His work constitutes a fundamental critique of pluralism and orthodox Marxism, which both assume that a shared interest is sufficient for political mobilisation to occur. It has generated empirical work in areas as diverse as the study of social revolutions (for example, Popkin 1979) and co-operation between states over such problems as the deterioration of the global environment (for example, Young 1989).

Early work in rational choice theory was carried out largely by economists, using similar methods as in standard microeconomics. Arguably the most important tool is game theory. Game theory deals with rational choice where there is strategic interdependence, others' choice of strategy effecting an individuals best choice and vice versa. Game theory has led to important developments in collective action theory, enabling us to explain why collective action failures can sometimes avoided if the number of individual decision-makers is small (for example, Taylor, 1987). Extensive use has been made of game theory to model nuclear deterrence, arms races, disarmament and other phenomena important to international relations specialists (see Nicholson, 1989). It has also been crucial to attempts to explain the formation of legislative coalitions (Laver and Schofield, 1990).

The sub-field of social choice theory developed when economists asked whether any satisfactory and broadly democratic way could be found of aggregating the preference of individual citizens so as to arrive at a social ranking of alternatives. An example of such a procedure is to use majority rule, ranking X above Y if X can gain a majority against Y. This method has long been known to lead to paradox where there are multiple alternatives (McLean, 1987, ch. 8). The key theorem, first proved by Kenneth Arrow (Arrow, 1951), is that no satisfactory democratic method of aggregation exists, so that the problem is not peculiar to simple majority rule. This result has led to further fundamental questions being asked about democracy (see, for example, Sen, 1970). For some authors, results like Arrow's, together with related results about tactical voting and agenda manipulation (for example, Gibbard, 1973), call into question the idea that democracy is the implementation of the popular will represented by a social preference ranking (Riker, 1982).

The central theme of the public choice sub-field is that the intervention of democratic governments to repair market failures often creates more problems than it solves. One argument is that the combination of the self-interest of bureaucrats in maximising their budgets, and bureaucratic control over information on the cost structure of state provision of public goods results in their over-provision, at the expense of the citizenry (Niskanen, 1971). Another important theme is rent-seeking: organised interests lobbying successfully for monopoly or quasi-monopoly powers and subsides from states, with consequent erosion of market efficiency and slower economic growth (see Olson, 1982). The literature on the political business cycle suggests that the search for electoral success through the manipulation of the economy leads to economic instability and a higher-than-optimal level of inflation (for example, Nordhaus, 1975). The normative thrust of public choice theory is towards constitutional limitation of the size and autonomy of the state and disengagement from corporatist entanglements. As filtered through neo-liberal think tanks, public choice was crucial to the development of 'Thatcherism' and 'Reaganomics' (Self, 1993).

Of course, explanations of political phenomena in terms of rational self-interest long pre-date the literature I have been discussing. The intellectual roots of post-war developments run back through microeconomics and welfare economics, nineteenth-century liberalism and utilitarianism, and the work of classical political economists such as Adam Smith, to the work of authors such as John Locke and Thomas Hobbes. The problem of social order and the normative justification of the state that has been central to Western political theory since the seventeenth-century hangs on whether self-interested rational individuals can provide the public good of social order without external coercion, a problem central to collective action theory (Taylor, 1987, pp. 125–50). If rational choice theory owes an intellectual debt to the liberal tradition, repayments have been made by suggesting lines of analysis and argument. For example, John Rawls' influential work (Rawls 1972) presents the idea that, within constraints set by the equal distribution of liberties and certain rights, it is just for society to maximise the well-being of the least well-off members of society (see also ch. 2 in this book). The argument is that individuals who (hypothetically) did not know what social position they would occupy (and were thereby impartial) would accept rationally a social contract embodying a principle protecting themselves against the case in which they turned out to be one of the worst-off (see Barry, 1989).

Rational choice is, then, both a positive approach to political explanation and an overtly normative enterprise. It strength is its ability to bring together a remarkably wide range of phenomena and concerns of political theorists under one heading. (For the most straightforward overview, see McLean, 1987.) I argue in this chapter that rational choice should not be regarded as a paradigm, however. Applications of rational choice theory are parasitic on a range of theories for assumptions about social structure and institutional variables, and for the fleshing out of what self-interest means; and very different models and normative consequences may follow depending upon the origins of the borrowings. For this reason rational choice is not necessarily wedded to the agenda of its public-choice variant. It is best regarded a set of techniques that can be appropriated by other paradigms so long as they take individual action seriously. However, the rational choice toolkit needs further refinement in the light of what we now know about individual decision-making.

In the first section of the chapter I describe the assumptions of the mainstream variant of rational choice theory in more detail. I then consider various lines of criticism that have been made of rational choice theory and how rational choice theorists have responded to these criticisms.

# The core commitments and assumptions of the mainstream variant

The most important commitment of rational choice theory is that there are important forms of political behaviour that are the result of choices made with a view to the efficient achievement of given ends (for an accessible account of the material covered in this section, see Hargreaves-Heap *et al.*, 1992, pp. 3–26 and 93–130). While recognising that human motivation is complex, mainstream rational choice theory assumes that individuals are self-interested. The concept of self-interest is potentially extremely elastic. Does it cover cases such as the individual who volunteers in time of war because of powerful 'warm feelings' from doing what his peers say is right? Some would argue that such 'moral motivations' should be excluded from rational choice models. I return to this question below.

Many mainstream rational choice theorists accept the principle of methodological individualism; that 'bed-rock' explanations of social phenomena should build upwards from the beliefs and goals of individuals. As we shall see, the sociological critique of rational choice theory disputes this claim.

The mainstream variant of rational choice assumes that individuals all have the rational capacity, time and emotional detachment necessary to choose a best course of action, no matter how complex the choice. The simplest problem conceptually is parametric decision-making under certainty in which each action has a known outcome (so there is no risk or uncertainty) and the relationship between actions and outcomes is unaffected by the actions of any other individual (so that they may be treated as fixed 'parameters'). Individuals are assumed to be able to rank-order outcomes or, which amounts to the same thing here, actions. Thus, for any pair of alternatives *a* and *b* they can say whether *a* is better than *b*, *b* is better than *a*, or that the two outcomes are indifferent. Also, preferences satisfy the transitivity property: this implies that if *a* is better than *b* and *b* is better than *c*, *a* is better than *c*. To say that *a* is preferred to *b* means no more than that *a* would be chosen above *b*, all references to utility or other 'unobservable' mental phenomena being seen as inessential. Rational individuals choose one of the highest ranked feasible actions/ outcomes available to them.

The first complication is that actions may lead to various outcomes depending on a random event; or individuals may not know for certain the consequences of their actions. It has been shown that, granted certain assumptions, individuals choose as if they were maximising expected ('average') utility, taking into account the various possible outcomes the action could lead to, and the probabilities of their occurrence. The utilities needed to represent decision-making here can be derived, at least in principle, from experiments in which individuals choose between lotteries over the outcomes, and can be interpreted as containing information about preference intensity – something inessential to predicting parametric choices under certainty.

The most important idea in game theory is that of a strategy equilibrium. In games where binding agreements between players are impossible, an equilibrium is a set of strategies, one for each player, such that no player can increase his/her payoff by changing strategy given that no other player changes strategy. Strategic interdependence poses the problem of a possible infinite regress of strategic calculation of the form: 'If s/he thinks I will choose *a* then s/he will choose *b*; but if s/he chooses *b*, I will choose *c*; but if I choose *c*, s/he will choose *d*, and so on'. This does not occur when strategies are in equilibrium. Suppose *A*'s strategy *s* and *B*'s strategy *t* are in equilibrium and it is common knowledge that both are rational. Then if *A* expects *B* to choose *t*, s/he can do no better than to choose *s*; and if *A* believes that *B* thinks s/he will choose *s*, then *B* will choose *t*, justifying *A*'s expectations. The argument goes the other way, from *B* to *A*, too. Thus, at an equilibrium, players' choices of strategy and expectations are consistent. In addition, equilibria are self-enforcing, whereas non-equilibrium strategy choices are not: even if the players say they will stick with strategies that are not in equilibrium, there will be incentives for at least one player to change. The notion of equilibrium has been extended and refined in several ways; for example, to allow for the possibility that players use mixed strategies under which the actions taken depend on the outcome of some random event such as the toss of a coin; or to allow for the possibility that coalitions of players can make binding agreements.

# ■ Four modes of criticism of rational choice theory

In recent years, a stream of critical commentary on rational choice theory has appeared in edited volumes and monographs (for example, Barry, 1970; Hargreaves-Heap *et al.*, 1992; Hindess, 1988; Lewin, 1991; Moe, 1979; Self, 1993). In order to provide a route map I examine four modes of criticism: (a) the internal critique of rational choice 'heretics' who wish particularly to emphasise bounded rationality; (b) the sociological critique, which centres on the way rational choice theory appears to play down social structure and holistic modes of explanation; (c) the psychologists' argument that individuals often do not act rationally in the standard sense and are motivationally and psychologically complex; and (d) the critique from mainstream political science, based on the implausibility of the assumptions made and the predictive failures of the model. Rational choice theory can respond to many of these criticisms and will continue to be important to political science and political theory. Nevertheless, I will argue that, in the light of the criticisms, the mainstream variant of rational choice should be modified.

## □ *The heretics*

If nothing else, one would expect rational choice theory to able to give an unambiguous account of what it means to behave rationally in all relevant contexts. However, this is not the case. There are particular problems in game theory, although decision-making under uncertainty is another area of concern. First, while there is general agreement that some equilibria do not make sense, there is little consensus on how to 'refine' the equilibrium concept so as to narrow down the alternatives (Hargreaves-Heap *et al.*, 1992, ch. 7). The problem is that the existence of multiple equilibria reduces the predictive power of the model. Other theories must be brought in to narrow the possibilities further (Johnson, 1993). For example, Schelling introduces the idea that some equilibria are prominent, having a quality of psychological or normative 'obviousness' which differentiates them from others (Schelling, 1960). Consider the 'divide the dollar' game, in which two players get to share a dollar only if their claims add up to exactly one dollar – a simple metaphor for distributional politics. Any pair of positive claims summing to a dollar is an equilibrium: if A claims $x$ cents, B's can do no better than to claim 100 minus $x$, because if he claimed anything different, he would get zero. The equilibrium idea does nothing to narrow the range of possible outcomes. However, a fifty-fifty split of the dollar is a plausible solution because it is normatively prominent in the absence of obvious differences in need. Second, there are numerous competing solution concepts for games between more than two players where binding agreements can be made between coalition members (Ordeshook, 1986, ch. 9). Each of these gives rise to a different understanding of rational behaviour in contexts such as legislative coalition formation.

Some rational choice theorists feel that the mainstream model makes highly implausible assumptions about the rational capacity of individuals. Herbert Simon's work (Simon, 1982; 1985) on bounded rationality has been particularly influential. In the face of limited information, limited time and limited cognitive capacity to process information, Simon envisages individuals using standard operating procedures as a heuristic device and as a shorthand guide to rational action. For example, Moseley argues that for the post-war period up to the early 1970s, the Treasury in Britain responded to changing macroeconomic conditions in an extremely simplistic manner, deflating when the dollar exchange rate was threatened and inflating when unemployment rose above 0.5 million (Moseley, 1976).

Decision-makers are better seen from this perspective as satisfiers rather than maximisers. In fact, they carry on what they are doing until the pay-off drops below a satisfactory level, amd then search for an alternative yielding a satisfactory pay-off; but the search will typically be very limited in extent and guided by procedural heuristics – and the search terminates as soon as a satisfactory alternative is found, even if it is far from optimal. Some have argued that such a pattern of decision-making, which commonly gives rise only to incremental policy change in political contexts, is normatively defensible when there is radical uncertainty (Braybrooke and Lindblom, 1963). However, it can certainly lead to sub-optimal outcomes, and it is arguably a poor way of making 'big' policy decisions, even if it works for everyday decision-making (see Etzioni, 1967).

Explanatory problems arise when the emphasis is upon procedures and levels of aspiration which define what is satisfactory and what is not. Where do the rules come from? Another difficulty is that models assuming bounded rationally are typically more complex and difficult to use to generate useful predictions. The parsimonious nature of the mainstream approach still commends itself to many rational choice theorists. Nevertheless, the questions posed here are important. For instance, is it plausible to assume that political parties seek to maximise their vote rather than get a satisfactory vote share when they have such imperfect knowledge of the effects of policy changes on voting intention and imperfect capacity to process that information (Kollman *et al.*, 1992)?

# ☐ *The sociologists*

Sociologists often claim that individual behaviour is largely a function of social structures. Choice is illusory for individuals and the rational choice approach based on individual choice is, therefore, unhelpful (Hindess, 1988, ch. 6). For instance, some argue that the Downsian approach is inferior to an account of voting in terms of the individual's position in the social structure. Social class, geographical location, gender, consumption and production location, and religion, among other variables, all have known correlations, of greater or lesser strength, with voting behaviour (Harrop and Miller, 1987). Critics of rational choice might concede that some voting takes place on the basis of self-interest but argue that it is an individuals' structural location that generates their interests and does most of the explanatory work in Downsian models of voting.

In fact, an individual's structural location typically does not account completely for what s/he does. With regard to voting, structural variables by no means account for all the variation among individuals: individuals' perceptions of economic performance are of considerable importance (for example, Sanders and Price 1992). Consider another example. Neo-institutionalists (see Chapter 1 in this book) often emphasise the way in which the institutional structures of government shape the world view of politicians and bureaucrats, mould their preferences and define the options they consider when making policy choices, and structure the emergence of decisions from conflicting strands of deliberation (see Hindess, 1988, ch. 5). Much of the time, individuals follow rules rather than make choices, and individual decision-making departs from the mainstream model (see next section). Classic case studies, such as Allison's study of the Cuban Missile Crisis demonstrate that organisational structures are very important, but that individual decision-makers such as President Kennedy still had enough autonomy to influence the outcome profoundly (Allison, 1971, chs 1 and 3). In general, it seems implausible either that individuals are fully autonomous or that their actions are determined completely by social structure (Hay, Ch. 9 in this volume; Hollis, 1977, ch. 1).

Even if social structure determines the individual's feasible set, beliefs and preferences, rational choice can add to the explanation by making predictions when the rational course of action is not obvious. This is especially likely to be the case where there is strategic interdependence of decision-making. Here, surprising predictions abound. Let us suppose that: the preferences of members of the working class and the bourgeoisie are completely determined by their structural location within capitalism; that the structure of the economy is such that workers control the rate of profit, via their control of wage rates; capital controls the rate of investment from the profits it earns; and that there are transitional costs for workers in moving to a socialist society. It is not at all obvious under what conditions an equilibrium involving class compromise rather than revolution will or will not exist, but game theory provides illuminating insights into this in terms of pay-off structures, discount rates and the degree of uncertainty each side faces (Przeworski and Wallerstein, 1982).

Because they favour methodological individualism, many rational choice theorists argue that social structures do not provide basic elements of explanations in the social sciences; rather we need to explain the structure using rational choice theory (see Elster, 1989a, ch. 2). This can be illustrated by looking at the debate between Theda Skocpol (1979), who tried to explain social revolutions without using voluntarist forms of explanation such as rational choice theory, and rational choice theorists such as Michael Taylor. Skocpol used the comparative case study method to isolate a set of sufficient structural conditions for a social revolution, three of which were: external stress upon the state in the geopolitical arena; breakdown in the state's ability to maintain internal order; and strong community structures among peasants. Taylor's point is that these structural factors can be seen as the result of decisions taken by individuals: decisions to attack another power; failures by state decision-makers to invest enough resources in social control; decisions made by the state which bolstered peasant communities in order to provide a bulwark against classes antagonistic to the monarch (Taylor, 1989). Taylor's critique is a powerful one, but surely structural factors shaped the decisions to which he alludes? To take one obvious example: why were there states rather than some other form of rule?

From one perspective, an actor is a locus of decision where actions are the consequences of decisions (Hindess, 1988, pp. 44–5), states, political parties, pressure groups and social movements often falling under this heading. The problem is that rational choice typically treats social actors as if they were individual decision-makers acting intentionally on the basis of a single set of beliefs and preferences. For example, the convention in the realist paradigm in international relations, and particularly in its game theoretic formalisations, is to treat the state as a unitary actor pursuing well-defined goals relating to security and power, something which is, at best, an heuristic simplifying device and at worst may lead to gross misunderstandings (Putnam, 1988). Also collective entities that can seldom, if ever, be treated as a locus of decision tend to be squeezed out of rational choice models. Yet individuals treat collectives such as social classes as having a reality and a life of their own, so that they are crucial to social explanation.

In my view, it is a practical impossibility for rational choice theorists to eliminate taken-as-given structural factors from any application of rational choice. Methodological individualism is simply not a coherent objective (Lukes, 1977). I do not believe that practising rational choice theorists typically exhibit much desire to squeeze out structure: rather, they often seek to illuminate how choices are made within structures, the agenda sometimes stretching to the consideration of how rational choices reproduce or transform structures. As such, rational choice can form part of a structuration approach (see Colin Hay, Chapter 10 in this volume).

The general points made here about social structure also arise in relation to norms. Drawing on the work of founding fathers of sociology such as Emile Durkheim, many sociologists emphasise norm-driven behaviour, with social norms understood to be derived from society's need for system integration. While recognising the possibility of anomic and dysfunctional behaviour, such holistic approaches typically play down instrumentally rational action.

Rational choice theorists sometimes admit norms into their arguments. But they see norms typically as generating costs and benefits to be set alongside other incentives, something that critics feel is not always an accurate description of how norms influence action (Elster, 1989b, pp. 106–7). For example, one way to explain why individuals bother to register a vote despite the infinitesimal chance that this will influence the outcome of a national election in favour of their preferred party, is to say that citizens gain pleasure out of doing their citizen's duty. In deciding whether to vote they set this incentive against the costs of voting (see Aldrich, 1993). The general implications of this line of thinking are: that people are more likely to conform to norms when conforming has low costs; and that they do not conform unreflectively.

In line with their bias against taking structures as given, rational choice theorists wish to explain why norms arise and how they are enforced. The first move is to see norms as solutions to collective action problems (see Gauthier, 1986). While many sociologists make similar conceptual moves, they then typically use functional analysis to explain norms in terms of the all-round benefits they bring. Rational choice theorists argue that this is inadequate because it ignores the corrosive effects of self-interest on collective action: those who do not adhere to the norm, or pay no part of the price of enforcing it, may none the less benefit if others conform (Taylor, 1987, pp. 29–30).

Axelrod's work shows that rational choice can illuminate how norms evolve through a process of social selection in contexts where there is a free-rider problem, but it also shows some of the limitations of the approach (Axelrod, 1986). Axelrod simulates a situation in which players have a strategy both in an underlying collective action game and in relation to punishing those who defect in the collective action game. He shows how co-operation may spread in the underlying game to become a norm, enforced by vengefulness against violators. However, he also shows that enforcement of the norm is likely eventually to crode unless there is some 'meta-norm' system which ensures that those who fail to be vengeful are punished. Axelrod's work shows that, in empirical application, we may be back once again to the structure/agency problem as we hit the practical limits of methodological individualism: taking the meta-norm system as given, Axelrod is able to show how his model illuminates the emergence of norms; but the suspicion is that he is unable to explain the meta-norm system. It is true that the game theoretic literature on collective action shows that free-riding on others' efforts to carry out threats may not be a problem in this context because, if *A* fails to carry out a threat, he can be punished by *B*; and if this second-order punishment is not carried out, *A* can punish *B*; and so on (see Fudenberg and Maskin, 1986). However, such a self-enforcing threat system seems empirically implausible.

Yet another variation on the basic argument concerns ideologies. Ideologies can be seen as structures of belief, assigning meaning to action. For many sociologists the key feature of human action is its mean-ingfulness to the individual (for example Winch, 1958). Rational choice may be seen as one way of investigating the meaning of others' actions, enjoining us to look at individuals' desires and beliefs, picturing these as leading to intentions and actions (Hindess, 1988, p. 59). However, many sociologists would argue that action can only be seen as rational or irrational within the context of a particular system of meaning, or discursive formation. Also, action often cannot be interpreted from an instrumental perspective. Indeed, symbolic and ritual action are crucial to politics (Edelman, 1964). Individuals identities are formed in complex social processes in which discourses are articulated and disarticulated, giving only limited autonomy to individual human subjects. Processes of identity formation of this sort are crucial to belief and preference formation, again suggesting that important elements of the rational choice model are given by discursive social processes unamenable to rational choice methods.

These criticisms are certainly significant, but counter-arguments exist: there is typically some individual autonomy from ideological determination; and ideological structures arise, are reproduced and transformed as the result of individual action, some of which is instrumentally rational. To expand on this, individuals often combine elements of one or more ideologies in novel ways with a view to furthering an interest instrumentally, and this can have profound political effects. Party competition can surely be illuminated by this idea. For example, Margaret Thatcher's Conservatism drew on liberalism and traditional strands of conservatism and was, to a degree, a deliberate construct.

Can rational choice do any more than this to illuminate how ideological structures change? I believe it can, as the work of William Riker on the manipulation of issue dimensions in democracies illustrates (Riker, 1982). Drawing on formal results from spatial theories of voting and elections, Riker shows that politicians may destabilise majorities by inserting extra issue dimensions into the debate, and may solidify majorities by encouraging the separate consideration of issues. For example, one interpretation of the play being made on the European Union (EU) by the Conservative Right is that bringing this issue to the political forefront will break the electoral coalition for centrist policies by attracting away some of those sceptical over Europe. This could generate a political vacuum which a revamped Thatcherite project might fill. While Riker sees such strategies as expressions of elite self-interest and anti-democratic, others have seen them as forms of statecraft which may be conducive to the general good (Nagel, 1993). One way to develop Riker's argument – not necessarily in the way Riker would develop it himself – is to suggest that behind the manipulation of issue dimensions there lies the construction or mobilisation of ideologies which 'organise in' or 'organise out' certain questions and the interconnections between them. Riker's argument makes transparent how such ideological movements may be linked to the electoral fortunes of parties and the legislative fortunes of policies.

It is often held that rational choice pictures individuals as isolated social atoms – autonomous sources of social causality in the social process. In contrast, the focus of much sociology is upon individual interrelatedness. It is not that relationships exist between fully constituted individuals: rather relationships modify individuals' identities in crucial ways. The atomistic picture painted by rational choice theory is said to be in line with other individualistic ideologies that support the social status quo by denying the existential reality of social groups, communities, social classes, and even societies. At the same time, forms of political action that affirm individuals' social identity and which are not based on self-interest are denied the validating stamp of rationality (see Sen, 1977). The very concept of rationality that rational choice theory celebrates is said to be historically and culturally specific to capitalist societies. Its logic is said to drive out other rationalities and forms of understanding, especially any notion of rationality which problematises the goals to which action is orientated (Dryzek, 1990, ch. 1). In short, the rational choice picture of the political world is a distorted reflection of a reality only approached in capitalism, generating forms of understanding of the political realm which prevent all but shallow criticism of the social status quo (MacPherson, 1970).

It seems to me that rational choice theory need not be committed to viewing individuals as isolated social atoms any more than it is committed to seeing them as self-interested: rational choice modeling starts with given beliefs and preferences, whatever their origin. The notion that instrumental rationality first arose with the capitalist market economy is surely indefensible historically: as one mode of human action it has always been important outside the immediate family circle (for example, Sahlins, 1972, pp. 191–204). I showed above that rational choice has been used as a tool by Marxists who are openly critical of capitalist society (for example, Przeworski and Wallerstein, 1982). It does not seem to me that their critique is blunted by using rational choice methods. Rather, they have achieved greater clarity within Marxism.

## ☐ *The psychologists*

Psychologists argue typically that individuals' motives need not reflect self-interest: envy is important and is incompatible with *self*-concern; drives such as revenge, guilt and greed may exist, whether or not they are acknowledged consciously. Critics have been especially worried by the exclusion of altruism from most rational choice models of politics (for example, Lewin, 1991). They argue that the empirical evidence suggests that individuals frequently act altruistically in political life. For example, while individuals' personal economic expectations may influence the way they vote, there is considerable evidence that the general state of the economy also matters, suggesting that voters are often also concerned about the well-being of others, (see Lewis-Beck, 1990, ch. 4). When individuals act in accordance with social norms, there also often seems to be some sacrifice of self-interest.

Normatively orientated rational choice is not wedded to the self-interest assumption. For example, social choice theory makes no assumptions about the motives that lie behind individual preferences, being concerned only with the problem of how they might be aggregated so as to make a choice for society. Rational choice theorists interested in explaining political phenomena have always been aware that altruism is important (for example, Downs, 1957, p. 29). Their position has often been that applications of rational choice should be confined to those areas where self interest dominates. For example M. Olson suggested that his theory of collective action would apply best to economic interest groups and not to philanthropic ones (Olson, 1965, pp. 64–5). The question then becomes one of how much room to operate would such a self-denying ordinance leave rational choice theorists. It might also be argued that models based on self-interest, even if they are empirically false, provide a standard against which actual behaviour may be compared (Mansbridge, 1990, p. 20)

One way around the problem of altruism is to suggest that individuals get pleasure out of the happiness of others. It is not difficult to model such a phenomenon in terms of positive utility interaction between individuals (see Collard, 1978). Margolis's model also allows for change in the relative weight attached to self-interest and others' interests, more weight being placed on self-interest given the extent to which the individual has been altruistic in the recent past (Margolis, 1990). Some argue for much more extensive use of this sort of modelling (for example, Mansbridge, 1990c). As with the case of more general forms of 'moral motivation' discussed briefly above, the danger is that the weight placed on the self might be used as a 'fudge factor', the model being immune to falsification because some combination of self-interest and altruism will always give the right prediction. The keys here are: (a) to make firm assumptions about the relative importance of the two motives in the particular empirical context concerned, so that the model is falsifiable; and (b) to look at other possible explanations of anomalies rather than starting by making *ad hoc* modifications to the motivational model (see Barry, 1970, pp. 19–23).

Altruism can take the form of disguised self-interest which confers evolutionary advantage. One example is that it may pay in evolutionary terms to help another person now in the expectation that s/he will help you in the future, so reciprocal altruism has an evolutionary basis. Game theoretic collective action theory has done much to clarify the conditions under which such reciprocal altruism may occur in contexts where it is consciously entered into, as well as where it is selected for in processes of social evolution: 'nice' actions must be conditional on others being 'nice' in the past, with punishment for those who were 'nasty'; the interaction must not have a definite time limit; the individuals should not be too short-term orientated; and short-term benefits being 'nasty' should not be too high. (see for example, Taylor, 1987).

Many psychologists regard synoptically rational decision making, approaching the ideal of the mainstream rational choice model, as being relatively rare (for example, Janis and Mann, 1977). Beside the cognitive limits emphasised by authors such as Herbert Simon, emotions and unconscious drives make the level of detachment necessary for the synoptic approach highly unlikely in many settings (Elster, 1989a, ch. 7). Decisions are often made more on the grounds of consistency with past actions, reduction of strains within the individual's belief system (cognitive dissonance), or normative orientation, than through a calculation of the most efficient means to given ends. The norms the individual adheres to and affective orientations s/he has may prevent feasible options being considered and relevant information being obtained, as well as biasing decision-making away from what instrumentally is rational (Etzioni, 1992).

Decision conflicts occur when individuals can find no alternative that satisfies all their goals simultaneously. This creates problems for normative decision theory (Levi, 1986) and it also tends to generate behaviour that is irrational. Decision conflicts are a source of stress. Whatever course of action is chosen there appear to be losses; there are simultaneous opposing tendencies both to accept and to reject a course of action (Janis and Mann, 1977, pp. 45–6). Decision conflicts also lead to vacillation, attempts to avoid making a choice at all, and forms of apprehensiveness that tend to lead to poor decision-making (Janis and Mann, 1977, ch. 4). Regret about past decisions, made when decision conflicts were not resolved, may immobilise the decision-maker. Where there is decision conflict, 'bolstering' – the retrospective, and perhaps unconscious, rationalisation of the idea that the chosen alternative is the best – is liable to occur if a choice is made at all (Janis and Mann, 1977, pp. 91–3). Where commitments to an existing path of action are strong, individuals 'bolster', carrying on in the same way, and freeze out consideration of other alternatives, even if they are aware that to do so is not necessarily desirable (Janis and Mann, 1977, p. 15). Case studies of areas such as foreign policy decision making suggest that such pathologies are probably widespread in political life (Janis, 1972).

New information is often not dealt with in a neutral way. Rather, it is fitted into existing patterns of belief and often ignored if it cannot be so construed. For instance, there is 'anchoring bias' or insufficient adjustment of initial probability estimates in the light of new information (Tversky and Kahneman, 1982, pp. 14–18). There are also framing effects whereby the impact of the same information depends crucially on how it is presented (Tversky and Kahneman, 1986, pp. 73–9). The focus of attention of individuals is very important in explaining their behaviour, as relevant and important aspects of reality typically are ignored (Simon, 1986, p. 31). Individuals rely on a number of heuristic principles and limited data to estimate risks, and commonly these result in mishandling of risk estimation (Tversky, 1982). These problems are crucial to explaining decision-making in areas such as foreign policy (Jervis, 1976).

There are widespread, systematic and fundamental deviations in behaviour from the predictions made by the expected utility model (Hargreaves-Heap *et al.*, 1992, ch. 3). For example, alternative descriptions of decision problems often give rise to different choices, even though they are considered to be the same when seen from the perspective of the conventional approach. Compared to what would be predicted on the basis of the expected utility model, people are often attracted unduly by small chances of large pay-offs and repelled unduly by small chances of bad ones (Hargreaves-Heap *et al.*, 1992, p. 38). Rather than holding subjective probability estimates that are analogous to objectively derived estimates of risk, individuals often have diffuse and ill-defined feelings about uncertainty and avoid ambiguity about the true risks they face (Einhorn and Hogarth, 1986, pp. 43–7). The desirability of options might effect perceptions of the chances of occurrence, as in the phenomenon of wishful thinking; or the probability of their occurrence might effect their perceived desirability, as in the phenomenon of sour grapes (Einhorn and Hogarth, 1986, p. 42; Elster, 1989a, pp. 17–20).

The idea that we are inhabited by multiple, conflicting selves seems to account for a number of observable forms of irrational behaviour, if only in a metaphorical manner (Elster 1985, Introduction). The idea has a very long history in philosophy and has been important to psychology, not least because of the work of Sigmund Freud. Violations of the transitivity assumption (see page 00) are common. Yet this assumption is fundamental to all mainstream models of decision-making. This can be connected with the idea that individuals have 'multiple selves' who see decisions from different points of view, leading to the impossibility of acting rationally in the conventional sense (Steedman and Krause, 1985). While there may be a meta-preference ranking which tells us which self should dominate in a particular context (Sen, 1977), decision conflict may be due to inner conflict between different selves. Quattrone and Tversky argue that unconscious self-deception – implying the idea of one self deceiving another – might account for why individuals go to the voting booth at elections (Quattrone and Tversky, 1988). The self-deception comes from believing that if *you* vote others like you will be encouraged to vote too, making it instrumentally rational to vote yourself. Weakness of will can be thought of as involving the inability of the 'higher self' to control impulsive urges, including the delay of immediate gratification in order to enjoy higher future pay-offs. The idea that we have both an instrumentally rational, self-interested self and a socially-orientated, norm-driven self provides one way of thinking about the individual tensions generated when self-interest collides with doing what is normatively right.

In the face of empirical evidence for apparent irrationality, the economist's traditional defences are: that in a competitive environment agents have to act 'as if' they were rational maximisers in order to survive; and that irrational behaviour will be spotted and exploited, leading to arbitrage in the market, which will drive out the inefficient in the long run (Friedman, 1953). This argument might seem to apply in politics, too. For example, a party may have little or no idea how to maximise its vote, suffer from organisational pathologies in relation to developing a winning policy platform, and may not act as a unified team. However, failure to cater to the tastes of the electorate could result in the long-run in its extinction (Elster, 1989c, p. 80). However, all the counter-arguments against the economist's defence apply with at least as much force, if not more, in politics: in a rapidly changing environment, equilibrium may never be reached; in many areas – including party competition – competitive pressures are highly attenuated by barriers to the entry of more rational competitors; the selection argument does not apply if the level of rationality is uniformly relatively low.

The evidence reviewed in this section suggests that the mainstream models of decision-making will often be descriptively inaccurate and will make correct predictions only in more limited domains of application than some rational choice theorists believe. Of course, it can still be claimed that the mainstream models provide a standard of rational behaviour against which actual behaviour can be compared; and that some decision-making will approximate the mainstream model. Parallelling the arguments for the bounded rationality approach, there is a strong case for a more descriptively accurate model of the way in which individuals deal with information and uncertainty.

## ☐ *The mainstream of political science*

Many empirically-orientated political scientists contest the utility of rational choice on the grounds that it makes implausible assumptions and fails in predictive terms. Take the case of electoral competition and voting. As we have already seen, rational choice may have problems explaining why people vote at all – some interpret the survey evidence to suggest that people vote for the party they identify with, and there is evidence that issue voting, where it occurs, is not based on narrow self-interest. Even if people are issue voters, the Downsian approach fails to allow for parties manipulating the structural basis of preferences (Dunleavy and Ward, 1981). On top of this, many argue that it is implausible that politicians are pure office-seekers, adopting policy platforms to win votes rather than out of conviction or social concern (for example, Lewin, 1991, ch. 3). The prediction that governments manipulate the economy to win elections seems to be false in many instances (see for example, Lewis-Beck, 1990, ch. 9). So, Downs predicts a high degree of ideological convergence in party systems which can be well-characterised by a single left-to-right dimension where voters are bunched in the middle of the spectrum. However, this is at odds with the empirical evidence on countries such as the USA and

Britain, where considerable ideological differences have existed over long periods of time, even though convergence is observed in some periods (see Budge *et al.*, 1987, ch. 3).

The point here is that rational choice theorists are engaged actively in modifying their models to allow for such problems; and this is all that can reasonably be demanded. Out of a post-Downsian literature which has moved a very long way (see Enelow and Hinich, 1990) I will pick one example. Donald Wittman's work on party competition (Wittman, 1983) suggests party elites moving away from their ideal policies in order to gain extra votes. However, they do so only in order to increase their chances of being able to implement policies they find relatively desirable as *policies*, and not to win office as such. Wittman shows that where parties are also uncertain about who will vote for them, equilibria in party competition typically will be divergent. Wittman also considers the effect of changing the size of the blocks of voters who vote on the basis of party identification rather than policy and is able to illuminate how this effects equilibria. There are numerous other examples of constructive engagement with contrary empirical evidence in diverse subfields such as bureaucracy (for example, Dunleavy, 1991, part 2), collective action theory (for example, Dunleavy, 1991, chs 2 and 3) and legislative coalition theory (for example, Laver and Schofield, 1990).

# ▌ Conclusion: the future of rational choice theory

As we have seen, rational choice theory has been subjected to a good deal of criticism as it has become more and more important to political science. It is equally clear that rational choice theory is by no means destroyed by these criticisms and has built up a range of responses. In the light of this; how should rational choice theory develop? And what is its status within political science? Human beings are psychologically complex, frequently act irrationally and operate within meaning systems that are difficult to comprehend fully when seen from a rational choice perspective. This suggests that the domain of application of rational choice theory will by no means cover the whole of political life, and also that other approaches to human action are as indispensable as rational choice itself.

In many areas of application the mainstream rational choice model is descriptively implausible, yet individuals do make somewhat rational decisions relative to reasonably well-defined goals. To stick to the mainstream approach is to put further development of rational choice theory in a straitjacket. Thus there ought to be concerted attempts to develop further and to apply non-mainstream variants of the model, allowing for bounded rationality; choice under uncertainty incompatible with the expected utility approach; and non-egoistic and 'moral motivations'.

As I have shown, rational choice theory can help to illuminate how structures arise and are transformed, but I cannot conceive of any rational choice model that does not introduce some premises about social structure from outside. Thus, rational choice theorists ought to give limited acknowledgement to the sociological critique, recognising that methodological individualism and fully reductive explanations are impractical. Rational choice theory can be put to use by a wide range of social scientists operating within very different paradigms because the results derived depend so crucially on ideas about structure imported from elsewhere.

In the light of my arguments here, the conclusion should be that rational choice theory is a useful set of research methods and heuristics for the toolkit of all political scientists. Its status is more akin to those of statistical techniques that are appropriate for certain types of data; it is not a stand-alone paradigm for understanding the whole of the political sphere.

# ■ Further reading

Two non-technical introductions to rational choice are: Laver (1981) and MacLean (1987). At the intermediate level the most sensible starting points are: Riker and Ordeshook (1973) and Dunleavy (1991). Dunleavy's book is less useful as a text but provides an excellent example of how a sceptical and empirically-orientated political scientist can make use of rational choice alongside other approaches.

Two books with in-depth technical coverage but virtually no critical commentary are: Mueller (1989) and Ordeshook (1986). For those who wish to take game theory further there are: Luce and Raiffa (1989); and Rasmusen (1989). There are two good collections of articles: Barry and Hardin (1982); and Elster (1986). From the numerous critical surveys available the most useful are: Barry (1970); Hindess (1988); Mansbridge (1990a) and Monroe (1991).

# ■ *Chapter 5* ■

# The Feminist Perspective
## Jenny Chapman

The emergence of radical feminism and the women's liberation movement in the late 1960s and early 1970s had a profound influence on how politics is defined by political scientists, as well as more diffuse effects on cultural values throughout the Western world. The political character of male – female relations and the idea that 'the personal is political' are widely accepted, and great changes have taken place in the way the law, the media and millions of ordinary people approach the subject of gender. Women's experience is accepted as valid and a field of study in the new area of 'women's studies' and in traditional disciplines. Issues which go to the heart of male power over women, but were treated as being 'non-political' and therefore 'non-issues' in the dominant culture – issues such as abortion, rape and other forms of violence against women – have been redefined and put squarely on the political agenda. Feminism has also become an object of political analysis in its own right, researched and taught by feminists and the subject of an ever-growing literature, written almost exclusively by feminists.

The fact remains, however, that much of the original feminist agenda for political analysis has still not been worked through by feminist political scientists, let alone the mainstream. With the passage of time, too, the radical ideas that had so much impact are radical no longer, while the vast amount of feminist theorising, publication and debate that has taken place since the 1970s has not only fragmented the women's movement but also obscured its original, unequivocally political character. In fact, it has led feminism in so many diverse directions that many feminists today would question whether a coherent 'feminist approach' to anything is either possible or desirable.

If I did not believe in the possibility of a 'feminist approach' to politics, I would not have agreed to write this chapter. However, the feminist perspective could never be easy to define, for it has always been a relative and shifting one. For well over a century feminism has been an active social movement, constantly promoting change and changing shape itself, in response to changes in society and the other social movements (such as socialism and 'the greens') with which it interacts. Patterns of internal conflict and diversity, reflecting women's dependence on men in a male-dominated society as well as the strategic dilemmas and conflicting goals which flow from their experience as women, were established long ago. The modern movement is also affected by its international character. Ideas and practice are communicated rapidly, but differences in social and political context produce distinctly different kinds of feminism. Thus, for example, Nordic state feminism in the 1980s clearly reflects its social democratic context and distinguishes it sharply from the philosophical bent of some French feminism, the strength of liberal feminism and diverse radical movements in the USA, and the anguished fragmentation of the British women's movement. It is impossible to do justice to such a complex subject in one chapter, and what follows is a selective account that reflects my own standpoint, as a feminist and a political scientist. It is arranged in three sections. The first introduces the original political agenda of modern feminism, from its origins in gender theory to its core political concepts such as 'the personal is political', the 'public and private spheres' and feminist democracy. The second section looks at some of the problems raised by this agenda and the subsequent fragmentation of feminism. The third section focuses on the uneven feminist presence in selected fields of political science and the challenges still to be met.

# ■ Radical feminism and the original political agenda of modern feminism

The radical feminism that emerged in the late 1960s was a holistic vision of the political, social, economic, psychological and cultural world of men, which identified the oppressive dualism of gender as the common factor underlying the whole and raised revolutionary hopes that women's liberation could transform it all. There was nothing mystical about this; it was grounded in women's experience of the limitations of 'equal rights', of their marginalisation in Left-wing and radical male-dominated movements and above all in the advances in knowledge and understanding made by women over the decades since access to education had been opened up. Few of the key concepts of modern feminism were either wholly new or even originally 'feminist'; it was their association in a new political perspective which was a revelation.

The concept of *gender* is a case in point. Although the distinction between biological sex and the cultural construction of gender was crucial to the radical perspective and is the fundamental distinction between radical feminism and its equal rights and socialist precursors, its roots lay further back. It was anthropologists, studying and comparing the wide range of non-'modern' societies which survived up to the middle of the twentieth century, who first realised how 'sex roles' varied from one society to another and identified the part played by culture in forming the assumptions made in all societies about what is naturally 'masculine' or 'feminine'.

Awareness of cultural relativity goes back almost to the origins of Western culture (Rachels, 1986), but gained great impetus from the Voyages of Discovery and the resulting contacts with diverse peoples and ancient oriental civilisations. In fact, the sense of relativity and scepticism which these produced were prerequisites for the emergence of the European Enlightenment, and co-existed with the logical positivism that is its defining characteristic for sociologists such as Zygmunt Bauman (Bauman, 1992). It was only isolated individuals (such as J.-J. Rousseau), however, who paid more than superficial attention to the implications of cultural relativity for male–female relations until the twentieth century and the entry of women to careers in anthropology and the social sciences.

There are many slightly different versions of the gender theory these women produced, but the following account (which follows Margaret Mead) identifies the essentials on which feminism was to draw. What they found was that all societies react to the biological difference between men and women by elaborating a dichotomy of male and female gender upon it. There is amazing variation, however, in how the sexes are perceived in different cultures; what is proper to one sex in one society may be assigned to the other elsewhere and the amount of 'difference' between the sexes may be much greater in some cases than others. The result is an almost infinite variety of gender stereotypes, which tell us little or nothing about the innate propensities of the individuals expected to conform to them, but are nevertheless deeply-rooted in society through its structures, and in individuals through the complex processes of socialisation (learning, identification and experience) in which we learn to see ourselves through interaction with society.

However, there is also a common thread in the way that 'male' and 'female' are shaped and valued. First, women's reproductive role (childbearing and lactation) is always at the core of female gender, while maleness is defined in terms of difference from the female. The result is that the acquired values of nurturing, service and subordination to the needs of others, always to a greater or lesser extent identified with women in extension of their reproductive role, are correspondingly absent from the male; in their place are competition, self-assertion and achievement. However, the activities and attributes peculiar to men, whatever they are held to be, are not just different from those of women; they are valued more highly too. Gender is not just a dichotomy of male and female, but a *hierarchy* of male *over* female. As a result, caring and nurturing values and activities are devalued, while competition and achievement, along with the inequality they inevitably produce *among men* as well as between the sexes, are prized highly.

Why did societies elaborate on reproductive difference and turn it into inequality? An existential tendency to dualism was one theory and innate male aggression another, but the crucial explanations were those advanced by post-Freudian anthropologists such as Mead, who located the male drive for status and achievement in the response of men to women's exclusive mothering. Lacking the secure, unsought identity that women had, and to a greater or lesser extent excluded from the experience of 'mothering', men defined themselves in terms of an elusive masculinity which must constantly be reasserted and imposed, not only on women, but on other men, who otherwise might prove more masculine. This need to *assert* their difference from women and to compensate for their own insecure masculinity (the 'fractured psyche' of men) explained plausibly both the hierarchical character of gender and the fact that men so often secure the sphere of 'male' attributes and achievements by deliberately keeping women out. There was no reason, however, to believe it was innate, any more than women's exclusive mothering must extend beyond their basic reproductive role.

The fact that this kind of gender theory is contentious nowadays (see below) does not alter the fact that it was absolutely crucial to the emergence of modern feminism and its core political concepts. If gender roles and values were cultural constructs (that is, not 'natural' and fixed), *they could be changed*. What radical feminism did was recast this as a political theory, by substituting 'power' and 'domination' for 'achievement' and 'superiority' in the account of male values and translating women's unequal status and restricted roles into political terms of subordination, powerlessness and oppression. This was what gave the statement that 'the personal is political' (originally a concept of the US civil rights movement) its enormous significance for modern feminism. Suddenly, the negative experience of so many women who could not 'fit' their gender stereotype or value their 'inferiority' was no longer seen as something purely personal, for which their individual failure 'as a woman' was to blame, but as part of a political relationship with men. Conversely, if the oppressive nature of female gender was political in character, then so was every woman's discontent. However, in order to realise this and make common cause with other females, women had to escape from their own internalisation of female gender and the low self-esteem, apathy and sense of helplessness that went with it. This was *consciousness-raising*, a form of adult political socialisation in which women meeting separately from men could overcome their marginalisation and recognise each other as full individuals whose experience was as valid as that of men. Problems women previously thought of as personal were discovered to be general to their sex and flowed not from their nature, but from the political system of gender in which they were oppressed *by men* (Chapman, 1986).

The very old distinction in Western civilisation between the private and the public spheres also acquired a radically new significance for feminism as the structural expression of male gender values (with women located in the 'private', largely domestic sphere, while virtually all valued, non-nurturing activities were reserved for the 'public' sphere, from which women could be excluded either outright or indirectly by their domestic ties and lack of 'public' skills). It was also the basis of male-constructed politics. The object of 'equal rights' feminists had been to gain access to the 'public' sphere on the same terms as men by overcoming the discrimination that excluded them, while 'socialist' feminists promised to do away with the 'private' sphere altogether, by communalising its domestic and childcare functions. In both these kinds of feminism, the values of the 'public' sphere were taken as the norm and the goal for women was the right to be like men.

From a gender perspective, however, the 'public' sphere was the product of male gender, reflecting its competitive and inegalitarian values both in its regulation of the private sphere (through laws and customs and the personal power of men in families) *and* in the hierarchical structuring of political, social and economic status among men. The dominant culture was permeated through and through with *sexism* – the assumption of male superiority – while *patriarchy* was originally adopted as the feminist term for male power and politics precisely because it captured the integral connection between the domination of women by men *and* the domination of men by other men (Randall, 1987). Female gender values had been left out in the formation of the public sphere, but men as well as women have to pay for this.

Thus the task of feminists was not to join the 'public' sphere, which would simply reinforce its dominance, turn women into yet another of its many 'out-groups' and continue to exclude the 'female' values that had been tied up and devalued in the 'private' sphere. Instead, the women's liberation movement was to be a profoundly revolutionary movement, which would not only liberate women from male oppression and their gender socialisation (the 'outposts of the enemy in one's head'), but also overcome the barriers between the public and private spheres and recreate society, culture and politics in new, non-patriarchal forms.

# ▌ What went wrong; fragmentation and the 'feminist perspective'

This immense project of women's liberation was to expose the whole gender-based system of sexism and patriarchal power, expressed in social, economic and political structures; in language and cultural images of men and women; in the alienation of women from their bodies, the repression of their sexuality and male control of women's reproduction; and in male violence against women. Sometimes exhilarating, but often deeply disturbing and painful, this labour has revealed inconsistencies and ambiguities in the strategy and goals of feminism that are inextricably bound up with both the theory and experience of gender. Some of these problems are illustrated by two fundamental issues that have never been resolved: motherhood and feminist democracy.

The logical strategy for motherhood indicated by gender theory was to promote 'shared parenting' which, by giving men an almost equal role in nurturing, could minimise their need for difference and expose both sexes to similar formative experiences that would shape a more androgynous society. From the start, however, feminists found it impossible to agree on how to value motherhood or fit it into their conception of a new society. In Shulamith Firestone's vision of an *androgynous* society free from artificial 'difference' and repression, motherhood was a biological trap which could only be overcome by the advance of science to the point where the human foetus could be reared outside the body. In complete contrast, Adrienne Rich equated the liberation of women with the liberation of *mothering* from the *institution of motherhood* (that is, from male control). Although Rich paid lip service to the goal of 'shared parenting', her vision of sisterhood and its basis in the bonds between mothers and daughters seemed to have more to do with women's traditional role and the elusive ideal of genders that are 'different but equal'. It certainly touched a chord with women who were reluctant to share their traditional sphere of fulfilment and maternal power with men. In addition, in societies where the incidence of women's single-parenthood is rapidly increasing, whether from choice or necessity, even advocates of shared parenting have found themselves obliged to support women in a form of motherhood that entails the ultimate exclusion of men from parenting and can only reinforce the system of 'different' but *unequal* (Chapman, 1993).

These positions with regard to motherhood signal some of the most divisive episodes in feminism since the early 1970s. The link between sex and gender – the point of departure of modern feminism-has become a battleground over the issue of *essentialism*, that is, blurring the distinction between biological sex and gender, so that the characteristics of men and women produced by culture are treated as being fixed and 'natural', either because men and women are believed to be innately different, or because their different reproductive roles have ineluctable effects. Thus the assertion of mothering led to some extremely essentialist platforms which depart from gender theory to identify women with nature, maternal power and a fixed cultural superiority to men (for example, Daly, 1979) and also let feminists out of the necessity of changing *men*. Although hardly any feminists endorse such claims, this thinking is often exploited nowadays by those who wish to dissociate feminism and women's futures from *any* links with their biology, a tendency which may also be fuelled by dismay at the 'long, often negative struggle' faced by the pioneers of personal politics (Snitow, 1990) and the natural inclination of feminist academics to prioritise their own especial interests. Thus Young (1984) is found to argue that if shared parenting 'entails monumental changes in all institutions in society' then 'relations of parenting cannot be changed without *first* changing other structures' (my italics), a *non sequitur* which in its turn is held to justify the proposition that 'women's mothering may be less fundamental than other institutions of domination'. From here it is but a short step to the categorical insistence of some contemporary feminists that gender is not derived from sex at all, but has been imposed on it; 'gender precedes sex' says Delphy (1993), an assertion which to my mind implies more than a trace of wishful thinking and a redefinition of 'gender' so profound that she ought to use a different word. Even this can look like a bulwark, however, against extreme forms of post-modernism which would redefine 'essentialism' as the derivation of meaning from *any* kind of structure (Hoff, 1994).

Overlapping problems arose from feminist political alternatives. A new, feminist definition of politics was implicit in the idea of 'the personal is political'; politics is in *all* the decisions that shape our lives, not only those made in the restricted arena conventionally described as 'politics'. This is not merely a matter of widening the focus from central institutions and political elites to local politics and community groups; it means that relations between individuals, even of the most personal and intimate kind, reflect the general situation of the broader groups to which they belong. However, if conventional ideas of politics are based on male gender values, there must be feminist alternatives. A feminist perspective should acknowledge the dualism of power *and* powerlessness, conflict *and* co-operation, and propose political forms which eschew power, conflict and the hierarchies which these produce.

Rejecting existing politics, many feminists set out to build a new political world of non-hierarchical, unstructured political forms and relationships which would reflect the web of particular relationships and personal responsibilities in women's nurturing role and form the basis of a new *feminist democracy*. These ideas found immediate practical expression in the women's movement, as feminist groups learnt to operate without the office-bearers and procedures that structure hierarchy in conventional groups and sought a form of decision-making that involved all members equally.

Although experience showed that political equality does not emerge spontaneously in unregulated groups (Freeman, 1974), inventive women in the movement soon found ways of structuring for equality of participation in their groups and, in the wider context of the movement as a whole, evolved the practice of 'networking' to enable some degree of co-ordination in the movement as a whole. These innovations have had an immense impact on the political practice of feminism and the 'alternatives' proposed by other social movements throughout the Western world, with effects ranging from the continuing general practice of women's groups in the USA and the UK (where a structured national organisation has never been set up) to the creative intervention of feminists in local and national Icelandic politics and their influence on 'green' politics (Chapman, 1993).

A more intractable problem was that feminists had to pursue their conception of democracy within the context of another, dominant form of politics. The rejection of male politics highlighted an underlying ambiguity in strategy and goals. By drawing alternatives to male politics from women's traditional role, were feminists not betraying themselves as being trapped within their female gender, and perpetuating a male-constructed 'difference'? Worse still, they might be falling into the trap of essentialism. If feminists believed that 'female' alternatives were better, were they not just seeking a *reversal* of dominance, female over male instead of the other way about? Confusion about goals overlapped with anxieties about how far *separatism* (the creation of a separate space in which women could act and interact autonomously outside male-dominated structures) should go. While some women saw this in terms of organisational strategy, either as a temporary stage until a more androgynous (that is, ungendered) society emerged, or involving a combination of separate organisation with participation in mixed structures and alliances with men, others were more pessimistic, especially if they took an essentialist view of 'men the enemy'; for them, separatism was not a means but the end, and should be as complete and final as could be.

Accusations of essentialism were to be a constant refrain of the debates that sprang up around the issues of feminist strategy and goals. Charges of *reductionism* were another. Gender theory certainly was reductionist in the explanatory sense, accounting for behaviour at one level by a theory of gender formation at a more fundamental level. However, this was seen increasingly as reductionist in its pejorative senses, that is, as fallacious reasoning which understands the whole in terms of its parts, or as in metaphysical reductionism which holds that processes at one level are nothing more than manifestations of processes at a lower level (Woodhouse, 1994). Feminists are especially exposed to charges of this kind by the anomalous position of women in a male-dominated society. Although their gender sets women apart from, and in a sense makes them 'outsiders' in, this society, their dependence on men makes them 'insiders' too, divided by all the same dimensions – of tribe, class, religion, race and so on, that divide men. In the reality of a prolonged struggle that had to take place inside the very society they were being 'liberated' from, feminists were soon to find that their early hopes of sisterhood gave way under attack from both established and oppositionist male interests, and from within their own ranks, for promoting feminism at the expense of other aims and reducing everything to the 'woman' question.

Many feminists came from the Marxist Left, where they had been disillusioned by the sexism of male socialists. These recruits, especially in the UK, found it difficult to abandon their conviction of the primacy of class struggle and deference to Marxist authority. Socialism, like liberalism, has always sought to 'disempower' feminism by marginalising it (Barth, 1986); the claim that there could be no solution to the 'woman question' until after a successful socialist revolution meant that in the opinion of socialists, feminism must be subordinated to the socialist movement. Now feminism seemed to be reversing these priorities; no real change in the nature of relations among men could be achieved without a fundamental change in gender. For socialists, it was essential to reconcile feminism and Marxism in some way that avoided this conclusion, a project which was a dominant theme in feminism for many years.

The term 'patriarchy' was adopted enthusiastically by many socialist-feminists, but a fierce debate erupted as to its historical or ahistorical (universal, trans-historical) character, its relationship to paternalist forms of political power, social contract theory and capitalism and the extent to which it is bound up with the history of the family as a social, political and economic unit (Pateman, 1988). Whereas the original feminist premise was that the power of *men over men* as well as that of *men over women* derived from gender, socialist recruits were anxious to separate the two, pointing to the family as the main sphere and instrument of women's subordination and leaving the rest of the field clear for the intellectual hegemony of Marxist class analysis. In practice, Marxist-feminist research tended to refute central socialist-feminist hypotheses about the harmony of interests between the patriarchal family and capitalist development, and socialist critiques of 'the family' came to be seen as somewhat misconceived (Mark-Lawson and Witz, 1990; Barrett, 1988). By that time, however, the feminist movement was already divided into apparently irreconcilable camps: radical and socialist.

The rise of black feminism, identifying racism as yet another distinct oppressive system, compounded the problem. Black feminism was the expression of a new confidence on the part of black women in the USA and Europe which not only mobilised black feminists but also added the effects of racism on women's situation to the feminist perspective and identified over-generalisations (for example, about the role of the family, the state and the labour market) stemming from the leading role of white women in the women's movement. It also led to links with Third-World feminists, which opened up new views of women's experience and aims to Western feminism, and exposed the ethnocentricity of some of its assumptions. Sadly, black feminism also had a negative impact. Its core was the assertion that the experience of black women was unique because of racism; white women could not speak for black. However, racism is experienced by black men as well as black women, and white women as well as men can be racists (even if white feminists have always had strong links with anti-racist movements); even the feminism of white women was a form of racism. The result was that black feminists ended by insisting that racism, like class relations for socialists, must be treated as a separate system of oppression from that of gender and that black women must organise apart from white.

This tendency to fragment can be attributed partly to two divisive influences that new waves of feminist recruits exerted on the women's movement. One is that of guilt, the effect of which was to create a 'hierarchy of oppression', in which the most valued were those judged to be most oppressed. The second influence was that of relativism and 'difference'. Most feminists were very ready to admit that every group's experience is to some extent unique and should be voiced, a particularly appropriate attitude in view of the 'deconstructionist' emphasis of the literary, linguistic and media studies that were becoming central to the new field of women's studies in the 1980s. The essence of 'deconstructionism' is the belief that all identities are socially constructed, in terms of a 'discourse' which reflects the perspective and interests of the dominant group and subordinates the rest. The only route to liberation is by deconstructing this discourse and 'privileging' one's own, oppressed identity. For a feminist, therefore, the object of deconstructing the dominant, masculine discourse is not only to reveal its secret, misogynist agenda, but also to liberate all the women's voices and experience it has denied. The trouble with relativism, however, is that if taken to what is often regarded, perhaps mistakenly, as its logical conclusion, it produces as many fragments as there are people; so too with deconstructionism: *no* identity can be immune from deconstruction. For feminism, the outcome was a movement of diverse and overlapping oppressed groups, whose feminism was only the common factor, not the primary one.

One of the most illuminating, but also most destructive episodes of deconstruction was the so-called 'sexuality' debate, which produced, at its height, the demand for 'political lesbianism', according to which heterosexuality was a construct of the dominant culture designed to keep women down, all sexual relations with men were a form of male power politics and women who were guilty of 'sleeping with the enemy' *could not be considered to be feminists;* lesbianism or celibacy were the only options open (Segal, 1994). This extreme form of separatism obviously overlapped with essentialist views of men as irredeemable, illustrating the pattern that has been repeated with each fragmentation episode: each strand interacts with, and feeds on, all the others to produce a seemingly endless proliferation of competing 'feminisms'.

At the theoretical level, however, liberation by deconstruction has not simply undermined the unity of feminists; it has also brought an *intrinsic* problem of modern feminism into focus. The revolt against the oppression of women puts feminists in the difficult position of trying simultaneously to articulate the women's voices which male-dominated cultures are suppressing (that is, to speak from the point of view of women who have been 'gendered' and advance their interests) *and* to escape from the tyranny of gender altogether. Each project is essential; the first enables feminism to mobilise its natural constituency while also bringing issues such as rape, lesbianism and violence against women into the open and revealing the power relations underlying them; while the second provides the dynamic of the liberation movement. However, the tension between them and the fact that they are both taking place inside living societies, produces endless ambiguity and conflicting strategies and goals. When we talk about women, what kind of women do we mean – women as a biological sex, 'women' as gendered cultures make them; or 'liberated women'? By speaking for 'women' as a social group and pursuing their interests according to a strategy derived from gender difference are we actually reinforcing gender as a construct (the so-called 'dilemma of difference') or, as other feminists would argue, is this the only practicable route to the empowerment of feminists and a gender reformation?

The fact that these intellectual dilemmas have to some extent become institutionalised in the field of women's studies has been a mixed blessing. On the plus side, it has created an autonomous, protected space in which some women are able to produce a pool of new knowledge and insights on which others can draw from within their disciplines. Without this, the study and legitimisation of issues such as rape, pornography and violence against women would not have taken place. The obverse is that this space may become a ghetto, insulating the outside world from feminist ideas which might subvert it (as in the case of political science), and fencing in the inhabitants from dialogue with a sufficiently wide range of others to prevent their becoming introverted, or even colonised by a hegemonic doctrine such as Marxism or post-modernism. Indeed, a markedly doctrinaire and even theological tendency runs like a continous thread through the debates of modern feminism, along with the tendency for feminist writing to become so intellectual and esoteric as to exclude the vast majority of women. Thus, while feminists of the 1970s and early 1980s had to grapple with the difference between socialists, socialist-feminists and socialist feminists 'without the hyphen', those of the 1990s are expected to pursue complex distinctions between feminists, 'post-modern feminists' and 'feminist post-modernists'.

Nevertheless, many feminists have continued on their way, welcoming diversity but still adhering to a recognisably feminist, political agenda. Recently, this has produced two different kinds of political science writing (Coole, 1993). One makes enthusiastic use of 'post-modern (deconstructive) strategies' (from which the 'feminist perspective' is tacitly exempt), but stops short of abandoning women as a social base. The other consists of 'modernist' works which address the material world in which social roles, economic activity and politics continue to be structured on a gender basis. There are corresponding differences of emphasis in their versions of culture, gender and feminist politics. For the 'modernist', culture is the result of interaction between ideas, experience and action in a structured world of social, economic and political relationships; gender has its roots in sex; and feminism is a political and social movement. Under the influence of post-modernism, culture tends to become a disembodied world of ideas, signs and signifiers, where sex is a merely a sign, feminism is a state of mind and political action comes close to being equated with discourse. Yet there is undoubtedly common ground between the central ideas and objects of feminism and post-modernism, even if post-modern strategies of political opposition seem to many feminists not only discursive but unacceptably relativist and even nihilist (Hekman, 1990).

One of the strongest themes in modern feminism has been its critique of the dualism of reason and nature in Western culture, according to which, culture (the fruits of reason) is attributed to men and base (that is, devalued), material nature to women (Plumwood 1993). In fact, the perception of dualism as a central problem of domination is now shared by radical feminists (the dualism of gender); Marxist-feminists (the dualism of class); black feminists (the dualism of race); and eco-feminists (the dualism of man versus nature). The need for a common approach to the problem of dualism/dominance is now being asserted most urgently by eco-feminists. In philosophical terms, this has produced a new/old 'reductionism' derived from the existentialist proposition (proposed by Simone de Beauvoir in her Introduction to *The Second Sex* back in 1949)(de Beauvoir, 1972) that the hierarchical dualism of gender is derived from an even more fundamental dualism in the development of human consciousness (the dualism of 'self' and 'other' which enables us to construct ourselves as subjects). Arguing that this has produced a distinctive 'master consciousness' in Western civilisation, Val Plumwood identifies a 'mutualism' with nature in some non-Western societies as an admittedly imperfect, but preferable, alternative. At the normative level, the emphasis is on integration; eco-feminism seeks to create 'a democratic culture beyond dualism', and a 'realignment of reason' with the cultural riches of diversity.

The need for integration and the view that 'difference' has gone too far are being expressed, albeit with caution, in many quarters, particularly by those whose concern for politics and social action leads them to view the recent history of feminism with some dismay (for example, Carroll and Zerilli, 1993; Lovenduski and Randall, 1993). Paradoxically, the fact that some of the 'differences', such as those between 'black' and 'white' women, seem a lot less categorical on closer examination (Nain, 1994) may even contribute to this more pragmatic tendency. At the same time, the present climate is also distingushed by the emergence of new male allies. Alliances with men always have been a factor in the history of feminism: destructive in their tendency to pull the movement apart in directions that reflect male interests, but also constructive, in their ability to produce limited but real rewards within male-dominated systems. The fact that these new male allies are also gender rebels (the gender dichotomy being the principal target of both 'gays' and heterosexual men who seek to alter masculine identities) certainly brings these alliances closer than previous ones to the central concerns of feminism. The prospects are far from clear, but neither are they altogether bleak.

# ▌ The 'feminist perspective' in political science in the mid-1990s

In addition to the fragmentation process, there are two other, rather obvious, reasons for the limited impact of feminism on political analysis. One is the small number of women in the discipline, perhaps partly because of a feeling, justified or not, that women are particularly unwelcome in such a male-dominated subject, or even to a belief that the study of politics is *inappropriate* for feminists, given the radical repudiation of male politics. Whatever the reason, there is certainly a limit to what a handful of people can achieve. Equally obvious is the natural inclination of men to resist an alien perspective for as long as possible. Since the most threatening and incomprehensible aspect of the feminist agenda was its holistic approach, it is not surprising that one response has been to sub-divide and compartmentalise it, into chapters here and there on feminism, and this or that aspect of the political science canon (which can be left unread), and into separate courses, or sub-sections of courses. The obverse of this has been the readiness of feminists to treat feminism as a subject in itself, instead of exploring their mutual concerns with people studying different mainstream topics. The result is that feminism has made more headway as an *area* of political analysis (for feminists) than as a living influence inside it.

## ☐ *Feminism and political thought*

Feminism calls for a complete reappraisal of the whole system of male political ideas and their epistemology; logically, neither should be studied without reference to the other. This dialectical approach is not a problem for feminists, whose ideas have developed in the form of critiques of male ideas and practice which lead to new insights. Where the heritage of political thought is concerned, feminist scholars have examined the implications of the treatment (or non-treatment) of women by male political philosophers; shown how the sexist assumptions of modern male scholars have distorted women's understanding of their own political traditions; and brought a feminist perspective to bear on social contract theory (Okin, 1979; Saxonhouse, 1985; Pateman, 1988). Jean Bethke Elshtain's *Women and War* (Elshtain, 1987), re-examining war, peace and politics as objects of Western political discourse, has rediscovered them as complex cultural constructions in which women have played a great variety of parts, as diverse mythological figures and images and also as individuals with personal experience that often overlaps with that of men. This not only brings new research topics into view but also, she argues, makes feminists more sceptical of grand utopian (for example, pacifist) projects.

However, there has been little reciprocal interest of men in feminist ideas and, as late as 1987, mainstream theory was still impervious to feminist theory of democracy (Pateman, 1987). Compartmentalism was almost certainly one reason for this: men did not read feminist texts. At the same time, feminist political scientists might not have made enough effort to assemble feminist political theory from its diverse and scattered sources in feminist writing and practice, or to explain its common ground with other theories. Pateman was not just the latest feminist to complain about the invisibility of feminism in the mainstream, but also one of the first to make it clearly visible, in terms of mainstream theories. However, it is where feminist challenges overlap with those being made by men that they are most likely to find an opening to the mainstream. The contemporary citizenship debate, fueled by the decline of the old Left and the rise of new male opposition interests, is a prime example.

Part of the impetus for the citizenship debate came from the feminist critique of liberal democracy and its gendered concept of the citizen, universal in theory, but really rooted in a public sphere derived from masculine values and the structural characteristics of the male gender role. Because of the identification of women with the 'private', domestic sphere and the limitations this places on their lives even now, it has always been difficult – originally impossible – for them to qualify as citizens (Saxonhouse, 1985; Phillips, 1993). Social contract theory, in spite of its emphasis on universalism, individualism and the consent of the governed, in fact reinforced women's exclusion (Pateman, 1988). Following custom and interest rather than logic, liberal theorists either tacitly assumed that women were 'naturally' subject to men, or claimed that they were 'contracted' by marriage to a subordinate, non-civic role; in practice, the 'individual' was male.

Predictably, formal political status has been a hollow gain. The exercise of civic rights and duties, such as participation and elite recruitment, depends on resources that are not available to women as they are to men. Rights may be 'universal', but if there are real differences of situation, cultural identity and resources among individuals (and especially between different 'kinds' of people) they will have different potential (and different value) for different social groups (Phillips, 1992). Similarly, laws will have variable outcomes; they may apply equally to all in theory, but if the situations of men and women are really different, then the results will be also. In a gendered society, the idea of 'gender neutral' law is a fallacy (Dahl and Hernes, 1988).

Unequal resources and the illusory autonomy of politics from social and economic differences are therefore crucial problems to be overcome if a more 'woman-friendly' citizenship is to evolve. Two lines of thought have emerged, both developing a group-based, rather than individualist, conception of citizenship and seeking, in very different ways, not only to de-gender it but also to avoid simply replacing one source of domination and exclusion with another; both are making important contributions to mainstream, as well as feminist, debate.

The first derives from the standpoint of social democracy and 'state' feminism. It links the concept of the citizen to the development of the 'mature' welfare state and what is called the 'care culture', a set of values and expectations derived from the welfare state experience but, it is hoped, also undermining both the paternalistic role of the state and the gender bias in society. The concept of 'welfare citizenship', most fully developed by Nordic feminists, is not just concerned with political status but also with social and economic rights and duties. Caring and welfare are matters of collective interest – everyone has a right to them – but they are also a matter of personal, civic obligation (Hernes, 1987; Siim, 1991). A gender dichotomy which has unpaid women providing 60 per cent of the care work carried out in a society, while the state provides the rest, is not compatible with this construction. The hope is that women, empowered by the state and supported by a culture that makes men susceptible to feminist pressure, will be able to put through innovative legislation which will either draw men into caring or else eliminate the distinction between paid and unpaid work.

A different argument for group-based citizenship seeks to address the recent proliferation, especially in the USA, of new collective cultural identities and mobilising groups (such as gays and Hispanics as well as feminists) which may be labelled deviant as well as marginal. The tendency of the dominant culture to impose its own 'exclusive' concept of the citizen has to be countered by 'inclusive' values, supported by appropriate political reforms which include radical decentralisation; obligatory out-group representation at the highest levels of the policy process; and participatory democracy, both inside disadvantaged groups and in community self-government: thus, hitherto excluded voices (differences) may be heard at every point (Young, 1989). In current 'female-gender talk', this is described as 'weaving stories together that invite dialogue across our differences' (Jones, 1993).

# ☐ Feminism, the state and the policy process

There is a predictably wide range of feminist perspectives on the state (Walby, 1990; Dahlerup, 1994). The radical view, condemning all institutionalised hierarchies as being inimical to the interests of women (and other out-groups) and insisting that feminists who attempt to achieve their goals 'from within' by participating in existing male-constructed systems must fail, since they cannot advance without 'selling out' to the system, was epitomised by Kathy Ferguson's *The Feminist Case against Bureacracy* (Ferguson, 1984).

The contrary case for participation in conventional structures, and the conditions in which the state may be an effective instrument for the achievement of feminist goals, are presented most positively by Nordic feminists such as Helga Maria Hernes, in her *Welfare State and Woman Power* (Hernes, 1988). Although the welfare state incorporates the values of the male-dominated labour market, it has played a crucial part in politicising women by invading the traditionally private sphere ('reproduction going public') and drawing women into the public sphere by employing them in low-level administrative and caring roles. Low pay, lack of promotion and awareness that men are taking policy decisions which affect women's lives lead to women's unionisation and political participation and, as their frustration grows, to their engagement with feminism as a social movement seeking fundamental change. The co-existence of a separate women's movement is seen as indispensable if anything is to be achieved, not only as a source of feminist consciousness and creative politics but also as a spur to women in conventional structures, and a potential threat to the system that will encourage far-seeing men to compromise with feminist demands.

The idea of the 'critical mass' is crucial to this strategy. As the proportion of women in legislative and other policy-making positions grows, so will their legitimacy in their own eyes and those of male politicians; they will feel able to act concertedly and as overt feminists who recognise women's interests, in a highly-gendered society, as being different from those of men. The critical point will come when women's presence in the system and their pursuit of women's interests are taken for granted by all concerned. Empowered by the state (instead of marginalised), they will be able to pursue the goal of a 'woman-friendly' social order, in which women will enjoy 'a natural relationship to their children, their work and public life' (Hernes, 1987, p. 15) and not have harder choices forced on them than society expects of men. Although this requires the pursuit of a 'difference' strategy in order to mobilise 'traditional' as well as feminist women and expose the gendered character of their experience, social roles and political interests, the ultimate goal for most state feminists is to overcome the tyranny of gender in favour of a more or less androgynous society.

Drude Dahlerup is also one of the few leading feminists (along with the Dutch scholar Joyce Outshoorn) in the field of modern policy analysis, using a feminist perspective to extend and apply the theory of non-decision making (Bachrach and Baratz, 1962; Lukes, 1974), which provides a framework for analysing the failure of out-group interests to reach the policy agenda or, if they get into the policy process at all, to make effective progress (Dahlerup, 1984; Outshoorn, 1991). In the USA, Gelb and Palley (1987) have focused on the possibilities of incrementalism, the 'mobilisation of bias' and the use of insider strategies, while Australian feminists are discussing strategies for 'playing' the state (Watson, 1990).

In Britain, the theory of policy analysis has been largely ignored by feminists apart from Gail Stedward (1987), and there has been very little interest in evaluating feminist policy strategy in this framework, except on the abortion issue. One reason is that anti-state orientations were strong in the UK, reinforced by disillusionment with Labour governments and research into women as helpless welfare clients of the patriarchal state (McIntosh, 1978). The creative approach, exemplified by Sheila Rowbotham's famous essay in *Beyond the Fragments* (Rowbotham *et al.*, 1980), was very decentralist, reviving the ideals of communitarian socialism and participatory democratic theory in the attempt to construct a feminist model for a new kind of socialism. Although the highest hopes of the 1970s died with the abolition of the Greater London Council (GLC), their legacy lives on in tenants' and other community action groups in which women are active, as well as in the women's movement itself, where local groups like Women's Aid often apply feminist decision-making principles and employ a flexible approach to participation in 'the system', with some success (Stedward, 1987; Lovenduski and Randall, 1993). It lives also in the absence of women from political elites and the isolation of those who try to work within the policy process. Latterly, however, reaction to the Thatcherite attack on the welfare state and the decline of the traditional Left have encouraged a more instrumental line towards the state. One result is a new interest in researching and evaluating the policy impact of feminism. Lovenduski and Randall (1993) not only provide a perceptive review of the theory and practice of the British women's movement, but also use a variety of methods to investigate and evaluate its policy strategy and inputs in five key areas: elite representation; equality policies; reproduction; childcare; and male violence.

## ☐ *Feminism and fieldwork*

Much of the social research carried out at the time of writing by public agencies, research institutes and academic sociologists is being conducted against a background of diffuse feminist influence and in areas of feminist concern; many of the researchers are women too. In political science, by comparison, feminist empirical research began well but has faltered. The first clearly feminist contribution to the empirical field was a badly-needed critique of American behavioural research (Bourque and Grossholtz, 1974; Lansing, 1974; Goot and Reid, 1975). Standard works on participation, attitudes and voting behaviour were revealed as sloppy and inconsistent in their treatment of the sex variable, and absurdly sexist in their conceptualisation of politics. Women were sometimes left out of investigations altogether, small variations were exaggerated into general-isations about broad (and, by implication, *fixed*) male – female differences, and some generalisations were made from absurdly few cases, in disregard of sampling rules. In interpretating data, the tendency was to draw on cultural stereotypes to explain the differences found in simple sex comparisons, instead of conducting the kind of rigorous analysis which would be applied to variation among men; differences which would disappear if the analysis controlled for socioeconomic background variables such as region, age and education, were attributed to women's nature (Lansing, 1974). Since male behaviour and assumptions about the nature of politics were taken as the norm, female differences were seen as being deviant (for example, Greenstein, 1965). Also, areas of activity in which women were more involved than men (such as school boards and local issues) were classed as non-political and omitted, apparently for that very reason, thus creating a false picture of low female levels of participation (Jennings and Niemi, 1979).

These revelations were followed by feminist research on themes of special interest such as socialization (Iglitsyn, 1974; Flora and Lynn, 1974) and the 'gender gap' in political participation (Welch, 1977, 1980), and a wealth of data-gathering on political recruitment, female candidacies and the composition of elites that continues to the present day. Much of this work was immaculately executed and some definitive in its field (for example, Christy, 1987). A work of a more innovative kind was Carol Gilligan's *In a Different Voice* (1982), a flawed but persuasive work on gender and moral reasoning which deeply offended many feminists at the time with its stress on 'difference', but is more in tune with feminist thinking now. In Europe, the gender dimension of attitudes and behaviour is the subject of cross-national surveys sponsored by the European Union (EU) and Danish, Swedish, Belgian and Dutch feminists also employ quantitative techniques freely in empirical research.

However, systematic research that draws on feminism for its conceptual framework and tries to advance the frontiers of *feminist* knowledge is very rare; in the UK, my own research on adult socialisation (Chapman, 1985); consciousness-raising (Chapman, 1987); political activism and personal experience (Chapman, 1991); and patterns of political recruitment, is almost unique (Randall, 1994). This research gap may be caused partly by an attack on empirical methods in the course of the feminist epistemology debate. Some lesbian sociologists, researching uncharted areas of women's experience from standpoints labelled 'deviant' in the dominant sociology, experienced all existing research methods as 'positivist', that is, representing the dominant culture and its structural arrangements as the only 'right' ones (Stanley and Wise, 1983, 1993). Although these influential authors disclaimed any demand for a completely different 'feminist method' of data collection and analysis, it is difficult to read their arguments against *any* use of dichotomies ('Cartesian binaries') and their criticisms of qualitative as well as quantitative research without interpreting them as a rejection of all systematic methods. To me, it seems that the failings of male behavioural methodology – its dominant-culture bias, the huge gaps where women's experience ought to be and the predilection for the most impersonal, closed and costly methods – were not attributable to the methods in themselves, but to the way they were applied. They could be corrected by the adoption of a clearly-specified, feminist perspective and a sensitive selection of techniques, in particular the combination of quantitative and qualitative methods. Instead, the demand for 'a new feminist methodology', in spite of positive contributions such as that of Harding (1994), seems to have widened the gap between feminist political science and most kinds of fieldwork.

This is especially unfortunate where the dimensions of difference are concerned, since one of the principal objects of systematic survey and in-depth research is to show how things vary, and surveys are also the only way that the variable experience of women in general, rather than the experience of feminist activists, is likely to be recorded. The fact that good behavioural research uses control groups also means that it is unlikely to be so woman-centred as to lose sight of *men* and their experience, or to reach unwarrantable conclusions about the extent of similarity or difference among women. The gap between feminism and fieldwork of all kinds, quantitiative or qualitative, is even more damaging where the women's movement is concerned. Feminism is naturally an absorbing subject for feminists, a brilliant succession of whom have examined and analysed its origins, objectives, ambiguities and achievements in historical and recent times (for example, Freeman, 1984; Taylor, 1984; Rendall, 1985; Banks, 1986; Phillips, 1987; and Rowbotham, 1992, to name but a few). However, very few attempts indeed have been made to relate the feminist movement to social movement theory (specifically Freeman, 1984; Dahlerup, 1986; Randall, 1987; Gelb, 1989; Chapman, 1993) and political science remains largely blind to its significance as the main theatre of women's political engagement and an incomparable resource for researching feminist 'alternatives'.

The absence of formal, national organisations, especially in the UK, certainly impedes the researcher; the flexibility which helps feminism to survive its disputes also renders much of what feminists do invisible to non-participants and makes the movement, with its lack of clear boundaries and formal membership, very difficult to pin down. However, this is not an adequate reason for neglecting matters so specific to political science as its size, composition and distribution, or the density and social basis of its various groups and tendencies; on the contrary, it is an argument for designing new research strategies to cope with these problems. It is astonishing, too, that Jo Freeman has had the negative, last word on alternatives to conventional, hierarchical politics since the early 1970s, considering that 'unstructured' and egalitarian forms of participatory democracy have been the common practice of many women's groups throughout this period and are known to produce very different results from those produced by conventional approaches. The fact that techniques for non-hierarchical decision-making do not *always* work (Rowbotham, 1986), and the problems that arise at the point where feminist practice intersects with the conventional system, are inadequate reasons for ignoring them.

# ■ Conclusion

The feminist political agenda had its origins in the early radical feminist proposition that the primary dualism was that of gender, which made all the others possible, and even inevitable, by separating artificially the human values of caring and mutualism from those of competition and dominance, and 'naturalising' the tension between them in the unarguable dichotomy of biological sex. The liberation of women was therefore an all-embracing, revolutionary project for changing everything, including male gender.

It has become axiomatic in academic circles to condemn the primacy of gender as reductionist and to deconstruct all systems of dualism/domination as separate, though inter-related, phenomena. This has added greatly to our understanding of diversity and made feminists a good deal more sceptical about 'grand theories', which may have a lot of truth in them, but never *all* the truth. However, the continuous assertion of difference, the relativistic and discursive influences of postmodernism, and the exaggerated claims being made about essentialist tendencies in modern feminism have inevitably undermined the coherence of feminism as a political movement. It is almost as a counsel of despair that some feminists are now returning to a more pragmatic and socially-structured concept of the 'feminist perspective' and turning with hope to new alliances with men.

There is a strong resemblance here to the cycle of first-wave feminism, which also started in revolt, developed in autonomy, but ended in fragmentation and alliances with men. The outcome then was a considerable advance in formal equality, plus some welfare legislation; the price was that the feminist movement collapsed and disappeared. This time round, the male allies include men in revolt against the tyranny of gender; the rewards for women may be that much greater, but it remains to be seen if the price is lower.

Meanwhile, the influence of the feminist perspective on political science has been uneven. This can be attributed partly to the changing character of feminism and partly to the compartmentalisation of feminism and mainstream topics. Integration with the mainstream was largely by default until the recent emergence of 'new' topics (such as the contemporary citizenship debate) where feminism makes common cause with new intellectual currents and interests among men. Also, although discourse analysis is one direction in which feminists are just beginning to expand the range of political science methods, lack of empirical research has marginalised some of feminism's most significant political objectives and left large areas of innovative political practice unexplored. We have a long way to go before either feminism or political science has opened fully to the other.

# ■ Further reading

Banks (1986) is a good introduction to the development of US and UK feminism. Chapman (1993) covers comparative political recruitment in Part 1 amd feminist strategies in Part 2, and Githens *et al.* (1994) offer articles and readings in contemporary feminist issues. Hekman (1990) is a very useful text, while Hernes (1988) explains the reasoning behind 'state feminism' and feminist policies for a 'woman-friendly' society; and Hirsch and Keller (1990) examine controversial theoretical and policy areas in contemporary feminism. Lovenduski and Randall (1993) is an extensive, accessible study, while Part 1 of Mead (1971) [1949] can be thought of as the foundation of modern feminist gender theory. Phillips (1993) is another useful text, and Plumwood (1993) explores feminism, ecology and the the dualism of reason and nature.

# ■ *Chapter 6* ■

## Discourse Theory
### David Howarth

Discourse theory is concerned with the role of meaningful social practices and ideas in political life. It analyses the way systems of meaning or 'discourses' shape the way people understand their roles in society and influence their political activities. Discourses are not, however, ideologies in the traditional or narrow sense of the term (that is, sets of ideas by which social actors explain and justify their organised social action). The concept of discourse includes all types of social and political practice, as well as institutions and organisations, within its frame of reference.

Discourse theory draws its inspiration from *interpretative* sciences such as hermeneutics, phenomenology, structuralism and deconstruction (see Dallmayr and McCarthy, 1977). These sciences are organised either around the interpretation of literary and philosophical texts, or the analysis of the way in which objects and experiences acquire their meaning. Placing itself in this tradition of thought, the discourse approach shares some resemblances with Max Weber's method of *verstehen*. In this methodology, the social science researcher attempts to comprehend social action through empathising with the agent who acts in society. The difference is that the discourse analyst examines the ways in which structures of meaning make possible certain forms of conduct. In doing so, s/he tries to understand how the discourses which structure the activities of social agents are *produced*, how they *function*, and how they are *changed*. In endeavouring to understand these objects of investigation, the discourse analyst gives priority to political concepts such as 'antagonism', 'agency', 'power' and 'hegemony'.

This chapter consists of four parts. The first part provides some background about the development of discourse theory; the second sets out in more detail some of the main characteristics of the perspective; the third shows how discourse theory tackles empirical problems by considering the case of Thatcherism, and the final part makes an assessment of the main criticisms of the approach.

# The emergence of discourse theory and its relationship to post-modernism

The concept of discourse is used in many different disciplines and approaches ranging from linguistics to literature and philosophy. In its more technical sense, discourse analysis refers to a neutral set of methodological devices for the analysis of speeches, writings, interviews, conversations and so on (see Fairclough, 1992, pp. 12–37). Conversation analysts, for example, have examined various aspects of conversation: their openings and closings; how topics are introduced, sustained and changed; how people narrate events in conversation; how people 'take turns' during conversations; and so on (see, for example, Heritage, 1984). Here, the concept of discourse is purely textual or linguistic, and its analytical focus restricted to small segments of speech or writing. For critical discourse analysts such as Michel Foucault, by contrast, 'discursive formations' refer to regular bodies of ideas and concepts which claim to produce knowledge about the world. In his historical accounts of scientific discourses, for example, Foucault endeavours to sketch out their underlying discursive regularities and connects their production and transformation to the broader social and political processes of which they are a part (Foucault, 1972).

Following Foucault's more critical perspective, this chapter focuses on the writings of Ernesto Laclau and Chantal Mouffe who have developed a concept of discourse that is concerned specifically with the analysis of political processes. In their various writings, Laclau and Mouffe have attempted to deepen the Marxist category of ideology by utilising the insights of post-modernist philosophy and theory. The label 'post-modernism' includes a wide variety of theorists who have questioned the foundational and essentialist assumptions of their respective traditions and disciplines. These include writers such as Michel Foucault, Jacques Derrida, Jacques Lacan, Jean Baudrillard, William Connolly, Jean-François Lyotard and Richard Rorty to name a few.

Unfortunately, in many ways the notion of 'post-modernism' is something of a misnomer. Even supporters of the idea, such as Richard Rorty, have voiced reservations about the way the concept has been employed in recent times (Rorty, 1991, p. 1). The reasons for these doubts centre on the misleading connotations it has engendered. For some, it is seen as a complete break with modern ideas such as 'reason', 'freedom', and 'autonomy' which emerged during the European Enlightenment. For others, it represents a historical period that comes after modernity. Still others equate post-modernism with the end of epistemology – the theory of knowledge – and thus a relativistic nihilism that rejects all knowledge claims and renders political and ethical commitments redundant. In all these interpretations, the continuities between modernity and postmodernity are overlooked. As we shall see, post-modernism is not a rejection of modernity, but a scaling down of its overreaching ambitions.

Bearing these misgivings in mind, how are the ideas of post-modernism useful to discourse theory? They are helpful in that they constitute an alternative attitude or sensibility toward the foundational drives of the modernist project. These drives have aimed to ground our knowledge, ethical beliefs and judgements on some objective and essential foundation, whether this be 'the way the world really is', our human subjectivity, our knowledge of history, or our uses of language. The post-modern attitude points out the necessary *limitations* in this project to master completely the nature of reality.

In this regard, three prominent post-modern themes are worth emphasising. First, there has been the critique of what Jean-Francois Lyotard has called 'meta-narratives', or the 'grand narratives of emancipation' in modernity. That is to say, there has been a questioning of the modernist recourse to some underlying and 'totalising' device of legitimation, as with the Marxist story of how history necessarily progresses in successive stages, to ensure the objectivity or truth of our knowledge and to justify socialist or Communist political projects. These universal and all-embracing narratives tend to obliterate other narratives, resulting in the triumph of consensus, uniformity and scientific reason over conflict, diversity and different forms of knowledge.

Second, there has been the 'anti-foundationalist' stance of the American pragmatist, Richard Rorty. Rorty's account of the history of Western philosophy and political theory is designed to show that there are no objective standpoints which guarantee truth or knowledge about the world, and that philosophical projects, from Plato to Immanuel Kant to Jürgen Habermas, have all floundered in this pursuit. The search for ultimate foundations assumes two separate realms – reality and thought – where efforts are directed at ensuring that our thoughts correspond to the 'real' world. Hence, in his *Philosophy and the Mirror of Nature*, Rorty criticises René Descartes, John Locke, and Kant's desire for a special theory of 'the mind' or of 'mental representations' to justify claims to knowledge. Their searches for the indubitable grounds of knowledge, morality, language or society being 'attempts to *eternalize* a certain contemporary [that is, historically specific] language-game, social practice, or self-image' (Rorty, 1980, p. 10). These foundational figures of modernity, which, according to Rorty, continue to exercise considerable influence on our contemporary viewpoints, all deny the historicity – or changing character – of our knowledge and beliefs and all assume that one can easily 'step outside' the traditions and practices of which we are a part and achieve a completely detached view of social processes.

A third important post-modern theme is its 'anti-essentialism'. In this regard, the French 'deconstructionist' Jacques Derrida is exemplary in showing the difficulties of trying to determine the essential characteristics of concepts and objects. Derrida's criticism of Western metaphysics shows the impossibility of demarcating the essence of things, and of fixing completely the identity of words and objects. For Derrida, the drive to 'close' philosophical texts and arguments – the effort to determine the essence of something – always fails because there exist ambiguities and 'undecidables' that resist ultimate fixation and blur absolute distinctions (see Bennington, 1993; Derrida, 1981; Gasche, 1986).

What, then, of the post-modern alternatives to the pretensions of the modern project? With respect to the 'meta-narratives' and 'grand narratives' of modernity, Lyotard questions their so-called universality, and stresses the need for dissent and tolerance of those narratives that are out of step with modern forms of knowledge (Lyotard, 1984, p. 75). Rorty's anti-foundationalism leads him to affirm the historicity and contingency of selfhood, language and community. Eschewing a 'trans-historical' point of view, he argues that things which were thought to be necessary or essential for one generation, may turn out to be accidental and empirical for another. In this sense, everything is a product of 'time and chance' and not determined by some overarching logic or principle. Hence, languages, communities and human beings are what they have become, and not eternal and unchanging entities. As he puts it: 'There is nothing to people except what has been socialised into them – their ability to use language, and thereby to exchange beliefs and desires with other people' (Rorty, 1989, p. 177). This awareness of our 'human finitude' – that we are mortal beings who happen to be living in a particular time and place – means that things are always vulnerable to change by our own actions and projects, and that we are not determined by a cosmic plan which goes on 'behind our backs'. Finally, in opposition to essentialist thinking, which emphasises identity at the expense of ambiguity and the 'play of differences', Derrida argues that there is no natural closure or fixity of meaning. Identity can only be achieved through deliberately denying ambiguity and excluding differences. For Derrida, however, these denials and expulsions haunt identities, preventing them from achieving fullness and thus always threatening to subvert them.

# ■ The core characteristics of discourse theory

While post-modernism has been influential in literature, philosophy and sociology, there is not much evidence of its deployment in the fields of political theory and analysis. Laclau and Mouffe have used the 'anti-foundationalist' and 'anti-essentialist' insights of philosophers such as Rorty, Derrida and Lyotard to expand the category of ideology and to elucidate their theory of discourse. I shall outline briefly the main concepts they have developed and utilised.

# ☐ *Discourse and articulation*

It is useful to begin by comparing briefly the categories of ideology and discourse. To simplify, ideology in Marxist theory refers to a domain of ideas and mental representations which is contrasted with the material world of economic production and practical action. Laclau and Mouffe reject this 'regional' conception of ideology. They also dissolve the distinction between a realm of ideas and a world of real objects, as well as the division between mental representations and practical activities, both of which have been employed by Marxist characterisations of ideology.

Instead of these separations, they argue that all objects and practices are discursive. In other words, for things and activities to be meaningful, they must be part of particular discourses. This does not mean that everything is discursive or linguistic, but simply that for things to be intelligible they must exist as part of a wider framework of meaning. Take a stone that we might come across in a field. Depending on the particular social context within which this object is located, it might conceivably be a brick for the building of a house, a projectile for use in warfare, an object of considerable wealth, or a 'find' of great archaeological significance. All the different meanings or identities the piece of material assumes depend on the particular type of discourse and the specific circumstances, which confer meaning or 'being' to the object (Laclau and Mouffe, 1987).

Hence Laclau and Mouffe's conception of discourse affirms the relational character of identity. The social meaning of words, speeches, actions and institutions are all understood in relation to the overall context of which they form a part. Each meaning is understood in relation to the overall practice which is taking place, and each practice in relation to a particular discourse. Hence we are only able to understand, explain and evaluate a process if we can describe the practice, and the discourse within which it is occurring. For example, the act of marking a cross on a piece of paper and placing it in a box – the practice of voting in an election – only becomes meaningful within the system of rules, procedures and institutions we call liberal democratic. The significance of voting is thus understood only in relation to the other practices and objects of which it forms a part.

The relational theory of discourse that Laclau and Mouffe develop means that discourses do not simply mirror processes occuring in other parts of society such as the economy. Rather, discourses incorporate elements and practices from all parts of society. This brings us to the process by which discourses are constructed. Here Laclau and Mouffe introduce the concept of *articulation*. This concept refers to a practice of bringing together different elements and combining them in a new identity. For example, the first majority Labour government set about welding together – or articulating – a number of diverse elements such as the welfare state; commitments to full employment and Keynesian demand management; the nationalisation of certain industries; and support for the Empire and the Cold War, in their establishment of the 'post-war political consensus'. This articulatory practice was not a reflex response to changes in the economy, nor did it simply express the interests of one social class. Rather, it was the result of a political project that unified a series of political, ideological and economic elements – each with no essential meaning of its own – which was able to win support from large sectors of British society during the 1950s and into the 1960s.

The theoretical basis of this conception of discourse is derived from the Swiss structural linguist Ferdinand de Saussure. Saussure argues that language is a system of formal differences in which the identity of words is purely *relational*. In doing so, Saussure divides linguistic units, which he calls signs, into 'signifiers' and 'signifieds'. Hence a sign such as 'father' consists of a written or spoken element – the word 'f-a-t-h-e-r' – and the concept we understand by this particular word. The relation between the word and concept is strictly formal and structural. In other words, there is nothing natural or substantial about the linkage: words do not have a special attachment to the concepts they imply, nor do they share any natural properties with the things they designate in the world. Saussure calls this the 'arbitrariness of signs'. Signs work as units of signification because they are part of the *system* of language we use. Thus, for example, the word 'father' obtains its meaning because it differs from other words in our language such as 'mother', 'son', 'daughter' and so on (Saussure, 1983). This relational conception of language is in marked contrast to a *referential* theory of meaning where words denote particular objects in the world.

## ☐ Discourse and political analysis

Laclau and Mouffe have extended this linguistic model to their understanding of social and political processes. The first move involves seeing social systems as being structured according to the rules of discourse. This emphasises the *symbolic* character of social relations. However, there are important differences between Laclau and Mouffe's conception of discourse and the Sausserian concept of language. The main difference is that Laclau and Mouffe argue that discourses are never *closed* systems of difference (and by extension 'societies' themselves are never closed). Thus, discourses never exhaust the available meanings and identities in societies. In presenting these arguments, Laclau and Mouffe draw on the post-modernist ideas discussed above. In order to show this, let us consider the post-modern or post-structuralist critique of Saussure.

The post-modern critique of Saussure's structuralist conception of meaning focuses on three difficulties. First, while Saussure argues that identity depends on the differences of the total system of language, he does not account for the identity of the system itself. Thus, there is no explanation of the *limits* of the linguistic structure or language. Second, Saussure's model focuses on the synchronic, rather than the diachronic, character of linguistic identity. Hence his account tends to be static and unchanging, rather than dynamic and historical. Third, Saussure's model does not allow for the ambiguity and plurality of linguistic meaning. In contrast to this, post-structuralists argue that language always contains the possibility that signifiers may be detached from a particular signified. Metaphors, for instance, can be constructed because words and images may be used to produce different meanings. In political life, signifiers such as 'freedom', 'democracy' and 'justice', for example, can assume a variety of different and competing meanings. Paradoxically, therefore, even though Saussure argues that the relationship between the signifier and signified is arbitrary, post-structuralists show that this position results in a complete fixing of the relationship between words and their meanings.

To offset these problems, Laclau and Mouffe argue that discourses are historically contingent and are constructed politically. Let us consider these dimensions. We have seen in the writings of Rorty and Derrida the historicity and contingency of identities. For Rorty, social agents, communities and languages are all historical products vulnerable to change and transformation. According to Derrida, identities are never fully constituted, because their existence depends on something external to, or different from, identity. These two perspectives do, however, pose a central problem for political analysis. If identities are never ultimately fixed, how is any identity possible? Are we condemned to live in a world of meaninglessness and chaos? That is to say, if we inhabit a world without any closure, is there no possibility of fixing the identity of discourses at all? Laclau and Mouffe resolve this problem by affirming the primacy of political practices in constituting identities. As we shall see in more depth, it is through the drawing of political frontiers and constructing antagonisms between 'friends' and 'enemies' that discourses acquire their identity.

## ☐ *Antagonisms*

The construction and experience of social antagonisms is central for discourse theory in three respects. First, the creation of an antagonistic relationship, which always involves the production of an 'enemy' or 'other', is vital for the establishment of political frontiers. Second, the constitution of antagonistic relationships and the stabilisation of political frontiers is central for the partial fixing of the identity of discursive formations and social agents. Third, the experience of antagonism is exemplary in showing the contingency of identity.

What exactly does the concept of antagonism refer to in the discourse approach? Let us contrast the discourse account with more traditional conceptions. Traditional accounts of antagonism have tended to focus on the conditions under which conflicts occur (see Chapter 3 and the discussion of the work of Gurr). For discourse theory, by contrast, antagonisms occur because of the impossibility of agents and groups acquiring a full and positive identity. This is because the presence of the 'enemy' in an antagonistic relationship prevents the attainment of identity by the 'friend'. Take the example of workers dismissed from their jobs as a result of a government drive to improve productivity in a nationalised industry through the introduction of new technology. For the workers, the actions of the government and management directly prevent them from achieving their identity as workers. For the management and the government, the workers are portrayed as preventing the modernisation of industry, or as trying to undermine the government. Thus, the experience of antagonism – the conflict between workers and management – demonstrates the mutual failure of identity both for the workers, on the one hand, and the government and managers, on the other, as they struggle to impose their will upon one another.

Antagonisms are subject to a process of construction and deconstruction. Take the case of a national liberation struggle in a colonised state. Typically, after the forcible imposition of colonial rule, there is an attempt by the colonizing power to create a system of differences which can accommodate the colonized in a system of non-antagonistic relationships. This is what Laclau and Mouffe call 'the logic of difference' and it can take place either through a partial process of assimilation, or through a policy of 'divide and rule', strategies which are always underpinned by the violent exclusion of those forces that resist these efforts at incorporation.

In many cases, resistance by the colonised results in an attempt to interrupt and challenge these divisionary logics. The manner in which this antagonism is organised generally centres on the creation of a frontier between 'the oppressed people' (the colonised) and 'the oppressors' (the colonisers). In doing so, the various manifestations of the colonisers – their language, traditions, institutions and so on – are made equivalent by being constructed as the 'enemy' of the people – as symbolising the 'anti-colonised'. Simultaneously, the different identities of the colonised are condensed around notions such as 'the people', or 'the nation', prevented by their colonial masters from realising their 'freedom', 'human dignity', 'social justice' and so on. Hence, the colonisers are presented as blocking the identity of the colonised. The particular floating signifiers that come to symbolise the antagonistic relationship – 'freedom', 'the people', 'democracy', 'human dignity', 'the nation' and so on – are, as we shall see, vitally important in analysing hegemonic practices and the manner in which political subjects are constituted.

## ☐ *Subjectivity and agency*

For an approach that is concerned with the way in which people conduct and understand themselves in societies, the question of social agency or subjectivity is of central importance for discourse theory (see also Chapter 9). This is best addressed by considering briefly an aspect of the so-called 'structure/agency' debate. Let us turn to the structuralist Marxist conception of the subject put forward by Louis Althusser. Opposing those for whom the subject is a unified and fully-fledged source of its own ideas and values, Althusser insists that subjects are constructed – 'interpellated' or 'hailed' as he puts it – by ideological practices. That is to say, the way human beings understand and live their lives as particular subjects – 'men', 'women', 'Christians', 'workers', and so on – is an ideological effect that centres and confers an imaginary identity to social agents about their real life conditions (Althusser, 1965; 1971, pp. 127–86).

While Laclau and Mouffe accept Althusser's view that the identities of subjects are discursively constructed, they reject the deterministic connotations of the Althusserian view. In Althusser's view, the subject gets reduced to the underlying social and economic structure. Laclau and Mouffe, on the other hand, distinguish between *subject positions* and *political subjectivity*. The former category refers to the positioning of subjects in various discourses. This means that individuals can have a number of different subject positions. A particular empirical agent might conceive of herself as being 'black', 'working class', 'Christian', a 'woman', an 'environmentalist', and so on. This need not imply a complete dispersal of subject positions, because various identities might be linked together in more all-embracing discourses such as nationalism, socialism, conservatism, Fascism, and so on.

If the notion of subject positions deals with the multiple forms by which agents constitute themselves as social actors, the concept of political subjectivity concerns the way in which social actors act or take decisions in novel forms. In order to go beyond Althusser's privileging of the structure over the agent, the discourse theory approach holds that the actions of subjects are made possible by the precariousness of those discourses with which they identify. Thus, subjects act in different ways when the contingency of their identities is revealed. This occurs when discourses begin to disintegrate during periods of social or economic turmoil, and when such dislocation is experienced by subjects as an identity crisis. In these situations, subjects endeavour to reconstitute their identities and social meanings by articulating and identifying with alternative discourses.

## □ *Hegemony*

In discourse analysis, struggles for hegemony and the establishment of hegemony by political projects are of the utmost importance. This is because hegemonic practices are central to political processes, and because political processes are vital for the formation, functioning and dissolution of discourses. Very simply, hegemony is achieved if and when one political project or force determines the rules and meanings in a particular social formation. As Humpty Dumpty puts it in his conversation with Alice in Lewis Carroll's *Through the Looking Glass*:

> "When *I* use a word," Humpty Dumpty said, in a rather scornful tone, "It means just what I choose it to mean. Neither more nor less."
> "The question is," said Alice, "whether *you* can make words mean so many different things."
> "The question is," said Humpty Dumpty, "who is to be master. That is all." (Carroll, 1987, p. 124)

Thus, the concept of hegemony centres on who is going to be master. That is to say, it is about which political force will decide the dominant forms of conduct and meaning in a given social context.

There are a number of aspects of the category of hegemony that we need to spell out. To begin with, hegemonic operations are a special type of articulatory practice in that they determine the dominant rules that structure the identities of discourses and social formations. This exemplary type of political practice presupposes two further conditions. First, hegemonic practices require the drawing of political frontiers. In other words, there must be a struggle between opposed forces and the exclusion of certain possibilities in the establishment of hegemony. Hence hegemonic practices always involve the exercise of power as one political project attempts to impose its will on another. Second, hegemonic practices require the availability of floating signifiers that are not fixed by existing discourses. Given the availability of contingent elements, hegemonic practices aim to articulate those elements into an expanding political project, thereby conferring (partial) meaning on to them.

## ■ Analysing Thatcherism

In order to provide a brief empirical illustration of the discourse theory perspective, let us consider the case of Thatcherism. The concept of Thatcherism has many different meanings and it has been analysed by various theoretical approaches (see Jessop *et al.*, 1988, pp. 5–9 and 24–51). Here we shall take Thatcherism to be a discursive articulation and approach its analysis from a discourse theory perspective. In doing so, I shall draw on the writings of Stuart Hall, and more particularly on his article 'The Great Moving Right Show', which was first published in late 1978. Hall's analysis of Thatcherism is premised on the critique of class reductionism and economic determinism (Hall, 1988, pp. 3–5). In contrast to other perspectives, Hall's relational approach does not enquire into the 'class character' of Thatcherism or the way in which Thatcherism 'corresponds' to economic laws or logics, but examines how economic crises and political processes are discursively constructed and 'lived out' ideologically and discursively by people in society (Hall, 1983, pp. 21–22).

Working with, and sharpening, the tensions of social democracy, the Thatcherite project represents, for Hall, the articulation of two seemingly contradictory sets of ideas and theories. These are neo-liberal economics (the social market, self-interest, monetarism, competitive individualism) and the older philosophies of organic Conservatism (nation, family, duty, authority, standards, traditionalism). These themes – sometimes referred to as a combination of the 'free economy' and the 'strong state' – were fused together by the drawing of a political frontier excluding certain practices and elements associated with consensus politics (Gamble, 1988). Around the theme of 'anti-collectivism', for example, the Thatcherite project was able to construct a series of equivalences. Hence 'collectivism' came to represent 'consensus politics', 'socialism', 'statism', 'inefficient corporatism', 'over-powerful trade unions' and so on. These ideas and practices, and the institutions in which they were embodied, were made responsible for the crisis of social democracy and for the long-term decline of the British economy and nation state. On the other hand, 'Thatcherism', or the discourse of 'anti-collectivism', was presented as the only alternative to these discredited practices and ideas. Thus 'Thatcherism' was made equivalent to 'individual freedom and enterprise' (as against the sterile power of state managers or the trade unions), the 'moral and political rejuvenation of the British people and state' (rather than its terminal decline), the 'restoration of law and order', 'decisive leadership' and the 'strong state' (as opposed to the breakdown of authority in society, the muddle of consensus politics, and an overburdened and weak welfare state).

Hall focuses on three important hegemonic processes involved in the Conservative Party victory of 1979. The first centres on the way that Margaret Thatcher was able to translate and disseminate the abstract themes of neo-liberal economics into a new political 'philosophy' ripe for popular consumption. This involved the disarticulation of the Keynesian orthodoxy, which had dominated the major policy institutes, state apparatuses and universities in the post-war period, and its replacement with a different orthodoxy. It also required the dissemination of these ideas into the popular arena. This was greatly aided, argues Hall, by the tabloid and 'serious' press. As Hall puts it:

Neither Keynesianism nor monetarism . . . win votes as such in the electoral marketplace. But, in the discourse of 'social market values', Thatcherism discovered a powerful means of translating economic doctrine into the language of experience, moral imperative and common sense, thus providing a philosophy in the broader sense – an alternative *ethic* to that of the 'caring society'. This translation of a theoretical *ideology* into a populist *idiom* was a major political achievement (Hall, 1983, p. 28).

The second process which Hall concentrates on is Margaret Thatcher's hegemonisation of the Conservative Party after winning its leadership contest in 1975. This involved a careful process of compromise and negotiation, enabling important Thatcherite figures such as Keith Joseph, Geoffrey Howe, David Howell and Norman Tebbit gradually to replace the 'wets' on the consensus side of the Conservative Party hierarchy.

The third important hegemonic practice was the articulation of Thatcherism's 'authoritarian populist' discourse in the country at large. Here, Hall examines the way in which the Thatcherite project was able to construct and mobilise populist discourse – the language of the people and the nation – in a distinctively authoritarian fashion. In other words, Thatcherism was able to present itself as restoring strong leadership and decisive government, while still addressing the genuine concerns of the people as a whole. This created what Hall calls a 'populist unity':

> The language of 'the people', unified behind a reforming drive to turn the tide of 'creeping collectivism', banish Keynesian illusions from the state apparatus and renovate the power bloc is a powerful one. Its radicalism connects with radical-popular sentiments; but it effectively turns them round, absorbs and neutralises their popular thrust, and creates, in the place of popular rupture, a *populist unity* (Hall, 1983, pp. 30–1).

How and why did this work? According to Hall, Thatcherism was effective because of its ability to 'explain' the crisis of social democracy while also providing an alternative model with which to replace it. As Hall puts it, this endeavour to 'construct the people into a populist political subject', was effective because it dealt with the issues and problems that people faced during the crisis years of social democracy. When the Labour Party's task of controlling and reforming capitalism via the state and 'corporatist bargaining' failed – and the 'winter of discontent' of 1978–9 was symptomatic of this failure – the Thatcher project was able to harness resentment against the old system and offer a radical alternative. In the division between the state and the people, Labour was thus presented, in Hall's words, 'as undividedly part of the power bloc, enmeshed in the state apparatus, riddled with bureaucracy . . . as "with" the state', whereas Mrs Thatcher, 'grasping the torch of freedom with one hand, as someone who is undividedly out there, "with the people"' (Hall, 1983, p. 34).

My brief presentation of Hall's explanation of Thatcherism has endeavoured to highlight the main concepts of discourse theory as I have outlined them. Although a good part of his account is based on an analysis of the speeches, statements, manifestos and writings of Thatcherism, Hall's concept of discourse includes economic and political logics, as well as the effects of key social institutions, so long as they are 'lived out' and experienced by different groups of people in British society. More concretely, Hall shows how the hegemonic project of Thatcherism successfully instituted a new political frontier in British society – thereby interrupting the already existing, albeit crisis-ridden, social democratic order – by constructing antagonistic relationships between those who were interpellated by her discourse, and those who were excluded. In doing so, Thatcherism was able to hegemonise those important signifiers such as 'the people', 'the nation', 'freedom', 'individualism' and so on, which began to float during the crisis of social democracy in the 1970s, while successfully negating and marginalising signifiers such as 'socialism', 'collectivism', 'the state' and so on, which had been central for the old social formation.

# ■ Criticisms of discourse theory

Despite the recent emergence of discourse theory, it has attracted some criticisms. These can be grouped into those critical of the *philosophical* assumptions underlying the category of discourse, and those opposed to the *substantive* concepts and arguments that have been developed for the analysis of social and political processes. Let us begin with the former.

## □ *Philosophical*

There are two main allegations which have been made about the philosophical assumptions of discourse theory. First, it is alleged that that the approach is *idealist* and, second, it is claimed that the approach is a variant of *relativism*. Beginning with the former, it is claimed by certain 'realist' critics that the category of discourse reduces everything to thought or language. Before assessing this claim, it is worth defining these key philosophical terms. '*Idealism*', in its broadest sense, refers to the reduction of reality to our concepts and ideas of it. '*Realism*', by contrast, refers to the fact that there is a reality independent of our ideas or conceptions. When defined in these terms, discourse theory rejects idealism and affirms realism. In other words, the discourse approach does not deny the existence of a reality outside our heads and external to our thoughts.

Where discourse theory parts company with some versions of realism is, first, in its claim that there is no 'extra-discursive' realm of *meaningful* objects and, second, in its rejection of the view that this independent realm of objects *determines* the meaning of those objects. From a discourse theory perspective, for objects to be meaningful they must be part of a wider discursive framework. Thus, meanings cannot be reduced either to the world of (extra-discursive) objects, or to a realm of ideas or concepts. Therefore, the meaning of our objects of investigation – and these include all practices, institutions, speeches, texts and so on – are dependent on the relational configurations (or discourses) that confer identity to them. (Earlier we noted the example of voting in an election). Moreover, as we have seen from the post-modernist themes which discourse theory draws upon, no discourses are completely closed or fixed. They are thus always vulnerable to change.

Let us turn to the question of relativism. It will be recalled that discourse theory accepts the 'anti-foundationalist' claim that there is no underlying and unchanging 'Truth' that can guarantee the objectivity of our knowledge or beliefs. Does this mean that discourse theory accepts the relativist viewpoint that every belief on a certain topic is as good as every other? (On this point, see Rorty, 1982, p. 166.) The answer is 'no'. The argument that the identity of objects is dependent on specific discourses does not mean that there can be no judgements about the truth or falsity of propositions asserted *within* certain discourses. Discourse theory asserts that in order for judgements to be made about empirical and moral claims there has to be a shared discourse – a common set of meanings and assumptions – within which these decisions can be made. Without this minimal condition, we would not be sure about the kinds of thing we were making judgements about. Given this, the truth or falsity of propositions depends on the consistency and persuasiveness of the claims that are asserted within a particular community of practitioners who share a common discourse.

Does discourse theory claim that all discourses are of equal validity and moral worth? This would be to remain within the paradigm of 'Truth' and the belief that we could adopt a trans-historical stance toward *all* available conceptual frameworks. The assumptions of discourse theory suggest that we are always part of a particular discourse and tradition. The question, then, is not about providing a grand philosophical justification for specific configurations – almost any opinion can be justified by some philosophical position – but of the particular state of our discourses themselves. In other words, can they be defended? How are they defended? Are they open to change and revision? Are they responsive to other traditions and discourses? This does not mean, however, that discourses which may be offensive (to the values of liberal democratic societies, for example) are to be welcomed and tolerated. Efforts can, and should, be made to criticise and change other discourses, as well as elements of the discourses we inhabit, as long as these modifications are not presented as universal truths that are not vulnerable to criticism and revision.

Finally, does this mean that there are no rational grounds to choose *between* discourses? Such a question is misleading. We are generally not in the position of choosing which discursive frameworks we want to inhabit. Moments of choice between discourses occur when our conceptual frameworks are no longer able to provide reasonable answers to questions that are posed when they are challenged by other perspectives. Hence, it is the *failure* of a particular form of rationality which requires us to reconstitute our discourses along different lines. While the choice between the different alternatives available may be deemed to be 'rational' (after the fact), unless we assume that there is only one possible candidate (an assumption which would push us close to a new form of universalism that would eradicate the notion of choice altogether), this new rationality will always involve force or an element of irrationality in its constitution (see Laclau, 1991, pp. 89–91). Thus, in keeping with the assumptions of discourse theory, every discourse is constituted through the exclusion of certain possibilities, a fact which prevents their ultimate closure.

# ☐ *Substantive*

Let us turn to the substantive criticisms of discourse theory as they have been presented. There are three important problems which need to be considered. It has been suggested that discourse theory results in: (i) the complete fragmentation and unfixity of social structures and relations; (ii) the abandonment of the concept of ideology and the undermining of its critical purchase; and (iii) the inability (or unwillingness) to analyse social and political institutions. Let us consider each of these criticisms in turn.

# ☐ The fragmentation of social structures

The first objection touches on two issues: the question of *limits* and the problem of *closure*. For some critics, discourse theory is *voluntaristic* because it does not acknowledge the *material constraints* (usually conceived of in economic terms) on political actions and practices. In other words, there is too much indeterminacy and too great a stress placed on the possibilities for action and change within the approach, with not enough attention on the limiting conditions of discourses (see Dallmayr, 1988; Hall, 1988; Woodiwiss, 1990). More concretely, these criticisms have focused attention on the role of the economy in the explanation of political processes (Geras, 1987; Jessop, 1990). Let us consider these points in more depth.

The discourse perspective does not deny that there are limits on the possible. In fact, every discourse constitutes a set of limits on the range of possible practices. In other words, a discourse always rules out certain options as false, meaningless or inappropriate for that given discourse.

Within a discourse such as Thatcherism, the ideas, practices and institutions of socialism or corporatism (and other forms of organising society) were explicitly ruled out. Hence a policy of nationalisation, for example, would not have been deemed appropriate for this discourse, unless the discourse itself was transformed in a certain way. Or, let us take the case of 'environmental limits', for example: do they not constitute a material constraint on discursive possibilities? The answer is 'yes', but only if they have been registered as an object of discourse. In other words, when scientists and ecologists discover the effects of our practices on the environment, these environmental limits become part of our discursive formations, thereby opening the way for a change in our attitudes and practices towards the environment.

What about the constraining role of the economy in discourse theory? According to the discursive perspective, the economy is not a foundation which determines other practices, or which secures the identities of political agents such as social classes. Instead of this view of the economy as a kind of natural substratum of society with its own autonomous laws and logics, it is treated as a discursive formation – concerned with processes such as production, reproduction and exchange – just like any other system of practices. Moreover, from a discourse theory perspective, economic practices are internally related to other practices. Rather than regarding the economy as a separate domain of social relations (alongside the ideological for example), economic practices are intimately connected to legal, political, cultural, sexual, psychological and ideological practices and processes. For example, there has been much recent discussion about the economic decline of Britain. But even a cursory glance at these debates will show that economic decline cannot be reduced to narrowly-defined economic variables. A combination of cultural, political, military, geo-political and legal factors have contributed to a highly complex historical process (see Gamble, 1988). Instead of talking, therefore, about the economy as being separable from the state and ideological realms, discourse theorists think about the articulation of these different practices in formations which Gramsci has called 'historical blocs' (see Gramsci, 1971). In this sense, for example, Thatcherism was an attempt to disarticulate the practices and institutions of the post-war consensus, and replace it with a new 'historical bloc' structured according to different principles and logics.

Finally, whereas some approaches to political analysis treat economic structures and processes as primary (if not determining), discourse theorists speak of the 'primacy of politics'. This is not to deny the centrality of economic processes and questions in political life, but to suggest that all discursive practices have a political origin. In other words, even 'economic systems' such as capitalism, are ultimately a product of political conflicts between different forces trying to impose their sets of ideas, practices and institutions on one another.

The second issue – the problem of closure – is neatly captured by Slavoj Zizek's claim that post-modernism privileges the fluidity and dissemination of meaning over its fixity (Zizek, 1989, p. 154). This critique is, however, somewhat misplaced in the case of Laclau and Mouffe's approach. They are insistent that every social formation *depends* on the drawing of political frontiers to attain its identity. Hence their approach always emphasises the '*partial* closure' and '*partial* fixity' of social relations. This is in keeping with the post-*structuralist* approach which they adopt where the emphasis is on the *weakening* of structures, rather than their complete dissolution.

## □ The abandonment of the concept of ideology

Is the critical edge of the discourse perspective blunted by its rejection of ideology as a form of 'false consciousness'? In other words, does its opposition to the category of ideology as a set of representations which mystify the true nature of things mean that there is no possibility for criticising existing discourses? (See Eagleton, 1991, p. 219.) In this regard, it is important to note that the concept of ideology does *not* disappear from the discourse approach, though it is not predicated on the science/ideology or the truth/falsity distinctions. The category of ideology is used to describe the drive toward the *total* closure of discourses. In other words, an 'ideological' discourse would be one in which there was no recognition of an outside or 'an other' which constitutes that discourse. In this sense, totalitarian and Fascist discourses – attempts to ground or close societies around a single principle – would be clear examples of ideological constructions.

Another dimension of the second criticism concerns the critical role of the discourse analyst. In the first place, practitioners of discourse theory do not claim to be conducting 'value free' or 'objective' investigations. It is a basic assumption of the perspective that the discourse theorist is always situated in a particular discursive formation. In other words, s/he has been constituted as a subject just like any other subject. What is challenged by the discourse theorist is the claim that values can be *derived* or *deduced* from the philosophical and theoretical assumptions of discourse theory. In this sense, anti-foundationalism does not give rise to a certain set of substantive political and ethical positions. It does, however, rule out positions based on foundational presuppositions. Shunning epistemological criteria for legitimating values means that discourse theorists justify their political and ethical positions in terms of their practical effects and the particular historical traditions from which they are derived (see Mouffe, 1993, pp. 13–18).

## ☐ The inability to analyse social and political institutions

Some commentators have emphasised the difficulties which the discourse paradigm has with regard to the analysis of political institutions and organisations (see, for example, Bertramsen *et al.*, 1990; Jessop, 1982). Though these writers have pinpointed the dearth of discursive analyses of institutions and organisations correctly, this critique needs to be tempered by the following observations. The discourse perspective strongly rejects those approaches that account for institutions such as the state by making reference to trans-historical and objective laws of historical development, or those which treat institutions as unified subjects or agents endowed with intrinsic interests and capacities. More positively, the perspective does, as we have seen, put forward alternative conceptual resources to make institutions and organisations intelligible. Institutions are con-ceptualised as *sedimented* discourses. In other words, they are discourses which, as a result of political and social practices, have become relatively permanent and durable. In this sense, there are no *qualitative* distinctions between discourses, only differences in their degree of stability. This means that relatively fixed discursive formations such as bureaucracies, states and political parties are legitimate objects of discourse analysis.

## ■ Concluding note

Discourse theory constitutes a relatively new approach to political analysis, although it has strong roots in past theoretical traditions and perspectives. Drawing on, and extending, the approaches of Marxist writers such as Antonio Gramsci and Louis Althusser, while taking on board ideas and assumptions put forward by post-modernist theorists such as Michel Foucault and Jacques Derrida, discourse theory examines the logics and structures of discursive articulations, and the ways in which they make possible the formation of identities in society. In doing so, it concedes political processes – understood as conflicts and struggles between antagonistic forces over the structuring of social meaning – a pivotal place in the understanding of social relations and how they are transformed.

While most attention in discourse theory has so far been directed at a clarification and development of its philosophical assumptions and theoretical concepts, empirical studies which have drawn on its theoretical framework are beginning to emerge. Jacob Torfing, in his co-authored book *State, Economy and Society*, has applied discourse theory to an understanding of economic regulation in advanced capitalist societies, thus laying the foundation for a reassessment of the modern welfare state (Torfing, 1991, 1994). In her recent book *New Right Discourse on Race and Sexuality*, Anna Marie Smith has examined the changing logics of racism and homophobia in British society in the post-war period (Smith, 1994). Aletta Norval has described and analysed the logic of apartheid discourse in a series of articles and a forthcoming book entitled *Accounting for Apartheid* (Norval, 1994, 1995). Finally, a recently published collection of essays entitled *The Making of Political Identities* (edited by Ernesto Laclau) has endeavoured to expand and apply the categories of discourse theory to contemporary political and historical situations ranging from the role of Rastafarian culture in Britain to an analysis of the former Yugoslavia, the struggles for Palestinian self-determination, and contemporary ecological and environmental discourses (see Laclau, 1994). These different interventions represent an attempt by discourse analysts to contribute a body of empirical knowledge to the discipline of political science, while at the same time challenging, and attempting to extend, its rather narrow positivistic bias.

# ■ Further reading

For those not acquainted with the traditions of thought – ranging from Marxism to post-structuralism, and linguistics to psychoanalysis – which Laclau and Mouffe draw upon, the reading of Laclau and Mouffe can be quite daunting. Perhaps the best place to begin is with the journal articles and interviews that they have published. Here are some further readings, which are presented in a suggested order of reading:

Dallmayr (1988), a very readable introduction to the main themes of Laclau and Mouffe's theoretical approach.

Laclau, E. (1988), also published in Laclau (1990), an accessible set of remarks about the emergence and development of discourse theory.

Laclau and Mouffe (1987), a response to a critical article by Norman Geras entitled 'Post-Marxism?' in *New Left Review*, which summarises the main theoretical categories and concepts that are developed in Laclau and Mouffe (1985), a complex and dense theoretical exposition of the discourse approach. It comprises a detailed 'deconstructive' reading of the Marxist tradition, and then puts forward an alternative framework of analysis; Norval (1994), an analysis of the logic and crisis of apartheid discourse in South Africa during the 1980s.

Smith (1994), a study of racism and homophobia in British society, demonstrating the demonisation of blacks, lesbians and gays by drawing on the writings of Nietzsche, Foucault, Derrida, Hall and Gilroy; Salecl (1994), a deployment of the categories of discourse theory, in conjunction with Lacanian psychoanalysis, to explain the disintegration of the former Yugoslavia and the rise of Serbian nationalism; and Torfing (1991), an account of capitalist regulation in advanced industrial societies from a discourse theory perspective, and an attempt to explain the character, dynamics and limits of the modern welfare state.

# PART 2

# METHODOLOGICAL QUESTIONS

# ■ *Chapter 7* ■

# Qualitative Methods
## Fiona Devine

Qualitative methods is a generic term that refers to a range of techniques including participant observation (overt and covert observation and involvement) and intensive interviewing (in-depth individual and group interviews). This chapter looks at the role of qualitative methods in eliciting people's views inside and outside the political system, and the ontological and epistemological positions of its practitioners. It evaluates the criticisms levelled against qualitative methods by comparing and contrasting the advantages and disadvantages of qualitative and quantitative methods. Two illustrations of qualitative methods are considered in detail: H. Heclo and A. Wildavsky's (1981) study of the Treasury and Devine's (1992) study of voters. It will be argued that qualitative methods have contributed to the study of mass political behaviour by seeking to understand political actors as conscious social beings who shape the world of politics as well as being shaped by it.

# ■ The role of qualitative methods in political science

Qualitative methods have played a major, albeit understated, role in political science: from the study of individuals and groups inside the formal political arena, to the political attitudes and behaviour of people (be they voters or members of elites) outside it. The origins of the different techniques lie in anthropology and sociology. Participant observation was first used in anthropology to study other cultures (Powdermaker, 1966; Spradley, 1980; Wax, 1971). It involves the researcher immersing her/himself in the social setting in which s/he is interested, observing people in their usual milieux and participating in their activities. On this basis, the researcher writes extensive field notes. The participant observer depends upon relatively long-term relationships with informants, whose conversations are an integral part of field notes (Lofland and Lofland, 1984, p. 12). They are the 'raw data' that are analysed, and the interpretation of the material forms the basis of a research report. The difficulties of gaining access to a particular setting has meant that the technique is associated increasingly with extensive observation and in-depth interviews.

Intensive interviewing techniques have been used widely in sociology. In-depth interviewing is based on an interview guide, open-ended questions and informal probing to facilitate a discussion of issues in a semi-structured or unstructured manner. In contrast to a predefined questionnaire, the interview guide is used as a checklist of topics to be covered, although the order in which they are discussed is not pre-ordained (Bryman, 1988, p. 66). Open-ended questions are used to allow the interviewee to talk at length on a topic. Finally, various forms of probing are used to ask the interviewee to elaborate on what s/he has said (Fielding, 1993, pp. 140–1). Intensive interviews are, then, 'guided conversations' (Lofland and Lofland, 1984, p. 59). Such lengthy interviews are usually conducted with only a small sample of informants. The transcriptions constitute the data that are analysed and interpreted. Interviewers also engage in observing the interviewee and the setting in which they are found, and these observations facilitate the interpretation of the material. In contrast to the highly-structured interview used in survey research, based on a tightly-defined questionnaire and closed questions, intensive interviews are open and flexible, allowing the informants to elaborate on their values and attitudes and account for their behaviour (Mann, 1985; Brenner, Brown and Canter, 1985).

From this brief description of qualitative methods, it should be clear that they are most appropriately employed where the aim of research is to explore people's subjective experiences and the meanings they attach to those experiences. Intensive interviewing, for example, allows people to talk freely and to offer their interpretation of events. It is *their* perspective that is paramount (Harvey, 1990). Qualitative methods are also appropriate in the study of processes. In-depth interviews allow people to tell their own story in language with which they are familiar. Where the discussion of issues flows naturally, it is possible to understand the logic of an interviewee's argument and the associative thinking that led them to particular conclusions. Finally, qualitative methods draw particular attention to contextual issues, placing an interviewee's attitudes and behaviour in the context of his/her individual biography and wider social setting. Qualitative methods therefore capture meaning, process and context (Bryman, 1988, p. 62; Rose, 1982).

Qualitative methods have long been used across a number of sub-fields of political science since participants in the world of politics have been willing to talk about their involvement in groups, their role in formal positions of power, their views about the political system and so on. Pressure group activists, for example, have been interviewed widely by political scientists studying policy communities (Grant and Marsh, 1977; Mills, 1993; Smith, 1990). Party officials and Members of Parliament have been interviewed for their views on the internal politics of political parties (Seyd, 1987; Whiteley, 1983) and, more recently, candidates have been interviewed to elicit their views on selection procedures (Norris and Lovenduski, 1993). Qualitative methods have been used extensively in the study of local politics in Britain (Dearlove, 1973; Gyford *et al.*, 1989; Lowndes and Stoker, 1992) and in urban politics in the USA (Jones and Batchelor, 1986; Stone, 1989). Qualitative methods have been used to a lesser extent in research on central government. The major impediment has been limited access (both real and perceived) into the seemingly secretive world of high politics. The exception is Heclo and Wildavsky's (1981) qualitative research (to be discussed below), which involved in-depth interviews with Treasury and other departmental ministers and officials.

The area in which qualitative research is almost absent is the field of election studies. The main method of enquiry has been a nationally representative cross-sectional survey, more recently supplemented with a panel survey, conducted after the election (Sarlvik and Crewe, 1983; Heath, Jowell and Curtice, 1985, 1993). The exclusive reliance on quantitative methods by political scientists has been the subject of criticism by Dunleavy (1990), who has argued that electoral studies have not contributed to an understanding of 'mass political behaviour'. Against this background, calls have been made for the greater use of qualitative methods in the study of voting (Devine, 1995). A qualitative study of working class socio-political attitudes and behaviour will be discussed below (Devine, 1992).

The use of qualitative methods is tied to a specific epistemological position. Issues of method therefore raise the long-standing debate between positivists and relativists about the similarities and differences of methodology between the natural and social sciences (Keat and Urry, 1975, p. 1). Quantitative methods, for example, are closely associated with a positivist epistemological position. As Sanders and Miller note in their chapters, early twentieth-century positivists and behaviouralists believed that the study of politics should be based on empirical observations and testable theories. Consequently, positivists have been concerned with the precise operationalisation and measurement of theoretical concepts (Henwood and Pidgeon, 1993, p. 15). There is a strong emphasis on behaviourial analysis, since behaviour can easily be translated into concepts, operationalised and observed (Lee, 1993, p. 13). The preference is for survey research with a standardised approach to interviewing based on a predetermined questionnaire and closed questions. Each respondent is asked the same questions in the same order. There is limited interaction between the interviewer and respondent, to avoid the respondent reacting to anything the interviewer might say over and above the interview schedule which might introduce bias. It is only by asking unbiased questions that objective truth can be obtained. The highly-structured interview is a form of communication under controlled conditions, as in an experimental situation (Fielding, 1993, p. 144). The interviews can be replicated easily and are reliable in reproducing the similar facts. The statistical analysis of the coded replies produce observed regularities which form the basis of explanation, generalisation and prediction. The major concern of survey researchers is with the predictive ability of their statistical findings (Bryman, 1988, p. 34).

Critics of positivism have argued that there is no external reality and only a socially constructed reality in which conscious people attach subjective meaning to their actions and interpret their own situation and the situation of others. People are not passive agents but are actively engaged in evaluating their own and others' actions. They shape the world as well as being shaped by it. The socially constructed world of meaning is fragile and ever-changing (Keat and Urry, 1975, p. 205). This ontological position implies that there is no rational objective science that can establish universal truths. No science can exist independently of beliefs and values and the concepts we create to understand the world. Theories cannot be tested by means of observation and experimentation. Nor is there any objective reality or truth against which to judge different theoretical positions, since beliefs and values influence such choices. With no criteria of external validity with which to judge competing theories, all theories are equally valid interpretations of the world (Benton, 1977, p. 76).

The problem with this relativist position is that it leads to a self-refuting paradox; namely, if relativism is true, then its truth is only relative. Relativism cannot be true if there are no universal standards of truth (Keat and Urry, 1975, p. 212). In seeking to avoid this relativist trap, few social scientists have argued there is no objective reality and no criteria on which to evaluating competing theories (Benton, 1977, p. 39). The social world is not constituted exhaustively by common meanings or a never-ending circle of negotiation and interpretation. Realists, for example, have argued that there is an objective reality independent of beliefs and values. It is possible to evaluate competing theories and establish truth, although proof cannot be established conclusively because there are only different degrees of positive confirmation (Keat and Urry, 1975, p. 217). The role of a rational objective science, however, is not to make predictions but to devise causal explanations about the world which involve describing both the observable and unobservable processes that link phenomena together. Explanation also involves describing and understanding people as conscious and social human beings, and their motives, experiences and subjective interpretations are an important component of causal processes (Bulmer, 1984, p. 211; Marsh, 1984, p. 88).

This epistemological position is associated with qualitative research methods. Intensive interviews are appropriate in seeking to understand people's motives and interpretations. It is by listening to interviewees talking that it is possible to gain some insight into their world views and see things as they do (Fielding, 1993, p. 157). There is a strong emphasis on describing the context in which people live their lives, form opinions, act (or fail to act) and so on. Rather than observe people in a controlled experimental situation, for example, participant observers go to great lengths to watch people in their natural settings, especially since subjective meanings vary according to the context in which they are found. Consequently, the emphasis is not on making predictions about behaviour but rather on seeking to capture the uniqueness of human experiences (Henwood and Pidgeon, 1993, p. 16). Explanation involves understanding and interpreting actions rather than devising general laws about behaviour (Keat and Urry, 1975, pp. 142–3). Explanatory understanding is unique to the social sciences and accounts for the use of different methods in the natural and social sciences (Keat and Urry, 1975, p. 175).

While the choice of methods is associated with an epistemological position, the distinction between quantitative and qualitative research should not be drawn too rigidly. To do so would be to argue that the different methods involved are mutually exclusive and cannot be employed in conjunction with each other. The choice of method should be made on whether it is suitable for addressing a particular research question (Bryman, 1988, pp. 108–9). Quantitative and qualitative methods involve collecting data in different ways, and the crucial question is whether the choice of method is appropriate for the theoretical and empirical questions that the researcher seeks to address. This lead us to confront criticisms of qualitative methods and tackle the issues of reliability, validity and objectivity.

# ■ Criticisms of qualitative methods

A number of criticisms have been levelled against qualitative methods and they need to be considered in the context of the debate regarding quantitative versus qualitative research. Quantitative research is portrayed as being representative and reliable. Systematic statistical analysis ensures that research findings and interpretations are robust. Overall, quantitative research is replicable and comparable, and generalisations can be made with a high degree of certainty. Social surveys produce 'hard' scientific evidence (Hellevik, 1984; de Vaus, 1990). In contrast, qualitative research is portrayed as being unrepresentative and atypical. Its findings are impressionistic, piecemeal and even idiosyncratic. Finally, qualitative research is neither replicable nor comparable and therefore not a basis on which generalisations can be made. Qualitative research produces 'soft', unscientific results. The major criticisms levelled against qualitative data, therefore, are that it is unreliable; that the interpretation of interpretations of the findings are difficult to evaluate; and that it is not easily generalisable (Bryman, 1988, pp. 84–5).

The issue of reliability revolves around the question of designing and generating a sample of respondents. As Miller outlines in Chapter 8, in quantitative research, a sample is usually designed to study a representative section of the population and close attention is given to the way in which that sample is selected. The characteristics of the respondents are closely defined according to the issue being studied, and the respondents' names are obtained from a sampling frame and chosen at random. The Electoral Register, for example, is the most widely used sampling frame of the adult population in Britain. The representativeness of samples is checked carefully to make sure that the final sample is not biased by non-response and, where there is significant under-representation, the sample is weighted to make up for missing sample members. There is also a variety of more complex sample designs such as clustering, multi-stage sampling and stratification to enhance precision (Arber, 1993, p. 86). Given that the aim of qualitative research is to focus on people's subjective accounts, intensive interviews are lengthy and time consuming. It is neither desirable nor feasible to interview a large number of respondents in a representative sample. This is not to suggest that qualitative researchers do not concern themselves with issues of sampling, possible sources of bias, and the implications of sample design on the interpretation of the findings. The way in which a group of interviewees is selected is as important to the qualitative researcher as it is the quantitative researcher. Qualitative researchers usually identify a group of potential interviewees according to social characteristics, patterns of behaviour, association with a particular locale and so on. Rather than generate a tightly defined sample according to a range of criteria, qualitative samples are more loosely defined to include a wide range of informants with different subjective interpretations of their lives. A small sample of approximately 30–40 interviewees is the norm. Although qualitative researchers rely on a small number of informants, they try to embrace a heterogeneity of experiences and accounts within the constraints of money and time. While qualitative methods cannot be representative, therefore, it is possible to seek diversity.

There is often no sampling frame from which to draw a random list of names to approach for interview, and 'snowball sampling' is the usual way of generating a sample. Interviewees are asked to nominate potential informants and the request is made at each subsequent interview until the required number is reached. 'Snowballing' a sample continues throughout the period in the field. The researcher effectively taps into a network of people, which can be of interest in itself. However, there are problems involved in generating a sample from one network of people with particular characteristics. In my own research on Luton car workers, for example, interviewees frequently nominated other family members as potential interviewees, and to have interviewed the nominees would have restricted the sample to a series of interconnected family networks. Only potential interviewees at the workplace were contacted for interview to extend the sample to a range of individuals and families (Devine, 1992). It is not surprising that most qualitative research reports devote a considerable amount of time to issues of how a sample was generated and the characteristics of the informants included in the final sample. A chapter devoted to these issues of method is often central to the research report rather than being relegated to the appendixes (as is often the case with the technical details of survey research). The design of the sample is, therefore, very important to the qualitative researcher.

The second criticism levelled against qualitative interviewing deals with the collection of data. Quantitative surveys, as Miller shows in Chapter 8, proceed on the basis of highly-structured interviews using a predetermined questionnaire and closed questions. Considerable effort is devoted to the formulation of unbiased questions that do not lead the interviewee to react in a particular way. It is especially important to avoid leading, double-barrelled or hypothetical questions (Lee, 1993, pp. 155–6; Newel, 1993, pp. 105–6). Response error is therefore reduced, as ambiguities are ironed out and the intention and meaning of the question is clear. In proceeding through the questionnaire, the interaction between the interviewer and respondent is minimal, to prevent the interviewer from influencing the respondent's answers. The interviewer is objective and interviewer variance is avoided. In a highly-controlled situation, the aim of survey research is to obtain consistent answers, further ensuring reliability as a way of getting at objective truth (Marsh, 1984; Newell, 1993, p. 114).

Qualitative interviewers use an interview guide with open-ended questions and probing – asking the informant to elaborate on specific points of interest – to discuss topics with the informant (Newell, 1993, p. 97). The relationship between the interviewer and interviewee is not aloof or unproblematical, since the interviewer participates in the conversation (Bulmer, 1984, p. 209). The relationship between the researcher and the researched cannot be so distant, especially if confidential personal information is to be revealed, and not least since sensitive topics are full of ambiguities that need probing (Lee, 1993, p. 111). A greater level of involvement is required so that the researcher inspires trust (Bulmer, 1984, p. 111). The relationship can also be problematical if the researcher becomes over-familiar. Partisanship calls into question the objectivity of the interviewer and the validity of the interpretation of the findings (Hammersley and Atkinson, 1983).

Playing an active role in facilitating conversations is not easy. Informants are often anxious to please and offer responses that they perceive to be desirable. They rationalise their behaviour, which may have been motivated by an outburst of anger or other feelings. They may seek to impress with shows of bravado and create the impression that they know more than they do. They may be keen to hide inconsistencies in their attitudes and behaviour (Benney and Hughes, 1956). Where the interviewee's responses are less than frank, the interviewer has to probe their initial responses and get them to elaborate on their accounts of a situation. Unlike the pre-specified prompting that is part of standardised interviews, probing occurs more spontaneously and may indeed involve the interviewer offering his/her own views, the views of others, or being asked by the interviewee to offer an opinion (Finch, 1984). The interviewer has to be careful not to direct the interviewees' responses in a certain direction. It is important not to be too directive and to question informants in as neutral a way as possible. The role of the interviewer is crucial in generating an open conversation and is valued by qualitative researchers for this reason. The nature of interaction between the interviewer and interviewee does have some impact on what is said or not said, and on how it is said. While it is difficult to judge the influence of the interviewer on the course of a conversation, qualitative researchers do not deny reactivity, and discuss its impact on the findings explicitly. Rather than control the effects of the interviewer, qualitative researchers prefer to acknowledge his/her role instead (Lee, 1993).

A third criticism concerns the analysis and interpretation of interview data. Is the interpretation placed on the material valid and how do we judge its validity? Surveys produce simple responses which are coded. Variables are subject to various forms of statistical analysis (see Chapter 8 for a description of the data analysis process). The interpretation of statistical data is not without its shortcomings (Abel, 1971, p. 68). There is a tendency to atomise people by taking them out of context, aggregating individual opinions and assuming the meaning of aggregation, or alternatively interpreting aggregate findings as individual properties (Marsh, 1984, p. 92). The validity of the data – whether the data represent what it is supposed to represent – is often questionable (Smith, 1987; 1988). It is also assumed that attitudes are a good indicator of behaviour while it is widely known that behaviour cannot be read off from attitudes. There is also the tendency to draw causal inferences from correlations in cross-sectional data without explaining the mechanisms involved in such relationships (Marsh, 1984). Nevertheless, it is possible to conduct a secondary analysis on a data set and re-analyze and reinterpret the main findings of the survey.

The analysis and interpretation of intensive interviews proceeds in a different manner. Transcripts are subjected to numerous readings until themes emerge. This process continues until an overall argument is established. The interpretation of the material is usually presented by means of an interplay of quotes from the interviews and commentary on the selected transcript. The researcher selects extracts from the transcripts which support points in an argument. The presentation of the material in this format makes it difficult to place such fragments and see how representative they are with regard to other material collected. Since transcripts are rarely reproduced in full, it is difficult to decipher how the researcher arrived at the interpretation of the interview material and thereby extremely difficult to formulate other interpretations (Rose, 1982, p. 139). These processes are often hidden from view so that it is not easy to assess whether an interpretation is convincing or not. There is a genuine problem of having no direct way of establishing the validity of an ethnography (Fielding, 1993, p. 166).

All data are subject to different interpretations and there is no definitive interpretation that tells the 'truth'. Nevertheless, the qualitative researcher needs to establish the validity of the interpretation and to demonstrate the plausibility of his/her interpretation. Various ways of enhancing the validity of interpretations exist. The interpretation of interview material can be discussed with a group of researchers to obtain a consensus on the interpretation. It is possible to ask the informant for his/her reactions to the interpretation of the interview data which may lead to a reinterpretation. The interpretation of the data should be made as explicit as possible by identifying majority and minority views on a topic of interest, for example. The plausibility of an ethnography can be enhanced by doing full justice to the context of the participant observation or intensive interviewing (Atkinson, 1990, p. 129). Finally, the internal consistency of an account can be assessed to establish whether an analysis is coherent with the themes that have been identified. External validity can be established by checking the findings with other studies (Fielding, 1993, p. 166). As Fielding (1993, pp. 169–70) suggests, 'Good qualitative analysis is able to document its claim to reflect some of the truth of the phenomena by reference to systematically gathered data. Poor qualitative data is anecdotal, unreflective, descriptive without being focused in a coherent line of enquiry.'

Finally, qualitative research is confronted with the problem of generalisability (see also Chapter 1). Unlike quantitative results, it is impossible to make generalisations about attitudes and behaviour from in-depth interviews. The qualitative researcher has to be tentative about making inferences from a small number of cases to the population at large (Rose, 1982, p. 38). Yet qualitative researchers can design research which facilitates an understanding of other situations. The findings of one in-depth study can be corroborated with other research to establish regularities and variations. Such a comparison would be a limited test of confirmation or non-confirmation of the findings (Marsh, 1984, p. 91). Research can be of phenomena which are predicted to become more typical in the future (Ward Schofield, 1993, p. 220). It is rarely the case that a sample of interviewees are so unrepresentative, or the interpretations so misleading, that any generalisations would be wholly specious. Finally, qualitative research findings are very often the basis on which subsequent quantitative research is conducted from which generalisations can be made. Qualitative findings, therefore, can have wider significance beyond the time and place in which they were conducted (Ward Schofield, 1993, p. 205).

Qualitative methods and techniques therefore have their limitations in a similar manner to quantitative research. As with all research methods, their disadvantages are invariably compensated by their advantages. While quantitative research is usually reliable, qualitative research tends to be valid. The crucial point is that the researcher should choose the most appropriate method of enquiry for the topic under investigation (Silverman, 1985, p. 20).

# ■ Illustrations of qualitative research

Qualitative methods have been used in research on a major problem of political science, namely, the issue of power. Heclo and Wildavsky's research on central government will be the first illustration of the use of qualitative methods in political science. It has been chosen for two reasons. First, the authors' approach to the study of power is interesting. Their starting point is that power is a complex phenomenon which entails the study of relationships. It is not a concept that is easily turned into indicators which can be measured (Bulmer, 1984, p. 44). Intensive research techniques are, therefore, the most feasible way of illuminating the intricate nature of power. Second, methodological issues are addressed explicitly in the monograph. Heclo and Wildavsky address the issues in their introduction, particularly the difficulties they encountered in studying central government relations.

Heclo and Wildavsky's research, documented in *The Private Governance of Public Money*, (originally published in 1974 and with a second edition in 1981), was conducted with two aims in mind. First, the authors sought to describe the expenditure process with specific reference to the nature of co-operation and conflict, and relationships between spending departments and the Treasury, and civil servants and politicians. Second, they sought to use the expenditure process to illuminate the 'characteristic practices' of British central government (Heclo and Wildavsky, 1981, pp. lxi–lxii). Their study is awash with anthropological language rather than with the usual concepts and terminology of political science. For example, they talk about 'penetrating' the political world, arguing that:

> The rules by which they live, the customs they observe, the incentives they perceive and act upon are important, not only to them but to the people they govern. To understand how political administrators behave, we must begin by seeing the world though their eyes. The world does look different depending on whether the participant is in Parliament or Government, spending Department or Treasury . . . We tell our tale largely from the viewpoint of participants, then, not to signify our agreement, but to explain their actions. The participant is the expect on what he does, the observer's task is to make himself expert on why he does it. (Heclo and Wildavsky, 1991, p. lxvii).

As such, the interviewee's views are seen as being of paramount importance in a study of power which involves a community of personal relationships 'operating within a shared framework' (1981, p. lxvii).

Heclo and Wildavsky's research involved interviewing approximately 200 Civil Service officials and ex-officials, ministers, former ministers and MPs in depth and making observations during the interviews. They address directly the problems of interviewing powerful people, who may be cautious about what they are prepared to reveal. In the process of negotiating access, for example, they had to demonstrate not only that they could be trusted but also that they were familiar with the subject so that respondents were 'reassured that they are talking to fellow insiders who will understand what is being said' (Heclo and Wildavsky, 1981, p. lxviii). The authors overcame this problem by talking initially to former ministers and civil servants who gave them details on how public expenditure was negotiated. In interviewing high-profile people about current government policies, there were limitations on what could be asked. Consequently, current cases and personalities were not discussed, and respondents were asked to describe negotiations over public expenditure in general rather than specific terms. In this way, Heclo and Wildavsky gained further access while still being able to identify the central features of the public expenditure negotiations.

For the most part, officials and politicians were willing participants in the research, although some doubted whether they could ever understand the process, while 'a few seemed to think that a little access, more sherry and much charm would yield a neat public relations return' (Heclo and Wildavsky, 1981, p. lxxii). The authors felt confident that they had 'captured' the community under investigation. They justified their particular interpretation with reference to the opportunity they had to observe people in their work and ask them to talk about their work. They listened to different viewpoints. In addition, they could write and think about the answers they were given while the participants themselves had neither the time, nor often the inclination, to undertake such reflection. Collecting the material furnished them with 'the larger picture' (Heclo and Wildavsky, 1981, p. lxxii).

Turning to substantive issues, Heclo and Wildavsky delved into the operation of the expenditure process by exploring relationships within the 'expenditure community', the norms and values which governed official behaviour, and the overall culture and climate in which the officials and ministers operated. They devoted considerable effort to describing the negotiations between officials, and the nature of the bargaining that went on between them. For example, describing some of the calculations, a Treasury official explained how he tried to 'create an atmosphere so they'll tell me things they shouldn't. And I do the same, sometimes sending [the department finance officer] a copy of the paper I have done for my masters. You can't expect to get something for nothing' (Heclo and

Wildavsky, 1981, p. 16). On this basis, they were able to identify the prevailing norms of the Treasury to restrain departments in their spending as part of the policy-making process. Heclo and Wildavsky concluded that the Treasury enjoys a subtle form of power which lies in shaping the 'assumptions and expectations' of spending Department officials. The dominant ethos is one in which 'expenditure is policy and policy is expenditure' (1981, p. 345). The Treasury view is ingrained in policy-making decisions so that 'policy is about making progress towards a certain goal at a certain rate of expenditure'. Social policies are designed with reference to issues of economic management rather than to redistributive questions (Heclo and Wildavsky, 1981, p. 356). Nevertheless, they argued that the Treasury is not all-powerful, since the expenditure process revolves around mutual dependence. Rather, 'Treasury influence rests not on a hard-nosed interpretation of formal powers but in personal networks, sensitive bargaining, and up-to-date information that operate to create habits of mind leading to anticipation of Treasury reaction' (1981, p. 380). The Treasury enjoys control because of the way in which departments anticipate its reaction to requests for more money and justify additional expenditure in a way that is most likely to fit in with the Treasury. The nature of power is extremely intricate within British central government.

Heclo and Wildavsky's monograph was well received as one of the few studies to offer insight into what they describe as the 'shadowy realm' of the 'political administrative culture of British central government'. More important, their use of qualitative methods – of extensive and intensive observations and interviews – allowed them to go beyond the formal organisational structure and to uncover the actual practices of the people involved in the expenditure process. It was only by talking to insiders that they were able to 'penetrate' central government successfully and proffer a highly sophisticated account of the power relationships between the Treasury and spending departments. It is extremely doubtful whether quantitative methods could have captured the intricate nature of power that Heclo and Wildavsky uncovered. The study is not without criticism. The emphasis on shared norms and values produces a picture of continual co-operation, and the absence of conflict is surprising. However, this picture may arise as a result of their concern with the internal workings of central government rather than, for example, external pressures on policy and expenditure. The study nevertheless illustrates the application of qualitative methods in the study of power.

The second illustration of the use of qualitative methods derives from the sub-field of voting behaviour (Devine, 1992). The study – *Affluent Workers Revisited* – comprised in-depth interviews with Vauxhall car plant workers and their wives living in Luton in the mid-1980s. The primary aim of the research was to examine whether members of the working class lead privatised life-styles in the 1980s. A second objective was to explore how life-styles may influence sociopolitical attitudes and behaviour. The research was a qualitative re-study of the *Affluent Worker* series conducted by Goldthorpe *et al.* (1968a, 1968b, 1969). In-depth interviews were conducted to establish whether Goldthorpe *et al.*'s findings had stood the test of time.

Generating a sample of Vauxhall workers and their wives in Luton was not easy. Against the background of poor industrial relations, the Vauxhall car company was unwilling to provide a list of employee names and addresses from which a random sample could be drawn. Instead, a list of names and addresses was drawn up with the help of the regional organiser of the Workers' Educational Association (WEA) and a trade union official of the Amalgamated Engineering Union (AEU). It was not a random list, although only a small number of (randomly chosen) Vauxhall workers were approached for an interview. In each interview, the informants were asked to provide additional contacts, which they did willingly. Nevertheless, five shop stewards appeared in the sample, and checks were made to ensure that they did not form a distinct grouping within the sample. Fortunately, only two of the shop stewards knew each other, one mentioning the other as a potential interviewee. The other shop stewards were unconnected and their names had been provided by different interviewees in the sample. Finally, their socio-political perspectives varied considerably in that one of the men was a long-standing Conservative Party supporter, while another was an equally loyal Labour Party supporter. They were not a source of bias in the findings.

The potential interviewees were initially contacted by letter followed by a brief visit to their homes to explain what the research was about, what was involved and, if they proved willing, to arrange a time and date for the interview. The interviews were conducted in the informants' homes, and each interview lasted approximately two hours. A wide range of topics was discussed, including the interviewees' geographical and residential mobility, their work histories, sociability with kin, neighbours and colleagues from work, conjugal roles, leisure activities, consumer aspirations and social, industrial and political perspectives. With prior agreement, the interviews were tape-recorded and transcribed later. The transcripts were read both as a whole and in sections across the interviews as a means of comparing and contrasting the interviewees' life-styles and sociopolitical proclivities. This internal analysis proceeded until topics and themes emerged which addressed the questions guiding the research.

The interviewees were invited to talk at length about their social and political perspectives. The issue of whether members of the working class have become more individualistic has been the major source of dispute in the class dealignment debate in the 1980s (Sarlvik and Crewe, 1983; Heath *et al.*, 1985, 1991, 1994). The interviewees' comments were placed in the context of this debate. The interviewees were asked whether they thought classes existed in Britain; if the *did*, what classes existed; whether they had changed over time; what class position they thought they occupied; how they felt about class generally; and how it affected their lives in particular. The overwhelming majority of the interviewees believed that classes existed; they identified different classes according to the distribution of wealth and income; and they associated themselves with the working class. The term 'working class' was used interchangeably with other terms such as 'ordinary people' and 'ordinary working people' and in using this definition, the interviewees included working-class and middle-class people who worked for a living. It was a 'mass' class separate from a small class of rich who inherited their wealth and a small class of poor people dependent on state benefits on which to live. The interviewees perceived that the class structure had changed and the differences between the middle class and working class were less distinct than they had been in the past. Nevertheless, they disapproved of class differences and they wanted a more egalitarian society. The findings concurred with Heath *et al.*'s (1985) argument that class awareness remains high, although they did not tap the diffuse nature of class identity by asking respondents what they *mean* by terms such as 'working class' and 'middle class'.

On their political perspectives, the interviewees were asked about their interest in politics; if they supported a particular party; if they had always supported the party in question, or if their attachments had changed; why they supported the party they did; their views on the other political parties; and how they might vote in the future. This line of questioning provided information on the interviewees' alignments and their voting histories as well as facilitating a discussion of the values underlying their allegiance to a particular party and their evaluation of the political parties in government and opposition. The interviewees could be divided into three groupings in terms of their political attitudes and behaviour: Labour Party supporters (24); disillusioned Labour Party supporters (24); and non-Labour party supporters (14). Attention will focus on the two first groups, who made up the majority of the sample (48 out of 62 informants) in the context of debate on declining working-class support for the Labour Party in the 1980s.

Among the Labour Party supporters, the interviewees spontaneously identified Labour as the political party which represented the working class. As one young women explained, 'I've voted for Labour in the past as a working-class party.' The interviewees looked to Labour to create an equal society. Some of interviewees expressed the modest proposal that Labour stood for giving working-class people 'a little bit more'. Other interviewees placed greater emphasis on ideals such as opportunity, independence and opportunity. As one interviewee explained, 'They give people opportunities. Nobody wants to be under the feet of other people. You should give people the opportunity to prove themselves, look after themselves.' The interviewees usually focused on improved standards of living for the working class. Labour, according to one interviewee, 'was the only party which will bring people's standards of living up to the level I would like to see. I think the average person should be able to afford to buy a house, have fridges, television sets, a car if they want it'. The interviewees wanted a more equitable distribution of wealth and income so that all members of society could enjoy a secure and comfortable standard of living. The Labour supporters were also highly doubtful about the party's ability to achieve greater equality. They referred to the 'winter of discontent' of 1978–9 which remained highly relevant as late as 1987. The interviewees recalled the conflict between the government's income policies and the competing claims of various unions for higher wages. The interviewees described the 'winter of discontent' as a 'fiasco', when the economy was in a 'mess', some blaming the Labour government while others blamed the trade unions. As one interviewee put it:

> They had percentage wage increases and the person at the bottom was still out in the cold. They were still as badly off after 10%. There was no light at the end of the tunnel. If everyone had got a £5 rise irrespective of their wages it would have been OK. Instead we had a big gap created and the bottom were left where they were.

The interviewees were not entirely convinced that the situation would not arise again. The economy would certainly not prosper and as a result, nor would they. Despite these criticisms, however, the interviewees felt that, as members of the working class, they could not vote any other way, and they would still vote for Labour in the (then) forthcoming election in 1987.

The disillusioned Labour supporters who had abstained or voted for another political party in the 1980s are, of course, the 'critical group' in debates about Labour's future. Like the Labour supporters, they spontaneously associated the Labour Party with the working class. They were also doubtful about the promises that Labour made to reverse the economic climate and achieve prosperity. They voiced similar dissatisfactions with the Labour Party along the lines of its more loyal supporters. They referred to the 'winter of discontent' and the less than harmonious relations between the Labour Party and the trade unions which left the economy in a poor state. The implications of this dissatisfaction on future voting among the disillusioned Labour Party supporters were diverse. Of the twenty-four interviewees, just under half of them (eleven) were not going to vote, as a demonstration of 'no confidence in the lot of them'. In constituencies (Luton North and Luton South) where the (then) SDP (Social Democrats) had a limited presence, only a small minority of informants (four) were going to vote for the SDP to 'give them a chance'. However, a sizeable number (nine) were going to vote Conservative. Voting Conservative, in the words of one interviewee, was a way of 'allowing things to stop the way they are' rather than the possibility of decline in the event of losing 'control'. The interviewees were fearful of what a Labour victory would mean, while voting Conservative meant that 'things would remain the same'. Their views were far from a positive endorsement of Conservative Party economic policies, although they were a damning indictment of Labour's likely economic success.

Overall, there was little evidence to suggest that there has been a permanent change in the political attitudes and behaviour of members of the working class in the 1980s as proponents of the class dealignment thesis argued (Franklin, 1985; Sarlvik and Crewe, 1983). This qualitative study complemented the findings of opponents of the class dealignment thesis indicating political dissatisfactions with the Labour Party's performance in government and opposition (Heath *et al.*, 1985, 1991, 1994; Marshall *et al.*, 1988). By talking to the interviewees at length, therefore, it was possible to gain some insight into *why* some former Labour voters had become disillusioned with Labour in the 1970s and 1980s, and thereby engage in debates on electoral behaviour.

# ■ Conclusion

Qualitative studies have made a significant contribution to political science from the study of power relationships in central government to voting in general elections. Participant observation and intensive interviewing have proved to be the most appropriate techniques in the study of such issues as people's motives and subjective interpretations of their actions, whether they are relatively powerful or powerless in the political sphere. These phenomena, and the theories that political scientists employ in seeking to understand and explain them, are invariably unquantifiable. Consequently, qualitative methods have been best employed in empirical research addressing such issues. Qualitative methods have their shortcomings, especially with regard to reliability, interpretation and generalisability. No single method, however, can resolve the complex issues involved in the study of politics. Qualitative methods, to repeat, have contributed to the study of mass political behaviour by seeking to understand political actors as conscious social beings who shape the world of politics as well as being shaped by it.

Political scientists have been loath to discuss methodological issues explicitly in their research. While they are engaged frequently in observing and talking to people about their involvement and activities in politics, it is rare to find a discussion about who they talked to; why they talked to them; the extent to which there was a frank discussion; or whether information collected in one interview was corroborated by information from another. As a result, political scientists have often failed to consider the advantages (and disadvantages) of qualitative methods in understanding political behaviour. Consequently, the virtues of qualitative methods in the study of politics remain unsung and the varied techniques play understated, albeit major, roles in political science.

# ■ Further reading

There are numerous books which discuss methods in the social sciences. The most useful title that considers quantitative and qualitative methods is Gilbert (1992), an edited collection. Complementing his earlier work, Silverman (1993) focuses on questions of analysis. Other examples of good qualitative research include Saunders (1981) and Billig (1978).

# Chapter 8

# Quantitative Methods
## W. L. Miller

Quantitative methods are not primarily about complicated statistics but simply about a concern for quantity. While alternative approaches to the study of politics pose their own fundamental questions – 'Is it morally justifiable?', 'Who did what and when did they do it?', 'How does it work?', 'Is it intriguing, persuasive or inspiring?' – quantitative methods are based upon the fundamental question 'How many of them are there?'. In itself that question is content-free and value-free, but the whole point is to apply it to data that are highly political in content. This chapter begins with a discussion of the different types of quantitative data and the different opportunities they provide. It outlines the statistical methods most frequently used to analyse quantitative data. It then reviews criticisms that have been levelled at quantitative research and briefly notes some of its past achievements and future prospects.

# ■ Types of quantitative data

Quantitative data comes in many forms. For extensive reviews see Manheim and Rich (1986), de Vaus (1991) and Miller (1983). One important distinction is between *experimental* and purely *observational* data. Of course, experiments involve observation, but they also involve manipulation; so they are not based on observation alone. Natural scientists can often manipulate nature in a carefully controlled way and observe the consequences. On a grand scale, students of politics usually do not have that option and might refuse to take it if they did. On a limited scale, however, it may be possible to add an experimental element to studies of public opinion by varying question wordings and getting people to think themselves into a variety of scenarios (Miller *et al.*, 1995), by pre-testing reactions to political adverts, or by manipulating the information made available to a small sample of co-operative citizens (Iyengar and Kinder, 1987).

A second important distinction concerns whether we undertake *primary analysis* of our own data or *secondary analysis* of someone else's. The arguments against secondary analysis are obvious: it limits the freedom and responsibility of the researcher. Forced to use data that already exists – official censuses and surveys, published Gallup polls, EU *Eurobarometer* polls, even published newspaper polls of uncertain design and origin – it is difficult for the researcher to break free from the conceptual frameworks, the mind-set, the priorities and the perspectives imposed by those who originally defined the topic and chose the appropriate quantitative measures. Researchers may even be tempted to claim that the available data measures what they want to analyse when it does not.

Against all that, secondary analysis of existing data has important advantages. Most obviously, it is available and usually cheap. Indeed, there may be no alternative: we cannot sit round a table in the 1990s and devise questions for a survey of opinion in the 1960s. Less obviously, but no less importantly, the secondary analyst does not need to make the large investment in time and skill that is necessary for data collection.

Another critically important distinction is between *aggregate data* and *individual data*. As its name implies, aggregate data is available only for spatial or temporal aggregates. Voting results for parliamentary constituencies are a good example of spatial aggregates; monthly Gallup opinion-poll percentages as published in the press are a good example of temporal aggregates.

The significance of the distinction between individual and aggregate data derives from a theorem, the 'Ecological Fallacy Theorem', (Robinson, 1950; Alker, 1965, pp. 102–5; Alker, 1969, esp. p. 79), which proves that a statistical relationship between aggregates need not be at all similar to the corresponding relationship between individuals. ('Ecology' here has nothing to do with healthy forests or polluted beaches: it refers to political and social environments – not to physical environments – and to their influence upon the behaviour of individuals.)

For example, the proposition P1 (about individuals):

*P1: people suffering economic hardship tend to vote for left-wing parties*
need not imply, nor be implied by, the corresponding proposition P2 (about temporal aggregates):

*P2: in hard times, left-wing parties get higher votes*
nor even the corresponding proposition P3 (about spatial aggregates):

*P3: in areas of economic hardship, left-wing parties get higher votes.*

While both P1 and P3 (but not P2) tend to be true, the degree of relationship found in aggregate data (P3) is usually not even close to what would be implied by the degree of relationship found in individual data (P1) – typically, it may be twice as strong (Miller, 1977; 1978). So a quantitative analysis of individuals can only lead to precise quantitative conclusions about individuals; an analysis of places only to precise conclusions about places; and an analysis of times only to conclusions about times. The fact that less prosperous areas tend to support the Labour Party certainly does not prove that less prosperous times will automatically produce more support for it. If it did, the best re-election strategy for any Labour government would be to wreck the economy in order to increase its vote. Even non-statisticians might suspect a logical fallacy in that strategy!

Next there is the distinction between *enumeration* and *sampling*. From 1790 in the USA and 1801 in Britain, governments funded, organised – and controlled the content of – regular population censuses. Basic statistics on taxation, unemployment, reported crime, imports and exports are other examples of attempts at complete enumeration. Alas, supposedly complete enumeration gives data great authority but does not guarantee accuracy in practice. In Britain, police figures on (spontaneously) reported crime are notorious underestimates; unemployment figures have been redefined so often to please the government that they have lost all credibility; and the Single European Market has made national import/export figures even more unreliable than they were before. Complete and accurate enumeration requires more co-operation from citizens (spontaneously or at least conscientiously reporting to government), and more impartiality from government (reporting back to citizens) than is normally available.

The idea of using a small, carefully chosen, sample to represent a much larger population was revolutionary. Sampling was cheap and so it extended the range and variety of information and let independent researchers, rather than governments or bureaucrats, decide what topics to research. Selecting small but representative samples presents obvious pitfalls and it took until the 1930s before it was generally accepted that the system used to select a sample was far more important than its size. While statisticians had long believed in the effectiveness of small samples, it was the 1936 success of the small-sample Gallup, Crossley and Roper polls over the *Literary Digest*'s badly chosen 2,376,523 respondent poll in predicting the US Presidential election result that established the credibility of small-sample polls (Teer and Spence, 1973, pp. 12–15). That insight legitimised samples as small (and cheap) as a mere 2000 to represent populations of 200 million and led to the explosion of data on political opinions and behaviour in the post-war years.

It is usual to distinguish three (sometimes four) *levels of measurement* ranging down from fully quantitative or 'interval' data (e.g. income in £) through ordinal or ranked data (e.g. 'would you describe your political position as: on the left, centre-left, in the centre, centre-right, or on the right?') down to merely nominal or categorical data which does not even indicate a position on a rank-order spectrum (e.g. 'what is your religion, if any?'). Ordinal and categorical data is only semi-quantitative, and analyses of such data either lead to relatively weak conclusions or depend upon persuasive but not always compelling assumptions. For example, political ideology could be measured on a scale from 1 = left, through 2 = centre-left, 3 = centre, 4 = centre-right, to 5 = right, but that implicitly assumes that the ideological difference between each pair of adjacent categories is the same whereas, in fact, those on the centre-left may be politically closer to the centre than to the left (or vice versa). Nonetheless such assumptions are often made in order to permit arithmetical calculations such as the average score of a particular social group on a left-right scale. Without associating numbers with ordinal categories, such detailed arithmetical calculations would be impossible; and without such calculations, it would be difficult (though not impossible) to compare the ideology of different social groups.

# ■ The data analysis process

Data analysis should be an on-going dialogue between theory and data, and a dialogue that extends through the data to the world beyond. It is simply nonsense to suggest that there is no world beyond the data. It is far more realistic to regard the construction and analysis of a data set as a dialogue, a conversation, between the researchers and the world of people and institutions they seek to understand. It is extremely unlikely that the researchers' knowledge of their subject matter will be limited to the particular research project on which they are currently engaged. They come to the conversation with considerable awareness of the other conversation partner. Certainly it is usually a conversation dominated, for good or ill, by the researchers who take the initiative in asking the questions and often in defining the range of acceptable answers – closer to a sympathetic interrogation than a balanced conversation between equals perhaps. Nonetheless the dialogue should, and usually does, retain the capacity to surprise its initiators.

Much of the real value of data analysis therefore does not involve 'number crunching'. It begins when the mere prospect of data collection and analysis forces researchers to clarify their concepts and distinguish between subtlety and complexity (good and researchable) on the one hand, and fudge and inconsistency (bad and not researchable) on the other. It continues by encouraging theoretical clarity about the nature of expected patterns and relationships. Reasoning about the structure of these relationships is more important than the choice of statistical procedure used to quantify them. Such reasoning can be represented diagrammatically by a pattern of arrows depicting chains of influence or causation, linking key concepts together. For obvious reasons they are often called 'causal diagrams', 'causal models', or sometimes 'path diagrams' because they depict the pathways of influence (Marsh, 1982, ch. 4; Stinchcombe, 1968).

# ☐ *Univariate analysis*

At its simplest, analysis may not involve any relationship at all. Its purpose may be to take that fundamental question 'How many?' at its most literal, focusing upon a single concept (and a single measure of that concept). There is no need for any kind of causal diagram here. To analyse a categorical variable such as voting choice it is sufficient to count the numbers who intend to vote for each party, or turn them into percentages. However, with ordinal or fully quantitative variables there are more opportunities for analysis. Usually we are interested in some measure of 'central tendency', that is the average or typical value; and some measure of the way values are spread around and about that average. For example, an analysis of income might include a calculation of average income, and a calculation of what percentage of people had incomes lower than half the average or greater than twice the average. Political scientists tend to be even more interested in measures of the spread or 'distribution' of income – that is in measures of income inequality – than in measures of average income.

# ☐ *Bivariate models*

Two variables $A$ and $B$ may be related in several different ways, each corresponding to a different causal model and associated analytic methods. We might hypothesise that $A$ causes $B$, or that $B$ causes $A$, or that each simultaneously influences the other, or that they appear to be related but only because both depend in part upon some third unspecified factor (this last situation is sometimes called a case of 'spurious correlation'). In all these cases cross-tabulations, scattergrams, and correlations are appropriate methods of analysis. Where there is a direct causal link between $A$ and $B$, running in only one direction, and that direction is known, then regression analysis can quantify how much the one depends upon the other. In political studies there is often a clear dependent variable: a political opinion, or even a party choice. For example, in the relationship between class and party choice in Britain, it is reasonable to suppose that class may exert a strong influence upon party choice but that party choice is unlikely to exert a significant influence upon class: luckily a vote against the British government does not lead to instant dismissal followed by exile to a collective farm (see Figure 8.1).

Two variables – such as choice of newspaper and choice of party – which simultaneously influence each other are a special case of a 'loop of causation' which is extremely difficult to analyse (see Figure 8.2). Appropriate analytic techniques are discussed in the next subsection on multi-variate models.

**Figure 8.1**  *Bivariate causal diagram 1: direct influence*

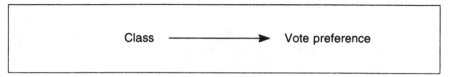

*Source*: Adapted from Marsh (1982, p. 86).

**Figure 8.2**  *Bivariate causal diagram 2: mutual influence*

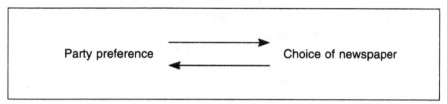

*Source*: Adapted from Marsh (1982, p. 80).

Where *A* and *B* are linked only by their joint dependence upon some third unknown factor, factor analysis can be used to estimate the nature of that factor. With only two indicators, factor analysis is unlikely to differ much from a common-sense approach in which we simply take the average of *A* and *B* as this unknown, underlying factor. The classic example is the idea of a 'general intelligence factor' underlying scholars' performances in different academic tests, which have nothing more in common (though each has its own peculiarities) than that they reflect general intelligence. Similarly, in political studies, we might devise two (or more) indicators of authoritarianism, or of liberalism, or of nationalism and use factor analysis to try and get behind the specifics of these measures to a more general authoritarian, liberal, or nationalist factor (see Figure 8.3).

**Figure 8.3**  *Bivariate causal diagram 3: joint dependence on unknown factor*

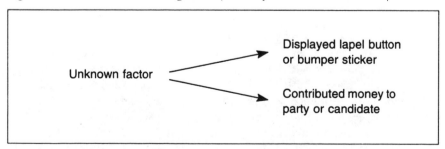

*Source*: Adapted from Verba, Nie and Kim (1978, p. 338).

# ☐ *Multivariate models*

With three or more variables, there are additional analytic possibilities which include multiple regression models, interaction models, path analysis models, and multiple factor models. The structural differences between these models are much more important than the particular statistical methods used to analyse them – a point which may be overlooked by enthusiasts for particular statistical techniques, or for particular computer programs.

The basic structure of the multiple regression model is that two (or more) so-called 'independent' variables exert some influence upon a 'dependent' variable. But, in addition, each independent variable exerts its influence upon that dependent variable in a way that is unaffected by simultaneous influences from other independent variables. For example, class and religion might both affect party choice. If the influence of class on party choice is the same within each religious group (and conversely, the influence of religion on party choice is the same within each class) then the data fits the model and a multiple regression program (or equivalent statistical program) can be used to calculate just how much effect class and religion each have upon party choice, to find out which has the greater effect, and so on (see Figure 8.4).

**Figure 8.4**   *Multivariate causal diagram 1: multiple regression model*

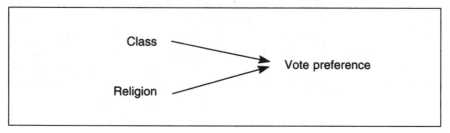

*Source*: Adapted from Butler and Stokes (1974, p. 161).

However, if class and religion have a variable influence – determined by age, for example – then the data fits an interaction model, so called because age interacts with class and religion in their effect upon party choice. In the 1960s, Butler and Stokes (1974, pp. 162–65) showed that class had more influence within more recent age-cohorts (i.e. amongst younger people) and religion had more influence within older age-cohorts – people who had entered the electorate when party politics had a more Liberal versus Conservative, Non-conformist versus Established Church flavour. (see Figure 8.5). Such data can be analysed by adding 'interaction

**Figure 8.5** *Multivariate causal diagram 2: interaction model*

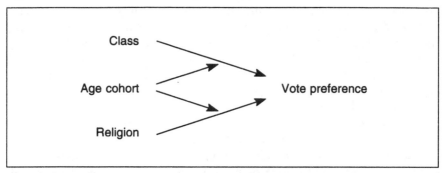

*Source*: Adapted from Butler and Stokes (1974, pp. 162–5).

terms' to a standard multiple regression model, or by using a special-purpose program such as AID (Automatic Interaction Detector – see Sarlvik and Crewe, 1983, pp. 103–15; Rose and McAllister, 1986, ch. 5). One variant of multiple regression methods, known as 'log-linear analysis', is usually programmed in such a way as to facilitate the addition of interaction terms (Heath, Jowell and Curtice, 1985; Heath *et al.*, 1991; Miller, 1988, ch. 13).

Path analysis models involve networks and chains of causation. They come in two kinds: 'recursive' path models, which do not include loops of causation, and 'non-recursive' path models, which do. Recursive path models can be analysed by repeated use of multiple regression analysis but non-recursive path models are very much more difficult to analyse statistically.

Unfortunately for quantitative analysts, loops of causation are very plausible in political studies. Consider, for example, psychological identification with a party and approval of its policies. Obviously approval of its policies is likely to increase general identification with the party, but the reverse is also likely: most people form an attachment to a party long before the specific issues of the day have arisen and they are disposed to look kindly upon new policies put forward by their own party and unkindly upon policies put forward by its rivals. The flat rate poll tax was never likely to have much appeal for traditional Labour voters but its initial appeal for many loyal Conservatives owed much to the fact that it was their own party's proposal. Wherever influence flows simultaneously in two opposite directions it is very difficult (though not impossible) to quantify how much flows in each direction. One possibility is to use the econometric methods popular with economists (see Markus and Converse, 1979).

Alternatively it may be possible to break the simultaneity of the causal loop by introducing a time element into the data. For example a panel survey that interviewed the same people on two occasions, once before the poll tax proposal had been introduced into public debate, and again afterwards, would allow us to quantify how many former Conservatives went on to approve the poll tax and remain Conservative, and how many revolted against the poll tax and abandoned their party. Panel-based analyses of mutual causal influences between economic optimism and support for the government appear in Miller, Clarke, Harrop and Whiteley (1990, ch. 4); between attendance at a party rally and support for that party in Miller (1983, pp. 232–6); between choice of newspaper and party support in Miller (1991, ch. 8) and in Harrop (1986).

Multiple factor models differ from bivariate factor models in a fundamental way. With three or more variables we can ask whether the correlations between them reflect their joint dependence upon two or more underlying factors, not just upon one general factor. The aim is seldom to uncover just one general factor, but equally seldom to uncover more than a very few underlying factors. One long-running aim has been to uncover a left–right dimension to political attitudes, plus one other cross-cutting dimension – such as a tough–tender or liberal–authoritarian dimension. (Eysenck, 1951; Heath *et al.*, 1991, ch. 11). Another has been to classify forms of political action into, for example, so-called 'conventional' forms (peaceable, legal expressions of opinion) and 'unconventional' (disruptive, aggressive, even violent action) by showing that attitudes to a wide range of political activities reflect underlying attitudes to just two general styles of activity: expressive and disruptive (Verba, Nie and Kim, 1978, pp. 317–39; Parry, Moyser and Day, 1992, pp. 50–62), see Figure 8.6.

**Figure 8.6**   *Multiple factor model*

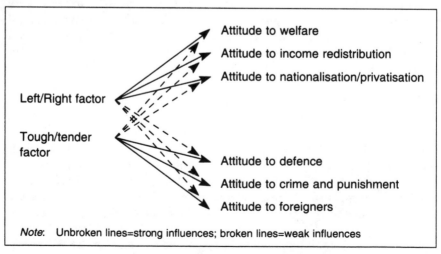

*Note*:   Unbroken lines=strong influences; broken lines=weak influences

*Sources*: Adapted from Eysenck (1951) and Heath *et al.* (1991, ch. 11).

The underlying factors uncovered by multiple factor analyses merely consist of weighted averages of the original variables. Ideally the weights should approximate either one or zero; so that each factor consists of a simple (unweighted) average of a subset of the original variables. Effectively the analysis therefore groups the original variables into a few subsets, each of which represents some underlying factor. Analysts then look at the variables in a subset and devise a factor name, or label, which succinctly describes what these variables appear to have in common. As part of a semi-mechanised dialogue with the data, this can be a valuable way of gaining insight and a good basis for the exercise of imagination.

## ☐ *Time-series models*

Most quantitative research in political studies is based upon individual data or spatial aggregates (constituencies, US states, countries) though it may be given a limited temporal aspect by comparing a few time-points, charting trends, or using panels. In contrast, time-series analysis usually focuses on a very large number of temporal aggregates – such as monthly economic statistics and published opinion polls spanning a period of ten, twenty or thirty years. Time-series analysis cannot reveal a deeper truth than analyses of individuals and spatial aggregates – only a different truth. Remember that the Ecological Fallacy Theorem proves that analyses of individuals justify conclusions only about individuals, analyses of places justify conclusions only about places, and analyses of times justify conclusions only about times. Nonetheless times are very important, and an understanding of trends can only be derived from an analysis of trends; it cannot be inferred from an understanding of individuals or places.

Time-series ways of thinking about data are fundamentally different from others. While particular time-series models differ greatly, they are all based upon fundamentally dynamic ideas such as: support for a party will automatically tend to return to its natural, long-term level unless forces exist to push it away from that level; the impact of a crisis event upon public opinion will be at a maximum immediately after the event and then fall away sharply in successive months until it no longer has any effect at all; the political influence of a condition (such as the level of unemployment) on the other hand, will not emerge until some time later than the condition itself, since it takes time for people to become aware of it and respond politically; political support in any month will not only depend upon all the influences acting in that month alone, but also upon the pre-existing level of political support – so that even the combination of all currently active influences will only produce a defined change, rather than set a defined level for support. For an impressive and up-to-date example of such reasoning look at Price and Sanders (1993) (see Figure 8.7).

**Figure 8.7** *Time-series model (simplified)*

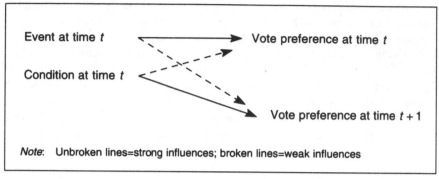

Note: Unbroken lines=strong influences; broken lines=weak influences

*Source*: Adapted from Price and Saunders (1993).

Time-series analyses in political studies have focused almost exclusively upon predicting trends in party (especially government) support from a combination of economic conditions such as unemployment, inflation, and living standards and discrete crisis events such as the invasion of the Falklands, the resignation of Prime Minister Thatcher, devaluation, a major strike, or the Gulf War (Clarke, Stewart and Zuk, 1986).

# □ Contextual or Multi-level models

Analyses of individuals, spatial aggregates and temporal aggregates can be combined (Miller, 1978). Contextual or multi-level analyses place individuals in a spatial and/or temporal context. Butler and Stokes (1974, pp. 133–6) cumulated over 120,000 NOP interviews to place individuals in spatial (parliamentary constituency) contexts. Similarly Marsh, Ward and Sanders (1992) pooled over 80,000 Gallup interviews to analyse individuals in temporal contexts (see also Miller, 1977; and Heath *et al.*, 1991, p. 110). Contextual or multi-level analysis requires either very large or specially designed data sets since individuals must be correctly assigned to contexts. In a typically clustered sample survey, respondents who live in a particular working-class constituency may all live in a single middle-class ward within it; so that the characteristics of the constituency as a whole do not describe the social context in which they live. Despite the difficulties however, contextual models are important because there is clear evidence that the same person will behave differently at different times, or in different places. Political behaviour is very much a matter of individual response to an environment that includes family, friends, neighbours and work-place associates, current press and television content,

**Figure 8.8**    *Context model (simplified)*

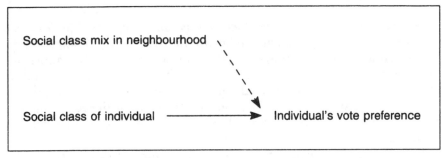

*Source*: Adapted from Miller (1978).

the state of the economy, and the political options on offer locally and nationally (see Figure 8.8).

## ☐ *Other quantitative methods*

Quantitative methods have been traditionally associated with statistical analysis. But they cover a lot more than that. Computer generated graphical displays are not designed to analyse so much as to ease communication. It is important that they are treated as a means of communication rather than as an end in themselves: the meaning of the graphic is more important than its beauty or the ingenuity of the computer program. In general, Edward Tufte's rule should be followed: maximise the meaning and minimise the ink (Tufte, 1983).

Computer simulations are designed neither to analyse nor to display known facts so much as to extrapolate from them. The most famous (or infamous) include the Treasury's economic forecasting model, and the Club of Rome's *Limits to Growth* study, but the method has been used in political studies also. Coplin (1968) is an early example. Simulation is speculation, not analysis, but controlled and disciplined speculation, based usually upon a combination of historical analysis and inspired imagination.

What should have emerged from the discussion of quantitative methods so far is their richness and diversity. Quantitative data comes in many forms and it can be analysed in many ways. Inevitably particular analyses of particular kinds of data rest upon certain explicit or implicit assumptions. But the imagination of the researcher is not forced into the straight-jacket of a narrow routine procedure and criticisms of particular applications of particular quantitative methods are seldom an argument against quantitative methods in general.

# ■ Criticisms

One criticism of quantitative methods is that they are *obscure and incomprehensible*. It is certainly unhelpful to focus too much attention on the technicalities of new statistical toys, but jargon and technicalities are not the preserve of those engaged in quantitative methods. In political studies, the focus should be on the major assumptions and principles on which an analysis is based, that is on the structures of the causal models that are being applied to the data. These are seldom difficult to understand.

It is alleged that quantitative methods *misrepresent* their subject. The GIGO principle (Garbage In, Garbage Out) always applies. If quantitative data is corrupt, irrelevant or misleading, it is unlikely to be improved much by statistical processing. There are often elementary faults in data collection and reporting. 'Russian' opinion surveys sometimes turn out to be samples of European Russia only, or of urban Russia only – for example, the European Union's *Central and Eastern Eurobarometer* gives opinion poll entries for 'European Russia', while Miller, Reisinger and Hesli (1993) is based on surveys of 'Russia west of the Urals', 'that portion of the USSR that is in Europe' and, in some chapters, Moscow alone. In the classic *Civic Culture* survey (Almond and Verba, 1963), subtitled *Political Attitudes and Democracy in Five Nations* the Mexican sample was restricted to urban Mexico (a minority of the population). In the sequel *Participation and Political Equality: A Seven-nation Comparison* (Verba, Nie and Kim, 1978) the Indian sample was restricted to four states, the Yugoslav sample to four republics, and the Nigerian sample excluded the Muslim northern region. *Small-town Politics* (Birch et al., 1959) was based upon just one small town, and the *Affluent Worker* (Goldthorpe, Lockwood, Bechhofer and Platt, 1968–9) was limited to a few affluent workers in Luton. Surveys carried out weeks or even months after an election are sometimes used to explain the vote, which means that attitudes and opinions after the election are used to predict behaviour in it – a causal process that apparently runs backwards in time. For example, interviews for the major study of the General Election of 9 June 1983 were carried out between 5 July and 5 October 1983 (Heath, Jowell and Curtice, 1985, p. 179).

Groups of people with particularly interesting combinations of characteristics may often be quite small with correspondingly high probabilities of sampling errors. So even in a relatively large survey Butler and Stokes (1974, pp. 111–12) at one point focused upon the twenty or so respondents who, during the course of their panel study, moved from council tenancy to owner-occupation. Findings based on such small sub-samples may be unreliable.

Government statistics may be wrong, biased and even intentionally biased. Moreover, the bias may not be consistent through time. British unemployment rates have been redefined so often and so optimistically as to cast serious doubts upon their validity. European integration has destroyed the accuracy of British import–export statistics. Survey respondents may tell lies to cover their embarrassment and they certainly adjust their memories to make them more consistent with their current preferences. They can be prompted into articulating opinions on issues that do not concern them, and persuaded to change sides on an issue by suitably manipulative wording. For direct evidence on the power of manipulation see Sniderman, Brody and Tetlock (1991, ch. 12) or Miller *et al.* (1995), or Miller, Timpson and Lessnoff (forthcoming).

More generally, the social and political context of data gathering may be unrepresentative of the context in which opinions are salient and actions are taken: a quiet one-to-one interview at home is a very different context from the midst of a political demonstration or riot (Muller,1979; Marsh, 1977; Barnes, Kaase, *et al.*, 1979). Conversely experimental attempts to assess the power of propaganda may focus far too much explicit attention on that propaganda, and measure its possibly transient effects at too early a point in their decay curve (Cohen, 1964; Iyengar and Kinder, 1987).

But if we are alert to these possibilities of misrepresentation it should be possible both to reduce the problems by design, and/or to take account of them when interpreting the results. We can extend the coverage of data collection or, at least, accurately describe the coverage achieved. We can use panel surveys to ensure that explanations of voting choice are based upon attitudes and opinions measured before the vote. Government statistics can sometimes be readjusted back to their original definitions, and international bodies such as OECD, the UN or the World Bank may be motivated to provide more consistent, and more internationally comparable, figures. Careful question wording can be used to minimise respondents' embarrassment at giving socially or politically 'incorrect' answers; the power of manipulative wording can be both measured and neutralised by pushing some respondents in one direction and others in the opposite; and the data gathering context can be moved closer to the action context by getting respondents to think themselves into particular scenario situations.

Quantitative methods are criticised for being *too narrowly focused*, like a search-light on a dark night that only illuminates a very small part of reality. In particular, questionnaires with very specific questions and a fixed range of allowable answers may prevent respondents from truly speaking their minds. This criticism betrays a groundless assumption that quantitative research is carried out by people who are totally ignorant of their subject matter, who have never looked at non-quantitative reports, nor carried out any kind of pilot study. It is as if quantitative researchers were some alien race of Martians in a hurry to get results. Where quantitative researchers are uncertain about their subject they can include 'open-ended' questions that do not have fixed answers (and then classify the answers later); they can cast individual questions in very general terms;

and they can ask a wide range of questions. Questions can be open-ended even though the interviewer has only a fixed set of expected answer categories, plus the fail-safe 'other–please specify' category which quantifies and, if necessary, interprets unexpected answers.

More important, specific questions and pre-set answers do not materialise out of thin air. They are likely to reflect the ideas and even the language found in non-quantitative accounts of the subject, in journalists' reports, in group-discussion transcripts, in debriefings of pilot interviewers, and in the advice of expert informants. Formal and informal qualitative research can provide a sound basis for later quantitative work. The purpose of pre-set questions is not to force opinion into a researcher-formulated framework but to present a framework that is known to be familiar to the respondent, and in which respondents can locate themselves without difficulty; their purpose is not to introduce unfamiliar ideas, but to count the frequency with which people subscribe to different familiar alternatives.

Quantitative methods are criticised for their alleged *causal inadequacy*. Marsh (1982, chs 4 and 5) and others quote Weber as demanding both 'adequacy at the level of cause' and 'adequacy at the level of meaning' – that is, a good theory should have both statistical justification and plausibility. Without a plausible explanation, we may discard a statistical link as mere coincidence. Conversely a plausible theory unsupported by statistical evidence is at best speculative, and at worst paradoxical. Politics is full of theories about how people should behave but, alas for the theory, do not (Brzezinski, 1989). And that applies to empirical descriptive as well as prescriptive theories in politics (Przeworski and Soares, 1971).

How well do quantitative methods perform in establishing causation? One criticism is easily dismissed: claims that causal reasoning is based upon a deterministic view of the world in which people are at the mercy of impersonal external forces and devoid of free will, misunderstand what is meant by causation. Causal models in political studies are not about determinism but about influences, usually only modest influences, and often rather weak influences. Moreover they often treat individuals' values and prejudices as a source of influence.

A more important criticism is encapsulated in the phrase 'correlation is not causation'. Correlations may be established quite easily but their causal nature remains in doubt. Surveys show a high correlation between peoples' party preferences and the partisanship of their newspaper, for example. But are they influenced by their paper, or do they merely choose a paper they find politically acceptable, or is their choice of both party and paper determined by something else, such as class?

Even with cross-sectional data it is possible to draw some conclusions about causation. First, several different theories may predict a correlation, but if the correlation turns out to be close to zero, all those theories are in trouble. So a correlation may provide corroboration, if not proof, of a theory about causation. Second, the possibility of 'spurious correlation' – that is, a correlation between two variables caused purely by their joint dependence upon a third – can be checked by multiple regression methods, provided the third variable has also been measured and included in the data set. Third, while the causal direction between party preference and newspaper choice is not obvious, with many other pairs of variables the direction is not in dispute. It is reasonable to assume that most social background variables (age, class, gender, etc.) are causally antecedent to most political opinion variables. Fourth, some data can be gathered about the (causally prior) past as well as the present: for example we can ask whether people have ever been patients in an NHS hospital and relate that (past) experience to their (present) support for an NHS. Since memories fade and change, this approach must be used with care. Memories of opinions, as opposed to experiences, are suspect. Since perceptions of other people's opinions (parents, for example) have been shown to be inaccurate even in the present (Niemi, 1973), attempts to relate people's political attitudes to their parents' politics when they lived in the parental home are doubly difficult – though Butler and Stokes (1974, ch. 7) provide an impressive attempt to use memories of long-dead parents' religion and party preferences to give some insights into a century of political change. Panels in which data is gathered on the same individuals at different points in time provide the best means of establishing causal sequences, though they have their own faults.

Quantitative methods are criticised for their *failure to reveal meaning*. Can quantitative methods do anything to establish meaning? Critics argue that quantitative methods may establish 'what' and 'when', but not 'why': motivations and meanings are inevitably hidden. It is a criticism that is either universal or invalid: if motivations can be established in relatively unstructured qualitative conversations then, in principle, they can also be established in the more controlled interviews typical of quantitative research – provided those interviews cover the right ground and ask the right questions. In this situation, the difference between quantitative and qualitative surveys is primarily a matter of the size and representativeness of the sample. Of course, the more flexible in-depth open-ended approach typical of good qualitative research is better able to uncover and explore unanticipated explanations and motivations – to get answers to questions that have not been asked. Philosophical reasoning and qualitative methods are extremely useful in establishing the range of possibilities, and the actual existence of possibilities. Quantitative research then seeks to count the relative frequency of alternative possibilities: it can assess which motivations are minority, majority, or preponderant motivations and which, though possible, are rare in practice.

While asking people directly about their motivations is as possible in quantitative studies as in any other, it remains highly suspect because people are not usually very good at introspection. They tend to retreat into socially-acceptable or culturally-plausible explanations of their own motivations and behaviour, to accept Press explanations as their own motivations. Retrospective self-descriptions of motivations, whether they appear in politicians' memoirs or in opinion surveys, must always be taken with a grain of salt. An alternative approach is to specify and measure the components or aspects of a complex concept and operate with these more elemental and less ambiguous variables. For example, when Campbell, Converse, Miller and Stokes (1960, pp. 301–6) in the 1950s asked 'why do Catholics tend to vote for the Democrats?', they broke the notion of 'Catholics' down into three elements: a self-conscious group, a set of people with similar socio-economic life experiences, or a social group only in the sense that being a Catholic made contact with other Catholics much more likely – a network rather than a group. All of these were quantifiable and analysis could show which of the three aspects of Catholicism best explained why Catholics at that time tended to vote so strongly for the Democrats despite the absence of overt religious issues in current political debate. Similarly we can answer questions such as 'what do Russians mean when they say they support democracy, or a market economy?' by measuring enough different aspects or components of the complex concepts 'democracy' and 'market economy' (Miller, White, Heywood and Wyman, 1994). Typical academic surveys based on structured interviews that take an hour or more and ask hundreds of questions allow thorough quantification of the different meanings that different people attach to such words.

# ■ Achievements and opportunities

More than other approaches to political studies, quantitative methods depend upon technology. So their use has been encouraged as much by technological innovation as by philosophical justification. From early in this century, logical positivists and behaviouralist thinkers argued for a science of politics based upon empirical observations and testable theories. But many practical-minded empiricists were less troubled by philosophical doubts than by technical and financial problems.

Two great technological advances in particular provided a major stimulus to the use of quantitative methods in political studies. First, the development of sample surveys in the century from 1824 when the *Harrisburg Pennsylvanian* first used them to predict the outcome of the US Presidential contest between Adams and Jackson (Teer and Spence, 1973, p. 13) through to the triumphs of 1936 brought down the cost of political data collection so much that it broke the government-dominated quasi-monopoly of quantitative information. Statistics were no longer 'official'. Second, the spread of electronic computers in the 1950s, swiftly followed by pre-programmed, easy-to-use, statistical analysis packages, did for data analysis what sampling had done for data collection. According to the authors of *Civic Culture*, for example, it was this 'revolution in social science research technology' that was 'the catalytic agent in the political culture conceptualisation and research that took place in the 1960s'. Political questions were important to them 'but the development of survey research methodology was the immediate and more powerful stimulus' (Almond, 1980, p. 15).

The greatest achievements of this post-war revolution in research technology lay in their studies of citizens. It had always been possible to study laws, major political institutions and top political elites with relatively primitive quantitative (or non-quantitative) methods simply because there were so few of them, but very little was known about citizens or middle-level elites because there were so many – though ignorance never inhibited speculation or assertion. Landmark studies of mass political attitudes and behaviour include: Butler and Stokes' (1974) *Political Change in Britain*, first published in 1969, which provided a particularly deep and realistic account of the evolving class basis of British politics; Almond and Verba's (1963) *Civic Culture*, first published in 1963, which compared the political culture of long-established democracies with that in ex-dictatorships or hegemonic regimes, its sequels (Verba, Nie and Kim, 1978) and rivals (Barnes, Kaase *et al.*, 1979); and McClosky's comprehensive studies of mass and elite attitudes towards civil liberties in America, culminating in his *Dimensions of Tolerance* (McClosky and Brill, 1983). At the same time, the use of quantitative methods renewed and deepened the study of political institutions, for example in Rae's (1967) *Political Consequences of Electoral Laws*, published in 1967, which analysed 115 elections in 20 countries, and treated institutions, not individuals, as the unit of analysis. Rae's pioneering work has been developed by Lijphart (1994) and extended by Powell (1982).

The computing revolution continues to gather pace. Computer-controlled interviewing, whether face-to-face or by telephone (known respectively as CAPI: Computer Assisted Personal Interviewing, or CATI: Computer Assisted Telephone Interviewing, though both are usually done by human, personal interviewers, since fully automatic totally computerised interviewing strains the co-operation of respondents in political surveys), makes it significantly easier to introduce randomised variations in question-wording and randomised variations in hypothetical scenarios, thereby introducing a much more experimental flavour into survey research (Sniderman, Brody and Tetlock, 1991; Miller *et al.*, 1995). As a by-product of computer printing technology, cheap CD-ROMs now give full-text access to many newspapers round the world, as well as to a range of classic texts in political theory. Some political science journals now provide regular reviews of political CD-ROMs. These full-text data-sets, like many other computerised databases, may initially be used only as bibliographic or library-reference tools, or as tidy, well-indexed versions of press-clippings files – an important enough advance in itself – but the boundary between words and numbers is being eroded and there are considerable possibilities for applying quantitative methods to analyse this huge new corpus of computable text data. At the least, statistical content analysis should be poised for a great leap forward.

# ■ Conclusions

Ideally, we would be happiest with an elegant theory, on an important subject, that proves consistent with a wide range of empirical evidence (including, but not limited to, quantitative evidence) and which resolves a moral dilemma or has agreeable moral implications. We may enjoy an elegant theory that is inconsistent with empirical evidence, though we will not believe it; and we may be inspired by a parable which is inconsistent with empirical evidence, because factual truth is not the point of the tale. Empirical evidence may be of great importance yet not be quantitative. There are no contradictions here. Empirical data and quantitative methods are not in conflict with elegance or inspiration, still less with relevance and importance. In political studies, as elsewhere, quantitative methods are as trivial or as important as the things we choose to count; and they are applicable to as broad or narrow a range of things as our wit, and our advancing technology, enable us to count. The faults in quantitative political analysis usually lie not with the statistical and computing methods, but with the data, with the structure of the postulated causal models, and ultimately with the analysts.

The challenge is to bring the methods of quantitative analysis together with matters of political importance, and to bring them very closely together. Quantitative analysis should be applied to important political topics, but it is not enough to combine a quantitative analysis with a discussion of an important political topic if the quantitative analysis does not significantly affect the discussion. The gap between the statistical and substantive conclusions should be as narrow as possible. Too wide a gap suggests a triumph of art over science.

# ■ Further reading

A good place to start further reading would be with de Vaus (1991) which provides an excellent introduction to the design and analysis of opinion surveys. Verba *et al.* (1978) and McClosky and Brill (1983) are two examples of survey-based books which deal with important political topics in a (relatively) non-technical way. Powell (1982) and Lijphart (1994) are good examples of quantitative analysis applied to non-survey data. Tufte (1983) is a good example of how to display quantitative data in graphical form.

# Chapter 9

# The Comparative Method
## Tom Mackie and David Marsh

Setting the boundaries of the comparative method and hence of this chapter is itself problematic. Certainly, comparison is very common in political science. So, in an analysis published in 1988, Hugh Berrington and Pippa Norris suggested that comparative politics was the largest single specialism in British political science. We do not intend to get drawn into definitional wrangles, rather we shall adapt the definition of Richard Rose. The comparative method involves the presentation of 'empirical evidence of some kind in an attempt to compare systematically and explicitly political phenomena' (Rose, 1991, p. 439). Rose adds that the comparison should be across countries, and this is where our definition differs. In the main, this chapter will follow conventional usage and focus on comparison between countries. However, logically, the comparative method can also be employed in intra-country comparisons (explaining differences in public policy among the fifty American states, for instance) or across time (comparing voting behaviour in Britain in the 1960s and the present day), and we shall occasionally refer to research of this type.

This chapter is divided into four substantive sections. The first section examines the reasons why the comparative study of politics is essential. The second section then identifies the types of comparative study. In the third section we deal with the problems involved in the various types of comparison. Finally, we chart the recent changes there have been in this area, many of which can be viewed as responses to such prior criticisms.

# ■ Reasons for comparative study

The major reason for comparative research reflects the basic nature of social science research; it is almost never possible to use the experimental method. Unlike physical scientists, we cannot devise precise experiments to establish, for example, the extent to which an individual leader affects policy outcomes. So, we could not ask Mrs Thatcher to resign in 1983 so that we could establish whether a different Conservative Party leader and prime minister, faced with the same political and economic circumstances, would pursue less radical policies. However, as we shall see, we can use other comparisons to approach the same question. More specifically, we can identify two major reasons why comparative analysis is essential: first, to avoid ethnocentrism in analysis; and second, to generate, test, and subsequently reformulate theories, and their related concepts and hypotheses, about the relationship between political phenomena.

## □ *Beyond ethnocentrism*

Hague *et al.*, (1992, p. 24) claim that, among other things, comparison is essential because it means that we find out more about other places. This claim is clearly correct, but it is far too narrow; it emphasises comparative description at the expense of comparative analysis. Certainly, comparison encourages a sounder knowledge of countries other than our own; in David Collier's words (Collier, 1993, p. 105) it 'sharpens our powers of description'. However, the key point is that it forces observers to escape from ethnocentrism (see Dogan and Pelasy, 1990, ch. 1).

Rose (1991) makes the point very well, in what represents a scathing attack on much British political science. He argues (p. 450): 'The tradition of writing about British (or more properly, English) politics is to assert *uniqueness through false particularisation*. Every institution, individual and event is described with nominal differences implying the absence of generic qualities' (author's emphasis). The opposite temptation, Rose argues, is 'false universalism'; here, authors assume that a theory developed in one country is applicable universally. More generally, they develop general theories that are regarded as being universally true without any consideration of national or historical context.

This point is easily made if we briefly examine the literature on the Thatcher period in Britain and what is often called the 'Thatcher exceptionalism thesis'. It has been common among students of British government to claim that 1979 marked a key break with the past; with the so-called post-war consensus based upon 'Keynesian' economics and social democratic policies developed and reinforced, in part, through negotiations between government and interest groups representing capital and labour (see Douglas, 1989, for a summary of this literature, which itself stresses Thatcherite exceptionalism). In this view, the advent of a Conservative government, with a strong decisive leader, committed to 'New Right' policies emphasising market solutions to economic problems and opposed to consultations with all interest groups, especially the trade unions, set Britain off in a new economic and political direction. Some authors even claim that these new policies, to an extent, provided a blueprint for changes elsewhere. While there is disagreement as to the exact extent of Mrs Thatcher's role in this transformation, all these authors see her role as being crucial; unlike previous post-war British prime ministers she was an ideologue committed to a radical change, which she carried through when in office.

There is a lively debate in the literature, which we shall not rehearse here, on the extent to which there was a transformation in the Thatcher era (see, for example, the debate between Moon, 1994, and Marsh and Rhodes, 1995). Our point is simple. Any claim that the Thatcher governments were 'exceptional' can only be established by comparative analysis. In fact, two claims are being made about the 'exceptional' nature of the Thatcher period and both need to be tested with comparative data, although they require different types of comparative analysis. First, it is claimed that the Thatcher governments were exceptional when compared with previous post-war British governments. To test this requires a systematic comparison over time. One would need to compare the Thatcher Government with other post-war governments; particularly, perhaps, with the Attlee Labour governments of 1945–51, which is the only other post-war British government generally regarded as being radical. Second, it is claimed that the policy changes that occurred owed most to the specific ideological commitments of the Conservative government and to the personality and political views of Mrs Thatcher. The clear implication is that the Thatcher governments were 'exceptional' in international terms. As such, we would need to compare the extent to which different governments, with different leaders, in different countries, pursued similar types of economic policy based on privatisation and market forces. To the extent that we found similar policy initiatives in different countries this would counsel caution before we claim too large an explanatory role for Mrs Thatcher's leadership; unless, of course, we could show that such policy changes occurred first in Britain and were subsequently transferred to other countries. To return to Rose's point, neither of these comparisons have been undertaken systematically.

## ☐ *Developing theory, hypotheses and concepts*

One of the aims of social science is to identify and explain the relationships between social phenomena. Theory provides both a way of organising and a way of interpreting data. Data or evidence then allows us to test hypotheses generated from theory, but only if we have developed robust concepts; that is, concepts which can be utilised across time and space. As a result of this testing, concepts may be adapted, hypotheses reformulated and, perhaps, theories recast. The point here is that comparative analysis plays a key role in these processes.

Of course, comparative analysis can be inductive or deductive (see Rose, 1991, p. 449). If we are operating deductively with hypotheses generated from a theory, then such analysis allows us to test these existing hypotheses. At the same time, much comparative research does not involve the testing of deductive models. Indeed, as Rose argues (1991, p. 448), invariably the concepts we use come before the theory. Of course, comparative analysis helps in the development of these concepts because it provides an excellent test of their robustness and transferability. After all, a concept is of limited utility if its meaning is totally culturally specific; if it cannot be used outside the country or culture in which it was developed. If such comparative analysis is inductive it will often generate new hypotheses (Collier, 1993, p. 105).

Nevertheless, comparative analysis is also important in the testing and development of theories. Again, the reason is clear. Most theories claim to have some level of general applicability. As such, the hypotheses generated from such theories should hold regardless of where they are applied. A good example is Mancur Olson's hypothesis (1965), derived from rational choice theory, that members do not, except under very unusual circumstances, join interest groups in order to gain influence over government policy (that is, for the collective good). Instead, they are motivated to join by selective incentives (perhaps, in the case of trade unions, discounts on insurance premiums, or, in the case of the Royal Society for the Protection of Birds (RSPB), cheap admission to bird sanctuaries). If this deductive model is correct, it should apply equally in the UK, the USA or Germany.

# ■ Different types of comparative analysis

Comparative political analysis is as old as the study of politics itself, although both what is studied and how it is studied have, as we shall see, changed significantly. There are three major types of comparative analysis: case studies of individual countries within a comparative framework; systematic studies of a limited number of countries; and global comparisons based on statistical analysis.

Both comparison between countries and case studies have a long tradition. Aristotle compared the different Greek city states while Herodotus compared the Greek and the non-Greek world. De Tocqueville's *Democracy in America*, first published in 1831, was a case study of a democratising society, not just a description of contemporary America. Of course, global, statistically-based, comparisons only date from the late 1960s. They depended on developments in computing and statistics and were thus associated with the growth of behaviourism.

# ☐ *Case studies*

Case studies are not inevitably, or perhaps even usually, comparative. Indeed, some authors reject the idea that case studies of individual countries involve the use of the comparative method. So, Sartori (1994, p. 23) tells us bluntly that the case study: 'cannot be subsumed under the comparative *method* though it may have comparative *merit*' (authors italics). Yet this seems a pedantic position to adopt. What is more, if it *were* adopted, a great deal of work published in journals dealing with comparative politics would be discounted. In this vein, Sigelman and Gadbois (1983) found that 62 per cent of the 565 articles published in *Comparative Politics* and *Comparative Political Studies* between 1968 and 1981 were case studies of single countries. Surely, as Rose argues (1991, p. 449), it is 'the presence or absence of concepts applicable to a multiplicity of countries [which] is the test of whether a study can be considered comparative'.

Of course, not all case studies are of the same type. Arend Lijphart developed a typology of case studies, although he was very sceptical of their use (Lijphart, 1971, pp. 691–3). He distinguishes between: (i) interpretative case studies which utilise an existing theory to illuminate the case; (ii) hypothesis-generating case studies; (iii) case studies which are designed to interrogate or test a theory (he called them theory-infirming case studies); (iv) theory-confirming case studies; and (v) deviant case studies. In our view, this classification includes one type, type (i), which is definitely not comparative. The other four types may be comparative, but are not necessarily so. We would argue that individual case studies are comparative if they use and assess the utility of concepts developed elsewhere (by elsewhere here we mean in another country, or in relation to a different jurisdiction in the same country or in the same country, during a different time period); test some general theory or hypothesis; or generate concepts to be use elsewhere or hypotheses to be tested elsewhere (for a broader justification of the case study method see Lowi, 1964; Eckstein, 1975; and Rhodes, 1994).

There are a large number of examples of the use of the case study approach in such a comparative framework. The election studies undertaken by the Michigan group in the USA provide a particularly good example of both the strengths and weaknesses of this approach. On the plus side, their work provided both the methodological guidelines for election studies elsewhere and also a theory of electoral behaviour which has inspired and informed work in a variety of other countries (Campbell *et al.*, 1960; Budge *et al.*, 1976; Converse and Pierce, 1986). However, there are problems with this analysis. A number of authors have argued that the Michigan model of voter choice is ethnocentric and, particularly, that its key social psychological concept of party identification does not 'travel' beyond the USA. They point out that in other Western countries, social structure, rather than party identification is what matters. In this view, psychological attachment to a social group is more fundamental than party identification and the latter is largely the consequence of social structure (Shively, 1979). In response to these criticisms, Philip Converse and Roy Pierce's study (1986) of voter choice in France in the 1960s is a theory-confirming case study which argues that the logic of the Michigan model works even in the context of a country for which it is least likely to apply.

# Systematic comparisons of a limited number of cases

Much comparative study involves what Hague *et al.* (1992, pp. 39–40) call 'focused comparisons'. This approach utilises more cases; it offers less detail than a case study but its conclusions are more generalisable. In essence, we are faced with a trade-off between detail and generalisability, or some might claim between description and explanatory power (for a fuller discussion of this question, see Ragin, 1991).

There is a good deal of such research, although there are fewer articles of this type published than articles which report case studies; Sigelman and Gadbois (1983) noted 12 per cent of the articles published in the two key American journals were of this type. There are also clear patterns as regards which countries are included in such 'focused comparison'. In part, this is clearly linked to the interest in area studies; so there is significant comparison between European countries and a, lesser, concentration on comparison among Latin-American countries. Not surprisingly, given both that most political scientists are American and that the USA is the dominant world power, comparisons involving the USA are also common, (see Page, 1990, p. 448, table 5, for the countries focused on in British studies of comparative politics, and Sigelman and Gadbois, 1983, table 2, p. 287, for the US data).

One question dominates the literature dealing with this type of comparative analysis: should comparisons focus on countries that are similar, or ones that are different? This question is worth a brief discussion. The terms of the argument are fairly straightforward. Advocates of the 'most similar' approach argue that: 'a comparison between "relatively similar" countries sets out to neutralise certain differences in order to permit a better analysis of others' (Dogan and Pelassy, 1990, p. 133). Ideally, of course, a researcher would chose two countries which were the same in all respects except the one which s/he wished to study; however, this is clearly impossible, given that there are too few countries and too many variables, a problem to which we shall return later. Not surprisingly, this is the research design adopted by authors engaged in regional studies (for examples of this type of approach, see Dogan and Kazancigil, 1994, ch. 6). The key problem with this approach is sometimes called the problem of 'overdetermination'; in Collier's words (1993, p. 111) 'the design fails to eliminate many rival explanations, leaving the researcher with no criteria for choosing among them'.

In contrast, the most different approach involves comparing countries where there is a maximum degree of differences in relation to the factors which are the most significant given the researcher's theoretical concerns. The aim of this research design is to 'force analysts to distil out of this diversity a set of common elements that prove to have great explanatory power' (Collier, 1993, p. 112). A good example of this strategy is offered in Sidney Verba, Norman Nie and Jae-On Kim's study of participation and political equality (Verba *et al.*, 1978). This study tries to test the generalisability of explanations of variations in levels of individual political participation developed by the same authors in the USA (Verba and Nie, 1972) across seven countries: Austria, India, Japan, the Netherlands, Nigeria, the USA and Yugoslavia. Of course, for such an analysis to be valid, the countries have to share certain characteristics, especially universal formal political rights. However, at the same time, and more importantly, they differ dramatically in many other respects: levels of economic development; culture; religion; and history. If Nie and Verba's theory developed in the context of the contemporary USA works in the case of the other countries then the validity of the theory is greatly strengthened. But, as the authors point out, this is a risky as well as a potentially very powerful strategy. It works only if you find uniformity across nations (as the authors did), but 'if one finds no uniformity, the results become unintelligible' (Verba *et al.*, 1976, p. 25; for further examples of this approach see Dogan and Kazancigil, 1994, ch. 7).

In our view, both of these research designs have utility, and which is chosen will depend in large part on the problems the research is addressing. In addition, the two approaches can be combined on occasion. This is clear in Collier's description of his recent research (1993, p. 112):

> My own recent work combines the two strategies by starting with a set of eight Latin American countries that are roughly matched on a number of broad dimensions. Among the eight countries the analysis focuses on pairs of countries that are nonetheless markedly different. The overall matching assures that the contexts of analysis are analytically equivalent, at least to a significant degree, and the paired comparison places parallel processes of change in sharp relief because they are operating in settings that are very different in many respects.

# ☐ *Global statistical analysis*

The 1960s saw a major expansion of quantitative or statistical comparative research in which the unit of analysis was typically the nation state. Much of this research was data, or machine, driven. Its expansion depended upon both the growth of machine-readable data banks of socioeconomic and political data (Banks and Textor, 1963; Taylor and Jodice, 1983) and the development of computers which could be used to store and manipulate these data. A good example of the use of such quantitative techniques to analyse a very large number of nations are the studies of the relationship between economic development and democracy (see Diamond, 1992, pp. 450–99, for a good review of the literature).

The key problem is that such global data has significant drawbacks. Mattei Dogan sums up the choices involved (Dogan, 1994, p. 64):

> The problem of global analysis is that it achieves very wide expansion at the price of losing almost all the intensive meaning achieved by comparisons among a less diverse set of nations. If the data are inaccurate, the statistical techniques should not be too ambitious. If the data are reliable, a sophisticated methodological design is justified and recommended.

# ■ Problems with comparison

The key problem with comparative research is the key problem with social research more generally. It is impossible to produce a flawless research design; the trick is to acknowledge, and cope with, as many of the problems as possible. We shall deal with four problems here, the first two of which we have already raised and for this reason they receive limited attention.

## □ *How many cases?*

As we have seen, researchers need to be careful in choosing how many cases they examine, trading off detail against generalisability, and they should also combine different types of comparative research wherever possible.

## □ *Too many variables, too few countries*

As has already been emphasised, it is rare, if not impossible, to find a country which is similar to another on all except one variable, so the types of tightly-controlled experiment that characterise the natural sciences are very unlikely (see Collier, 1993, pp. 113–14, for a discussion of the limited number of attempts to use the experimental method in comparative politics). The number of countries in the world, in a legal sense at least, is finite at any given time. As such, there is a limit to the number of cases the researcher can use; a limit that is tighter because for many countries the quality of data available is inadequate to enable any useful comparative analysis. Nevertheless, there are plausible responses to this problem. In essence, researchers attempt to concentrate on fewer variables.

One way to proceed is to use a research design which identifies most similar cases in order to reduce the number of variables in a given study. Alternatively, some researchers reduce the number of variables by operating with a parsimonious model/theory. For this reason, there has been significant interest in the use of Rational Choice Theory among some, particularly American, students of comparative politics. There are examples of the use of this perspective to simplify the research design in studies which compare a considerable number of nations, for example Olson's analysis of the relationship between political structures and economic growth among developed countries (see Olson, 1982), and in the comparative case-study literature, for example the material which examines the growth of interest groups and new social movements (for a critical review of some of this literature see Marsh, 1994).

## ☐ Beyond bias

Hague *et al.* (1992, pp. 29–30) regard bias as one of the key problems of comparative research. By this they mean that the values of the researcher affect the results of the analysis. Only an extreme positivist would disagree with this position, but it seems to us that it misidentifies the issues raised. In our view it is better to talk of problems of measurement and problems of interpretation. So, for example, quantitative studies are only as good as the data they employ. The concepts underlying the data are sometimes unclear, and even when they are clear the data employed may not be of good quality. A relatively straightforward example of such difficulties involves the measurement of economic development; a crucial concern for those researchers interested in the question of the relationship between economic development and democratisation (see Diamond, 1992 and Lipset, 1994 for an overview). We are told by Hague *et al.* (1992, p. 46) that developing countries, with half of the world's population, produce only 18 per cent of the world's output. In contrast, the International Monetary Fund's (IMF) figures show that developing countries' share of the world's output to be a third (*Economist*, 15 May 1993, p. 95). The difference between these two estimates result from the use of different indicators of output. In estimating gross domestic products, the IMF (unlike Hague *et al.*, 1992) uses purchasing power parities, which take into account differences in prices between countries. Moreover, even the IMF estimate may undervalue production in Third World countries where, unlike in the richer countries, much economic activity, especially in agriculture, is not traded commercially at all.

Even if agreement can be reached on concepts, problems of data quality remain. All countries have a 'black economy', which is not measured in official statistics because citizens conceal economic activity from the government to avoid taxes and the regulation of business. This part of the economy is obviously impossible to measure accurately, but its size clearly varies greatly between countries. Taking the black economy into account, Italy's gross national product (GNP) is greater than Britain's. However, according to the official statistics the reverse is the case. Despite all these problems, GNP is still widely used in comparative research (Dogan, 1994, p. 46).

Non-economic indicators can also be problematic. Vanhanen's (1990) quantitative study of democratisation in 147 countries uses an index of democratisation based on two indicators: *electoral competition*, defined as the combined share of the vote for the smaller parties; and *participation*, defined as the percentage of the population that voted in national elections. Vanhanen finds that throughout the 1980s the top-ranking country on this index was Italy. Unfortunately, this discovery sits poorly with survey evidence which shows that Italians are much more sceptical of the quality of their democracy than the citizens of any other EU country (*Eurobarometer*, 1993, pp. 19-36). It is also at odds with the massive rejection of the regime in the 1994 Italian election (Brand and Mackie, forthcoming).

## ☐ *Same phenomena, different meanings*

The most fundamental, and intractable, problem with comparative research relates, more broadly, to the epistemological underpinnings of social science research generally. Traditionally, most comparative politics research implicitly operated within a positivist position, which emphasised that through systematic observation, and the generation and testing of hypotheses, it was possible to establish relationships between variables that were consistent and generalisable across time and space (for an outline of the basic epistemological positions see the Introduction to this volume). This was particularly true of quantitative research based on a large number of cases, given that that approach was strongly associated with the behaviourist position, which itself was inherently positivistic. However, the positivist position has been questioned increasingly in social science by researchers operating with a relativist position who have argued that the world is socially constructed, that political phenomena, and consequently the relationships between them, do not exist independently of the way in which they are socially constructed. So, for example, a relativist would argue that a concept like democracy is not given; it does not exist independently of the way it is experienced, or of the meaning that individuals and groups attach to it. Similarly, economic growth is a social construct, having different meanings in different societies. As such, macro quantitative, studies which analyse the relationship between democracy and growth are of very limited utility because they impose an objective 'reality' on a diverse, socially constructed, world.

Obviously, we cannot resolve these basic epistemological problems here. However, they must be recognised. Crass positivism is untenable and any comparativist must recognise that the meanings and understanding of concepts is affected by the cultural context of both the researcher and the country being studied (see Collier, 1993, p. 113).

# ■ Changes in comparative politics

Comparative politics has changed significantly in recent years, for three main reasons: first, there has been a rapid increase in the scale of the endeavour, which is reflected in its wider scope (see Page, 1990, p. 440); second, students of comparative politics have responded to the changing concerns of the profession more generally; and third, the sub-discipline has adapted in the light of the criticisms associated with the problems specified above.

More specifically, we identify four developments in comparative politics since the 1950s: greater rigour in research design; a move from comparison of institutions through comparison of processes to comparison of policies; the decline in quantitative studies; and a response to the challenges of globalisation.

## □ *Greater rigour in research design*

Lee Sigelman and George Gadbois make the point very well (1983, p. 300):

> If we were now given a dozen articles and told only that six of them had been written during the 1950s and the other six during the 1970s, we dare say that we could correctly classify all twelve, or come very close to it. The studies of the more recent vintage would be more theoretically and conceptually attuned, more sophisticated in terms of their approach to data collection and analysis, and more likely to incorporate explicit comparative elements into their design.

## □ *From institutions to political processes to public policy*

In the first half of the twentieth century, comparative studies focused typically on the institutions of the state. Many of them had a strong legalistic bias (Eckstein, 1963, pp. 3–32). In the 1960s, partly as a result of the behavioural revolution, attention shifted from formal institutions to political processes (see Hague *et al.*, 1992, pp. 31–7; and Page, 1991, p. 441); although, of course, there are still a significant number of comparative institutional studies.

In the 1950s and 1960s the most influential paradigm was functionalism. Functionalists, such as Almond and Powell (1960), argued that all political systems performed key political functions designed to reproduce the society; the emphasis was upon the reproduction of processes and the stability of the social and political system. Functionalists rejected the study of formal institutions in favour of what they argued were universal political processes carried on by different institutions in different political systems. By the late 1960s functionalism was in retreat in social science generally, both because of its inherent conservatism, given its emphasis on reproduction and stability, and because of its positivism, it was increasingly argued that it was culturally specific, using concepts in one setting which were inappropriate in others, and failing to appreciate the social construction of 'reality'.

The demise of functionalism as a dominant paradigm in comparative analysis has not meant the end of the interest in comparing political processes or political behaviour, although authors have become more sensitive to the ways in which similar processes and behaviour can have different meanings in different cultural settings. However, the growing area of comparative research since the early 1980s has been the study of comparative public policy. This interest reflects partly the growing focus on public policy research in the discipline generally. In turn, this focus on policy owes something to the significant policy changes (the spread of privatisation, the questioning of social democratic policies and so on) that have occurred since the 1970s in those countries which interest many comparativists (Britain, the former West Germany, France and the USA). In addition, the process of globalisation, which we shall discuss below, has also stimulated an interest in comparative policy, given that developed states at least were faced increasingly with similar constraints and opportunities, to which they often responded with similar policy 'solutions'.

The move from the focus on institutions, through the concentration on political processes and political behaviour, to the interest in comparative public policy, is well reflected in the figures of both Sigelman and Gadbois, and Page. Sigelman and Gadbois' survey of articles on comparative politics published in the two key American journals appeared in 1983. They showed that just under 10 per cent of the articles dealt with institutions, while about 33 per cent dealt with political processes and behaviour (we have recalculated the figures from table 3, p. 293, excluding political parties from either category given that articles on this subject could deal with their institutional or behavioural aspects; 10 per cent of the articles dealt with parties). Sigelman and Gadbois only identified 7.5 per cent of the work as examining public policy. In contrast, Page's analysis of work published by British political scientists in books and three journals (*British Journal of Political Science, Political Studies* and the *European Journal of Political Research*) appeared in 1990 and is probably a better reflection of current trends; although, as behaviourism was always a stronger influence in the USA it may be that there will still be more focus on processes and behaviour among American scholars. Page's analysis shows that, as far as books are concerned at least, there is a roughly equal representation of the three types of work (all figures recalculated from Page, 1990, table 6, p. 449): institutional analysis (31 per cent), political behaviour (32 per cent) and public policy (30 per cent). When articles are considered, and there are far fewer of these, the figure are: institutional analysis (25 per cent), political behaviour (46 per cent) and public policy (29 per cent).

## □ *The decline of 'over-quantitative' studies*

In the 1960s there was a move towards large-scale, global, quantitative analysis, although, as Page points out, there was never much enthusiasm, or sufficient resources, for such methods in Britain (see Page, 1990, pp. 446–7 esp. table 3). However, as Collier (1993, p. 111) emphasises: 'Quantitative cross-national research in the sub-field of comparative politics . . . have not come to occupy as dominant a position as many people expected.' This reaction results from a number of clear problems that emerged with such large scale statistical analysis. First, many researchers felt increasingly that the cost of such research was high and, particularly given the growing constraints on resources for academic research, the returns were poor. Second, as we saw earlier, researchers began to recognise that such global comparison involved 'concept stretching' (see Sartori, 1984), which meant that there were major problems concerning the validity of the data and, thus also of the results. Third, the relative success of comparative historical study, based upon structured comparison between a small number of cases, has directed attention away from global studies (see, for example, Barrington Moore, 1966; Skocpol 1979; Collier and Collier, 1991; and, most heroically, Mann, 1986 and 1993; for a critique of this approach, see Goldthorpe, 1991; for a debate on its strengths and weaknesses, see Hill and Rock, 1994).

None of this means that global studies have no place in comparative analysis. However, it is clear that they have to be used with care; the researcher must acknowledge, and attempt to overcome, the problems of concept stretching and interpretation. It is also worth pointing out, following Collier (1993, p. 111), that the advent of new, more sophisticated, statistical techniques may 'breathe new life into this approach'. However, statistical sophistication is no substitute for a better research design, nor does it solve many of, let alone all, the problems of interpretation.

# □ *The challenges of globalisation*

As Hague *et al.* argue (1992, pp. 28–9), there is an increasing need to think globally as well as comparatively, given that it is difficult to treat countries as though they were truly independent of one another. Certainly, the economic, strategic and cultural aspects of globalisation, which are discussed at more length in the Conclusion below, are important constraints on the autonomy of states. In addition, there is also a political dimension to globalisation, given the growing importance of supranational political organisations. This is particularly important in European comparisons because of the increasing significance of the EU. For example, no comparative study of industrial policy-making in two or more European countries could fail to examine both the way in which the EU affects industrial policy-making in each country or the way in which each country affects EU policy.

These processes of globalisation present problems, challenges and opportunities for political scientists generally, and comparative politics specifically. At one and the same time it makes comparative analysis more difficult and more necessary. In such a world, comparative analysis is more difficult because it means researchers need to broaden their concerns in order to understand more about the common global problems that all countries face; albeit to different extents and in different ways. They must also appreciate that any explanation of political processes and outcomes inevitably needs to acknowledge the articulation between economic, political and ideological/cultural factors. Gone are the days when political scientists could insulate the study of politics from broader social and economic processes.

At the same time, globalisation emphasises the necessity of comparative analysis. We need to analyse in what way, and to what extent, the globalisation processes affect political institutions, behaviour and policy in particular states; this is merely to re-emphasise, and to an extent recast, what Gourevitch (1978) called the 'international sources of domestic politics'. At the same time, we must study the way in which individual states contribute to the processes of globalisation.

One example of how aspects of globalisation have influenced the concerns of comparativists can be found in the growing literature on the process of policy transfer or lesson-drawing. As Rose emphasises (1991, p. 3):

every country has problems, and each thinks that its problems are unique . . .
However, problems that are unique to one country . . . are abnormal . . .
confronted with a common problem, policy makers in cities, regional
governments and nations can learn from how their counterparts elsewhere
responded.

Policy transfer, emulation and lesson-drawing all refer to a process in
which knowledge about policies, administrative arrangements, institutions
and so on at one time and/or place is used in the development of policies,
administrative arrangements and institutions at another time and/or place
(see Dolowitz and Marsh, 1995). A focus on policy transfer is only one
minor way forward for comparative analysis, but whichever way
researchers choose they must acknowledge the importance of globalisation.

# ■ Conclusion

The comparative method is an essential tool of political research. Given
the virtual impossibility of using a tightly-controlled experimental design
to study the relationship between political phenomena, then a comparative
design is often the best alternative. As we have seen, there are problems in
using the method, but many, if not most, of them are problems associated
with all social research. For example, any social researcher has to
acknowledge, and face up to, basic epistemological problems. Comparativists, like other social scientists, need to appreciate that reality is, in an
important sense, socially constructed.

It seems to us that comparative analysis is developing all the time. Gone
is the over-emphasis on institutions and the later flirtation with
methodologically sophisticated, but epistemological naive, quantitative
global studies. There is now more research using sounder research designs
and acknowledging the strengths and weaknesses of different types of
comparison. The cross-fertilisation of ideas this involves is important if
comparative analysis is to flourish, and it is very important it does flourish
in an increasingly interrelated, 'globalised' world.

# ■ Further reading

Collier and Collier; edited book (1991) provides a useful overview of recent
developments in comparative politics while Collier (1993) is the most sophisticated
recent account.

Ragin (1987) discusses the differences between a case-oriented and a variable-
oriented approach and argues that small-N case studies are a valuable research
strategy.

Diamond (1992), an exhaustive review of the quantitative/statistical literature on the socioeconomic correlates of democracy. A good example of the strengths and limitations of this school of comparative politics.

Two classic works are Lijphart (1968) which was the starting point for the development of Lijphart's 'consociational' model of democracy, and Verba *et al.* (1978) whose comparison of participation and political equality in seven countries providing a 'most different' approach to comparative analysis.

# ■ *Chapter 10* ■

# Structure and Agency
## Colin Hay

Every time we construct, however tentatively, a notion of social, political or economic causality we appeal, whether explicitly or (more likely) implicitly, to ideas about structure and agency. The way our explanations are formulated reflects a deeper set of understandings about the (relative) autonomy of actors or agents in the settings in which they find themselves. What model of the nature of political actors are we creating in our explanations? Are these actors the unwitting products of their context, helpless individuals with minimal control over their destiny, floundering around in a maelstrom of turbulent currents; or are they knowledgeable and intentional subjects with complete control over the settings which frame their actions? Are the effects we wish to explain the products of actors displaying their agency, making unconstrained choices; or are these effects the products of the unfolding logic of a structure (or set of structures) over which agents (individual or collective) have no control?

We can ask these questions of every political situation we are interested in explaining and we will no doubt come to different answers depending upon the specific nature of each action setting. None the less, our answers to these questions are highly significant. Clearly, it makes a difference whether we explain the electoral success of the Conservatives in the British General Election of 1992 as a consequence of John Major's charisma, personality and leadership (an agency-orientated account, however unlikely); or as nothing to do with John Major or even the Conservative Party at all, but rather as a product of the influence of a biased media in constructing perceptions of the incompetence and unreliability of the Labour Party (a more structural account, perhaps equally inadequate).

In this chapter I hope to demonstrate that structure and agency logically entail one another – a social or political structure only exists by virtue of the constraints on, or opportunities for, agency that it effects. Thus, it makes no sense to conceive of structure without at least hypothetically positing some notion of agency which might be effected (constrained or enabled). If, for instance, we are interested in the structures imposed by the surface and atmosphere of Mars, we necessarily do so by considering the potential constraints placed upon human agents hypothetically deposited on to this alien landscape – Is there an atmosphere? If so, is it breathable? Can we walk on the surface? How difficult will it be to extract valuable minerals from the planet's rocks? and so on.

Furthermore, I wish to argue that within every social or political context (however mundane) we witness a variety of accomplished, complex and sophisticated displays of agency. As we shall see, such displays are generally the product of intentional action informed by some 'knowledge' (however intuitive and however misinformed) of the structures that define the setting for that action. Such knowledgeability is a condition of effective action (action likely to achieve intended outcomes – whether explicitly acknowledged or not). When orientated to a specific task, intention or motivation yields *strategy*. At its most straightforward, strategy involves the selection of objectives and the search for the most appropriate means to achieve those objectives within a particular context at a particular moment in time. Here it is important to emphasise that appropriate strategies change with time. Agency, then, is the product of *strategy* and *intention*. The ability to formulate strategy (whether explicitly, or more probably, intuitively) is the condition of all action (this is summarised in Figure 10.1).

**Figure 10.1**   *Intention, strategy and action*

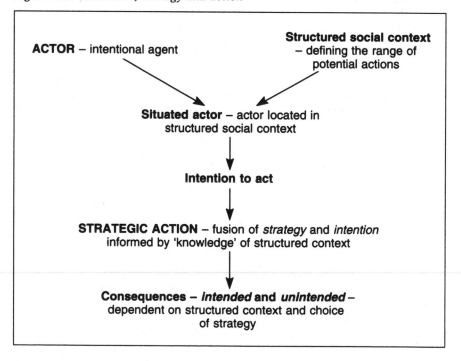

**Figure 10.2** *Interrogating conceptions of structure and agency in political explanation*

- Who is the agent in our explanation?
- Is our agent individual or collective?
- If collective, how is this collectivity sedimented and/or mobilised?
- If there is no agent, how do the effects we describe appear?
- Have we contextualised our agent within the broader structural and strategic context?
- How relevant is this context in accounting for the consequences (both intended and unintended) of the actions that we have identified?
- Have we considered adequately the extent to which this relevant context constrains and/or enables our agent?

Conceptions of structure and agency are implicit in *every* explanation and attribution of causality to social and/or political actors. As a consequence, we can benefit greatly from seeking to render explicit the conceptions of structure and agency that we necessarily appeal to, and by asking ourselves a series of related questions, thereby interrogating the notions of causality we formulate (see Figure 10.2).

Furthermore, ideas of structure and agency are central to any notion of *power*. This would not come as any great surprise to students of French, since the verb *pouvoir* meaning 'to be able' also doubles as the noun *pouvoir*, meaning 'power'. Indeed, if we probe a little deeper in to the English language, a similar link may be found. Etymologically, 'power' is derived from the Old French verb *poeir* and ultimately the Latin *posse* meaning 'to be able'. Similarly, an 'agent', as defined in the *Penguin English Dictionary*, is 'one who acts, or *exerts power* to bring something about' (emphasis added) and in the *Oxford English Dictionary* as 'a person . . . that *exerts power* or *produces an effect*' (emphasis added). Hence, power is fundamentally bound up with the idea of the victory of the *agent* or *subject* over its other – *structure* or *object*. Power is a question of agency, of influencing or 'having an effect' upon the structures which set contexts and define the range of possibilities of others. This suggests the need for a *relational* conception of both structure and agency: one person's agency is another person's structure. Attributing agency is therefore attributing power (both causal and actual). The actions of ministers and governments produce the structures that constrain junior civil servants and state functionaries, the effects of whose actions similarly constrain the rest of us.

This lies at the heart of the fundamental distinction between the natural sciences on the one hand and the social sciences on the other. The difference lies in the fact that the social and political sciences must deal with active and intentional agents, however constrained. The natural sciences, by contrast, are concerned with the elucidation of trans-historical structures and what might be termed *metastructures* – the structures and laws that govern the evolution of dynamic systems such as the geological plates which make up the earth's surface. Within the natural sciences the only approximation to the concept of agency in social science is 'that not yet accounted for' – that is, the effects of as yet unexplained structures. These differences are usefully summarised by Bhaskar (1979) and define the limits to the possibility of developing a social scientific *naturalism* (in which the methods of the natural sciences might be applied to social science):

1. Social structures, unlike natural structures, do not exist independently of the activities they govern;
2. Social structures do not exist independently of the agents' conceptions of what they are doing in their activity; and
3. Social structures may be only relatively enduring.

# ◼ Positions in the structure–agency debate

Since notions of structure and agency are so thoroughly bound up with questions of power, causality and political explanation, the question of structure and agency lies at the heart of the philosophy of the social and political sciences and, as a consequence, has attracted a lot of close attention. The ways in which political scientists deal with such issues reflect their underlying philosophical assumptions about:

(i) The nature of the social and political world and of 'social being' in particular. Such a theory or philosophy of social being is referred to as an ontology; and
(ii) The nature of what constitutes an adequate and valid explanation of a political event, effect or process – a theory of knowledge or epistemology.

So different positions with respect to structure and agency reflect different epistemologies and ontologies. These epistemological and ontological concerns in turn influence the very process or methodology of political enquiry. We can usefully distinguish between different approaches on the basis of their answers to the following questions:

● To what extent are individuals' actions the product of socialisation and hence structures over which they have minimal control, to what extent are they the product of rational choice or intention on the part of autonomous subjects? (Ontological)

- To what extent is the autonomy of actors constrained by the structures these actors 'bear' – their positions within a patriarchal and racist society; their position with respect the relations of production, and so on – and the contexts in which they find themselves? (ontological)
- How should we seek to explain a particular political effect – as the consequence of the intentions and actions of the immediate actors involved, or in terms of the logic or structure of the broader relations of which these actors form a part? What constitutes an adequate explanation? (Epistemological)

If we do this a number of distinct positions emerge, among which the following have proved the most influential: (a) structuralism; (b) intentionalism; (c) structuration theory; and (d) critical realism.

**Figure 10.3**   *Positions in the structure–agency debate*

|  | 'Insider' account (agency-centred) | 'Outsider' account (structure-centred) |
| --- | --- | --- |
| Simple view of structure–agency | Intentionalism | Structuralism |
| Dialectical view of structure–agency | Structuration theory | Critical realism – strategic-relational approach |

## ☐ *Structuralism*

Structuralism, and its alter ego, functionalism, are now little more than terms of abuse within social and political theory. Very few, if any, contemporary theorists would volunteer the label 'structuralist' to categorise their own work, and even fewer would wish to be described as functionalist. None the less, the structuralist position was at one time highly influential and still represents a crucial point of departure for many current approaches to the perpetual problem of structure and agency. Basically, a structuralist viewpoint privileges structure within the structure-agency relationship, seeking to account for observable social and political events, processes and outcomes in terms of the operation of *unobservable* social and political structures of which actors are merely bearers (*Träger*). Structuralist modes of thought are examples of what

Wendt (1991) terms 'outsider' accounts which operate at some distance from actual human agents, preferring instead to contextualise actors within the structures that are understood to constrain them and that generally lie outside their immediate perceptions. Structuralism operates with what might be labelled a 'simple' or monocausal view of the relationship between structure and agency in which structure is largely seen to *constrain* and even *determine* agency (see Figure 10.3). Within structuralist accounts, explanations are not sought in terms of the motivations, intentions, strategies and actions of agents, since these are seen as mere artefacts of ultimately determinant structures. Notions of causality must, instead, arise out of a consideration of the complex interplay or 'overdetermination' of structures and systems which have their own 'relative autonomy' (Althusser, 1969; Poulantzas, 1973).

Structuralism is associated closely with *determinism*, *functionalism* and all forms of *teleologism* (the view that social and political processes, particularly processes of change, can be accounted for in terms of an historical end-state to which they are believed to evolve inexorably). Thus, for instance, many versions of the Marxist philosophy of historical materialism are seen as forms of economic determinism in which all aspects of social and political life are explained in terms of the economic relations which underlie them, and in which the evolution of structures as diverse as the state and the family are seen to be driven by the incessant unfolding of economic relations towards an historical end point – Communism.

Within functionalist modes of thought, specific social and political outcomes are explained, not in terms of the motivations and intentions of the actors involved, but in terms of the consequences of their effects. Thus, from such a perspective, the emergence of more consensual forms of capitalism related to the extension of the franchise, the creation of the welfare state, and the more general expansion in the ideological apparatuses and resources wielded by the state might be accounted for in terms of the state's 'function' of securing the conditions for the continued accumulation of capital. The problem with such modes of explanation is that the *mechanisms* whereby these effects are secured are never elucidated. Thus functionalism often becomes in fact a surrogate for explanation, a form of pseudo-explanation. This has the effect of diverting attention from the full complexity of processes, such as the evolution of state structures, which in fact have to be accounted for in terms of the dialectical interplay of structure, strategy and struggle.

Structuralism has over the years been exposed to a number of devastating critiques:

1. It underestimates systematically, and at times ignores completely, the activity of individuals, explaining away their real autonomy and denying that they have an effect or make a difference.

2. Thus structuralism paints a picture of the social and political world in which we are all mere automata, passive dupes of structures beyond our comprehension and over which we can exert no influence. As a consequence, it is incapable of distinguishing between Fascist author-itarianism on the one hand and liberal democracy on the other – each is considered to be equally 'bad'. Such an undifferentiated view of political systems is not of much practical use and certainly does not provide the basis for informing political intervention (which presum-ably makes no difference in any case).

3. Relatedly, the deterministic and teleological view of social and political development which structuralism supports is accused of encouraging fatalism and passivity (often against its own best intentions). For, if the course of human history is ultimately (pre)-determined and leading inexorably towards some end-point, then all we can do is sit back and wait for the inevitable unfolding of history's inherent logic.

4. Finally, there is a fundamental contradiction within structuralist modes of explanation. Put simply, if structuralist thought is indeed correct, and we are all merely passive dupes of the structures we bear, could the structuralist position ever be expressed? How is it that structuralist scholars from their ivory towers could step outside the structures which inevitably constrain and construct the rest of us, in order to describe them? Structuralism thus appears to rely on an extremely patronising and condescending distinction between the 'enlightened' theorist and the masses, which is logically unsustainable.

# ☐ *Intentionalism*

Structuralism's 'other' is intentionalism. If structuralism is an 'outsider' account, then intentionalism is an 'insider' account that focuses on social practices, human agency and the rich texture of social and political interaction. Intentionalism too works with a 'simple' or monocausal view of the relationship between structure and agency, conceiving of structures (where such a notion is appealed to) as the product of intentional action. The concepts of constraint and context are largely absent from such accounts, which tend to take issues of social and political interaction largely at face value, constructing explanations out of the direct intentions, motivations and self-understandings of the actors involved and using explanatory concepts which lay actors might themselves use to account for their actions.

Intentionalism is closely associated with the notions of *indeterminacy, contingency, voluntarism*, and, above all, *methodological individualism* (the view that in formulating social and political explanations we should start and finish with the individual). Thus intentionalists tend to reject deterministic explanations which seek to account for specific events and outcomes in terms of theoretical abstractions that are imported by the theorist (like the capital-labour relation), in favour of explanations couched in terms of the directly observable events themselves. Thus links between specific contexts or settings of interaction tend not to be drawn, since explanations are sought which reflect the uniqueness and 'richness' of social and political interaction in a given setting. The focus is largely upon the *micro-practices* of social interaction as opposed to the *macro-embeddedness* of action within broader social and political structures. In contrast to notions of determinacy, intentionalist accounts tend to stress the contingent nature of social and political processes – that is, the idea that outcomes cannot be predicted in advance and are, by contrast, the product of specific intentional acts whose effects we might scrutinise but whose existence is largely the product of chance and intention neither of which is subject to social and political investigation.

In emphasising the contingent nature of social and political effects, intentionalists are often accused of *voluntarism* – the view that in order to understand political outcomes we must merely consider the motivation and intentions of actors as if there was some one-to-one correlation between the intent and the effect of action. If structuralist accounts tilt the stick too far towards the pole of structure, where everything can be accounted for without recourse to a notion of agency, then intentionalism is guilty of the converse, failing to consider the structural constraints on the realisation of actors' intentionality.

Whereas structuralism has now been relegated to a mere term of abuse, intentionalism lives on, most notably in the work of the rational choice theorists, public choice theorists, analytical Marxists, pluralists and journalists (Downs, 1957, 1967; Elster, 1979, 1982, 1983, 1989a, 1989b, 1993; McLean, 1987; Roemer, 1987; Przeworski, 1985; Sen, 1977; see also Dunleavy, 1991). These theorists focus on individuals as selfish and independent utility maximisers, as rational strategic calculators and as intentional actors (Dunleavy, 1991, pp. 2–7; Kontopoulos, 1993, pp. 89–90). The individualist emphasis of rational choice theory is reflected in Elster's recent description of his own work as 'political psychology' (Elster, 1993) and it has been widely and variously criticised. These critiques (see ch. 4) have stressed the 'illogical' nature of much human behaviour; the importance of the *unintended* consequences of action (whether rational or irrational); the partial and often misleading information individuals use to inform their strategic calculations; and the need for a *relational* conception of rationality – no 'pure' rational action exists outside of, and unaffected by, the situational context and social structures in which it is embedded – hence, an understanding of context is in fact a condition of any notion of rationality (Boudon, 1981; Dunleavy, 1991; Kontopoulos, 1993).

# ☐ *Structuration theory*

Probably the single most influential recent contribution to the question of structure and agency within social and political theory is Anthony Giddens' theory of *structuration*. This is an ambitious theoretical attempt to transcend the *dualism of structure and agency* (the rigid separation of structure and agency such that they are seen as independent and analytically separable aspects of the social world and not as internally related or mutually constitutive of one another). Giddens prefers the idea of a *duality*, in which structure and agency are seen as two sides of the same coin, to that of a *dualism* in which structure and agency are externally related – two separate coins which periodically knock against one another. His theory of structuration is motivated by a recognition of, and frustration with, the rigid demarcation of accounts of structure and agency into the two closed and hostile camps of structuralism and intentionalism.

Giddens' aim has been to develop a hybrid theory capable of reconciling, on the one hand, a focus on the structures which are the very condition of social and political interaction, with, on the other hand, a sensitivity to the intentionality, reflexivity, autonomy and agency of actors. This he has attempted to achieve through the development of a *dialectical* under-standing of the relationship between structure and agency, reflected in his two central concepts – *structuration*, and *the duality of structure* (Giddens, 1976, 1979, 1981, 1984). With the notion of *structuration*, Giddens introduces the idea of the mutual dependency, and internal relatedness, of social structure and human agency. Within this framework, the production and reproduction of society is seen as a skilled accomplishment on the part of social actors. Thus social processes and practices are 'brought about by the active constitutive skills of . . . [society's] members . . . as historically located actors, and not under conditions of the their own choosing' (Giddens, 1976, p. 157). This leads Giddens towards the recognition of the *duality of structure*, by which he means that 'social structures are both constituted by human agency, and yet at the same time are the very medium of this constitution' (ibid., p. 121; see also, Sztompka, 1993, pp. 200–1).

Given Giddens' claim finally to have transcended the artificial dualism of structure and agency, it is hardly surprising that structuration theory has proved to be so influential, informing a multitude of theoretical elaborations and applications in areas as diverse as political sociology (Stones, 1991), political theory (Cerny, 1989), international relations (Wendt, 1987; Dessler, 1989), social and political geography (Gregory, 1990; Storper, 1985) and feminist theory (Wharton, 1991). Giddens' central achievement has been to place the question of structure and agency back at the core of social science. His theory of structuration challenges us to render explicit the often implicit conceptions of structure and agency that necessarily inform our theoretical reflections and empirical investigations. In so doing, Giddens has begun to take us beyond the rather fatuous and factionalist struggles between the 'two hostile camps' of structuralism and intentionalism. His demonstration that structure and agency are internally related in social practices clearly represents a significant theoretical development.

None the less, structuration theory is not without its problems. On closer scrutiny it can be seen that the overturning of the dualism of structure and agency is achieved more by theoretical sleight of hand and definitional fiat than by analytical rigour. For, if we consider Giddens' idiosyncratic definition of structure as the 'rules and resources' implemented in interaction, and his comment that 'agency refers not to the intentions people have in doing things but to their *capability* of doing things in the first place' (Giddens, 1984, p. 9, emphasis added), then it is apparent that the dualism has effectively been transcended by *redefining* the terms which comprise it. As Layder observes perceptively, 'in Giddens' theory, structure does not mean anything like the same thing as it does in conventional approaches' (Layder, 1994, p. 138). No dualism, in fact, ever existed between the concepts Giddens deploys. The pre-existing dualism between structure and agency (as conventionally defined) is in fact merely displaced. Indeed, if we search for the notion of structure more familiar within social and political theory then we discover it lurking in Giddens' largely undeveloped concept of 'system'. As Outhwaite notes, to redefine structure in this way 'is to push onto the concept of social system much of what has been meant by "structure" in other social theories' (Outhwaite, 1990, p. 67). The former dualism between structure and agency may have been defined away, but its form lives on in the new, and largely unrecognised, dualism between *system* and *agency*. The redefinition of structure is thus exposed as a condition of Giddens' claim to transcend the dualism of structure and agency (see Bauman, 1989, pp. 42–6; Thompson 1989, pp. 62–6).

Sadly, the notion of system does not feature prominently in structuration theory and as a consequence Giddens is led towards an 'insider account' of structure (system) and agency. His substantive work certainly reflects the rich texture of social (inter-)action (Giddens, 1991, 1992), but this is achieved by detaching the micro-practices of everyday life from their broader social and political context. Giddens thus develops a form of sophisticated intentionalism.

Ironically, where Giddens does consider the properties of social systems he does so by temporarily 'bracketing-off' (Giddens, 1984, pp. 289 ff.) the dimension of agency and intentionality, thereby mirroring the structuralism of which he is so critical (Giddens, 1985, 1990). Similarly, where he considers social interactions and micro-practices, he does so by 'bracketing-off' institutional analysis (Giddens, 1991, 1992). The theoretically unresolved dualism between system and agency thus returns to haunt Giddens' substantive sociology of modernity, resulting in a dualism of macro-institutions and micro-practices. This has led Nigel Thrift to describe structuration theory as all micro-situations and world-empires with nothing much in between (Thrift, 1985; Stones, 1991).

None the less, Giddens' achievement should not be underestimated. Though his own attempt to formulate a sophisticated view of the internal relatedness of structure and agency is not altogether satisfactory, his recognition of the central importance of questions of structure and agency, and the need to transcend the dualism between these terms, represents a fundamental theoretical development.

## □ Critical realism

A further attempt to overcome the dualism of structure and agency, based on a dialectical understanding of the relationship between the two, is found in the work of the critical realist, Roy Bhaskar (Bhaskar, 1975, 1979, 1986; Outhwaite, 1987; Sayer, 1992) and in the closely related *strategic-relational approach* developed by Bob Jessop (Jessop, 1990). Despite the obvious similarities with structuration theory, critical realists approach the dualism of structure and agency from a more structuralist starting point, positing the existence of layers of structure which condition agency and which define the range of potential strategies that might be deployed by agents (whether individual or collective) in attempting to realise their intentions. In this sense critical realism is an 'outsider', or structure-centred account of the relationship between structure and agency. None the less, this view of the dialectic of structure and agency is not unlike that of Giddens. Indeed, Bhaskar comes close to the notion of the *duality of structure* when he suggests that 'society is both the ever-present *condition* (material cause) and the continually reproduced *outcome* of human agency' (Bhaskar, 1979, p. 43; original emphasis).

Similarly, Jessop, in an application of his strategic-relational approach, argues that 'the form of the state is the crystallisation of past strategies as well as privileging some other current strategies. As a strategic terrain the state is located within a complex *dialectic of structures and strategies*' (Jessop, 1990, p. 129; emphasis added). This introduces the important notion that systems, and the structures that comprise them, are *strategically selective*. The structures and *modus operandi* of the state, for example, 'are more open to some types of political strategy than others' (Jessop, 1990, p. 260). Systems, to adopt a sporting analogy, are not level playing fields – their complex, sloping contours favour certain strategies and actors over others. It is critical realism's self-appointed task to elucidate and map out the contours of social and political structure as a critical guide to political strategy and intervention.

In developing this dialectical understanding of the internal relationship between structure and agency, critical realists have retained the orthodox usage of the terms 'structure' and 'agency'. In so doing, they have developed a somewhat different conception of the dialectic from that of Giddens. Thus, whereas Giddens sees structure and agency as opposite sides of the same coin which can only be viewed one at a time (we cannot view both sides of a coin simultaneously), critical realists prefer to see structure and agency as the two metals in the alloy from which the coin is moulded. Hence, structure and agency, though *theoretically* separable are in practice completely interwoven (we cannot see either metal in the alloy by looking at the coin, but we can see the product of their fusion). The properties of the coin (society) derive not merely from the sum of its component metals (structure and agency), but also from their complex chemical interaction.

The premises of a critical realist or strategic-relational ontology can be summarised as follows:

1. All human agency occurs and acquires meaning only in relation to already preconstituted, and deeply structured, settings.
2. Such settings simultaneously constrain and enable the actors (whether individual or collective) that inhabit them by determining the *range* of potential appropriations and the direct consequences of such actions.
3. What constitutes a structure is entirely dependent upon our vantage point. For instance, the action of others (a crowd for example) represents a structure from the perspective (vantage point) of an individual who is not part of that collectivity. This is an inherently *relational* conception of structure.
4. Structures, do not determine outcomes *directly*, but merely define the potential range of options and strategies. Since actors only have a partial knowledge of such structures they only have partial access to this hypothetical range of strategies.
5. Action settings can be conceived of in terms of a nested hierarchy of levels of structure that interact in complex ways to condition and set the context within which agency is displayed.
6. The nature of the constraints (and range of opportunities) imposed on action by structured settings are twofold: (i) *Physical:* referring to the spatial and temporal properties of the (potential) action setting; and (ii) *Social:* (here the notion 'social' is employed in its widest possible sense) − referring to the products of the intended and unintended consequences of previous human action or inaction on a structured context.
7. These constraints may also be seen as *resources*. Constraint also implies opportunity.
8. Strategic action is the dialectical interplay of intentional and knowledgeable, yet structurally-embedded actors and the preconstituted

(structured) contexts they inhabit. Actions occur within structured settings, yet actors have the potential (at least partially) to transform those structures through their actions. This impact of agents upon structures may be either deliberate or unintended.

The critical realist framework, like Giddens' theory of structuration, stresses the importance of the *consequences* (both intended and unintended) of agency, and the impact and effects of strategic action upon the structured contexts in which that action must be situated. In this respect, both theories represent a considerable advance on their structuralist and intentionalist predecessors. They are equally capable of dealing with Heraclitus's truism that we cannot walk into the same river twice – too much water has flowed in the meantime (Ollman, 1993, pp. 28–9). Indeed, they both pose the question of the influence of agents and intentionality upon such flows. Within the critical realist framework this is approached through the notion of strategy. Actors appropriate a structured context which is *strategically selective* (favouring certain strategies over others) by way of strategy. This is formulated on the basis of a partial knowledge of the structures within which they find themselves and the anticipated behaviour of others (which, from the vantage point of the agent, and within a relational approach, represent a form of structure). Strategies are operationalised in action, and such action yields effects, both intended and unintended. Since individuals (and groups of individuals) are knowledgeable and reflexive, they monitor the consequences of their actions routinely (assessing their impact, and their success or failure in securing prior objectives). Hence, action produces:

(i)     *Direct effects* upon the structured contexts within which it takes place and within which future action occurs – producing a partial transformation of the structured context (though not necessarily as anticipated); and

(ii)    *Strategic learning* on the part of the actor(s) involved, enhancing awareness of structures and the constraints/opportunities they impose, providing the basis from which subsequent strategy might be formulated and perhaps prove more successful (see Figure 10.4).

This can be illustrated by considering an environmental pressure group seeking to influence political decision-making about transport policy through lobbying and the mobilisation of protest. The effects of such strategic action are twofold:

(i)     It may have some (limited) influence on subsequent policy and the presentation of policy and it might also mean that environmental issues are seen as (more) important considerations when similar issues return to the political agenda in the future; and

**Figure 10.4**    *Strategic learning*

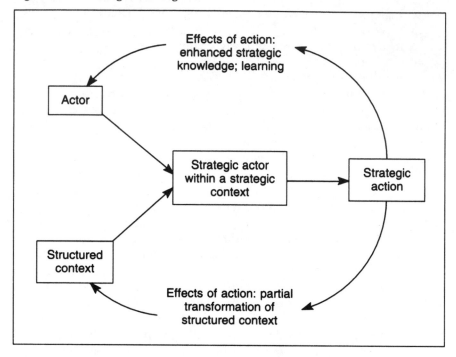

(ii)    In terms of the strategic learning on the part of the pressure group, the experience of lobbying and of attempts (successful and unsuccessful) to influence the media enhances the movement's strategic knowledge, having a potential influence on the strategies pursued in subsequent campaigns.

# The Maastricht vote: holding the whip('s) hand?

The above discussion demonstrates the theoretical advantages of a dialectical approach to the question of structure and agency. In this section I illustrate one variant of this view, the critical realist or strategic-relational approach, showing how it might be utilised to shed some light upon the process of ratification of the Maastricht Treaty in the UK Parliament.

On 22 July 1993 John Major's Government was defeated in a Commons motion on the ratification of the Maastricht Treaty by 324 votes to 316 despite the support of 9 Ulster Unionists; 23 Conservative MPs voted against the government (*Hansard*, 22 July 1993). As a consequence, John Major was stripped of the immediate parliamentary authority to ratify the treaty and tabled an emergency motion for the following day, in which he mixed the issues of confidence in the government strategically with the terms required for the ratification of the treaty. The vote of confidence was subsequently won, and a rather incident-prone government lurched onward. An earlier Labour amendment in favour of the Social Chapter of the treaty (which would have committed the government to, among other things, a minimum wage) was only defeated on the casting vote of the Speaker, Betty Boothroyd.

The outcome of this series of votes can be interpreted as the complex and contingent product of the dialectic of structure and agency (mediated by strategy) at a number of different levels. On the face of it, this was the product of a number of intentional actors (in this case MPs) engaged in the physical action of registering a vote. At a mundane level, this involves the accomplishment of walking through the appropriate lobby – that is, of understanding correctly the social meaning attached to a specific action at a particular moment in time, and being able to achieve this successfully (being there at the right time, not getting lost between the chamber and the lobby room, and so on). This is perhaps the most banal level at which we might identify agency, strategy, intention and structure. It relies on drawing out categories exclusively from the unfolding of the event as it presents itself to us (or as it is presented to us in the media or in the pages of *Hansard*). Yet this does not tell us very much about the specific outcome of the vote, its significance, or its wider ramifications. Hence it is appropriate that we contextualise the actors involved at a number of other levels – making a number of appropriate abstractions.

This can be illustrated by demonstrating how the notions of structure, strategy and agency might be operationalised at *one* particular level. At perhaps the most abstract level that might still shed some light on our case study: we might consider the impact of the economic and political structures of Britain *as a capitalist society* on the strategy of the Major Government in the lead-up to the Maastricht vote. It must be stressed that the following analysis is purely illustrative, and would have to be complemented by a consideration of structure, strategy and agency at a number of other levels if it were to escape the charge of partiality.

At this level, we might situate the Maastricht vote, and the strategy pursued by the Major Government, in the context of the constraints imposed (and the opportunities provided) by the imperatives of capitalist accumulation. For instance, in a democratic capitalist society such as Britain, the legitimacy of the state is dependent to a considerable extent (though not exclusively) upon some degree of economic success measured in terms of the accumulation of capital. Thus perceived, economic success is a necessary (though insufficient) condition of continued political legitimacy. In the light of this, the framing of the Maastricht vote might be seen as one aspect of the Major Government's *accumulation strategy* (Jessop, 1990) – its attempt to secure economic growth for Britain and political legitimacy for itself. It might, for instance, be argued that the decision by the government to favour a ratification of the Maastricht Treaty was driven by the perception that this would secure a place for Britain in a developing European trading bloc that might provide some degree of economic security for Britain in the face of the increasingly volatile, footloose and flexible (strategic) decisions of multinational capital. Pursuing this line of argument, it might be suggested that Maastricht was regarded by the government as something of an economic necessity (however politically undesirable). If this is indeed the case, we have a good example of reflexive and strategic calculation based on some knowledge and informed perceptions (however partial, however inaccurate) of broader and dynamic structures (in this case, the structures of contemporary capitalist accumulation).

Similarly, the strategic decision by the government to reject the Social Chapter of the Maastricht Treaty might be accounted for in terms of its ongoing strategy of seeking to construct for Britain a particular niche within Europe. Such a strategy involves 'selling' Britain as a low-skill, low-wage and relatively un-unionised economy, providing an attractive distribution and assembly site for non-European capital wishing to penetrate a potentially lucrative, though increasingly protected, European market. This ongoing strategy might very well have been compromised by the employment legislation enshrined in the Social Chapter of the Maastricht Treaty. The result was the government's counter-strategy of seeking to ratify a version of the treaty from which the Social Chapter clauses had been excised.

The strategy formulated on the basis of such calculations was realised in various displays of *agency*: notably, the framing of the text of the motion; the (strategic) activity of government Whips in constraining, enticing, and in one case physically manhandling, Conservative MPs to get them to vote with the government; the transporting of sick and infirm Conservative MPs to the lobbies; and John Major's 'informal discussions' with James Molyneux, the leader of the Ulster Unionist Party on the eve of the vote. The enticements were alleged to have ranged from bottles of vintage claret seen in the possession of the government's Chief Whip entering a meeting with 'Euro-rebel' Toby Jessel, to £10,000 bonuses for loyalty and knighthoods in the New Year's Honours List, according to Frank Dobson (*Independent*, 23 July 1993). The now infamous incident of manhandling involved the government's Deputy Chief Whip, who was so exasperated at seeing Bill Walker, MP for Tayside North, filing through the Opposition lobby that he tried physically to prevent him from registering his vote. The list of the sick and infirm summoned to the Chamber included Michael Heseltine who was recovering from a heart attack, and John Patten, who was brought to the Commons in an ambulance, suffering from an intestinal complaint. All nine Ulster Unionists ultimately voted with the government.

Even within such a partial analysis, then, the Maastricht Treaty is seen to take on greater political and economic significance. The very motion which framed the initial vote is seen as the product of a complex process of strategic calculation and decision-making, based on a particular appropriation by the government of a particular economic and political context that favoured certain strategies and discriminated against others.

Clearly, we might choose to contextualise the Maastricht vote in a number of different ways. An account like the one above, which does not consider the impact of public opinion in the light of the legacy of Thatcherism, or the motivations, intentions and strategic decisions of Conservative 'Euro-rebels' is clearly incomplete. None the less, I hope it has shown that by contextualising specific events in relation to different levels of structure, strategy and agency, that we can illuminate the contexts shaping political decision-making, the formulation of political strategy, and the outcome of political action.

# ■ Conclusions

There is surely something in Carlsnaes' claim that 'the problem of structure and agency is . . . *the* central problem of social and political theory' (Carlsnaes, 1992, p. 245). The question of the relationship between structure and agency provides us with an extremely important set of considerations when both carrying out and evaluating pieces of political research. As a consequence, it is crucial that we seek to identify the implicit models of structure and agency that underlie and inform our own attempts to account for processes of social and political change.

In so doing it is crucial that we bear in mind the two related issues of the *contextualisation of agency* and the *strategic selectivity of structure*:

*The contextualisation of agency* In attributing political causality it is essential that we contextualise social and political action within the structural context in which it takes place. We must ask ourselves constantly how processes *external* to the immediate unfolding of the events we are interested in have an impact (often in ways that are not immediately obvious) upon the context and the strategies, intentions and actions of the agents *directly* involved.

*The strategic selectivity of structure* The structures we identify are both enabling *and* constraining – they define the range of potential strategies and opportunities available to actors. Whether we choose to describe the structures we identify primarily as resources (enabling action) or constraints (limiting opportunities for action) depends on the 'abstraction of vantage point' (Ollman, 1993, p. 43). For example, from the perspective (vantage point) of someone wishing to guard their property, the fact that hungry German Shepherd dogs bite is a resource; from the perspective of an unwitting trespasser, on the other hand, it is something of a constraint! Thus structures impose a strategic selectivity. They provide resources and opportunities for the powerful, while simultaneously constraining the powerless and the subordinated. The question of structure and agency, therefore, is the question of political power, the question of who holds the whip hand.

# ■ Further reading

Introductions to the question of structure and agency in political science are noticeable only by their absence. The best available accounts are provided by the sociologists Layder (1994, chs 6–8), Sayer (1992) and Sztompka (1994, chs 13–15). Carlsnaes (1992) and Dessler (1989) produce useful and accessible attempts to relate these issues to political science and international relations. Giddens' structuration theory is most clearly stated in *Central Problems of Social Theory* (1979, ch. 2) and *The Constitution of Society* (1984, esp. ch. 1), but Craib (1992) provides the most useful introduction. Bhaskar's work is notoriously difficult. His most important contributions to the question of structure and agency are to be found in *The Possibility of Naturalism* (1979) and *Reclaiming Reality* (1989). However, Collier (1994) provides a remarkable clear and accessible account of critical realism, and this is probably a better starting point. The strategic-relational approach is best demonstrated by Jessop (1990) and is applied by Hay (1994).

# PART 3

# THEORIES OF THE STATE

# ■ *Chapter 11* ■

# Pluralism
## Martin Smith

Pluralism as a theory is an enigma. Despite being the dominant theory in political science, it is remarkably undertheorised. Consequently, there are many different interpretations of pluralism (see Table 11.1). It is at the same time normative, prescriptive and descriptive. It is normative in that pluralism is seen as the best form of government; it is prescriptive in providing a model of what all governments ideally should be; and it is descriptive in its analysis of government. This under-theorisation and confusion of ends makes it very difficult to define pluralism.

Frequently, there have been attempts to characterise pluralism, crudely, as a belief that the state is neutral; that societal groups are potentially equal in their influence, and that access to the political system is open (Jessop, 1983; Dearlove and Saunders, 1991). However, as Paul Hirst points out, one of the most prominent pluralists, Robert Dahl argued that pluralism 'does *not* mean that *all* the citizens are included in the political process. Dahl makes it evident and emphasises the fact that many citizens are inactive, that income and wealth and political resources are unequally distributed' (Hirst, 1990, p. 40).

This chapter seeks to provide a clarification of the main features of pluralism. It will demonstrate the way in which much mainstream political science literature has been at least implicitly influenced by pluralism. It will highlight some of the problems of pluralism and will look at how it has developed as a result of criticism. Finally, it will examine the resurgence of interest in pluralism from contemporary radical political theory.

# ■ Characterising pluralism

The key feature of pluralism is difference or diversity. The complexity of the modern liberal state means that no single group, class or organisation can dominate society. Pluralism sees a separation between the state and civil society; a difference between economic and political power; and a

Table 11.1 *Models of pluralism*

| | Classical pluralism | Reformed pluralism | Plural elitism | Neo-pluralism | Radical democracy |
|---|---|---|---|---|---|
| **Government** | State highly responsive to group pressure. Site of group conflict. | Fragmented state. Responsive to groups but differential access. | Fragmented state. Differential group access with highly resourced groups privileged. Degree of state autonomy. | State biased towards business interests in economic policy. | State dominated by privileged professional and economic groups. |
| **Groups** | Groups easily formed with varying resources. Continual conflict with variations in winners and losers. | Certain groups with privileged access. There is group exclusion but role for excluded groups in forcing policy change. | Elite groups with privileged access but different groups dominate in different policy areas. | Role of business interests crucial. Structural power limits importance of group behaviour. | Certain groups privileged but excluded groups important in developing alternative forms of politics. |
| **Power** | Observable phenomena that are dispersed in liberal democracies. | Observable and relatively dispersed. | Observable and unobservable. Tendency to concentration but dispersed in certain policy areas. | Unobservable–structural and ideological. Highly concentrated in 'grand' issues and dispersed in 'secondary' issues. | Ideological and concentrated but opportunity for dispersal through alternative political forms. |
| **Democracy** | Exists through groups and potential groups controlling government. | Democracy threatened by policy communities but excluded groups and media can limit influence. | Groups in segmented policy sectors limit effectiveness of democracy. | Little democratic control of 'grand issues'. | Democracy unlikely through traditional political structures but potential for developing alternative forms of democratic participation |
| **Civil society** | Distinct and non-political. | Integrated into state through policy communities. | Distinct and with limited influence. | Distinct and with limited influence. | Thriving alternative to state and highly political. |
| **Points of convergence** | Importance of groups in the political process. | Importance of groups in the political process. | Importance of elite groups in political process. | Importance of groups in secondary issues. | Importance of groups in the political process. |

variation in the interests that are successful in particular policy areas. Power is non-cumulative and dispersed. Hence the role of the state is to regulate conflicts in society rather than to dominate society in pursuit of particular interests.

Pluralists have an underdeveloped theory of the state. The notion of the state assumes an all-encompassing authoritative organisation that governs society. Pluralists are wary of using a concept which they see as too broad and talk of the government rather than the state. Consequently, the pluralist notion of 'the state' is of a set of institutions such as the executive, legislature, civil service and judiciary that are distinct from civil society. Through the mechanisms of elections and pressure politics the government is reflective of society's demands and constrained by the countervailing powers of civil society and other organisations. For Dahl (1967, p. 24) 'there are multiple centres of power, none of which is wholly sovereign'.

Even within the state there are numerous constraints on other state actors. So, for example, there are constraints on the executive from the legislature and judiciary. More importantly, there are constraints within government from other departments. Pluralists do not deny that there is a tendency for certain groups to establish close relationships with particular departments or agencies. One of the principal theorists of pluralism, David Truman, acknowledged that 'institutionalised relationships between an agency and its attendant interest groups' could develop (Truman, 1951, p. 10) and this could lead to other interests being ignored. However, Wilson (1977, p. 45) maintains that there is 'Whitehall pluralism'. Even if one department disregards the interests of a particular group, their views are represented 'by the fact that other departments have checks and have different departmental views correspondingly'. The Ministry of Agriculture may be very close to the farmers and attempt to allow the farmers' interests to dominate agricultural policy, but the Department of Trade and Industry will ensure that trade issues are considered; the Department of Environment will press for environmental interests to be considered; and the Treasury will act so that tax payers do not have to subsidise farmers too much.

For pluralists, the state is often seen as a site of conflict between departments that represent a range of interest groups. Authority is dispersed even within the government (Eckstein, 1963, p. 392) and hence no single interest is able to dominate the state. Yet, the state is rarely neutral but reflects the range of group pressures it faces. Easton (1967, p. 172) believes that 'policy arises from the interaction of various social elements'. The process of making policy within the state is an attempt to bargain between a range of conflicting interests. Politics is a constant process of negotiation that ensures conflicts are resolved peacefully (Dahl, 1967, p. 24).

Politics as the resolution of conflicting interests means that groups are a crucial element in the political process. A. Bentley argued that the analysis of politics is the analysis of groups. The policy process is essentially a continual process of conflict and exchange between different groups, with the government being classified as just another group:

> All phenomena of government are phenomena of groups pressing one another, forming one another, and pushing out new groups and group representation (the organs or agencies of government) to mediate adjustments. It is only as we isolate these group activities, determine their representative values, and get the whole process stated in terms of them, that we approach to a satisfactory knowledge of government. (Bentley, 1967 [1908], p. 269)

It is by organising into groups that individuals can represent their interests to government. Pluralists define the state as a discrete organisation making policy in response to the myriad of groups pressing on the government. Consequently, there are a vast array of pluralist pressure group studies that examine the methods and success of pressure groups. Pluralists do not see all pressure groups as having equal resources, access or influence. For instance, pluralists acknowledge that business is in a privileged position. Dahl (1961, p. 76) recognised that 'the goals of businessmen are legitimized by a system of beliefs widely shared throughout the community'. For Finer (1966, p. 27), the importance of economic interests to the economy meant that 'their cooperation must be won, rather than their services commanded. They do not direct but they may veto'.

Yet there are a range of constraints on economic groups. First, economic groups are only interested in a limited range of issues and thus do not try to influence the majority of policies. Second, economic groups do not have shared interests and are as likely to be in conflict with each other as to be in a coalition to defeat the less economically dominant. Third, the existence of one powerful group is likely to lead to the development of a countervailing power that will act as a constraint (Galbraith, 1963, p. 125). The creation of a business association will, for instance, lead to the establishment of a countervailing trade union.

Fourth, although Dahl (1961, p. 228) acknowledged inequality in the distribution of resources for influencing political outcomes, he also realised that there were a range of different resources available for influencing public officials and that, 'Individuals best off in their access to one kind of resource are often badly off with respect to many other resources'. In other words, if a group is well resourced in terms of finance it is likely to have limited resources in terms of votes. As Finer (1966, p. 118) argued:

> The comparative strength of rich associations is an argument which does not impress me; partly because the uses to which this wealth can be put are so circumscribed, partly because there are such effective ways for poor associations to influence public policy, and partly because the capacity of publicity to mould political attitudes is so highly problematical.

Rich groups might have very close contacts with senior ministers, but poor associations can use the media and campaigns to attract attention and influence policy. Consequently, resources are dispersed, admittedly unequally, between a range of groups and elites, and it is impossible for a single class or interest to dominate society.

Fifth, Truman claims the government takes account of the interests of 'unorganised and potential groups' and, therefore, they do not need 'organised expression except when these needs are flagrantly violated' (Truman, 1951, p. 448). Government is prepared to take account of groups that are unorganised either in order to ensure that they do not become organised – a kind of 'anticipated reaction' – or because the government is highly motivated by the need to win an election (Beer, 1982). Politicians are therefore driven to act in the interest of the electorate rather than for organised groups.

Finer believed that it is the duty of government to take account of the counter-claims of interests whether or not they are represented, concluding 'on the whole it does work' (Finer, 1966, p. 128). Although certain groups are advantaged in terms of resources and access, the pressure group system as a whole, and the nature of the state, ensures that there are checks on potentially powerful groups.

Despite the recognition that conflict between groups is endemic within liberal democracy, this conflict rarely threatens to undermine political stability. The political system as a whole is maintained by a consensus which defines the limits of political actions and the framework of policy outcomes. Dahl (1967) maintains that although severe business/labour conflicts frequently occurred in the USA, these never threatened the political and economic system. An ideology that promoted wide support for democracy and capitalism was accepted because of the absence of a socialist party; the fact that coalitions were often conglomerates; the level of economic growth; the absence of a high degree of class differentiation; and because workers never became a majority of the population (Dahl, 1967, pp. 439–40). (What Dahl fails to mention is that any signs of a growing socialist movement in the USA were harshly suppressed by the state.) Almond and Verba (1963, p. 491), in their study of political culture in five nations, maintained that: 'If there is no consensus within society, there can be little potentiality for the peaceful resolution of policy differences that is associated with the democratic process.' For democratic society to work effectively there has to be a degree of consensus concerning the fundamental values of a society shared by the competing groups.

The importance of consensus to the pluralist conception of society underpins the pluralist notion of power. Power for Polsby (1963, p. 5) is 'the capacity of one actor to do something affecting another actor, which changes the probable pattern of specified future events'. Or for Dahl, 'A has power over B to the extent that he can get B to do something that B would not otherwise do' (Dahl, 1957, pp. 202–3). The central questions of the pluralist approach are: Who is involved in the decision-making process; and who was successful in getting their preferences accepted as decisions? Who was it who could be *seen* to influence outcomes? According to N. Polsby, 'The researcher should study actual behaviour, either from first hand or by reconstructing behaviour from documents, informants, newspapers and other appropriate sources' (quoted in Lukes, 1974, p. 12).

The pluralist conception of power dictates pluralist methodology. Pluralists examine observable behaviour and observable outcomes. Hewitt (1974) highlighted the nature of pluralist methodology when he studied national decision-making in Britain. He focused on a number of issues within the following policy areas: foreign affairs, economic policy, welfare policy and social policy. He then analysed which groups were involved in each issue area and discovered that, 'Very few organisations were involved "significantly" in more than one issue'. He concluded:

> From the evidence presented, it is clear that policy making does not appear to be elitist in the sense that any single elite interest is dominant. Instead the picture of national power that is revealed suggests a 'pluralist' interpretation since a diversity of conflicting interests are involved in many issues, without any one interest being consistently successful in realising its own goals. (Hewitt, 1974, p. 61)

Pluralists focus on who does what, and who is successful in achieving his/her goals. The advantages of this approach are that:

1. It does not assume anything about the distribution of power (Polsby, 1960):
2. It is possible to determine empirically who does or does not have power. By omitting concepts such as false consciousness, dominant ideology and hegemony, pluralists develop a theory of power that is testable empirically.
3. By developing a notion of modern society and polity as fragmented, diverse and democratic, they provide a more accurate description of the distribution of power than do monolithic Marxist or elitist theories.

Pluralism provides an intuitively plausible account of the policy-making process in modern liberal democratic societies. It points to the fragmentation of both society and the state. Modern society is divided into a variety of groups with different interests and a range of resources. These groups use their resources to influence a diverse polity with its own conflicts and divisions. The complexity of the state, society and the policy process means that it is impossible for a single group or class to dominate. In order for a democratic society to survive there has to be accommodation by the state of the various societal groups (Dunleavy and O'Leary, 1987, ch. 2).

# ■ Problems of pluralist analysis

There are a number of problems with the pluralist analysis of the policy process and state–group relationships. This section will examine some of the internal inconsistencies of pluralism and examine the criticisms of pluralism from alternative theoretical traditions.

Pluralism is far more subtle and complex than many of its critics have suggested. Pluralists are aware of inequalities in society, and between groups, and recognise that through institutionalised relationships some groups have privileged access to the government. However, despite this sophistication, pluralism still sees power as being widely dispersed and non-cumulative – success in one policy area does not increase power in other policy areas. It also maintains that there is no connection between economic and political power. Consequently, pluralists maintain a benign view of the political system which leads them to overestimate the ease of access to the policy process. Pluralists suggest that if groups do not have access, it is because they have not tried assiduously, or that their interests have not been sufficiently threatened. They deny that it is possible to exclude groups for a long period. However, there are a range of empirical studies which demonstrate the exclusion of groups from agriculture (Smith, 1990a); nuclear policy (Saward, 1992) and prison reform (Ryan, 1978).

Pluralists do not take adequate account of the mechanisms that exist within the policy process for the exclusion of undesirable groups. For example, for groups to be represented on a government advisory committee they have to be seen to be legitimate. This means that they have to conform to the 'rules of the game', which involves behaving in certain ways and accepting particular views and values. These views and values conform to the interests of the dominant groups in the policy process. For example, the group 'Radical Alternatives to Prison' were not given access to prison policy because their policy goal was radical alternatives to the prison system (Ryan, 1978).

This notion of the ease of access to the political process is related to problems with pluralist methodology. Because pluralists are concerned with observable behaviour, they see evidence of consultation as an indicator of access, and therefore influence. If $A$ supports a policy $Z$, and the government consults $A$ and chooses policy $Z$, $A$ is seen to be influential. However, all that is demonstrated is a correlation between consultation with $A$ and outcome $Z$. The relationship might not be causal. By focusing on the observable, pluralists may miss the real reasons for policy. They do not examine the ideological and structural context within which policy is made (Smith, 1990b).

The influence of pressure groups does not derive from their resources but also from the institutional, historical and ideological context within which decisions are made. This context biases the decision-making process so that certain interests are privileged over others. For example, teachers' unions have always been in daily contact with officials at the Department for Education. This is a degree of access unavailable to other groups in education. Similarly, groups that share the ideology of dominant actors are much more likely to gain access. To grasp the influence of groups it is important to assess the historical development of a policy area, to examine how groups became involved, what pressure groups were excluded and what policy-making institutions developed.

Pluralists fail to recognise, because of their positivist method, the role of ideas in shaping policy outcomes. In other words, they concentrate on observable behaviour and thus are unable to evaluate how ideology may shape the actions of policy-makers. This failure to understand ideology leads to the assumption that society is underpinned by a consensus of values. Moreover, this consensus is seen as being politically neutral and the result of shared interests. However, the degree of consensus is in itself questionable and even where consensus does exist, it is not neutral but serves a particular set of interests. Dahl points out that the acceptance of the market capitalism is part of the consensus in the USA. He even states that:

> Fortunately for the politicians it is easy to avoid the hostility of the (economic and social) notables, for living conditions and the belief system has not – at least so far – generated demands for local policies markedly antagonistic to the goals of businessmen and notables. (Dahl, 1961, p. 84)

Dahl has identified the dominant system of beliefs as being partly responsible for the dominance of the interests of capital.

It is also questionable whether countervailing powers are as important as pluralists assume. Is it really the case that consumer groups provide a constraint on the power of producers? Consider the situation of consumers and producers in relation to the Thatcher and Major Governments. The Conservative governments have been influenced by New Right ideology and committed to the extension of the market. Consequently, consumer policy has shifted from one of consumer protection to one of improving the market choice of consumers. The Thatcher Government set up a deregulation unit, abolished the Department of Prices and Consumer Protection, and attempted to lessen the impact of EC (now EU) consumer legislation (Smith, 1993). With a *laissez-faire* ideology and a stated goal of increasing the competitiveness and profitability of industry, can it be maintained that the government gave similar consideration to the interests of consumers and producers?

Pluralists may accept the weakness of consumer groups, but would see consumer interests being protected through 'Whitehall pluralism'. However, the concept of Whitehall pluralism is questionable. On many occasions, other departments will not have the opportunity to represent alternative interests. In most instances, policy is made within departments without reference to Cabinet or Cabinet committees (Smith *et al.*, 1993). Even when policy is referred to interdepartmental committees, the extent to which other departments will represent alternative interests is limited. It is usually the case that ministers are too busy to read the papers of other departments in order to offer constructive alternatives. They are also wary of criticising colleagues when they may want these colleagues' support for their own department's policy (Headey, 1974, pp. 48 and 77–8).

In addition, it is doubtful that potential groups exercise much influence over decision-makers. Departments do not represent their interests, not least because it must be difficult to recognise these interests. Moreover, it is unlikely that potential groups offer much of an electoral threat. It is rare in the UK for a single issue to sway large numbers of voters, and the members of potential groups are likely to have many conflicting interests. If a politician appeals to one potential group, he or she could lose the votes of another. It is also the case that most potential groups have great difficulty in organising. Consumers and the elderly do not meet collectively; they lack resources; they often have conflicting interests; and they have very little, and diffuse, economic power. The threat to their interests has to be extremely great for them to organise into actual groups (see Olson, 1965). Indeed, the concept of a potential group is questionable. It presumes some a priori group identity. However, group identities develop within the context of group formation. As Arblaster (1993, p. 105) notes: 'General interests, like the interests of patients and potential patients, which is what we all are, by their very nature, are not susceptible to organization or mobilization in the same way as the interests of specific, permanent groups'.

Perhaps the central problem of pluralism is the tendency to treat business as just another group, but one that is well served in terms of resources. Clearly, business has advantages not available to other groups. First, businesses have ready-made organisations in the form of firms and, consequently, they do not face the collective action problems of other interests (Olson, 1965). Where businesses do have to join together, the benefits of their actions are often enjoyed by a small number of firms and so the incentives to organise are high (Olson, 1965).

Second, because of its key role in the economy, business has resources unavailable to other groups (Lindblom, 1977). The actions of business affect the lives of many people, and the success of economies as a whole. This, as C. Lindblom points out, gives business a privileged position. Governments need successful economies for their own survival and are therefore inevitably responsive to the interests of business. Third, business has access to financial resources far greater than those of any other group. Fourth, through ownership of the media, business has much greater access to sources of information than have any other groups. Fifth, business operates within a favourable ideological framework. More or less automatically, business groups are seen as legitimate interests that operate within 'the rules of the game'.

It is apparent that in terms of the policy process, pluralist's focus a great deal on the role of groups. In doing so, they underestimate the importance of the state and state actors. Most policies are initiated within the state by state actors. They are not necessarily developing their policy in response to group pressures, but have their own interests which they wish to pursue (Nordlinger, 1981). Frequently, groups are incorporated not because of their pressure but because they are useful to state actors in the development and implementation of policy. It is the state that has the resources and legitimacy to develop and implement policy whilst state actors can, and frequently do, ignore the interests of groups. Consequently, in examining policy outcomes, the more appropriate focus of analysis may be state organisation rather than group action.

An important problem, in terms of British pluralism at least, is that the development of pluralism is culturally and historical specific. The pluralism of Bentley, Truman and Dahl developed to analyse politics in the USA. In the USA the notion of a strong central state does not exist. At the national level there are competing power centres such as the legislature, judiciary and executive. In addition, there are important federal and local centres of power. These multiple power centres mean that state actors have an interest in encouraging interest groups into the policy process as a resource for developing and implementing policy, and to provide political support in internal conflicts. In addition, the weakness of parties, and the failure of working-class organisations, combined with regional, ethnic and economic divisions means that people often look to interest groups, rather than to parties, to represent their interests. The USA is a political system where interests groups play an important role in the policy process, and the political system is more open to their pressure. It might be the case that a theoretical tradition that developed in the open US system is not applicable to the elitist and closed British state, where ideas of Parliamentary sovereignty and secrecy prevail (see Judge, 1993; Tant, 1993).

Consequently, it was changing historical conditions that led to a theoretical critique of pluralism. The Vietnam War, the civil rights movement and the persistence of inequality suggested that there were flaws 'in the pluralist heaven'. From the 1960s, pluralism was challenged by a range of alternative theoretical traditions that presented empirical and conceptual criticisms of the pluralist case. Bachrach and Baratz (1962) challenged the notion that power was always exercised through observable behaviour, and proposed that it could be reproduced through keeping issues off the agenda. Gavanta (1980), among others, questioned Dahl's and Polsby's notion of community power and demonstrated that power within communities, even in the 1960s and 1970s, was still concentrated and cumulative. Mills (1956) and Domhoff (1967) illustrated the range of interconnections between the elites of business, finance, the military and politics that existed in the USA. There might be different elites in various areas of society but these elites were linked through a range of connections and interchangeable personnel. Following Mills, Miliband (1969, p. 61) tested the pluralist thesis empirically and found:

> that in terms of social origin, education and class situation, the men who have manned all the command position in the state system have largely, and in many cases overwhelmingly, been drawn from the world of business and property or from the professional middle class.

For Miliband, it was not the case that power was dispersed, nor was there a separation between economic and political power.

The theoretical and empirical critique of pluralism was maintained in the 1970s by two very different traditions. First, it was argued that liberal societies were becoming increasingly corporatist. Rather than there being a relatively open process of group/state interaction, groups were developing increasingly integrated relationships with the state. In particular, economic policy decisions were made through a process of bargaining between state actors and the peak economic actors. In Britain, a range of corporatist relationships could be identified in areas such as incomes policy (Crouch, 1977), health policy (Cawson, 1982) and economic policy (Middlemas, 1979).

Second, a normative theory of overload was developed. It argued that there were too many groups demanding too much from the government, which was creating overload within the political system. This was making Britain ungovernable (see, for example, Brittan, 1975). Governments were expected to find solutions to numerous policy problems, and the cost of intervention was bankrupting the state and causing the economy to stagnate. Consequently, rather than pressure groups being good in terms of controlling the state and maintaining the democratic process, they were extending the state too far and undermining democracy by protecting special interests. The concepts of corporatism and overload inspired the New Right critique of pressure groups. Pressure groups were seen by the New Right as distorting the democratic system. The political process was dominated by groups rather than voters. The result was economic stagnation, as special interests rejected restructuring in order to protect their existing privileges.

The dominant political tradition of the 1950s and 1960s was undermined by theoretical inconsistencies, subject to theoretical criticism from Marxists, elitists and the New Right, and challenged empirically because of a range of events in the UK and the USA. The underlying conception of society was questioned by the political events of the 1960s and 1970s, and the development of corporatism questioned the benign role of pressure groups. The democratic defects of liberal democracy seemed greater than even the most sophisticated pluralists had allowed, and the growth of radical movements that were excluded from the policy process suggested that power was not widely dispersed. However, these problems did not result in the abandonment of pluralism. Rather, a range of pluralist writers attempted to refine their models of power and state–group interaction.

# ■ Pluralist responses to criticism

## □ *Reformed pluralism*

J. J. Richardson and A. G. Jordan (1979 and Jordan and Richardson, 1987a, 1987b) have recognised that the relationship between the state and pressure groups has changed while maintaining the underlying principles of pluralism. What might be called 'reformed pluralism' accepts many of the criticisms of classical pluralism. It acknowledges that government–interest groups relations are often institutionalised, and that certain groups are excluded from the policy process. Richardson and Jordan (1979, p. 13) admit that '"perfect competition" rarely exists except in theory. In practice we have at best an oligopolist situation and at worst a monopolistic situation'. A group will try to capture a department, which may result in clientelism, with shared priorities and identification between the government agency and the interest group. This has led to the creation of policy communities which blur the distinction between the governed and the governors, and where there is 'cooption and a consensual style' (Richardson and Jordan, 1979, p. 57). According to Richardson and Jordan, such a model provides for a 'better account for policy outcomes than do examinations of policy stances or of parliamentary influence' (Richardson and Jordan, 1979, p. 74).

However, the key feature of the modern state for reformed pluralists is complexity and fragmentation. The modern polity is segmented. Although there may be closed and institutionalised relationships in one policy or sub-policy area, in other policy areas different groups and interests will be involved, and policy-making may be much more open. The modern polity is one of conflict between multiple clienteles over the 'collective allocation of scarce resources'. In order to maximize 'legitimacy and autonomy state bureaus create stable networks of clienteles, funding sources and interbureau alliances' (Laumann and Knoke, 1987, pp. 8–11).

Despite these institutionalised arrangements, reformed pluralists do not accept that the state has become a corporate state. For Richardson and Jordan, the notion of a policy community is meant to be a flexible concept. There is:

flexibility in the system, not all groups are active in all aspects of even one area as narrowly defined as education. On different aspects of policy, different sets of participants are involved. While some groups are very much part of the department's 'legitimised clientele', others enjoy less comfortable co-existence with the department. Thus it is not possible to give a static and exhaustive listing of groups in a community. (Jordan, 1981, p. 105)

This conception of flexibility, within structured and institutionalised relationships, leads Jordan *et al.* (1992) to suggest that even areas such as agriculture, which have previously been seen as dominated by very closed relationships with a limited number of groups, are in fact more open than has been presumed:

The number of interests consulted, the number of interests which civil servants at MAFF acknowledged as influential, and the changed tactics of the NFU in recent years, all tend to support a view of a very dense and specialist policy making terrain (Jordan *et al.*, 1992, p. 8).

Reformed pluralism accepts that relationships between groups and the state can be structured and institutionalised. Yet at the same time it tries to retain some of the key features of pluralism. Richardson and Jordan argue that there are no monopolies of power; policy communities include countervailing powers; and the pressure group universe is highly populated. They believe that these structured relationships are disintegrating and becoming confused, and increasingly open to groups (Jordan and Richardson, 1987a, pp. 117–18).

Reformed pluralism tries to acknowledge the criticisms of pluralism but at the same time retains its key features. Rather than stress the institutionalised forms of state group interaction, they emphasise the ability of groups to break up these relationships. This pluralism is reflected in Richardson and Jordan's view of the consultation process. Although they admit that consultation is often cosmetic, they make continual references to the ease of being consulted, the desire of departments to consult and their long list of consultees (Jordan and Richardson, 1987a, p. 145). They also refer to the constraints from Whitehall pluralism and the extent to which there is overlapping membership of policy communities. Hence, their position is very close to that of Truman and Dahl concerning the way overlapping membership of groups prevents a single group from dominating. Richardson and Jordan fail, like classical pluralists, to contextualise the decision-making process. They confuse a large number of groups being involved in decision making with a large number of groups being influential. Groups may be consulted but may exercise little influence, and it is important to understand why some groups have more influence than others.

In the USA the response to the criticism of classical pluralism took a number of forms. As with reformed pluralism, there was an acceptance of what McFarland (1987) calls 'elite pluralism'. Writers such as McConnell (1966) and Lowi (1969) argued that it was increasingly the case that producer groups were coming to dominate particular areas of policy or subgovernments. Within these subgovernments, policy is dominated by an iron triangle of Congressional sub-committee, bureaucratic agency and interest group, who are responsible for the particular policy and who close off the policy area to groups that threaten their interests. This is a different form of the policy communities outlined by Jordan and Richardson.

Nordlinger (1981) attempted an alternative response to the criticism of pluralism. He maintained that policy was not necessarily determined by groups but rather that state actors have their own interests in policy, which they are prepared to defend in the face of group criticism. He therefore acknowledges the role of state officials in determining policy outcomes. For Nordlinger, pluralism exists within the state as various state officials conflict in order to achieve their particular interests.

McFarland (1987), in his sophisticated defence of pluralism, synthesises sub-sectoral government and state autonomy in the 'triadic theory of power'. McFarland distinguishes between iron triangles or 'sub-government power' and 'triadic power'. He accepts that policy areas can be dominated by producer interests. However, the theory of triadic power acknowledges that while economic producer groups will organise in order to lobby the government, in certain situations there will also be countervailing groups that oppose the interests of the producers. At the same time, McFarland appreciates that 'state agencies are normally assumed to have a significant degree of autonomy' (McFarland, 1987, p. 141). So rather than sub-governments being dominated by iron triangles, within each policy area there is a triad of a state agency with some autonomy, a producer group and countervailing groups. This basic analytic unit is then 'complicated by adding such factors as legislators, presidential policy-makers and the judiciary' (McFarland, 1987, p. 141).

McFarland points out that triads might exist but this does not necessarily mean that all interests are organised. However, it may be the case that countervailing power can limit the strength of producer groups, and this increases the autonomy of agencies. He also argues that in areas of high politics – 'the politics of making general decisions' – presidential policy-makers may greatly restrict the autonomy of agencies. So, in areas such as deregulation, the intervention of presidential actors can allow a situation where the power of producers is greatly reduced and this increases triadic power. As the reform cycle ends, there may be a shift back to sub-government.

McFarland's theory is clearly a useful way of understanding relationships between governments and groups. It is a very sophisticated form of pluralism that recognises the power of producers, the potential of agency autonomy and also the ability of other groups in particular circumstances to restrict the power of producers and the autonomy of the state. It places policy-making in a context. Its limitations are that, despite its claims, it is not really a theory of power but an analysis of the policy process that is only applicable in particular situations. Moreover, it bears little relationship to pluralism, being much closer to an elitist analysis of the policy process. An alternative development of pluralism is 'neo-pluralism'.

# ☐ *Neo-pluralism*

A more radical response to the criticisms of pluralism has been from an approach called neo-pluralism. Neo-pluralism first developed in the USA with the recognition that business was often in a superior position to other groups and enjoys certain advantages over the consumer and the market (Dunleavy and O'Leary, 1987, p. 275). McConnell developed the view that 'the major corporate units of American business exercise great power'. With this power, and the economic needs of war, close relations developed between business and government. Consequently significant parts of government are controlled by business interests (McConnell, 1967, p. 129). For neo-pluralists, countervailing powers are not sufficient to check the interests of business (Dahl, 1982, p. 51).

The major development in the theory of neo-pluralism came from an exponent of classical pluralism, Charles Lindblom. For Lindblom, business is advantaged by two important factors. First, government is dependent on a successful economy and so has a tendency to provide inducements and advantages to business. The requirements to meet the needs of business means that it achieves 'a privileged position in government' (Lindblom, 1977, p. 175). Second, in a market economy, many decisions are taken by business concerning investment and employment. Despite the impact that these decisions have over other people's lives, they are not subject to democratic controls (Lindblom, 1977, p. 172).

These factors led Lindblom to argue that business does not have to operate through the traditional lobbying channels of other pressure groups. Business benefits from structural power:

> Any government official who understands the requirements of his position and the responsibilities that market orientated systems throw on businessmen will therefore grant them a privileged position. He does not have to be bribed, duped or pressured to do so. Nor does he have to be an uncritical admirer of business to do so. He simply understands, as is plain to see, that public affairs in market orientated systems are in the hands of two group leaders, government and business, who must collaborate and that to make the system work government leadership must often defer to business leadership (Lindblom, 1977, p. 175).

The importance of business to the government means that the government will respond automatically to business's interest. Power is structural rather than observable. Lindblom's position is closer to some Marxists than it is to pluralists. He acknowledges that power can be exercised in an unobservable way through structures, anticipated reaction and ideology.

Yet neo-pluralism still displays some of the features of classical pluralism. It continues to stress the importance of groups and the existence of competitive policy areas. Lindblom distinguishes between grand issues – which are generally closed to the public and concern the major interests of society; and secondary issues – which are not of crucial importance to the state or a key economic interest, and where the policy process is more competitive (Lindblom, 1977, p. 142). Thus neo-pluralism provides a complex and sophisticated view of the modern state. It recognises that business is privileged, but that it does not completely dominate the policy process. It could be argued that it is a much more realistic analysis of power in the modern state than classical pluralism.

Nevertheless, there are a number of problems with neo-pluralism. Neo-pluralism tends to treat business in a very unified and unproblematic manner. It fails to specify the division and conflicts within business and thus the notion of a business veto is oversimplified. Consequently, it does not really specify the nature of structural power and how it operates (Marsh, 1983, p. 7). Vogel points to the decline of business power since the 1960s and the fact that, with the rise of public interest groups such as consumers and environmentalist, business does not appear to be that successful in vetoing policy (Vogel, 1989).

Perhaps what is most important about neo-pluralism is that it represents a convergence between pluralism and Marxism (see Chapter 14 of this book). Changes in modern industrial societies and the collapse of Communism in Eastern Europe have led to the questioning of the traditional theoretical boundaries in political science. To an extent, pluralism has been revitalised by radical political traditions such as post-modernism which are, in part, searching for a theoretical alternative to Marxism.

# ■ Postmodernism: the rediscovery of pluralism?

One of the great ironies of political science is that whilst classical pluralists such as Dahl and Lindblom are shifting towards positions more aligned to Marxism, a number of 'post-Marxists' and post-modernists are redis-covering some of the principal arguments of pluralism.

Again, historical events have influenced the development of pluralism. The crisis of Marxism, resulting from the collapse of Communism, has led a number of Marxists to reconsider the importance of parliamentary democracy and the need to recognise diversity and plurality in civil society (Hindess, 1980). Marxists have also been prepared to accept that the state is not a unified monolith. They see it as conflictual, fragmentary and therefore open to a wider range of interests other than solely business (Jessop, 1990). Consequently, some Marxists have shifted their analysis from privileging class groups and have been prepared to recognise that groups representing other interests can have some influence on policy outcomes. Indeed, Jessop (1990, pp. 248–9) uses the term 'Marxist pluralists'.

The resurgence of pluralism has been taken further by the proponents of post-modernism and radical democracy. Many post-modernists reject what they see as the Marxist belief in a single truth or explanation and its tendency to see inherent characteristics in classes. Frequently, their ideas reflect many of the concerns of pluralism (McLennan, 1989). As McClure (1992, p. 114) points out: 'this most recent incarnation of pluralism bears certain affinities to its predecessors'. Indeed, Hirst (1990, p. 47) argues that there is much in classical pluralism that is worth saving. He suggests that pluralism can provide a much more accurate model of how modern liberal democracies operate than can Marxism:

> pluralism provides a theoretical framework which can accommodate both considerable inequality based on socio-economic inequality, and a significant measure of the diffusion of power and influence. It also provides indicators of possible forms of reform that would reduce inequality and would permit the enhanced influence and power of non-wealthy strata. (Hirst, 1990, p. 47)

There are a number of areas where the pluralism of radical democracy and classical pluralism overlap. Both are mistrustful of the state and see voluntary organisations as desirable for controlling the state and as alternative mechanisms for the distribution of public goods. They

> have been articulated in critical opposition to unitary, monolithic or totalizing conceptions of the political domain, particularly in so far as these presume some singularly sovereign or unique agency overseeing or determining political processes and/or social relations. (McClure, 1992, p. 115)

Consequently, they accept that there can be no organisation that has a monopoly of knowledge. Wainwright (1993) highlights that knowledge is socially constructed; it is impossible for a single person, group or party to know everything; and knowledge can be organised in range of ways. Ideally, knowledge should be demystified and developed in a pluralistic mode through a range of social movements. Thus, central to radical democracy is a strong belief in the richness of civil society and the importance of social movements as a way of controlling and circumventing the monopolising tendencies of the state. Like classical pluralists, radical democrats see social movements as crucial elements in society. Civil society is complex and pluralistic, with individuals belonging to a vast array of social groups that have no essence but develop as a result of struggle and social interaction (McClure, 1992, p. 115). Wainwright sees the social movements that have developed since the early 1970s as having challenged the traditional position of social democratic movements and as being an important source of social change (Wainwright, 1993, p. 193).

However, unlike the pluralism of the 1950s and 1960s, it is not meant as a realistic portrait of society but as a radical critique of the distribution of power in capitalist societies which offers the alternative of participatory and communitarian politics (Phillips, 1993). In addition, there are significant differences between the epistemologies of radical pluralism and classical pluralism. Classical pluralism, with its positivist method, maintains the existence of an objective truth. Radical democrats are extreme relativists, arguing that social reality is socially constructed and subject to a range of interpretations, one of which is not inherently more valuable than another.

Yet radical democrats make some similar mistakes to classical pluralists. They do not really develop a convincing theory of the state. Radical democrats fail to conceptualise the relationship between the state and civil society and thus are not very effective at developing practical suggestions for overcoming state power. This leads, like classical pluralism, to an over-emphasis on the role of social groups (or social movements). All hope for social change and a radical alternative is vested in social movements which have the potential to bring about radical change. Yet little account is taken of the role of the state in defining and limiting these groups. Moreover, they are also calling for a radical politicisation of society, where differences can be preserved. But will all social interest be allowed to develop, and who will protect the interest of minorities in a highly politicised and weakly governed society?

# ■ Conclusion

The main problem in examining pluralism is that no single pluralist theory exists. It is often self-consciously atheoretical and so its assumptions are implicit rather than explicit (see Jordan, 1990). This leads to a great deal of confusion among pluralists and their critics about what pluralism is and what it is trying to do. At the same time, pluralism is descriptive, prescriptive and normative. It is also a theory that has been influenced greatly by its historical and social milieux. It developed within a particular system and has changed significantly according to social and political circumstances.

Despite this confusion, pluralism does offer some useful pointers for analysing modern society. Unlike Marxism and elitism, it is aware of the need to understand the complexity of modern society and the implications this has for the state and groups. Modern liberal democracies are complex and difficult to govern. It is hard to sustain an argument that society as a whole is ruled by a particular class or group. Is any class or group unified enough to rule, and even if it were, does it have the ability to rule information-rich societies that are traversed by a range of social and economic cleavages?

However, society may be complex and lacking a ruling class, but this does not mean that power is widely dispersed. It is undoubtedly the case, as reformed pluralists point out, that policy-making in liberal democratic society is segmented. In each policy area, different interests prevail. It is also apparent, as neo-pluralists suggest, that there are certain groups in modern society that have the resources to dominate particular areas of policy making. There is social closure, and access to the policy process in key areas is heavily restricted.

The problem for pluralists is, in a sense, epistemological and methodological. While they are often able to produce empirically useful material, their concentration on the observable means that they are unable to take account of the ideological and the structural as these are not immediately discernible. The limits of pluralism lie not in its suggestion that power is a complex phenomena, but in its failure to examine the context in which decisions are made, and the way that such decisions favour some interests over others.

# ■ Further reading

The best example of classical pluralism is Dahl's (1957) account of politics and decision-making in New Haven. It provides a rich and sophisticated pluralist study which highlights the strengths and weaknesses of pluralism. Other useful examples of classic pluralism are Polsby (1980) and Truman (1951). A British example is provided by Finer (1966). British reformed pluralism is outlined in Richardson and Jordan (1979), and American in Heclo (1981). An important account of the development of pluralism is McFarland (1987). Neo-pluralism is represented in the later work of two key proponents of classical pluralism; Lindblom (1977) and Dahl (1982). The influence of pluralism on radical democracy is discussed in Hirst (1990), and the best outlines of radical democracy are in Phillips (1993) and Wainwright (1993).

# ■ Chapter 12 ■

# Elitism
## Mark Evans

At the core of the elitist doctrine lies the belief that the history of politics is the history of elite domination. Elitist theory therefore challenges the key premises of most Western liberal assumptions about politics, the organisation of government and the 'proper' relationship between the state and civil society. As Gaetano Mosca (1939, p. 50) puts it:

> In all societies – from societies that are very meagrely developed and have barely attained the dawnings of civilisation, down to the most advanced and powerful societies – two classes of people appear – a class that rules and a class that is ruled. The first class, always the less numerous, performs all political functions, monopolises power and enjoys the advantages that power brings, whereas the second, the more numerous class, is directed and controlled by the first.

Hence, the nature of any society – whether it is consensual or authoritarian, dynamic or static, pacifist or totalitarian, legitimate or illegitimate – is determined by the nature of its elite. Moreover, the goals of every society are both established and manipulated by its elite (Prewitt and Stone, 1973, p. 3).

This chapter discusses the theoretical, empirical, philosophical, organisational and institutional concerns of the main theorists who would classify themselves as elitists, and evaluates their contribution to our understanding of contemporary political science. Its aim is to review the content and nature of elite theory. The scope of the chapter is circumscribed by space: it is by no means exhaustive, nor does it attempt to be. The chapter is divided into three sections. The first section discusses the emergence of classical elitism. In the second section we analyse the position of democratic elitism. The third section examines the contribution of some modern elitist perspectives which seek to understand the operational bases of the autonomy of the capitalist state. In sum, the chapter broadly argues that the elitist position is a cumulative one which rests on three central claims: a belief in the inevitability of elite rule and the irrationality of liberal democracy; a rejection of the economistic Marxist conception of the economy as the ultimate determinant of societal dynamics; and a belief in the potential autonomy of the state from social and economic forces.

# ■ Classical elitism

Although the seeds of the perspective were sown in the ideas of Plato, Niccolò Machiavelli and others, elitism as a theory of social power is most associated with the works of Vilfredo Pareto, Gaetano Mosca and Robert Michels. Their common thesis was that the concentration of social power in a small set of controlling elites was inevitable in all societies, and they rejected the feasibility of Karl Marx's vision of evolutionary change towards a classless society with power equality. This section provides an overview of the core propositions of classical elitist thought, focusing on: Pareto's reworking of Machiavellian realism and the circulation of elites (Pareto, 1935); Mosca's idea of *The Ruling Class* (Mosca, 1939); and Michels' main work, *Political Parties* (Michels, 1911), which drew attention to the inevitability of an 'iron law of oligarchy'. Each one of these texts engage in a critique of Marxism and pluralism that emphasises the rejection of both class domination and the diffusion of power on pluralist lines. A critical discussion of these texts will enable us to identify a partial, if weak, theory of elite domination.

Pareto argued that historical experience provides testimony to the perpetual circulation of elites and oligarchy. Every field of human enterprise has its own elite. Pareto borrowed two categories of elites from Machiavelli: 'foxes' and 'lions' (Pareto, 1966, pp. 99, 110), in order to illustrate the nature of governing elite structures. The two categories stand at opposite ends of a continuum of governance. 'Foxes' govern by attempting to gain consent and are not prepared to use force, they are intelligent and cunning, enterprising, artistic and innovative. However, in times of crisis their misplaced humanitarianism leads them towards compromise and pacifism. Hence, when final attempts to reach a political solution have failed, the regime is fatally weakened. 'Lions' represent the opposite pole. They are men of strength, stability and integrity; cold and unimaginative, they are self-serving and are prepared to use force to achieve or maintain their position. 'Lions' are defenders of the status quo in both the state and civil society. They are likely to be committed to public order, religion and political orthodoxy. For Pareto, the qualities of 'fox' and 'lion' are generally mutually exclusive. History is a process of circulation between these two types of elite. Pareto's ideal system of governance would reflect a balance of forces that exhibits characteristics of both 'fox' and 'lion'. This incessant process of elite renewal, circulation and replacement illuminates the thesis that an elite rules in all organised societies.

Pareto's focus on the concentration of power in the hands of a political elite represented a rejection of both vulgar Marxist economism and the weak but popular liberal/pluralist view. It undermined the Marxist conception of the state as a mere tool of the working class. It rejects Marx's claim (Marx, 1983, p. 203) that 'the history of all hitherto existing society is the history of class struggle'. Within this approach, liberal-democratic constitutions give expression to bourgeois demands and cement the dominant ideology. Hence, for Marxists, the state is a reflection of the economic conditions and the nature of class struggle. No capitalist state can be called democratic in the sense of securing liberty and rendering the exercise of political power accountable because the state ensures the long-term interests of continued and expanding capital accumulation. At the same time, Pareto's elitist claims also weaken the pluralist conception of the state as a co-ordinator of the national interest in a plural society. Within the pluralist paradigm the polity is comprised of a multiplicity of competing groups, all of which seek to influence the decision-making process. Rule purports to be in the interest of all and not that of any one section or alliance of sections. The duty of government is to harmonise and co-ordinate.

Mosca argued that elites were inevitable as all societies are characterised by the dictatorship of the majority by the minority. He posited the existence of a ruling, but not necessarily economically dominant, class from which key office holders were drawn. Within Mosca's formulation, each ruling class develops a 'political formula' which maintains and legitimates its rule to the rest of the population. Elite circulation will usually occur through inheritance but, from time to time, power will pass into the hands of another class due to the failure and collapse of the 'political formula'. Mosca's conceptualisation of the 'political formula' has much in common with the concept of 'hegemony', which springs from the views of Karl Marx and Friedich Engels in *The German Ideology* (1846); the ideas of the ruling class are in every historical stage the ruling ideas. Hence, the class that is the dominant economic group in society is, at the same time, its ruling intellectual force (Evans, 1975, pp. 82–6). In other words, an economistic Marxist would say that those people owning the means of production also control the process of government and can use this domination to impose their views on society. This results in a false consciousness among the proletariat, whereby they accept their sub-ordinate position in capitalist society and do not question the existing social and political structure. Mosca failed to develop the concept of 'political formula' in any systematic way, unlike his Marxist contemporary, Antonio Gramsci. The centrality of the ideological dimension to an understanding of the dialectic of power domination and control is an important consideration that Mosca's research clearly overlooked.

Michels' work needs to be understood in the context of his own personal struggle against the German academic establishment. He wrote from the standpoint of a radical socialist whose ability to secure an academic post at a German university was impared by his ideological position. However, it was the German Social Democratic Party, and its propensity for oligarchy, and not the establishment, that bore the full brunt of his frustrations. Michels' (1962, p. 364) central explanation of the inevitability of elites represents a further critique of pluralism and Marxism. With regard to the former, Michels argued that the practical ideal of democracy consisted in the self-government of the masses in conformity with the decision-making of popular assemblies. However, while this system placed limits on the extension of the principle of delegation, it fails, 'to provide any guarantee against the formation of an oligarchical camerilla' [political structure]. In short, direct government by the masses was impossible. Michels applied a similar argument to political parties. In his view, the technical and administrative functions of political parties make first bureaucracy and then oligarchy inevitable. Hence, for Michels (1962, p. 364), 'Who says organisation, says oligarchy.' This maxim clearly determined his conception of the nature of elites. The notorious notion of the 'iron law of oligarchy' provides the key to Michels' thoughts on the nature of elite structures, because it ensures the dominance of the leadership over the rank and file membership. Elite circulation is maintained by the inability of the masses to mobilise against the leadership view. This ensures their subjugation to the whim of the elite. In essence, it is the very existence of this system of leadership that is incompatible with the tenets of liberal democracy and pluralism.

The work of Robert Michels is remembered more as a series of sound bites than as a seminal contribution to political thought. As a case in point, his phrase the 'iron law of oligarchy' has been conceptualised more by others than by himself. For example, the notion of organisation as the basis of oligarchy has been developed much further in the research of Max Weber (1947) and organisational theorists such as March and Simon (1958), among others. The major impact of Michels' work has been on pluralist thinking in so far as it has compelled pluralists to acknowledge the existence of elites, although they continue to reject the argument that elites act cohesively (see Chapter 11).

The integration of elites is generally assumed by Pareto, Mosca and Michels without any rigorous empirical investigation. Pareto failed to demonstrate a theory of elite domination in his native Italy. Mosca showed that governments in the past were often characterised by a self-serving elite, but did not establish that this was always the case. Further, while Michels argued that Western European political parties were characterised by elite domination, it was a difficult proposition to sustain empirically. Perhaps not surprisingly, then, subsequent elite theorists have disagreed strongly about the relative degree, causes and consequences of elite integration in Western industrialised societies. In the USA a lengthy debate has ensued over the structure of power and influence at the national level, which has centred on the degree to which this structure of elite domination has coalesced or expanded (see Moore, 1979). This debate will be considered in the third section of this chapter. First, however, I shall examine the work of the democratic elitists. The views of the classical elitists and those of the democratic elitists are summarised in Table 12.1 (pp. 234–5).

# ■ Democratic elitism

Democratic elitism is associated with the work of Max Weber (1864–1920) and Joseph Schumpeter (1883–1946) which emerged in critique of the weak liberal view of democratic theory. Both these thinkers believed that participation in politics was circumscribed by powerful social forces. In their view, liberal democracy at its very best was a restrictive enterprise for selecting decision-makers and ensuring their legitimacy through elections. At worst, it was an attenuated form of governance aimed at securing the hegemony of a ruling political elite.

Max Weber's political thought emphasises the independent influence of the 'political' as opposed to the 'economic'. He therefore rejected any notion that the history of ideas could be reduced to economic factors. Hence he was opposed to Marxist analyses of 'ideology' and 'super-structure'. He further argued that the advance of bureaucratic organisation was an inevitable component of the growth of capitalism and had undermined the efficacy of the liberal democratic model. He viewed democracy as a means for securing good government rather than popular control and political equality and refuted any natural law of democratic government embodied in classical democratic theory.

Weber's views on state power and domination are central to our understanding of the theoretical development of elitist thought. They represent a significant and sophisticated development. Weber argued that the state is characterised by three main elements:

- a differentiated set of institutions and personnel;
- centralisation, in the sense that political relations radiate from the centre to cover a territorially demarcated area; and
- a monopoly of authoritative, binding rule-making sustained by a monopoly of the means of physical violence (Mann, 1988, p. 4).

For Weber, elite domination within the state apparatus was inevitable. As Weber himself puts it, 'All ideas aiming at abolishing the dominance of men over men are illusory' (Weber to Michels, 1908, quoted in Mommsen, 1974, p. 87). The crucial feature of the state is located within its role as the major authoritative association within a given territory. For the state to maintain its central position it has to claim a monopoly of the legitimate use of force. Domination, or as Weber termed it, 'the authoritarian power of command' (Roth, 1978, p. 946) is a necessary and inevitable feature of this process. State domination requires:

- a minimum of voluntary compliance;
- an acceptance of commands as valid norms; and
- a belief in the legitimacy of the form of domination.

Hence, force, although always present, is not enough to ensure the stability and survival of a regime; all systems have to provide a source of legitimation for their form of governance.

As Table 12.2 shows, Weber suggested three types of legitimate domination. The first, 'traditional', rests on a belief in the 'sanctity of immemorial custom'. The second, 'charismatic', centres on a devotion to the exceptional sanctity of heroism or exemplary character of an individual person. The final type, 'rational', focuses on a conviction as to the legality of enacted rules (Runciman, 1978, pp. 226–50). It is important to note that these three pure types did not represent historical stages. Any empirical situation could involve elements of any of the three, in different combinations. How do these ideal types of legitimate domination relate to different institutionalised state forms? 'Traditional' domination centred on patrimonial states and feudalism; 'charismatic' domination was an inherently unstable form caused by what Weber termed 'the routinisation of charisma'; and 'rational' domination was seen as the major state form in Western societies. Weber (Roth, 1968, p. 1117) argued that charismatic domination was the 'creative revolutionary force of history', but that it was the fate of charisma to decline with the development of permanent institutional structures. Bureaucracy was viewed by Weber as the epitome of a formally-organised structure based on rational principles. However, he also believed that bureaucracy first arose in patrimonial states and, as such, lacked certain features deemed to be essential to modern democracies.

Table 12.2  *Weber's conception of domination*

| Forms of domination | Source | Leadership | Change |
|---|---|---|---|
| **Traditional** | Non-rational | Customary | Static |
| **Charismatic** | Affectual (emotional) | Personal | Dynamic |
| **Rational** | Rational | Impersonal Rulers | Dynamic |

*Source*: M. Evans (1984), Department of Government, University of Manchester, mimeo.

**Table 12.1** *From classical elitism to democratic elitism*

| Main features of perspectives | Representative theorist | | | |
| --- | --- | --- | --- | --- |
| | Pareto | Mosca | Michels | Democratic elitists |
| Explanations for the inevitability of elites | History shows that there is a perpetual circulation of elites. | All societies are characterised by the dictatorship of the majority by the minority. | The technical and administrative functions of political parties makes bureaucracy and oligarchy inevitable. | Politics involves an unceasing struggle for power and the primacy of nation state interests over all others. |
| Nature of elites | Every field of enterprise has its own elite. | A ruling but not necessarily economically dominant class from which office holders are drawn. | 'Who says organisation, says oligarchy' (1962, p. 364). | An hierarchy of domination is inevitable as 'all ideas aiming at abolishing the dominance of men over men are illusory'. |
| Elite structures | Governing ('foxes' and 'lions') and non-governing. | Each ruling class develops a 'political formula' which justifies its rule to the rest of the population. | The 'iron law of oligarchy' ensures the dominance of the leadership over the rank and file membership. | A focus upon elite domination within the state apparatus, but elitism is a feature of modern organisational forms in all spheres. |

| | | | | |
|---|---|---|---|---|
| **Elite circulation** | A circulation of individuals between the upper and lower strata in the same field of activity and a circulation between governing and non-governing elites. | Circulation usually occurs through inheritance, but from time to time power will pass into the hands of another class because of the failure of the political formula. | The incompetence of the masses constitutes the foundation of elite domination and ensures their subjugation to the whim of the elite. | Weber suggests three pure types of elite domination: traditional; charismatic; and rational, from which different types of elites and elite circulation emerge. |
| **Assessment of the role of elites** | Some governing elites are progressive, others conservative – no clear strand of progress. | Unlike Pareto, Mosca believed in human progress and accepted a general trend of progression, with some exceptions. | Every system of leadership is incompatible with the tenets of democracy. | Weber argues that charismatic domination is the creative revolutionary force of history, but that this has receded as a consequence of the emergence of permanent institutional structures. |
| **Point of convergence** | Rejection of Marxian economism and liberal democracy. | Rejection of Marxian economism and participatory liberal democratic forms. | Rejection of socialism and liberal democracy. | Rejection of socialism and participatory liberal democratic forms. |
| **Focus of empirical enquiry** | Failed to demonstrate a theory of elite domination in his native Italy (Bottomore, 1966, p. 53). | Demonstrates that government in the past was often characterised by a self-serving elite, but did not show that this was always the case. | Attempts to establish a theory of elite domination in Western European political parties based upon weak empirical evidence. | Primarily a sociologist of great standing, whose interest to political science is limited in scope. His major contribution lies both in his classification of the legitimacy of regimes and in his analysis of the rule of bureaucracy. |

A pure type rational bureaucracy involves:

- the organisation of functions on a continuous and regulated basis;
- a functional division of spheres of competence;
- hierarchical organisation with control of higher over lower levels;
- working rules which may be technical, or norms requiring training;
- officials who are separated from the ownership of the means of production or administration;
- officials who cannot appropriate their office;
- administration which involves a written record; and
- a bureaucratic administrative staff.

Hence, there exists a hierarchy of domination which contains a system of rationally consistent rules and job specialisation among the officials, who administer the rules in a highly impersonal way. As Weber puts it:

> The development of modern organisational forms in all spheres (state, church, army, party, economy, interest groups, voluntary associations, charitable bodies etc.) is simply identical with the development and continuous increase of bureaucratic administration. (Roth and Wittich, 1968, p. 223)

Weber was a liberal who thought that politics inevitably involved an unceasing struggle for power, and that nation state interests should supersede all others. At the same time, he was clearly a liberal in anguish (see Momsen, 1974, p. 95) who argued that the central issue was not that there was too much freedom, too much individualism or too much democracy. He was concerned with establishing how one could preserve any individual freedom. How is it possible to check and control the power of state bureaucracy? As Weber puzzles, 'How will democracy even in this limited sense be at all possible?' (Roth and Wittich, 1968, p. 1403) Here, he broadens the scope of his critique of liberal democracy and power relations from one which focused on the relationship between, and contradictions of, democracy and capitalism, to one which emphasises the role of the state in securing elite domination.

Schumpeter's approach involved a mixture of competing methodologies; a tool-bag of Weberian, utilitarian and Marxist method. He shared Marx's view of the inevitability of the collapse of the capitalist state under the weight of its own contradictions (see Schumpeter, 1976, part III) and, like Marx, argued that large corporations dominated the production and distribution of goods. Despite this, Schumpeter was a reluctant socialist who rejected Marxist class analysis and class conflict. As David Held observes, for Schumpeter:

> the definitive element of socialism was the planning of resources: an institutional pattern which allowed a central authority control over the production system. Interpreted in this manner, socialism was not necessarily incompatible, as Weber had asserted, with democracy. (Held, 1987, p. 169)

For Schumpeter, the most important task for socialists was to develop the most appropriate model of democracy to meet the demands of 'big government'. Here, he highlighted the importance of the planning of resources in economic and political life. In particular, he emphasised the need to re-examine the role of both bureaucratisation and democratisation in providing the conditions for a centralised governing tradition. It was within this context that he embraced the need for a leadership model of democracy. He rejected explicitly what he perceived to be the classical doctrine of democracy, and was a vociferous advocate of the leadership state. Because, in Schumpeter's view, 'the people' are, and can be, nothing more than 'producers of governments', a mechanism to select 'the men who are able to do the deciding' (Schumpeter, 1976, p. 296). Hence he refuted the notion of the 'popular will' as a social construct that had no rational basis, as a 'manufactured' rather than a genuine popular will (ibid., pp. 256–68). 'Popular will' is therefore the 'product and not the motive power for the political process' (ibid., p. 263). Within this formulation, democracy and socialism can only be compatible as a form of 'competitive elitism', and if the conditions for its successful functioning are met (Held, 1987, p. 177).

Schumpeter's theory of democracy reflected support for competitive party systems in which democracy merely served as a source of legitimation for the governing elite. He quite clearly failed to recognise that, rather than safeguarding the last remnants of individual liberty, the competitive party system merely enabled political elites to manipulate and distort the political will of the citizen. As Macpherson (1977, p. 89) observes, Schumpeter appeared to confuse a 'competitive' political system with an oligopolistic one, in which:

> there are only a few sellers, a few suppliers of political goods . . . Where there are so few sellers, they need not and do not respond to the buyers demands as they must do in a fully competitive system. They can set prices and set the range of goods that will be offered. More than that, they can, to a considerable extent create [their own] demand.

Political elites are thus both inevitable and necessary.

Following Weber, the democratic elitist model developed a broad view of the state. The state has both capacity and autonomy as a regulator and distorter of markets. The democratic elitist model also emphasises the unattainability of classical participatory democratic forms of political organisation. Joseph Schumpeter's 'equilibrium model' develops this theme, arguing that a division of labour between political activists and a passive electorate was crucial for strong, efficient government and the defence of liberty. Schumpeter accepts the inevitability of hierarchy, observing the democratic process as a forum for legitimate elite competition: 'it is simply an institutional arrangement for reaching political decisions not an end in itself' (Schumpeter, 1976, p. 126). It is not surprising that Schumpeter's conclusion should claim that: 'dictator-ships might better serve the popular interest than democracies'.

# ■ Modern elitist perspectives

This section reviews four modern elitist perspectives. Table 12.3 provides an overview of the main features of these perspectives.

## □ *National elite power network studies*

The study of national elite power networks (NEPNs) has long been a focus of study in the USA and the UK. The key concern of this literature has been to identify the degree to which national elite structures are unified or diversified. The origins of these studies lie in the pluralist–radical elitist debates of the 1940s and 1950s in the USA. These had two chief protagonists: C. Wright Mills (1956) who in *The Power Elite* (see Dahl, 1958 for a critique) provided an account of the role of power elites within the US Executive; and Walter Burnham who, in *The Managerial Revolution*, argued that a new managerial elite was in the process of establishing control across all capitalist states. However, it was the work of the radical elitist C. Wright Mills that had the most impact on future NEPNs.

Mills' theory involved a three level gradation of the distribution of power. At the top level were those in command of the major institutional hierarchies of modern society – the executive branch of the national government, the large business corporations, and the military establishment. The pluralist model of competing interests, Mills argued, applied only to the 'middle levels', the semi-organised interaction between interest group and legislative politics which pluralists mistook for the entire power structure of the capitalist state. A politically fragmented 'society of the masses' occupied the bottom level. Mills' (1956, pp. 167–9) work suggested a close relationship between economic elites and governmental elites: the 'corporate rich' and the 'political directorate'. He maintained that the growing centralisation of power in the federal executive branch of government had been accompanied by a declining role for professional politicians and a growing role for 'political outsiders' from the corporate world (ibid., p. 235). Despite this, Mills contended that it would be a mistake 'to believe that the political apparatus is merely an extension of the corporate world, or that it had been taken over by the representatives of the corporate rich' (ibid., p. 170). Here, Mills wanted to distinguish his position from what he termed the 'simple Marxian view', which held that economic elites were the the real holders of power. For this reason, he used the term 'power elite' rather than 'ruling class', a term which for him implied too much economic determinism (ibid., pp. 276–7). Crucially, Mills argued that political, military and economic elites all exercised a considerable degree of autonomy, were often in conflict, and rarely acted in concert.

*The Power Elite* provided the most important critique of pluralism written from an elitist perspective. It emphasised that far from being an independent arbiter of the national interest, the state was actually dominated by a NEPN of politicians, military and corporate bosses who moulded public policy to suit their own ends. Mills' analysis was given an empirical fillip by a series of 'community power' studies which demonstrated the validity of the elitist interpretation of American politics (see Polsby, 1963, for an interesting critique). In the debate that ensued throughout the 1950s and 1960s, pluralists emphasised the mistaken nature of the claims of the community power theorists (see Chapter 11). NEPN theorists in the USA such as Mills and Domhoff found a considerable amount of elite integration, although with various bases in the national power structure. According to Mills (1956, p. 292):

> The conception of the power elite and of its unity rests upon the corresponding developments and the coincidence of interests among economic, political, and military organisations. It also rests upon the similarity of origins and outlook, and the social and personal intermingling of the top circles from each of these dominant hierarchies.

The existence of a broad, inclusive network of powerful people with similar social origins, in different institutions, is an important feature of this view of the power structure. However, the NEPN literature identifies three key dimensions of political elite integration:

(i)    Social homogeneity (Mills, 1956; Domhoff, 1967) which emphasises shared class and status origins.
(ii)   Value consensus (Prewitt and Stone, 1973), focusing on agreement among elites on the 'rules of the game'; and,
(iii)  Personal interaction among elites, both informally through social and personal interaction and formally through membership of common organisations.

The third dimension is reflected in the interlocking directorates of major US corporations. These ties are seen to foster integration, cohesiveness and consensus within the business community. Many social scientists, particularly in the USA, have examined the sociometric ties among elites in individual communities (for example, Laumann *et al.*, 1977) following the pioneering work of Mills.

In the UK, NEPNs have rarely reached any degree of sophistication. A number of historians have considered the fate of the English aristocracy

Table 12.3  *Modern elitism*

| Main features of perspectives | Representative perspective | | | |
| --- | --- | --- | --- | --- |
| | Power elite studies | Revisionist pluralism | Corporatism | Neo-corporatism |
| Explanations for the inevitability of elites | Democracy limited because its perceived detrimental effect on political and economic efficiency. Competition between rival political elites and parties. A constitutional settlement which patterns social relationships and politics. | Power is open to competition between numerous groups but political participation and political equality are circumscribed by unequal access to both resources and the decision-making process. | Corporatism emerges as a normative or ideal state form, a consequence of the fusion of state and private sector interests (e.g. large firms or organised labour). | Neo-corporatism is a concept for understanding policy-making. |
| Nature of elites | C. Wright Mills emphasises the emergence of a power elite; Walter Burnham, a managerial elite; Polsby, machine politics. | Multiple pressure groups, but a corporate bias exists. | Social partners. Sectional interests are uniquely privileged in policy-making. | Monopolies of interest representation exist within the policy-making process. |
| Elite structures | Closed policy networks. | Closed policy networks. | Institutional setting for legitimate elite domination through tripartism. | Closed policy networks but not necessarily tripartite. |

| | | | | |
|---|---|---|---|---|
| **Elite circulation** | Contingent upon bargaining role of sectional interest. | Contingent upon bargaining role of sectional interest. | Contingent upon bargaining role of sectional interest. | Contingent upon bargaining role of sectional interest. |
| **Assessment of the role of elites** | Contrary to pluralist opinion, the state was not an independent arbiter of the national interest. | No one group dominates all policy networks. A pluralism exists on the terrain of 'low' politics. | Corporatism observes a general downgrading of liberal democratic and pluralist forms of state–group intermediation. | Neo-corporatists observe that hierarchies develop in associational forms. |
| **Point of convergence** | In critique of pluralism/democratic theory as the hegemonic approach in American political science. | In critique of pluralist ideal-typical political forms and the need to create new countervailing mechanisms to offset a democratic deficit. | In critique of pluralist and socialist ideal-typical political forms. | In critique of pluralism. |
| **Focus of empirical enquiry** | Mills, for example, focused on identifying and classifying a national elite network of politicians, military and corporate bosses. | British accounts focus on re-establishing pluralism through constitutional reform. | Schmitter (1979, p. 38) for example, provides empirical evidence to suggest that Brazil, Spain, Portugal. Greece, Austria, Italy and Germany all have forms of state–group intermediation that approximate to the corporatist model. | As a concept for understanding policy making emphasis is placed upon identifying powerful social and economic interests in policy networks. |

(for example, Winchester, 1981) dwelling on the changing nature of the relationship between landed and mercantile interests. William Guttsman (1963) analysed the decline of the upper class and the rise of the middle class as a principal source of elite renewal. Anthony Sampson (for example, Sampson, 1982), in his exhaustive accounts of the anatomy of Britain, has argued that the aristocracy no longer rules and, indeed, that there is no longer a real social elite at all. Further, Sampson contends that the various hierarchies of British society have become gradually more open in their recruitment, and the diversity of these hierarchies is such that there is no single centre of power.

# ☐ *The corporate power debates*

The aim of this sub-section is to provide a simple overview of the central considerations within elitist thought on the analysis of the relationship between business elites and government. This is a particularly fertile area of analysis as it provides a further example of convergence between competing theories of the state that is crystallised in the 'structural approach' to the study of corporate power; an approach that is implicit both in the work of Charles Lindblom (1977, 1982) and in neo-Marxist analyses of the liberal-democratic state (Marsh, 1983). These debates focus primarily upon the relationship between economic power and political power as it is exerted through the modern interventionist state. The ensuing discussion will argue that, first, the neo-pluralist position has more in common with elitism than pluralism; and, second, that the corporate power debate in the USA provides a major source of convergence between revisionist pluralist, elitist and Marxist theories of the state.

Neo-pluralism, as descibed in Chapter 11, is a critical theory which may be identified with the work of Charles Lindblom (1977, 1982). It rests on the structuralist view that because of the dependency of Western democracies on capitalist economies, the disproportionate influence of business corporations over the state is an inevitable structural necessity, 'for the state to operate in conditions of stability and therefore of political equilibrium – business needs must first be met'. Lindblom criticises liberal democratic theory for failing to take into account the 'privileged position of business'. Lindblom's work has not gone without criticism. While many pluralists have modified their methodology to cope with these critiques of corporate power, and have reconsidered aspects of democratic theory, a number of political scientists, who may be viewed as methodological pluralists, have dissented from the new conventional wisdom. Vogel criticises Lindblom's position on the basis that it exaggerates the role that investment decisions play in the performance of the economy. Moreover, he suggests that Lindblom 'underestimates the options available to politicians to manipulate business decisions and fails to appreciate that businessmen are not unique in requiring inducements to perform their social role' (Vogel, 1987, p. 385). This leads Vogel to the conclusion that while corporations undeniably exercise significant political power, its scope and magnitiude may be accounted for within a pluralist framework of interest group politics:

> My contention is not that individual companies, trade associations and inter-industry coalitions do not weild significant political power, of course they do. It is rather that we do not require a distinctive methodology for measuring the political power of business in capitalist democracies. Business is not unique. There is nothing about the nature, scope or magnitude of the power wielded by business that cannot be accounted for within the framework of a sophisticated model of interest-group politics. (Vogel, 1987, p. 408)

Lindblom is also held to be culpable for his failure to analyse the divisions within business, to recognise the power potentialities of other groups, or to take into account the flexibility involved in the relationship between business and the state (see Marsh, 1983).

In contrast to neo-pluralists, neo-conservative political scientists consider corporate political power to be on the decline (see Steinfel, 1979). Jeanne Kirkpatrick (1979), for example, identifies the emergence of a new class, a knowledge elite that threatens the political aspirations of corporate power. Kirkpatrick argues that this new class has been in the forefront of efforts to shift various responsibilities from the private sector to the government, and has had a significant role in developing public policies hostile to business and the market system (Kirkpatrick, 1979, p. 46). Aaron Wildavsky, on the other hand, has defended the corporation as a bulwark of pluralism and a sanctuary for private life against the bureaucratic power of the state (Wildavsky, 1978, p. 234). James Wilson (1973) uses a tool bag approach in assessing competing theories of political power (Marxist, elitist, bureacratic and pluralist). Wilson concludes that no single model provides an accurate description of the political system as a whole, and that different models are applicable in different policy areas. None the less, Wilson may still be considered to be a pluralist because while some groups are able to dominate particular areas, their power is not necessarily transferable to other policy areas or to the overall structure of power.

The structural dimension of corporate power implicit in the work of revisonist pluralists such as Lindblom (1982) has important implications for democratic theory and pluralism. It places decison making firmly within an elitist context, or what Lindblom has termed the 'imprisoned zone of decision making' (1982, p. 324). This suggests a very strong form of elite domination that does not fit happily with democratic theory. Once again, the pluralist response represents a remarkable retreat from the classical position. It is recognised that power is open to competition between numerous groups, but political participation is circumscribed by unequal access to both resources and the decision-making process. Further, multiple groups exist, but a corporate bias predominates. However, in their view, the integrity of the pluralist position is maintained because no one group dominates all policy networks. In both the above cases, the paradigmatic shift within pluralism towards the elitist and Marxist position is striking.

## ☐ *Corporatism and neo-corporatism*

Corporatism emerged as a strand of Catholic social doctrine that was adapted and subsequently modified (some would say vulgarised) in the authoritarian regimes of Benito Mussolini's Italy (1922–43) and Antonio Salazar's Portugal (1933–74). It was later resurrected in several European democracies under the name of 'neo-corporatism'. Like many such concepts in social science, different people have used it to mean different things, but Philippe Schmitter (1974, pp. 93–4) provides the most exact conceptual definition:

> Corporatism can be defined as a system of interest representation in which the constituent units are organized into a limited number of singular, compulsory, noncompetitive, hierarchically ordered and functionally differentiated categories, recognised or licensed (if not created) by the state and granted a deliberate representational monopoly within their respective categories in exchange for observing certain controls on their selection of leaders and articulation of demands and supports.

Hence, corporatism is a model of state–group intermediation in which the interests of the state and certain private sector interests fuse. These interests (principally large firms, but also to some extent organised labour and other private interests such as the professions) enter into negotiations and compromise with government agreeing to certain concessions and undertaking certain functions of government. In turn, the government supports them financially and forwards their interests in policy-making. Corporatist theory received an enormous boost in Britain during the period of the 1974–79 Labour governments, when initiatives such as planning agreements, incomes policies and the National Enterprise Board (NEB) seemed to indicate a move towards a system of private ownership coupled with state direction. Corporatism is therefore best understood as an ideal state form which represents a fusion of state and private sector interests (Cox, 1988). Elites emerge within this context of social partnership because of the need for governments to increase Gross Domestic Product (GDP) in order to stay in power. Hence, sectional interests almost inevitably become uniquely privileged within policy-making. The most distinctive feature of corporatist theory lies in its structures of elite domination. An institutional setting for legitimate elite domination is created in which elite circulation is dependent upon the bargaining resources of the various sectional interests.

Corporatists have observed a general downgrading of liberal democratic and pluralist forms of state group intermediation (Schmitter and Lehmbruch, 1979). As such, corporatism represented a critique of both pluralist and socialist ideal-typical political forms. However, Corporatism was very much a product of its time, and while Schmitter (1979, p. 38) did provide some empirical evidence to suggest that Brazil, Spain, Portugal, Greece, Austria, Italy and Germany all had forms of state–group intermediation approximating the corporatist model, it remained equally possible to provide examples to the contrary.

Neo-corporatism emerged in the wake of a wave of pluralist critiques of Corporatist methodology (see for example, Cawson, 1985). They contended that there was nothing within corporatist method which had not already been accounted for in revisionist and methodological currents of neo-pluralism. Corporatism was also criticised by Marxists, who argued that it ignored the ideological dimension of analysis and granted an unwarranted autonomy to the state in mediating between competing sectional interests. The neo-corporatists reshaped their argument accordingly. As Cox (1988, p. 297) observes:

> Instead of accepting that the concept might not be as widely applicable as they first thought, to save its integrity they redefined it so that its meaning subtly shifted from being a descriptive concept about an ideal-typical political form of the state to become a catch-all phrase for special interests bargaining with the state.

They argued that, as hierarchies develop in all associational forms, corporatism could be used as a concept for understanding policy-making. Neo-corporatists identify the existence of monopolies of sectional interests within the policy-making process. This is reflected in closed policy networks, but not necessarily tripartite ones. Within this formulation, elite circulation is still dependent upon the bargaining resources of the sectional interests involved.

Whether or not the corporatist state form ever existed is still open to much debate. Many of the claims made in the literature are certainly stronger on assertion than on evidence (see Cox, 1988, p. 295) and remain vulnerable to the Marxist charge that they fail to specify whose interest this new bargained corporatism serves. In sum, it still provides a poor understanding of how and why policy networks operate in the fundamentally elitist way that they do. In this sense, corporatism and neo-corporatism provide insufficient methodological tools for analysing power monopolies within policy networks.

# ■ Conclusion

Overall, this chapter has made two central arguments. First, elitism still provides an important focus for the work of political scientists and political sociologists, particularly in the USA, and has presented a compelling critique of the liberal democratic model. Second, when contrasted with other theories of the state, the elitist position appears to be both theoretically unsophisticated and conceptually underdeveloped. There are four central reasons for this. First, despite a large number of empirical studies, many of which have been cited in this chapter, elite theory remains difficult to sustain in an empirical sense. Second, as Birch (1993, p. 202) reminds us, 'there is no adequate and convincing theory showing that democratic systems must always be elitist in practice'. Third, elite theory offers an insufficient conceptualisation of the relationship between elite circulation and the nature of state crisis and legitimation (see Hay, 1993, 1994 for a broader discussion from a post-Marxist position). Fourth, elite theory offers a limited account of the structure of elite networks, both within the nation state, between centre and region, and outside the nation state, between nations (see Higley *et al.*, 1991, pp. 35–45). Yet, despite this, elite theory still contributes much to the tool bag of the political scientist. As Domhoff (cited in Olsen and Marger, 1993, p. 180) puts it:

> Thus, the argument about the American power structure is as much philosophic as it is empirical. While the debate continues, however, we should continue to remind ourselves that members of an upper class making up less than 1 per cent of the population own 20 to 25 per cent of all privately held wealth and 45 to 50 per cent of all privately held corporate stock; they are overrepresented in seats of formal power from the corporation to the federal government; and they win much more often than they lose on issues ranging from the tax structure to labor law to foreign policy.

The future of elite theory continues to look bright, because there is now a distinct global dimension to the discourse, of the kind suggested by David Held's conception of global interconnectedness (Held, 1991). His view may be summed up as a rejection of the underlying premises of democratic theory that democracies should be treated as:

> self-contained units; that democracies are clearly demarcated one from another; that change within democracies can be understood largely with reference to the internal structures and dynamics of national democratic politics; and that democratic politics is itself ultimately an expression of the interplay between forces operating within the nation-state. (ibid., p. 199)

Thus the growing integration of economics, technology, communications and law, together with the transnational character of capital, has eroded nation state sovereignty of the kind jealously guarded in the British context, and undermined state capacities. The density of current global politics and its impact upon state theorising has been dramatic. As McGrew (1992, p. 12) comments:

> It encompasses not just political relations between states, and relations between states and international organisations, but also a vast array of transnational interactions which cut across national societies, as well as transgovernmental relations which permeate the institutional structures of the state itself.

While the credibility of the elitist approach increased in response to the dramatic rise in the size and complexity of the capitalist state, its future development is likely to reflect a concern with the emergence of new social and political forms as a consequence of globalisation pressures. Analysing how far increased globalisation has facilitated changes in state form must be a key concern for contemporary elitists. Elitists have a new, fertile ground for analysis that will inevitably entail confronting an important source of weakness in the elitist approach: its national specificity.

# ■ Further reading

For three sound overviews of elitist theory, see Dunleavy and O'Leary (1987, ch. 4), Held (1987, ch. 5) and Birch (1993, chs. 11 and 12). A collection of both classic and recent articles written from an elitist perspective can be found in Olsen and Marger (1993). For a critique of Mills' power elite thesis, see Dahl (1958). See Domhoff (1967, 1970), Prewitt and Stone (1973) and Moore (1979) for the most compelling accounts of elite theory in the US literature. Lindblom (1977) deals with the key issues at stake in the political analysis of business groups. For the classic corporatist approach, see Schmitter (1974) and on varieties of corporatism see Williamson (1985).

# ■ *Chapter 13* ■

# Marxism
## George Taylor

In his celebrated text *History and Class Consciousness*, G. Lukács sought finally to resolve the thorny issue of what constituted the essence of orthodox Marxism (Lukács, 1922). As he observed, it had become an increasingly precarious task to challenge or reject particular theses without forfeiting the right to the title 'Marxist'. Such a thankless task has not become any easier with the passage of time. In part, this can be attributed to the problems experienced within the Marxist tradition during the 1970s. The doubts which had surrounded structuralist Marxism had developed into a full-blown crisis as the pivotal role accorded to class struggle was questioned increasingly. This was a problem accentuated by the emergence of new issues such as feminism and environmentalism, the persistence (some would say success) of the welfare state, and the transformation of work relations under capitalism. Although not always directly concerned with the debates on state theory, these issues have nevertheless had a profound impact on its development (for a more detailed account of these themes, see Taylor (1994)). It is also important to recognise that Marxist state theory has also had a profound effect on other traditions, and has influenced the work of notable political scientists such as Andrew Gamble and Charles Lindblom.

This chapter is divided in two main parts. The first traces the development of the core themes of the Marxist theory of the state through the works of Karl Marx, Antonio Gramsci, Nicos Poulantzas and Bob Jessop. Attention is focused on five sets of changes: the struggle with economism; the growing emphasis on state autonomy; the increasing stress upon the manufacture of consent as the basis of hegemonic domination; the move away from privileging social class; and the increased attention paid to the role of calculating subjects, with the consequent emphasis on strategic selectivity (Table 13.1 offers a brief outline of the positions of key authors on these issues). The second part of the chapter explores a series of critical stances taken by the radical Weberian, feminist and environmentalist traditions.

# ■ Marx on the state

It is possible to discern in Marx's writings at least two analytically distinct accounts of the relationship between the state and particular classes. The first, and by far the most influential, is the view of the state as an instrument of the dominant class which performs the crucial function of co-ordinating its long-term interests. From this perspective, most commonly associated with the Communist manifesto, Marx argues that the 'executive of the modern State is but a committee for managing the affairs of the whole bourgeoisie' (Marx, 1973, p. 69). Here, Marx depicts class struggle in terms of a simple clash between two opposites, with a declining number of the bourgeoisie and an explosion in the size of the proletariat.

The second view embodies a more subtle appreciation of the relationship between the state and particular classes. Such a view can be seen clearly in Marx's essays on contemporary political events in France, *18th Brumaire of Louis Bonaparte* (1852) and *Class Struggles in France* (1850), where he is eager to stress the plurality of classes and the manner in which the state appears capable both of dominating civil society and of restricting the power of the bourgeoisie. While this analysis suggests that agents of the state do not simply perform the function of co-ordinating the long-term interests of the dominant class, Marx was nevertheless convinced that the state's role could not escape indefinitely the constraints imposed by those who own and control the means of production (Held, 1987, p. 119).

There are, then in Marx's work, two distinct approaches to the relationship between the state and particular classes. On one hand, the state is viewed as being relatively autonomous from the dominant class, and on the other, it is depicted as an instrument serving the interests of the dominant class. It should be noted, however, that these early essays do not establish a coherent and reasoned analysis of the state. As Jessop notes, at best they can be considered as a set of arguments which display an interest in the relationship between the state and class struggle within a general framework of historical materialism (Jessop, 1982, p. 9).

Marx's failure to elucidate this relationship in a more systematic manner meant that the task fell to the next generation of Marxists, most notably Georgi Plekhanov and Karl Kautsky. However, stimulated by the desire to establish a scientific Marxism (dialectical materialism) capable of replacing bourgeois science, these authors emphasised the determining role of the

Table 13.1  *Developments in the Marxist theory of the state*

| Author | Position on economism | State autonomy? | Coercion or consent? | Is class privileged? | Structure/agency/strategy |
|---|---|---|---|---|---|
| Marx | Later work develops economistic theory of history. But there are many less economistic insights, particularly in earlier work. | Two views. State as instrument of the ruling class (Communist manifesto). State having limited autonomy (work on mid-19th-century France). | Emphasis on rule by coercion and on overthrowing the capitalist state by force. | Class is privileged as a social force. | Largely a structuralist interpretation. Little, if any, role for calculating subjects. |
| Gramsci | Key author in struggle with economism. Considerable emphasis on superstructure. However, economic relations are still determining in the last instance. | Significant state autonomy but the state forwards the interests of capital. | Emphasis on manufactured consent, and thus hegemonic domination, as the basis of capitalist rule. Overthrowing the capitalist state depends on a successful hegemonic struggle. | Class is privileged as a social force. | Significant emphasis on the role of calculating subjects, particularly intellectuals. But failure to integrate this emphasis significantly with broader structuralist interpretation. |

| | | | | | |
|---|---|---|---|---|---|
| **Poulantzas** | Another key author in struggle with economism. Attempts to escape economism by utilising concept of structural selectivity. Ultimately an interesting failure. | Develops, from Althusser, the concept of relative autonomy. The state needs autonomy in order to forward the interests of 'capital in general'. | Emphasis on role of manufactured consent, backed by force. Key emphasis on the way the state uses law to 'individualise' society in order to displace class struggle. | Class is privileged as a social force. | Although there is some discussion of strategy there is no space for agency or calculating subjects. |
| **Jessop** | State of the art modern Marxist. Totally rejects economism but acknowledges the difficulty of escaping its clutches. | Rejects relative autonomy. Whether or not the state is autonomous is an empirical question. State is potentially totally autonomous but its form and function reflects the outcome of past strategic struggles. | Emphasis on hegemonic domination and struggle. The outcome of past struggles shapes the terrain on which present struggles are conducted. | Class is not privileged. There are a number of cross-cutting bases of structured inequality. None is necessarily dominant. | The emphasis is upon strategy. Strategic decisions taken by calculating subjects, agents, in contexts structured by the outcome of past strategic struggles. |
| **Block/ Skocpol** | Statist Marxist with Weberian leanings. Rejects economism. Emphasises that the key division of labour is between capitalists and state managers. | Rejects relative autonomy. State is potentially totally autonomous. However, the interests of state managers and capitalists usually coincide for structural reasons; normally re-election depends upon a successful economy. | Emphasis on manufactured consent. | Privileges class and the control of the state apparatus. | Has strong structural residues. However, emphasises the strategic decisions of state managers. No real attempt to address the relationship between structure and agency. |

productive forces at the expense of the relations of production (economism). Economism is a variant of Marxism which overemphasises the determination of social life by the economic base and therefore underestimates the importance of ideology and political action in the formation of history. It also embraces the view that there exist a set of objective laws of historical development. Put simply, this second generation of Marxists produced an evolutionary–determinist conception of history in which capitalism was governed by a set of immutable laws that lay beyond the scope of man (economism) (Merrington, 1978). As a consequence, Marxism had been cleansed of its humanist and philosophical bias and was now firmly rooted in a scientific prescription of the inevitable collapse of capitalism. This position, undoubtedly influenced by the publication of Charles Darwin's *Origin of Species,* was well suited to the political practice of the second international workers' movement. More importantly, for the purposes of this chapter, it was the rejection of this political and theoretical orthodoxy that formed the starting point of Antonio Gramsci's attempt to reformulate the Marxist theory of the state.

# ■ Antonio Gramsci

The power and originality of Gramsci's arguments lie undeniably in his attempt to re-establish human subjectivity as the principal feature of Marxism. In the orthodox Marxism of Kautsky and Plekhanov priority lay with the objective conditions of capitalism; human subjectivity (consciousness) was therefore seen as the simple manifestation of a series of deeper economic processes. In contrast, all of Gramsci's most significant contributions to Marxist theory represent an attempt to restore the voluntarist side of Marxist theory: a concern with the role of ideas, consciousness and human subjectivity. Such an endeavour is evident in his rejection of economism, his more sophisticated appreciation of the relationship between ideology and consciousness, his wider appraisal of the autonomy of the state, and his novel interpretation of the role of intellectuals in the class struggle (Gramsci, 1971).

As Merrington has noted, the starting point for Gramsci's work can be found in his explicit rejection of economism (Merrington, 1978). For Gramsci, the variant of Marxism espoused by Kautsky and Plekhanov, in attempting to develop a pseudo-science capable of predicting the volatile forces of capitalism, had neglected the most crucial feature of the dialectical approach: the interplay between the objective and subjective in the historical process. In so doing, it had reduced the complexity of the superstructure, the role of the political, the ideological and the cultural, to the status of mere emanations of the economic base (Merrington, 1977, p. 143). This is often referred to as the base/superstructure model in which the state is denied autonomy, and can be understood only in terms of its function of reproducing the relations of production, the relationship of exploitation between the proletariat and the bourgeoisie. In this context, Gramsci argued that economism was not only unable to account for important political events such as the rise of Fascism in Italy, or the increasing importance of Catholicism, but was incapable of grasping the complexity of the class struggle itself (Gramsci, 1971, pp. 158–85).

However, as Merrington has noted, the key to understanding Gramsci's theoretical originality lies in the fact that the private ownership of the means of production is a necessary, but not a sufficient basis, for capitalist domination (Merrington, 1977, p. 144). If we are to understand the complexity of any particular conjuncture, then it is essential, in Gramsci's opinion, to examine the political, the cultural and the ideological dimensions of class struggle. Thus, while he was willing to concede that the basic course of human history is explained by the development of the forces of production, he was also eager to emphasise that its trajectory would be shaped in accordance with the particular circumstances of each country (Gramsci, 1971, p. 240).

For Gramsci, then, historical change cannot be understood in terms of a simple linear development (Communism inevitably follows capitalism), but should be appreciated in all its complexity. It is open and contingent and there are crucial political, ideological and cultural dimensions to the development of consciousness. 'Consciousness' here refers to more than the economic experience of exploitation; it involves an understanding of how people are subjected to the effects of competing ideological views of the world.

Before Gramsci, the problem of order within Marxism had been explained in terms of force, repression or the overpowering dominance of bourgeois ideology. In the *German Ideology*, for example, Marx and Engels argued that the ideas of the ruling class were in every historical period the ruling ideas and that the class which is the ruling material force in society is at the same time its ruling intellectual force (Marx, 1845). In developing the concept of hegemony, Gramsci's position deviated from that of Marx and Engels in two important respects. First, Gramsci emphasised the grave importance of ideological superstructures *vis-à-vis* the economic structure (the autonomy of the state). Second, his views on hegemony display an important emphasis on the role of consent within civil society as opposed to the use of pure force by the state (Carnoy, 1984, p. 69).

According to Gramsci, the rule of a particular class contains two separate dimensions: coercion (dominance), and social–moral leadership. Hegemony refers to the way that class domination is based not simply upon coercion but upon the cultural and ideological acquiescence of subordinate classes. The political cannot therefore be understood as either force or consent: it is both force *and* consent. In this context, a class may be deemed to be hegemonic only when it has gained the active consent of the subordinate class (Femia, 1987, p. 24). Consent, here, should not be understood to be a permanent state of affairs, rather it conveys the impression of a struggle between competing ideological positions that are shifting constantly to 'accommodate the changing nature of historical circumstances and the demands and reflexive actions of human beings' (Carnoy, 1984, p. 70).

The concept of hegemony is crucial to Gramsci's theoretical framework, since its aim is to redefine the nature of power in modern society; and to attribute a greater degree of importance to the struggle taking place at the ideological, political and cultural levels. However, although Gramsci was eager to emphasise the autonomy of the superstructure, he nevertheless recognised that it was intimately connected to the relations of production. Although hegemony is ethical–political, 'it must also be economic, must necessarily be based on the decisive function exercised by the leading group in the decisive nucleus of economic activity' (Gramsci, 1971, p. 160).

The concept of the state assumes a wider and more organic sense in Gramsci's work, an alternative arena for struggle, with a corresponding increase in the level of importance attached to its role and function in modern society. Thus Gramsci argues that the state consists of the 'entire complex of political and theoretical activities with which the ruling class not only justifies and maintains its dominance, but manages to win the active consent of those over whom it rules' (Gramsci, 1971, p. 244).

The conception of power is extended to include a vast array of institutions through which power relations are mediated in society: education, the mass media, parliaments and courts, are all 'activities and initiatives which form the apparatus of the political and cultural hegemony of the ruling classes' (Gramsci, 1971, p. 258). The increasing importance accorded to the state in Gramsci's work is evidenced by the fact that he considered the struggle over consciousness to be as important as the struggle over the ownership of the means of production (Carnoy, 1984, p. 75). It is not simply an issue of the experience of exploitation, but how subordinate classes receive competing ideological interpretations of that reality. For Gramsci, the political struggle of the class and party was undertaken with the specific aim of establishing an alternative hegemony and, by implication, the political struggle needs to embrace the ideological, cultural and moral currents of society (Showstack-Sassoon, 1987, p. 118).

Within this wider, organic sense of struggle, Gramsci assigns an increasing level of importance to the role of the intellectuals. As he observed, there is no organisation without intellectuals, and therefore the political unity of any revolutionary organisation required a corresponding level of ideological coherence, in which the party, the intellectuals and the masses are brought into an organic relationship (Gramsci, 1971, p. 334). This issue, which revolves essentially around how the unity between the economic structure and the superstructure is achieved, occupied the central theme in *Southern Question* (1971). As with other areas of Gramsci's work, the objective was to unmask the complexity of the concrete situation (conjuncture), to examine the terrain of political struggle and inform the activity of the party (Showstack-Sassoon, 1987, p. 180). Crucially for Gramsci, theory could not 'be the result of a rationalistic, deductive, abstract process . . . one typical of pure intellectuals', but a process that is verified only in relation to political practice (Gramsci, 1971, p. 189).

The central thrust of Gramsci's work, then, was to reassert the role of the subject within Marxism. As such, his work is dominated by a more systematic appreciation of the role of ideology, the capitalist state and a rejection of abstract theory. The tradition of French structuralism, which rose to prominence in the 1960s and 1970s, is diametrically opposed to this position. As its critics have often noted, structuralism is a theoretical tradition bereft of a subjective core. There are no subjects in history as structuralism formulates it, only individuals who occupy objective structures (Geras, 1978).

# ■ Nicos Poulantzas

From the outset it is important to recognise that Poulantzas's theoretical position shifted dramatically between the publication of *Political Power and Social Classes* (1974) and *State Power and Socialism* (1978) as he sought to remove the structuralist residues of his earlier publications (see Jessop, 1985). However, in a number of important respects, Poulantzas's later views on the capitalist state still owe a great deal to the influence of French structuralism, and in particular, the work of Louis Althusser. This was most visible in his rejection of economism, his sustained commitment to the concept of relative autonomy, and his belief that history could not be understood in terms of a linear form of development (historicism).

In the opening statements of *State Power and Socialism* Poulantzas presents a crucial paradox for contemporary state theory. It is obvious, he argues, that we are 'hemmed in more tightly by a state whose most detailed practices demonstrate its connection with particular, and extremely precise, interests' and yet at the same time 'while the bourgeoisie continue to derive many benefits from such a state, it is by no means always contented with it' (Poulantzas, 1978, p. 12).

Adopting Althusser's concept of relative autonomy, Poulantzas argued that if the capitalist state was to function successfully as a class state, acting in the long-term interests of the bourgeoisie, then it must retain a degree of autonomy from the dominant class. As Jessop notes, the exclusion of any open class bias enables the capitalist state to present itself not as a class state, a state for particular interests, but as a state operating in the interests of the general public (people–nation) (Jessop, 1985, p. 68).

As Poulantzas points out, in the process of securing class hegemony, the state 'acts within an unstable equilibrium' of compromises between the dominant classes and the dominated 'and as such may adopt measures which are of a positive benefit to the masses' (Poulantzas, 1978, pp. 31, 127–45). Yet, while Poulantzas accepts fully Althusser's view that the political and ideological levels are relatively autonomous, he is at pains to stress that this is because the political and ideological levels are 'already present in the actual constitution of the relations of production that they play such an essential role in their reproduction' (Poulantzas, 1978, p. 27). In other words, the role of the political and ideological is not limited to reproducing the external conditions in which production takes place; rather, it is a crucial component in the social relations of production.

For Poulantzas, the capitalist form of production involves inherently a process of class identification and class struggle. If these relationships are to be reproduced it is imperative to see that the state plays an extended role. It is not concerned simply with the negative function of ideological mystification, but is actively involved in the positive reproduction of the capitalist production process (Poulantzas, 1978, p. 63). This is a significant step forward from the position held by Althusser. As Poulantzas noted, as far as Althusser was concerned, the state:

> acts and functions through repression and ideological inculcation and *nothing else*. It assumes the State's efficacy lies in what it forbids, rules out . . . according to this conception, the economic is an instance capable of self-reproduction and self-regulation, in which the State serves merely to lay down the negative rules of the economic game. (Poulantzas, 1978, p. 30)

According to Poulantzas, capitalism has promoted the view of democracy, 'one person one vote', as a sufficient condition for a mass democratic society. In so doing, it has displaced the struggle from the economic to the political sphere. This is a crucial theme within Poulantzas's later work, since this forms part of a process in which class subjects are atomised into individual juridicial subjects, thereby diffusing the potential for conflict between classes. This process of (individualisation) serves not only 'to mask and obscure class relations (the capitalist State never presents itself as a class State) but also plays an active part in the divisions and isolation of the popular masses' (Poulantzas, 1978, p. 66). In addition, Poulantzas identifies the division between mental and manual labour, the role of bourgeois law and the people–nation as crucial themes in this process of reproducing atomised individuals.

For Poulantzas, capitalist production is characterised by a social division of labour in which intellectual work is separated from manual work, a separation of technology from work and the use of science to rationalise power. The framework of state apparatuses, in Poulantzass opinion, rests on the permanent exclusion of the masses who are subjected to manual labour. In this way, the state not only has an important hold on the generation of new knowledge but also on how that knowledge is used (Carnoy, 1984).

Within Poulantzas's work on bourgeois law there are two distinct themes. In the first of these, and in contrast to the notion of consent within Gramsci's work, Poulantzas is not averse to stressing the repressive element of law. He argues, for example, that 'law is the code of organised public violence' (Poulantzas, 1978, p. 77) and that the state 'has a monopoly of legitimate physical violence' (Poulantzas, 1978, p. 80). However, there is also a second distinctive theme to Poulantzas's views on the law, in which its function is to reproduce individual political subjects by presenting their unity in the people–nation (Poulantzas, 1978, p. 87). Once again, it is a process that serves to obscure class relations and avert political crisis. In this context, Poulantzas argues that, 'confronted by the struggle of the working class in the political arena, capitalist law, as it were, damps down and channels political crises, in such a way that they do not lead to a crisis of the State itself (Poulantzas, 1978, p. 91). Within this theoretical framework, bourgeois law performs the dual function of legitimising the dispossession of the worker from the means of production, and reunifying systematically the subject under the umbrella of the people–nation. For Poulantzas, the state is actively involved in constructing both unity and disunity. It reproduces atomised individuals as juridicial subjects (preventing the unity which emerges in class-based relations of production), and reconstructs unity within the concept of the people–nation (Poulantzas, 1978, pp. 93–120).

While a large part of *State Power and Socialism* details the processes by which the state reproduces individuals as juridicial subjects, the most significant contribution of this text is to develop a view of the state as an arena of class struggle. Thus, for Poulantzas, it is impossible to understand the form and function of the state without including its role in mediating class conflict. Moreover, while the state may act in the long-term political interests of a dominant class fraction, this does not preclude the presence of the popular classes in the state. As Poulantzas argues:

> The State apparatuses consecrate and reproduce hegemony by bringing the power bloc and certain dominated classes into a variable game of provisional compromises. The State apparatuses organise and unify the dominant power bloc by permanently disorganising – dividing the dominated classes. (Poulantzas, 1978, p. 140)

This later work does not simply emphasise the presence of conflict over state power, but rather stresses the fact that this conflict takes place within the institutional apparatus of the state itself. Here, the state is presented as a fractured polity, riven with contradictions and divisions. The different branches or sectors of the state act as power centres for different class fractions or alliances within the dominant power bloc. It is in this sense that the state is perceived as a strategic field, site, terrain or process of

interconnecting power networks (Poulantzas, 1978, p. 132). For Poulantzas, the often chaotic and incoherent nature of state policy is attributable
to the way in which the struggle between different class fractions is
mediated by the institutions of the state. Here, Poulantzas identifies a
process of structural selectivity that consists of a set of institutional
mechanisms which serve to advance or obstruct (filter) the strategies of
particular class fractions (Jessop, 1985, p. 127).

In summary, then, Poulantzas's work reflects the development and
transformation of a structuralist view of the state into one that is more
historically specific, where social movements play a key role. There are
two crucial themes embodied in this position. First, the capitalist state and
the relations of production have undergone significant change and can only
be understood as being historically specific, or associated with a particular
stage in the development of a mode of production. Second, there has been
a displacement of class struggle from production into the heart of the state.
The forms and functions of the state are not determined by the class
struggle in some abstract sense, but are the historical expression of those
relations in the form of struggle (Carnoy, 1984). Within this conception of
the state as a strategic terrain, state policy is explained in terms of strategic
causality, a process involving strategic calculation without individual
calculating subjects (Jessop, 1985, p. 127).

Although the concept of relative autonomy was crucial to Poulantzas's
theoretical framework its function and meaning shifted considerably
between the publication of *Political Power and Social Classes* (1974) and
*State Power and Socialism* (1978) (Jessop, 1985). In his earlier work, the
concept referred to the level of institutional autonomy required to organise
the unity of the dominant class fraction(s) in order to secure their
hegemony over the nation–people (Jessop, 1985, p. 132). Here, the crucial
question is, as his critics have pointed out, 'How relative is the relative
autonomy of the state?' In reply, Poulantzas argued that

> the degree, the extent, the forms, etc (how relative, and how is it relative) of the
> relative autonomy of the State can only be examined . . . with reference to a
> given capitalist State, and to the precise conjuncture of the corresponding class
> struggle . . . I cannot, therefore, answer this question in its general form
> precisely on account of the conjuncture of the class struggle. (cited in Jessop,
> 1985, p. 134)

As Jessop observes, there is an explicit tension here between necessity
and contingency in relating institutional forms and the class struggle. Put
simply, while Poulantzas wanted to avoid the charge of economic
reductionism, by introducing an element of contingency, he did not want
to abandon the Marxian view that the capitalist state must, in the long run,
reproduce bourgeois class domination (Jessop, 1985, p. 134). In his later
work, the unity of the state is no longer seen in terms of the functional
imperative of reproducing class domination. Instead, Poulantzas argues

that the long-term political interest of the bourgeoisie emerges as a result of a multiplicity of diversified micro-policies which reflect the nature of class struggle. However, as Jessop notes, this does not provide an adequate solution to the problem, since Poulantzas would need to address the awkward issue of how this macroscopic necessity (the need to ensure bourgeois class domination) emerges out of microscopic diversity (the chaotic nature of state policies). More disturbing, perhaps, is the fact that had Poulantzas been successfull in identifying how the relative autonomy of the state ensured class hegemony, it would have undermined his view that crises of hegemony occur (Jessop, 1985, p. 135).

Since the publication of *State Power and Socialism* the emphasis has shifted as the status of class analysis within the Marxist tradition has come under closer scrutiny. Authors such as Jessop now emphasise the role of disaggregation in social analysis; the importance of avoiding essentialist forms of explanation; and the need to address the role of calculating subjects within the state apparatus (state autonomy/strategy). Thus, within Jessop's work, the tension between necessity and contingency in relating institutional forms and the class struggle has been resolved by a tendency to abandon the primary role accorded to class struggle (particularly the role of the proletariat) in favour of a wider, more flexible conception of struggle which acknowledges the need to disaggregate social analysis and embrace the particularities of divisions along the lines of gender and ethnicity.

# ■ Jessop: a strategic-relational approach

The most important area of concern within contemporary Marxist theory of the state involves the continuing dialogue over the rejection of economism. In general terms, there has been a concerted move away from economism, retreating from the primacy of the economic within social analysis and, in turn, embracing an approach that stresses the dialectical and contingent quality of relationships. This tendency perhaps finds its most complete expression in the work of Jessop, who insists upon 'the multiplicity of possible causal mechanisms or principles of explanation' and refuses to 'privilege economic determinations in the first, intermediate or last instance' (Jessop, 1982, p. 228).

It is important to recognise that while Jessop insists upon the multiplicity of determinations, and refuses to privilege any (single) point of reference, he does not rule out causal explanation, provided that causality is conceived in terms of contingent necessity. Thus Jessop states that 'While a combination or interaction of different causal chains produces a determinate outcome (necessity), there is no single theory that can predict or determine the manner in which such causal chains converge and/or interact (contingency)' (Jessop, 1982, p. 224).

Within Jessop's frame of reference there is explicit recognition of the need to disaggregate social analysis. Moreover, as Jessop acknowledges explicitly, the interests of capital in general cannot be identified outside the framework of historically specific accumulation strategies. However, in at least one important respect, Jessop's work differs significantly from that of B. Hindess and P. Hirst because, while he is unwilling to privilege the economic dimension within social analysis, his work at both empirical and theoretical levels appreciates that a correspondence between the state and the economy, understood in terms of the need for reproduction, is a possibility, but that it must be constructed in the course of a struggle (Hindess and Hirst, 1977; Jessop, 1987).

For Jessop, any attempt to conceptualise the relationship between the state and civil society faces the difficulty involved in distinguishing between instrumentalism and structuralism in relation to economism. The instrumentalist position assumes that the state is a neutral institutional ensemble accessible to all political forces equally, and that it is capable of possessing a variety of objectives and goals. In contrast, a structuralist approach equates the nature, form and the activities of the state with the basic structures of the economy. The emphasis within the structuralist tradition is on the constraints to which the state is subject in a capitalist society and the claim that, irrespective of the views of state managers, policies will be designed to ensure the continued reproduction of capital.

Jessop's contention is that both approaches contain debilitating weaknesses. If one accords the state a form of neutrality and thus views it as unbiased in its effects on the interest realisation of different social forces, one is forced to explain the nature, form and the policies of the state purely in terms of those who are in control. In contrast, structuralism seeks to explain the form of the state, its functions and modes of intervention in terms of determining structures, the needs of which must be met to some degree or another.

At the most general level of abstraction, Jessop detects within capitalism a number of key defining characteristics. Primarily, it involves a basic circuit of capital and a fundamental social relationship: the value form (capital/wage labour relationship). However, the exact nature of that circuit of capital, the specific operation of the value form and the relationship between them, must be understood as being problematical and historically specific. In Jessop's view, then, although it is impossible to understand capitalism without reference to the complexities of the value form , the value form itself does not determine fully the course of capital accumulation. Indeed, the very substance of value depends on capital's ability to control wage labour, a process that is, in turn, contingent upon a struggle shaped and moulded by factors beyond the confines of the value form.

Jessop's treatment of the state and the extent to which it pushes forward the interests of capital reflects this indeterminism. He regards the interests of capital, the unity of the state and the relationship between capital and the state as being problematical. Following Poulantzas (1978), Jessop stresses the need to distinguish between capital in general and particular forms of capital. Jessop concedes that there are necessary interests which capital in general must realise if capitalism is to be reproduced. However, there is an extensive array of problems and contradictions which question whether these aims can be achieved successfully. Thus, while Jessop would concede that a correspondence between the state and economic region is possible, he is at pains to stress that it is a correspondence which must always be constituted in the course of dialectical struggle, the outcome of which is always in question.

For Jessop, the state consists of a plurality of institutions with no pre-given unity and no necessary relationship to the capitalist mode of production and/or the economically dominant class (Jessop, 1982, p. 222). State power may be deemed to be capitalist only to the extent that it either creates, 'maintains or restores the conditions required for capital accumulation within a given situation' (Jessop, 1982, p. 221). While he recognises that the state may, and indeed possibly *will*, enjoy autonomy, the extent of that autonomy must be explained. It is crucial to recognise, therefore, that political and economic forces are themselves shaped by the institutional structures and effects of state intervention; thus relations between the state and the social relations of production are always reciprocal and dialectical. Within such a theoretical arrangement, state power is conceived as being a complex social relationship which at any given time reflects the particular balance of social forces. Hence, both the relationship between classes and that between class and non-class forces, particularly gender and ethnic divisions, are a basis of economic, social and political domination. Jessop's framework attempts systematically to remove the economically reductionist and functionalist overtones associated with the work of Poulantzas, (Jessop, 1985).

For Jessop, the basic contradictions involved in the circuit of capital and the value form ensure periodic crises of capital accumulation. The possibility that the capitalist class inevitably enjoys the unity essential to sustain these contradictions is opposed vehemently. Such unity can be constructed only through struggle. Moreover, it is a unity that cannot be developed in any simple form by the state, given that the state itself does not possess any essential unity. Accordingly, Jessop does not assign to the state any form of innate power, rather:

> The State is a social relation, State power is a form determined condensation of the balance of political forces . . . the State as such has no power, it is merely an institutional ensemble: the power of the State is the power of the forces acting within the State. (Jessop, 1982, p. 149)

This should not be taken to imply that Jessop views the state as a neutral body, able to be captured and used by any social force. Rather, in Jessop's view, the state is a crucial site of struggle between social forces, the structure of which has been shaped by past struggles. In this sense, Jessop's approach begins from the simple premise that if capitalism is to be reproduced, state unity is an essential prerequisite. His originality lies in the emphasis he places on the way in which this unity needs actively to be constructed in and through the struggle between social forces. As such, there is no particular state form that can resolve indefinitely the inherent contradictions within relations between capital and labour. For Jessop, this means that class conflict will be reproduced at the very heart of the state apparatus. Thus, in Jessop's opinion, the effectiveness of state power depends ultimately upon the balance of forces in any given situation. Strategies for organising a secure social base (corporatism, for example) will vary with the particular stage of development, the form of the state and the location in the world economy. This complexity necessarily means that 'blanket generalisations' are inappropriate and that it 'would be wrong to suggest that any given state form best secures an adequate social base in all situations' (Jessop, 1990, p. 129).

For Jessop, the state is now viewed as being a strategic terrain and the emphasis has focused increasingly on strategic considerations. Thus Jessop argues that 'The State is not simply something towards which one must adopt a political strategy but is something (or better, a social relation) which can be fruitfully analysed as the site, the generator, and the product of strategies (Jessop, 1989, p. 3). According to this view, any theory of the state must produce an informed analysis of the strategic calculations and practices of the actors involved and of the interaction between agents and the state structures. However, the relationship is always dynamic and dialectical; state structures effect both strategic assessments and strategic conduct, which, in turn, effect change within state structures.

Not all of Jessop's work is pitched at such a high level of abstraction. Indeed, if the interests of capital in general can no longer be identified outside the framework of historically specific accumulation strategies, and there can be no ultimate state form that is able to serve as an unambiguously favourable political shell for advancing these interests, this suggests that there is no abstract theoretical solution to the question of how the political class domination of capital is secured. The answer, in Jessop's opinion, is to be found at the level of specific conjunctures in terms of the complex interaction between the circuit of capital, accumulation strategies, state forms and the balance of political forces. A successful capitalist state is one which has a unified form with a strategic selectivity that privileges the bourgeoisie. It is unified through a hegemonic project incorporating political, ideological and economic aspects which legitimise the dominance of the capitalist class, or more probably one fraction of it, over other social forces.

Within such theorising there exists a tension between, on the one hand, recognising the possibility of a correlation between an effective accumulation strategy and a successful hegemonic project and, on the other, the theoretical need to question the likelihood of such an occurrence, given the mass of contradictions among possible strategic options and the nature of strategic conduct involved in the operation of capitalism. Even so, Jessop's primary concern is with empirical regularity, involving a correspondence between an effective accumulation strategy and a successful hegemonic project. As the previous remarks imply, there can be no macro-necessity in social relations and as a result we must reject on principle the notion that somehow there is a totality 'out there' which remains fixed and constant. Jessop rejects the possibility of any comprehensive or complete strategy, because this would presuppose either the presence of a global subject, omnipresent and omnipotent, or some form of super-determination. There is never just a single calculating subject; rather, we are faced with a plurality of calculating subjects and a plethora of competing and contradictory strategies. The totality is thus conceptualised as possessing no determining centre or inner essence. There are no universal or unifying strategies. Strategies are always particular, relational, relative and conjunctural. They present themselves only as possible methods in which to organise and articulate a number of smaller sites of power and/or agents (Jessop, 1989). (For reasons of space it is not possible to discuss Jessop's recent embrace of a modified form of Regulation Theory. For critical comments on this, see Bonefield (1987) and Clarke (1988).)

Contemporary variants of the Marxist theory of the state have therefore not gone uncriticised. Authors from a wide variety of perspectives have argued that the transformation of the post-war economies, the entrenchment of the welfare state and the threat posed by environmental degradation have all questioned the pivotal role accorded to the concept of class within the Marxist framework. The remaining sections of this chapter explore briefly the core themes of such critical postures, focusing on the contentious issue of state autonomy and the challenge presented by the environmentalist and feminist traditions.

# ▋ Fred Block and Theda Skocpol: bringing the state back in

The work of Block and Skocpol is related, although Block retains more Marxist residues than does Skocpol. As the title of Skocpol's essay suggests (Skocpol, 1985) the accent within American political theory in the last two decades has been to focus upon the specificity of the state, its institutional autonomy and its capacity as an actor to realise policy goals. The objective within this particular variant of state theory has been been to reject the 'grand' theorising of structuralism and produce 'solidly grounded and analytically sharp understandings of the causal regularities that underlie the histories of states' (Skocpol, 1985, p. 28). Thus Skocpol argues that the state should be seen as both an organisation through which an official collectivity may pursue distinctive goals and as a set of institutions which influence the meanings and methods of politics. Consequently, structuralism is charged with the failure to address adequately the idea of state autonomy and the importance of state actors in realising specific policy goals (Skocpol, 1985, p. 28).

As emphasised, Block's work retains strong Marxist residues, but he rejects the concept of relative autonomy because it assumes that the ruling class has 'some degree of political cohesion, an understanding of its general interests, and a high degree of political sophistication' (Block, 1977, p. 10). Instead, Block suggests that the starting point for analysis should be the division of labour between those who accumulate capital and those who manage the state apparatus. Within this division of labour, Block contends that capitalists are only conscious of the specific short-term economic interests of their firms and are unaware of how to ensure the reproduction of the social order. Accordingly, attention needs to be diverted towards the crucial function of state managers (calculating subjects) in reproducing the conditions for sustained economic growth. In this context there are two themes that need to be addressed. First, we need to explain the structural constraints that reduce the likelihood that state managers will oppose the interests of business. Second, it is necessary to explain why state managers may actually extend state power, even in the face of capitalist resistance (Block, 1977, p. 7).

Within Block's theoretical position, the capacity of capitalism to rationalise itself is no longer viewed as being the sole responsibility of the capitalist class, but is the outcome of a conflict between the capitalist class, the managers of the state apparatus and the working class. For Block, the problem is one of how to explain the tendency of the state to serve the interests of the dominant class without succumbing to the problems of instrumentalist or functionalist forms of explanation. Block's response is to suggest that the placement of members of the dominant class in key positions within the state is an insufficient basis for reproducing capitalism, because:

> for one thing, ruling class members who devote substantial energy to policy formation become atypical of their class, since they are forced to look at the world from the perspective of managers. They are quite likely to diverge from ruling class opinion. (Block 1977, p. 13)

Block's preference is to view state managers as collectively self-interested maximisers who have interests that are linked to the specific needs of continued economic growth. This does not assume that state managers are capable of resolving the problems of capitalism, or producing the most favourable responses to crisis; rather, it conveys the idea that the actions of state managers are taken within the constraints imposed by political realities and economic orthodoxies.

# ▎ Broad churches and rainbow alliances: the ▎ challenge of feminism and environmentalism

For Marxists, the appeal of the concept of class rests on the dual function it performs as both a descriptive category and an explanatory variable. In this sense it is possible both to assign people to a particular class (bourgeiosie/proletariat), and to suggest that this will influence a particular form of political behaviour. Such arguments have, in the 1990s, been roundly condemned by elements within both feminist and environmentalist traditions, on the grounds that they are either 'sex blind' or neglect to consider one of the most pressing problem facing society: environmental degradation. From the outset, it is important to recognise a wide variety of position within both the environentalist (see Eckersly, 1992) and feminist traditions (see Humm, 1992).

For authors such as Hartmann, recent attempts to integrate Marxism and feminism have proved unsatisfactory because they have subsumed the feminist struggle into the larger struggle against capital (Hartmann, 1992). Consequently, many of the weaknesses in Marxism, such as economism or the way in which it has homogenised class interests, has prevented it from theorising adequately on the position of women and other non-class oppressions (Segal, 1991, p. 284). Here the principal objection is that Marxist categories are rooted in relations of appropriation and exploitation which fail to consider the particular gender of the exploiters and those whose labour is appropriated (Barrett, 1992). In contrast, a great deal of contemporary radical feminism now concentrates upon the 'particularities of women's lives', or the specific identity around which a feminist struggle can be sustained (Segal, 1991, p. 280). It is a position which replaces the central role accorded to the 'relations of production' within Marxist theory with an exploration of consciousness-raising or, as Mackinnon prefers, the 'collective critical reconstitution of the meaning of women's social experience, as women live through it' (Mackinnon, 1992, p. 119). For the more radical variants of feminism, then, Marxist categories are inappropriate to an adequate understanding of the ideology of familialism, particular forms of household organisation, sexuality and male power that are crucial to the subjugation of women under capitalism.

In a similar fashion, the environmentalist movement has sought to challenge the economic orthodoxy of Marxist theory: the all-pervasive role of class struggle, its reliance upon a productivist ethos and the continued domination of nature by humanity. Accordingly, Marxist theory is charged with possessing an intellectual legacy that is incompatible with current environmental concerns (Eckersley, 1992, p. 77).

For authors such as Gorz, there is now a myriad of antagonisms superimposed upon the contradiction between capital and labour. It is no longer possible, therefore, to answer the question of who will perform the crucial function of carrying out the socialist revolution by means of traditional class analysis (Gorz, 1991, p. 289). Within this critique, two themes are sythesised: a rejection of the role accorded to the working class in the socialist project, and the need to embrace an environmentally-informed vision of society that emphasises the *limitations* to economic growth (Gorz, 1980, 1982). For Gorz, the subject of a socialist project can no longer be found in the capitalist/wage labour nexus but must be located in the worker (as citizen) who is confronted by the imperfections of modern capitalism (Gorz, 1982). Thus, Gorz states that where socialism understands itself as the 'planned development of not yet existing economic structures . . . it reconstructs a society so that it is devoted to the economic development of capital accumulation' (Gorz, 1991, p. 289). The most pressing problem for Marxism, then, is that it is rooted ultimately in a conception of society that neglects to consider one of the most serious problem facing society: ecological degradation.


# ■ Conclusion

Among those authors who retain allegiance to the Left it has become an accepted practice to replace the role of class struggle with an amalgam of metaphors designed to invoke a wider, more flexible appreciation of the disparate elements involved within the socialist project. It is now more commonplace, for example, to argue in terms of 'alternative sites of struggle', or to emphasise the importance of social movements. This trend, which is now firmly entrenched, has occurred largely as a result of a systematic attempt to rid Marxism of essentialist or reductionist forms of explanation in favour of concepts which stress the partially contingent nature of social reality. This represents a crucial departure, since it also rejects the view that society inevitably follows a particular path, and that class struggle inevitably leads to the 'end' of history, Communism. Such theoretical developments have been influenced by rapid changes taking place within capitalism: the transformation of work relations, the growth of the Keynesian welfare state and the decline of trade union power – all of which appear to have combined to sound the death knell for class politics, ensuring that the central role for the working class in the struggle for socialism can no longer be guaranteed. Within such work, the rise of environmental and feminist protest groups represents a potential new source around which to form a political struggle, one in which a 'broad church' or 'rainbow alliance' of eco-feminist-socialist groups has the potential to transform society.Such developments have had an important bearing upon contemporary Marxist theory of the state. Few authors are now willing to defend a universal theory of the state, rather, they propose specific historical analysis within a universalistic conception of the relationship between the state and economy. The instrumentalist concern with who rules the state has been abandoned firmly in favour of an approach which argues either that the class nature of the state is expressed through the 'structure' of capitalist development, or that the state is a political apparatus through which control is contested between the dominant/subordinate classes and social movements.

# ■ Further reading

On Marx, see Ollman (1971) and Rigby (1987). On Marxist state theory, see Carnoy (1984) and Jessop (1982). Among the best secondary work on Gramsci is Showstack-Sassoon (1987) and Merrington (1978). On Poulantzas, see Jessop (1985). Humm (1992) is possibly the best introduction to feminist thought, while Eckersley (1992) and Gorz (1980) deal with environmentalism and Marxism.

# Chapter 14

# The Convergence between Theories of the State
## David Marsh

The last three chapters indicate there has been a convergence between the three major theoretical traditions dealing with the relationship between the state and civil society (see Dunleavy and O'Leary, 1987; Etzioni-Helevy, 1993). The aim of this chapter is to establish both the extent of, and the reasons for, this convergence. The chapter is divided into four main sections, each of which addresses a specific question: 'What do the current positions have in common?' 'Why has there been a convergence? What differences remain between the three positions?' and 'How should the study of power, or more specifically the relationship between the state and civil society, progress?'

## ■ The basis of the convergence

The developments in the three positions have not produced a consensus. There are a number of authors who still advocate a fairly pure form of one of the three positions (so Geras, 1987, develops a largely economistic Marxist analysis, while Janda *et al.*, 1994, offer a mainstream traditional pluralist interpretation of the distribution of power in the USA). In addition (and I shall return to this point later), there are still significant differences between the converged positions. However, there *is* a clear convergence. Indeed, this convergence is well reflected in the difficulty one has in locating some authors within a specific position. So, Lindblom (1977) may regard himself as a pluralist of sorts but, as Martin Smith's analysis suggests (Chapter 11), his work fits as happily, if not more so, within the elitist tradition. Similarly, Mark Evans indicates in Chapter 12 that, although the elitists Skocpol (1979) and Scott (1991) owe much to the legacy of Max Weber, they also were influenced by the Marxist tradition. Finally, Domhoff (1967) and Miliband (1968) are elite Marxists.

As George Taylor makes clear in Chapter 13, the history of Marxist thought, at least since Gramsci, can be characterised as a struggle with economism. More specifically, we can identify six features of the modern Marxist theory of the state which most authors writing in that tradition share. First, they reject economism; that is, the view that economic relations determine class relations, which in turn determine the form, functions and thus outputs of the state. Second, there is a consequent rejection of determinacy. Relations between the economic and the political are seen as being contingent rather than causal. Third, they deny that *a single* theory of the state is possible. Marxism provides a set of tools with which to examine historically specific relationships between the state and civil society, rather than a theory that explains the form and actions of the state in all capitalist social formations and at all times. Fourth, class is no longer seen to be the only major basis of structured inequality and hegemonic struggle, as *the* crucial social force shaping political institutions and outcomes. Indeed, for many authors, class is no longer even ascribed primacy. Rather, gender, race, nationalism and so on are also crucial bases of structured inequality, inequality which is also inscribed in the state form. On some occasions, and in relation to some political outcomes, these social forces may have a greater influence than class. Fifth, there is a strong emphasis on disaggregation, an emphasis on the need to recognise that the unity of the state, of the classes, and indeed of other social forces, cannot be assumed. All are characterised by divisions, so there is a plurality which is mediated, if not resolved, through politics. Sixth, structural explanation is still important, but increased space is given to intentional explanation. So structures based on class and other social forces may constrain and facilitate, but they do not determine, outcomes. Agents, whether individuals, groups or classes, attempt to maximise their autonomy and push forward their interests within these constraints. So the emphasis increasingly is upon the strategic judgements of calculating subjects acting within a context characterised by structured inequality.

As Smith indicates (Chapter 11), pluralism has also developed significantly since the 1960s. Three changes are particularly important here. First, pluralists have acknowledged increasingly that power is concentrated, and that interest groups only extend participation to a limited extent, largely because some sections of the population are under-represented, but also, *pace* Michels (1962), because interests groups, like all political organisations, are structured hierarchically. Second, there has been increased interest in the role of the state (although most pluralists prefer to talk of the government rather than the state; a concept they see both as too inclusive and as associated with Marxism). In particular, a number of authors have stressed the importance of institutional pluralism. In this view, pluralism is, to a large extent, ensured by competition between sections of the state, or between one interest group and its sponsoring section or department within government and another interest group and its sponsoring section or department. Third, and clearly related, pluralists increasingly have acknowledged the importance of political structures in shaping political outcomes. So there has been a growing emphasis in the pluralist position, although not exclusively in this position, on the importance of policy networks. Some of this work has stressed that these networks are based on interpersonal relations, but most emphasise that the networks involve relationships of dependency between institutions or organisations, and are thus structural. In this way, pluralism (which historically has emphasised intentional explanation, with interest groups as agents attempting to maximise their self-interest relatively freely) has accepted increasingly that access to government is not easy or open; rather, some groups are privileged by their role in sub-governments or policy networks, while others are excluded. Overall, pluralism, like Marxism, is increasingly a broad church. It offers no general theory and seems, to a large extent, to rest on the existence of a great deal of empirical evidence of plurality (see Vogel, 1989). So pluralists suggest that, despite the fact that some groups enjoy privileged status and thus exercise more influence, no one group/interest dominates policy-making in a broad spread of areas at any one time, and the influence of any particular group ebbs and flows over time. To the pluralist this is *prima-facie*, and indeed sufficient, evidence that the USA, and the UK, are pluralist societies.

If Marxism and pluralism have evolved, so has elitism. In essence, there have been two main changes in the elitist position. First, it has become more flexible in the post-war period, dropping the residues of the theories of history associated with the classical elitists, Mosca (1939) and Pareto (1935, 1966). So while elitists still believe in the inevitability of elites, they no longer see a clear and unchanging pattern in the circulation of elites underpinned by a functionalist argument that the type of elite necessary for the development of society (in Pareto's terms 'lions' or 'foxes') will emerge.

Second, as Evans' chapter (Chapter 12) makes clear, there has been a renewed concern, not always or mainly successful, to ground the elitist position on a firmer theoretical base. So while much of the work of the democratic elitists was in effect largely an empirical critique of pluralism, more recently elitists have flirted with corporatism before gravitating towards what might be characterised as a radical Weberian position. As Evans shows, the work of Skocpol (1979), and indeed of Scott (1991) in the UK, represent, to an extent, an attempt to integrate Weberian and Marxist ideas. In Skocpol's case, this is linked to an emphasis on the autonomy of the state, on a statist perspective, which has clear overlaps with the work of Block (1977, 1980) – a Marxist, and Nordlinger (1981) – a pluralist. This emphasis on the state is one of the key aspects of the convergence to which I now turn.

These brief overviews in the context of the last three chapters suggest a number of elements of convergence. In essence, there is a convergence towards an elitist position. The modern Marxist position, well represented in Jessop's strategic relational approach; the radical Weberian elitist position, well reflected in the work of Skocpol (1979), and in the UK by the analysis of Scott (1991); and the elite pluralist or countervailing power position, best expounded by McFarland (1987), share a great deal in common – although, as we shall see later, there are still significant differences, particularly between pluralism and the two other positions. In more detail, there appear to be six aspects of the convergence.

## ☐ Structured privilege

Each position accepts that political competition does not take place on a level playing field. Rather, a group (individual) may enjoy a privileged status because of its (his/her) structural position. However, there is a important difference between the pluralist view and the other two views, as most pluralist would emphasise the importance of political structures but play down the utility of broad social categories, such as gender, to explain political outcomes. To the pluralist, a variety of other divisions cross-cut it, for example class/status, education, knowledge and political interests, and interest groups form to represent the various, and very different, interests of women. It is the conflict between interest groups that is at the core of politics and that shapes political outcomes, although some groups are 'more equal than others' because they enjoy privileged access to the government through their inclusion within policy networks.

## ☐ The role of agency

Just as pluralists have acknowledged that political structures at least shape political institutions and outcomes, so Marxists and elitists have accorded a greater role to agency. Of course, some elitists, *pace* Pareto, always emphasised the role of individual leaders in shaping outcomes, and stressed the importance of personality. However, classical Marxism emphasised structural, and indeed functional, explanation, so agents were 'bearers' of structures. In contrast, modern Marxists, such as Jessop, emphasise the role that the strategies adopted by calculating subjects have on both the shape of institutions and on the outcomes of political struggle.

## ☐ Limited number of structural bases of privilege

There is a shared emphasis on a limited number of bases of structured inequality and privilege, although again there is more overlap here between

Marxism and elitism, because pluralism emphasises almost exclusively political structures; so a pluralist would acknowledge that policy networks or sub-governments affect outcomes, but deny the importance of structured inequality based on class or gender. The focus is particularly upon: (i) economic/property resources, a basis of division obviously most associated with Marxism, but also crucial in the Weberian tradition; (ii) gender; because of the influence of feminist theory (a topic to which we shall return later) gender inequality has received increasing attention; (iii) political resources, control of agenda and membership of policy networks; and (iv) knowledge, a basis of division closely associated with the Weberian position and emphasising the role of professionals.

## ☐ *Statism*

There has been an increased interest in each position on the role of the state; on the need to take the state seriously. Historically, both Marxism and pluralism are, in different ways, societal-based theories. Classical Marxism saw the state as an epiphenomenon: economic relations structure class relations, which determine the form and actions of the state. In this view, studying the state is of little importance. Classical pluralism concentrated on the role of interest groups in society; the government merely acted as a 'weather vane' responding to the competing pressures from various interests. Again, the role of the government was limited and thus not the key focus of attention. More recently, as we have seen, both traditions have developed a strong statist perspective. So, Marxists such as Block stress the independence of 'state managers', while aiming to explain why their interests tend to correspond to those of the capitalist class. On the other hand, pluralists such as Nordlinger also emphasise the autonomy of the democratic state, and view pluralism as much in terms of conflict between the different interests of sections of government as in terms of conflict between interest groups within civil society.

## ☐ *Contingency*

Pluralism has never been deterministic. So a society was pluralistic to the extent that power was diffuse; although, of course, most pluralists believed that the distribution of power in the UK, and particularly in the USA, was pluralistic. In contrast, both classical Marxism and the classical elitism of Mosca and Pareto developed theories of history which underpinned their theories of the state; both offered a general theory of who ruled, how they ruled, in whose interest they ruled, and how rule circulated. This is no longer the case for most Marxists or elitists. Few Marxists now accept the Marxist theory of history (although, for a spirited defence of it, see Cohen,

1978). To contemporary Marxists such as Jessop, a state may be a capitalist state, forwarding the interests of capital, but such a relationship is contingent, not necessary, and is a matter for empirical investigation, not theoretical assertion. Modern elitism is either based on an empirical refutation of pluralism or is underpinned by a broadly Weberian position, and Weber was a relativist in epistemological terms who rejected the idea of a theory of history and developed no theory of the state.

## □ *The primacy of politics?*

If anything, most contemporary developments in all three traditions ascribe primacy to politics (although for more economistic readings from within Marxism, see Ward, 1993; Taylor, 1992). This does not mean that they always and inevitably regard the state as the starting point for any analysis; politics is not usually conceived in such narrow institutional terms. Rather, political outcomes are viewed as the product of conflict between interests/social forces for the allocation of scarce resources in a context characterised by structured inequality. Obviously, pluralists always accorded politics primacy but this is a new development within Marxist thought that owes most to Gramsci, but also something to the influence of post-Marxist theorists such as Laclau and Mouffe (see Chapter 6 in this volume). So Jessop's concept of strategic selectivity suggests that the form of the state is a product of the outcome of past hegemonic, and therefore essentially political, struggles. In addition, he suggests that the state form privileges certain present interests and strategies. In essence, this is a politicist view.

## ■ Why convergence?

Theories change for two related reasons: the world they are attempting to describe or explain has changed; or the hypotheses and predictions a theoretical position generates may not be substantiated by empirical investigation, leading to criticisms by its opponents or, increasingly, by its supporters, and, consequently, to important modifications in the theory,

In the post-war period there have obviously been major economic, social and political changes that have forced theorists, particularly pluralists and Marxists, to reconsider their positions. For example, as Smith points out in Chapter 11, the growth of political dissent in the USA in the 1960s, as a result of anti-Vietnam protest and inner-city riots in response to racial inequalities, had a crucial influence on the development of pluralist thought. Against this background, it was difficult for political scientists to be complacent about viewing America as a perfectly-functioning, pluralist democracy. Clearly, some people/groups were excluded systematically, while other people/groups enjoyed privileged access to policy-making and power. Such events were clearly influential in the growth of elite pluralism, with its recognition that a limited number of hierarchically-structured groups enjoyed a close relationship with the government, within policy networks or even iron triangles, while pluralism was retained because such groups or networks competed with one another for influence on a government, which was not identified with any particular interest.

Marxists have also had to respond to the fundamental changes in the post-war world. In particular, the centralisation and abuse of power in the Soviet bloc, despite the abolition of private ownership, made it increasingly difficult to argue that economic relations determined social and political relations. At the same time, growing globalisation and the variety of forms the state took in different capitalist societies also mediated against a simplistic conceptualisation of the relationship between the state and civil society.

However, if we want to explain the recent convergence most attention must be paid to the debates between theorists, although, of course, these debates are informed by empirical evidence concerning the relationship between the state and civil society, which, in turn, reflect the theorist's understanding of the changes in the world.

## ☐ Marxism

Marxist thought clearly has been influenced by criticism from inside and outside the tradition. Four crucial contributions from within the tradition, identified by Taylor in Chapter 13, are worth re-emphasising.

First, the work of Gramsci marked the first important break with economism. Gramsci's concentration on the role of political or hegemonic struggle, the importance of ideology, and the manufacture of consent and the significance of the actions of agents (in his case parties, workers', councils or intellectuals) introduced themes which have been taken up and developed in contemporary Marxist state theory. It is also worth emphasising here that Gramsci's work was influenced significantly by the tradition of Italian social and political thinking which traces back to Machiavelli and which also influenced the Italian elitists, Mosca and (especially) Pareto.

Second, the work of Poulantzas (1974, 1976, 1978) was crucial to developments in this area. Poulantzas's attempt to theorise the relative autonomy of the state has been particularly influential. More specifically, his argument that the state's autonomy is constrained by the outcome of past class struggles, which are inscribed upon the state form, and thus privilege certain class interests over others (that is, the concept of structural selectivity) has provided a starting point for much subsequent work; authors like Jessop (1990) reject the notion of relative autonomy, and are critical of the idea of structural selectivity, but develop their own positions through a critique of Poulantzas.

Poulantzas's work has also been influential in relation to methodology, and thus to the structure/agency debate; although here it was his exchange of articles with Miliband in 1969 and 1970 which stimulated renewed Marxist interest in methodological questions. Poulantzas (1969) argued that the relationship between the capitalist class and the state was a structural one which existed regardless of the backgrounds or actions of those individuals who occupied elite positions in the capitalist sector or in the state apparatus. Miliband, in contrast, in both *The State in Capitalist Society* (1968) and his replies to Poulantzas (Miliband, 1970, 1973), was concerned to show that members of these two elites, and indeed other elites, shared common backgrounds and interacted together, with the consequence that the political elite generally forwarded the interests of the capitalist class. So Miliband saw the role of agents as being crucial, if necessarily constrained by structures. As we have already seen, contemporary Marxists have accepted the role of agency and there is no doubt that this change owes something to the Poulantzas/Miliband debate.

Third, the move towards statism in modern Marxism is clearly associated with the work of Block, who links statism with relative autonomy. He argues that 'state managers' are most concerned to forward their self-interest, and not the interests of capital; hence they are autonomous. Their self-interest lies first and foremost in winning elections. However, as elections are increasingly, in effect, referendum on the government's handling of the economy, and as economic performance depends upon decisions on investment and so on taken by capitalists, then 'state managers' will forward policies that are in the interests of capitalists in order to encourage them to take business decisions which lead to improved overall economic performance. So, while state managers are autonomous they will tend to forward the interest of capital in order to forward their own interests. In Block's view (Block, 1979, 1980), this relationship will only cease beyond a contingent 'tipping point', that is if and when the state managers think that their interest would no longer be served by supporting capital – perhaps in a period of massive depression. Block's ideas have had relatively little influence on some Marxists; for example, Jessop hardly considers his work, although both derive similar ideas from Poulantzas. However, Block's work has been developed interestingly by others, for example Ward (1993).

Fourth, Jessop's work (especially 1990) is probably the most interesting of the modern Marxist material on the state. In particular, Jessop offers the most sophisticated attempt to confront economism. He denies explicitly the primacy of class; emphasising the importance of other social forces, especially gender. In addition, his emphasis on strategy recognises that outcomes are not determined structurally; rather, they are the product of strategic decisions taken by calculating subjects, in contexts which privilege certain strategies over others. As such, his view that state forms are the outcome of past strategic struggles between social forces builds upon Poulantzas's work, but marks a step forward in two ways: it recognises the importance of social forces other than class; and acknowledges the dialectical nature of the relationship between structure and agency. In addition, Jessop stresses contingency; emphasising the need for historically specific analysis using theoretically-informed concepts, rather than suggesting that a theory of the state is possible. Jessop's work has weaknesses (see Hay, 1994, for a sympathetic criticism of Jessop) but the key point here is that he has had significant influence on the development of contemporary Marxist theory and any future developments are likely to build upon a critique of his work.

However, Marxism has clearly also been influenced by outside criticism. Here, two contributions are worth highlighting. First, as Taylor shows, feminist thought has had a significant influence on Marxist state theory. Feminism raises crucial questions concerning the definition of politics, revolving in particular around the distinction between the public and the personal and the nature of power (see, for example, Phillips, 1992). At the same time, it situates group conflict against the background of structured inequality and argues that structured inequality based on gender leads to political inequality. Such theoretical arguments are underpinned by empirical evidence which suggests, in Jenny Chapman's phrase (Chapman, 1993, p. 4), two almost iron laws that shape women's participation in politics:

> i) wherever political rewards exist which are desirable to men, relatively few women will be found seeking, and even fewer securing them; ii) wherever there is a hierarchy of such rewards, then the higher up the hierarchy we look, the smaller the proportion of women will be.

To all feminists the private crucially affects the public. In particular, unequal sexual division of tasks within the family limits female participation. In addition, patriarchal attitudes underpin institutions and processes, privileging the access of men. Finally, there is considerable evidence that women's issues, such as childcare provision, contraception and abortion are at best marginalised on the political agenda (see Chapter 5).

Of course, there are major differences among feminist writers about the causes of dominance and about strategies for political transformation. Radical feminists accord gender primacy; suggesting that it is the key basis of structured inequality shaping the states form and thus political outcomes. In contrast, feminists who still operate within the Marxist tradition, broadly defined, see gender as the second key basis of social division which, together with class, shapes political institutions and outcomes. These two bases of structured inequality may reinforce one another, but neither can inevitably, or always, be assigned primacy. This emphasis on gender as a key bases of inequality is clearly evident, if perhaps underdeveloped, in the theoretical work of Marxists such as Jessop.

Second, Marxists have also drawn upon work from the other two main traditions. Once again, we can use Jessop's work to illustrate this process. In particular, Jessop's conceptualisation of the relationship between structure and agency, which is a crucial relationship for his strategic relational approach, is clearly influenced by the work of Gidden's (1979), who is, in broad terms, a Weberian. Jessop is critical of Gidden's structuration approach, as Hay in Chapter 10 shows, but his own position, while it owes a great deal to Gramsci, has also developed in part through this critique of Giddens. In addition, Jessop has shown interest in the literature on policy networks and institutional pluralism, which fits happily with the emphasis in his work on the need to disaggregate the state and to examine how political structures privilege certain strategies.

## ☐ Pluralism

Pluralism has changed almost as much as Marxism in the last three decades. Much of the change has resulted from debates within the position. Three crucial contributions to that debate are worth emphasising.

First, pluralists were clearly influenced by the empirical and methodological criticisms of the position from the 1960s onwards. Some of these were by elitists who were attempting to establish empirically that the distribution of power at both the local and the national level were elitist rather than pluralist (see, for example, Hunter, 1953, and Mills, 1956). This work, together with the Marxist empirical analysis of Miliband, probably accelerated the move towards elite pluralism by authors such as Dahl (1982) and Lindblom (1977).

Nevertheless, it was the methodological, and subsequently empirical, critique of two pluralists, Bachrach and Baratz which was particularly influential. They argued (Bachrach and Baratz, 1962) that the usual pluralist methodology was inadequate because it utilised a decision-making approach and thus concentrated on the first, most obvious, face of power; power was measured in terms of the capacity to make a government do something it would not otherwise have done. In contrast, Bachrach and Baratz suggested that interests can exercise more power if they have the capacity to control the political agenda. To Bachrach and Baratz, if one examined this second face of power, it became evident that power was concentrated, not diffuse. This critique also represents a move towards structural rather than intentional explanation, and towards an emphasis on sub-governments or policy networks, given that the second face of power and agenda-setting is normally associated with closed government. Indeed, others have developed Bachrach and Baratz's critique to suggest that more emphasis should be placed on the structural position and ideological/hegemonic domination of interests (see Lukes, 1974). The methodological criticisms of pluralism by Bachrach and Baratz and others were refuted by some pluralists (see Polsby, 1963, 1980), but nevertheless increasingly were accepted, and pluralists have acknowledged the importance of agenda-setting and the role of political structures in effecting policy outcomes.

Second, the works of Robert Dahl (1982) and Charles Lindblom (1977) have been influential. Both were leading figures in American political science and strongly associated with the pluralist position. Yet both increasingly stressed the limited nature of pluralism in the USA. Dahl developed the concept of polyarchy, which became one of the pillars of elite pluralism. To Dahl and other elite pluralists, a limited number of groups did enjoy privileged access to the government, and some interests in society were under-represented, if represented at all. However, pluralism was preserved because these privileged groups competed with one another. In addition, and most important for Dahl, the government was autonomous; it was not identified with any particular interest. The emphasis in Dahl's work was on the role of individual politicians; as such he stressed the role of agents rather than structure.

Lindblom (1977) moved even further from classical pluralism and argued that business enjoyed a special position in capitalist liberal democracies. His view shared much in common with that of F. Block. To Lindblom there is an imprisoned zone of policy-making, which broadly covered those areas of policy in which the interests of business are most directly affected – economic, industrial and industrial relations policy. In these areas the government forwards the interests of business because the decisions taken by business determine the level of economic performance, which in turn affects the re-election chances of the government. Outside the imprisoned zone, a more open pluralism persists. So Lindblom emphasised the structural constraints which affected government policy-making; a position which distinguished him significantly from Dahl. In the light of this, it is not surprising that Lindblom characterised himself as a '.4'(i.e. 40%) pluralist (Lindblom, 1982). More importantly here, however, Lindblom's views have had considerable influence on subsequent pluralism. First, some pluralists, Dahl amongst them, have acknowledged that the position of business needs serious consideration and even that business interests may be first among equals in pluralist democracies. Second, Lindblom's work has clearly influenced some authors to take structural constraints more seriously.

Third, E. Nordlinger's work (Nordlinger, 1980) on the autonomy of the democratic state has also been influential. He suggests that pluralism places too much emphasis on societal interest groups and not enough on the state; that pluralism is too societaley-centred an approach. As such, he develops a statist reading of pluralism, arguing that state officials have particular and distinct preferences. More specifically, he identifies three forms of state autonomy: weak state autonomy, when state officials act on their own preferences in situations where societal preferences do not differ from theirs; medium state autonomy, when state officials attempt to alter societal group preferences which differ from theirs; and strong state autonomy, when state officials forward their preferences regardless of the preferences of societal interest groups. To Nordlinger, all types of autonomy are possible in democratic societies and it is an empirical question as to which dominates. Nordlinger's work, together with that of those authors who emphasise the existence of sub-governments and policy networks, has been influential in the move towards institutional pluralism and structural explanation within pluralism.

Two criticisms from outside the pluralist tradition have had some influence on its development. First, the neo-liberal element of New Right theory also had some influence on the development of pluralism. The New Right do not have a theory of the state; rather they offer an analysis of why the pluralist, liberal democratic state is not working and a view of what should be done to make it function more effectively. To the New Right, and indeed to some pluralists, particularly in Britain (see King, 1975), by the 1970s the pluralist system was deeply flawed. There were two explanations for this failure, although to an extent these were mutually exclusive. One explanation blamed interest groups. It was argued (see Brittan, 1975) that interest groups were becoming too powerful and demanding more and more from the state; this was commonly known as the 'government overload thesis'. Governments were responding to these demands in order to win votes in a competitive two party system. As such, there was a crisis of over-government; the state was interfering more and more in society and the public sector was growing at the expense of the private sector, with disastrous consequences for the economy. The other explanation placed more blame on the state. The expansion of the state was explained in terms of the pursuit of self-interest by politicians and state officials. Politicians and political parties expand services in order to win votes and state managers, whether ministers or bureaucrats, have an interest in the growth of spending in 'their' own policy area in order to increase their importance, job satisfaction and/or job security/prospects.

A number of pluralists embraced the notion of over-governance, although for many in Britain it was associated with the view that the real problem was the supposedly overwhelming power of the trade unions. More broadly, the critique of pluralism explicit in New Right thought certainly led some British pluralists to support the 'Thatcherite' position and argue for a general strengthening of the power of the state in relation to interest groups, while specifically supporting a restriction of union power.

Second, despite this, it is probably the theoretical and empirical work on sub-governments that has had most influence on the development of modern pluralism. I have treated this body of material as a criticism of pluralism from outside the tradition, although many of the authors producing work in this broad area would regard themselves as pluralists. In essence, I have done this because the origin of the work on sub-governments was as an elitist critique of pluralism, particularly in the work of Theodore Lowi (1969), an author usually characterised as a pluralist elitist. Nevertheless, the way in which Lowi's ideas were taken up, developed and criticised by pluralists amply illustrates the convergence between pluralist and elitist positions.

Lowi argued strongly for the need to disaggregate when looking at the distribution of power and the process of policy-making. For Lowi, there was pluralism in certain policy areas in which benefits were non-divisible (for example, government regulations) and there were well-organised interest groups. On the other hand, plural elitism occurred in those areas in which benefits were divisible (for example, government grants or tax subsidies). Here, particular interests enjoy privileged access and close relations with government; they control and defend their own turf and trade benefits with other interests in similar positions to preserve the power bases of each. To Lowi, the latter, distributive, mode of politics had come to dominate the American political system in the 1970s. As such, a wide range of decisions had been turned over to sub-governments, in which the interest group, the Executive agency and the Congressional Committee made policy within an exclusive, closed and secret policy network. Lowi's work was very influential among pluralists, who accepted the existence of limited elite pluralism and the importance of sub-governments, which gave some interests privileged access to policy-making and excluded others. It also emphasised the importance of a disaggregated approach to government and to policy-making. In addition, it focused on the way in which political structures, like sub-governments or policy networks, could have a crucial effect on political outcomes. However, Lowi played down the possibility of state autonomy; a theme which, as we saw, the work of Nordlinger in particular has introduced into modern pluralism.

# ■ The remaining differences

Despite the convergence there are still important differences, particularly, although not exclusively, between pluralism and the two other positions.

First, pluralism still differs significantly from the other two positions. It places more emphasis on the role of agents – particularly, although not exclusively, interest groups. In so far as it is concerned with the role of structures, and that concern is limited, the emphasis is upon political structures, both the formal institutions of government and, increasingly, the structural manifestations of sub-governments or policy networks. As such, politics is the starting point for the analysis of power, and the focus of that analysis should be on the interaction between interest groups and the government. To the pluralist, the autonomy of the state and the primacy of politics is axiomatic; given this, it is perhaps not surprising that pluralism has been the preferred position of most political scientists. In contrast, both Marxism and elitism stress that politics takes place in a context characterised by structured inequalities. Many emphasise increasingly the autonomy of politics and take the state more seriously; but all emphasise that an understanding of the effect of structured inequalities based on class, gender, race and so on, is crucial if we are to explain the form that the state takes and the outcomes of the political process.

Although pluralists have accepted some of the methodological criticisms made by Bachrach and Baratz and others, they still stress decision-making analysis. In order to study power, the pluralists emphasise the importance of concentrating on political outcomes; of studying what interests want and how far, and how consistently, they can persuade the government to do something it would not otherwise have done. This can result in a type of abstracted empiricism in which any evidence of plurality is used to criticise the elitist position. In this way, Vogel (1989) criticises Lindblom, whom he views as an elitist, by classifying him as a structural determinist and then presenting evidence to show that business does not always get its way, or on all issues that concern it. This approach is of limited utility, as not only does it over-simplify Lindblom's position but it also fails to appreciate the methodological weaknesses of the pluralist position which were outlined by Bachrach and Baratz and Lukes.

Of course, most pluralists do accept that interests can have influence through their ability to set the agenda. However, because they stress agency and the actions of interest groups, politicians and bureaucrats, they neglect the importance of structures, and indeed ideology, in affecting outcomes and thus fail to appreciate that the relationship between structure and agency (as Hay showed in Chapter 10) is a dialectical one. Marxists and elitist adopt that position increasingly, which has significant methodological implications. It points towards comparative and, particularly, historical analysis. Certainly, dialectical relationship cannot be analysed using a case-study approach which focuses on a limited number of political decisions. This type of methodology is used to some effect by authors such as Block, Jessop and even Skocpol.

Second, while Marxism and the radical Weberian strand of elitism offer very similar analyses of the distribution of power within capitalist society, there are differences. In particular, many Marxists do retain economistic residues. For example, while Jessop's theoretical work plays down the primacy of economic relations, his empirical work often sees political change as being driven by economics; so he views 'Thatcherism' as a response to economic crisis (see Hay, 1994).

In addition, the two positions often differ on normative questions. Both see contemporary society as characterised by structured inequality, but most elitists regard that as inevitable; the dominant social force may change, but there will always *be* one. In contrast, most Marxists are interested in practice; in understanding society in order to change it. So, to take Jessop once again as an example, he is interested in understanding the reasons for the successes and failures of 'Thatcherism' as a hegemonic project to a great extent in order to establish how a successful democratic socialist hegemonic project could be developed and advanced.

# ■ The way forward

Each of the theoretical positions examined here needs to address some specific problems. In addition, the convergence I have identified suggests that political sociology might benefit by focusing on a limited number of key areas. Here I shall deal first, and at most length, with pluralism, which is the dominant position in political science, although this dominance is often implicit rather than explicit.

## □ *Pluralism*

Contemporary pluralism, by acknowledging that power is, at least to an extent, concentrated, clearly offers a more realistic model of the distribution of power in advanced liberal democracies than does the classical pluralist model. The big strength of pluralism is that it acknowledges, and indeed trumpets, plurality. This is a strength, because contemporary society is characterised by plurality; as all the positions examined increasingly accept.

In addition, the best pluralist work does not assert an answer to the question it poses; rather it postulates a pluralist distribution of power and generates a series of hypotheses which can be tested, about the nature of decision-making and outcomes. However, this is not true of all pluralist work. In this way, McFarland's 'countervailing power' model is much superior to Vogel's 'plurality' model. Vogel criticises Lindblom, accusing him of structural determinism. Vogel then argues, with evidence, that business interests do not always achieve their policy objectives; that the influence of business ebbs and flows over time and space. Unfortunately, Vogel's argument is flawed, for three reasons. First, Lindblom is not a structural determinist (Marsh, 1983). Second, contemporary Marxists and elitist would gainsay determinism; to both, structures may constrain and facilitate but they do not determine. Third, Vogel's 'evidence' that the interests of business are not always forwarded does not refute Lindblom or prove pluralism; it is evidence of *plurality*, (which the other positions do not deny), not of pluralism. In contrast, McFarland offers a sophisticated discussion of the state of modern pluralism. On the basis of this discussion, he generates a series of eighteen propositions. These propositions offer both a way of organising the existing literature and a way of structuring future theorising and research. They can also provide a basis for empirical investigation. Certainly, McFarland's work suggests a plausible and systematic way forward for pluralist analysis.

As Vogel's shortcomings suggest, the basic weakness of pluralism, as Smith makes clear in Chapter 11, is that it is under-theorised. In essence, pluralists such as Vogel deal in 'abstracted empiricism'. They present the existence of plurality as prima-facie and compelling evidence of pluralism. However, as we saw, none of the theories we examine here deny the existence of plurality. The key problem is that modern pluralism deals with only two of the four questions any theory of power needs to address: 'Who exercises power?'; and 'How do they exercise power?' It fails to confront the other two, (and some would say more important) questions: 'Why do some people have privileged access to power?'; and 'In whose interest do they rule?' Classical pluralism, with its origins in democratic theory, had an answer, although sometimes it was implicit rather than explicit. To A. Bentley, the outcome of the various representations of groups, if it did not serve the interests of all, ensured a balance, allowed for gradual change and economic progress for all. The sub-text, rarely made explicit, was that the interests of all – the 'national interest', even – was forwarded even though not everyone benefited equally. Now pluralism is couched in more negative terms: there is plurality, no one group dominates and the system is open, in an important, if limited, way. The difficulty with all this, as Smith makes clear, is that while some pluralists acknowledge the privileged position of business, their attempts to reconcile this privilege with the existence of pluralism are unconvincing.

In part, of course, this weakness reflects the methodological inadequacies of pluralism. Pluralists largely ignore the way that social and economic structures constrain political outcomes. They place almost total stress on agency explanations, emphasising the roles of interest groups and politicians/bureaucrats. As such, power is measured in terms of the agent's intention and capacity to affect outcomes. This neglects important aspects of power. A brief consideration of the position of the financial sector in British politics amply illustrates this point. A variety of authors from different theoretical positions agree that British economic policy favoured the interests of the financial sector, even over (and against the interests of) the manufacturing sector (see Coakley and Harris, 1983; or Scott, 1979, 1991). Yet the financial sector in Britain is represented by weak interest groups and, indeed, such groups only came to the fore in the 1970s. The influence of the City was not exercised through interest groups;

rather, it rested upon two facts: the economic decisions of the City affected overall economic performance crucially, and, thus the government's re-election chances; and the financial institutions were major holders of government debt (Marsh, 1986). Pluralists need to come to terms with the structural aspects of power.

One other problem with pluralism is identified by Smith. Historically, pluralism was a culturally specific theory. It was developed in the USA, where classical pluralists such as Bentley thought that the key problem for democratic theory was the problem of representation. Interest groups extended democracy by ensuring broader representation than was possible in a two-party system in a large, complex society. Less attention was paid to the role interest groups might play as a check upon the power of the state, since the checks and balances of the US Constitution were assumed to perform this function. In contrast, in Britain, pluralists such as H. J. Laski were very concerned about the growth of state power and saw interests groups as a potential check on that growth. Not surprisingly, given the dominance of US political science, it was the American concerns that dominated, until in the 1960s they showed increasing concern about the growth of Executive power.

Even so pluralism remained, to an extent, culturally specific. As an example, both Lindblom's work and the emphasis of Lowi and others on sub-governments is essentially informed by the US case. Lindblom fails to appreciate that civil servants and politicians may have different interests because in the USA many senior bureaucrats are political appointments (see Marsh, 1983). Similarly, Lowi's sub-governments usually involve relationships, and negotiations, between the interest group(s), the Executive agency and a key Congressional Committee. This is only an appropriate model in a political system with a strong legislature – not the case in Britain or most other European political systems. In such cases the key link is between the interest group(s) and a government department, although an Executive agency may also be involved. This has potentially important theoretical implications, because in Europe the sub-governments or policy networks are clearly even more closed than they are in the USA, given the minimal involvement of a democratically-elected legislature. Pluralism certainly needs to broaden its horizons beyond the USA.

## ☐ The future of Marxism

Marxism's key problem is that it remains involved in an unresolved struggle with economism. Even Jessop, who rejects economism and whose work is consistently interesting, in his own empirical work treats political change as a response to economic crisis. C. Hay (1994) argues that this is because some of Jessop's empirical work neglects the insights of his theoretical analysis but it needs to be recognised that much Marxism is still characterised by strong economistic residues. Jessop and Hay would regard that as a major failing. However, while the economic clearly does not determine the political, and other social forces effect the form and outputs of the state, Marxists may well suggest that economic forces are the key (but not the *only*) constraint on state autonomy. After all, some pluralists, as well as many Weberians, argue that capital or business occupies a uniquely privileged position in capitalist liberal democracy. This appears to me to be the key dilemma for Marxists: is it possible to assert the primacy of economic relations without endorsing the functionalism and determinism of economism? In the end, any such formulation would need to suggest why an autonomous state normally enacts policies which tend to forward the interests of capital (for an alternative to Jessop's analysis, see Ward, 1993).

## ☐ *Elitism*

Obviously, elitism is a position with a large number of adherents. Indeed, one reading of the evidence on convergence presented here, although not necessarily a 'correct' reading, is that it illustrates the superiority of the elitist position; or, to put it another way, we are all elitists now. Certainly, evidence of concentration of power and the limited bases of structured inequality point in this direction

However, despite this, it must be acknowledged that much elitism is still atheoretical, resting upon an attempt to refute pluralism empirically. There is little agreement among elitists as to the key basis of structural inequality. Some elitists stress control of economic resources, or more often, like Scott, or even Skocpol, economic and political resources. Others want merely to assert the inevitably of elites and the variety of bases of structured inequality. This form of democratic elitism is really no different from elite or 'reformed' pluralism and should be acknowledged as such. If elitism has a future as a distinct position, it surely lies in the radical Weberianism of Skocpol or Scott, or Dearlove and Saunders (1984).

Not surprisingly, given their reluctance to specify the key basis of structured inequality which underpins political domination, most modern elitists also fail to confront the key problem of elite circulation. Classical elitists had theories of history. Modern elitists reject such theories, but acknowledge the impermanence of elites without offering any idea of how one elite may replace another. Once again, this means that elitism is an empirical refutation of pluralism rather than a distinct position. It may be that the distribution of power in contemporary capitalist liberal democracies is elitist, but that does not mean that any particular elitist model/theory can explain that distribution.

# □ *The future focus*

If this characterisation of the convergence between various theories of state/civil society is accurate, then it would seem to suggest to me that political sociology needs to break free from an approach which concentrates on expounding and criticising these three positions. Instead, perhaps it should concentrate upon three themes which are crucial and which all three positions address. Two of these themes – the growth of statism and the centrality of the structure–agency debate – have been dealt with at some length in this chapter, and, indeed, the latter is the subject of Chapter 10 in this book. The third theme, 'globalisation', will be returned to in the conclusion. For this reason, each receives only brief attention here.

This brief review of convergence emphasises the growth in the importance of statism in each position. In particular, there is general agreement about the need to take the state seriously; or as one book title puts it, to bring the state back in. No contemporary theoretical position sees the state as a simple agent of one or more social forces; all acknowledge the autonomy of the state. At the same time, most authors accept that the unity of the state is not given, or inevitable; rather, it is politically constructed. So analysis has to recognise the divisions and the way those divisions relate to, are reflected in, or reflect, the divisions in civil society. In addition, it must establish to what extent, and how, the unity of the state is constructed. These are important questions for all social scientists, but they are crucial to political scientists because the state and state–civil society relations are at the core of our discipline.

As Hay emphasises in Chapter 10, the structure/agency debate is one of the most important in social science. Hay outlines the positions that have been taken on this debate and they clearly relate to the three positions on state–civil society relations discussed in this section. Marxism and elitism have focused traditionally on structural explanation, while pluralism has utilised intentional/agency explanation. However, as we have seen, the positions have converged in this debate. In my view the way forward is identified by Hay. All the positions need to recognise that while politics may decide outcomes, the process takes place in a context that is characterised by structured inequality; a structured inequality which, unlike pluralism, is rooted in class, gender, race and knowledge as well as control of political resources. As such, the relationship between structure and agency is crucial and the relationship is clearly a dialectical one.

All the positions discussed pay insufficient attention to the international dimension, although Marxism and elitism are less guilty of this omission than pluralism. However, the processes of globalisation, which a number of authors in this volume discuss, means that any attempt to analyse the power structure in an individual country has clear limitations. Political decision-makers in individual countries are subject to a number of cross-national constraints: geopolitical and strategic considerations affect economic policy as much as foreign policy, the influence of some supranational organisations, particularly in Britain's case the EU, is growing, the internationalisation of capital, the growth in the economic, and thus political, power of trans-national corporations and, perhaps particularly, the liberalisation, and thus increased flexibility, of the financial markets are three key aspects of globalisation which obviously constrain both individual governments and the EU. In addition, advances in telecommunications increase cultural homogeneity and give both politicians and the electorate more chance to observe the policy problems faced, and the putative solutions adopted, by other countries. All these constraints need to be acknowledged in both the development of theory and in the choice of methodology. The theories need to take the international dimension more seriously and we need more comparative analysis.


# ■ Further reading

Schwarzmantel (1994) offers a sound introduction to the various theoretical positions although not one which offers more than the three relevant chapters in this volume. Dunleavy and O'Leary (1987) provide more extensive treatment of the positions and raise, although they do not develop, the issue of convergence. However, their treatment of Marxism is very poor. The best discussion of convegence is provided by Etzioni-Halevy (1993).

# Conclusions
## David Marsh and Gerry Stoker

This concluding chapter first outlines our approach to political science before examining two of the key problems which the discipline must acknowledge and confront. The first section argues for a political science that is diverse and rich in theory and method, capable of reaching out to other disciplines and with the capacity to tackle issues of concern to society. The second section explores the implications of the multi-theoretical approach that we advocate. It argues that if the richness of diversity is to be exploited it necessitates a sophistication in using and criticising alternative approaches; combining different approaches or theoretical perspectives demands considerable care and skill in articulating and integrating the various elements. The final section highlights two key challenges which we argue political science must confront: epistemological questions and globalisation.

# ■ Doing political science

This book started with a plea for political scientists to be more self-reflective in approaching their work. It has not been our aim in this book to champion one position; indeed, the positions adopted by our authors are too diverse to allow such sleight of hand. However, we would emphasise that authors should acknowledge explicitly both their theoretical and epistemological positions. We shall return to these two points later.

However, this does not mean that we advocate 'armchair theorising' at the expense of doing research; quite the contary. This book will have failed if it does not help to provide the motivation and excitement necessary to engage in the hard slog of doing political science. Finding answers to questions, subjecting your findings to public debate and discussion, and developing and refining your ideas in the light of the comments of others provide the essential dynamics of political science. The practitioner of political science engages in public debate and has his/her work tested against the demands of logical coherence and adequate evidence. It is in the context of doing empirical work that people learn the art of compromise in terms of meeting theoretical and methodological challenges.

The breadth of approaches offered in this book is considerable. In our view, such diversity is a strength; examining political events from different conceptual and theoretical approaches can offer alternative explanations of, an insights into, phenomena. We oppose those who argue that political science should give priority to forms of knowledge production that make use of quantification or mathematical proof. Certainly, appropriate quantitative measures can help us to tackle research questions. Similarly, mathematical reasoning can enhance one's ability to elaborate ideas. Yet historical, institutional or discourse analysis can also offer insights that are not available through such methods. More broadly, as Fiona Devine argues in Chapter 7, qualitative analysis should be seen as a full partner to quantitative studies. We want a political science that captures the richness of human experience and not one that, in the search for professional esteem, makes a fetish out of particular techniques or forms of knowledge production.

In doing political science, we want to find ways of overriding the debilitating effect of narrow specialisation. There is a proliferation of diverse special interests within the discipline. Such diversity reflects the growth in the political sciences and, in some senses, it is a cause for celebration. Each sub-discipline has its own journals, conferences and networks. Yet such a development can mean that researchers become trapped in one branch of the discipline and unaware of relevant and important developments in other branches. Another problem is that research takes place within networks of researchers who tend to share the same methods and core arguments, and pay little attention to other schools of analysis. Electoral studies tends to be quantitative and positivist in style. In contrast, European studies has been dominated by descriptive historical and institutional investigations. As such, the problem of specialisation is an issue potentially of missed opportunities. Again, our book is aimed at attempting to tackle the issue by exposing the richness of political science and the variety of approaches and methods which are available.

A further characteristic of good political science, in our opinion, is that it should have the capacity to reach out to other disciplines. There is a core of political science, and political scientists should seek to sustain their own identity, but they should have a capacity to relate to the literatures and concerns of other disciplines. Held and Leftwich (1984) suggest that to ensure a break from narrow discipline boundaries, political science should become less subject-centred and more problem-orientated. If the focus is on a social problem, such as poverty, then in order to provide a 'rounded' explanation the researcher will be encouraged to reach out to other disciplines for insights and enlightenment. Those undergoing training to be a political scientist should also have access to, and an understanding of, the other disciplines of social science.

The final feature of political science we should like to emphasise here is that it should be relevant. For us this means avoiding the trap of highly abstract and abstruse theoretical and methodological debates. The ultimate failure occurs if these debates become a game in themselves, where participants have to learn a new language and jargon before they can join in, and having joined become part of an exclusive world shut off from wider debate and political activity. Given the content of this book, it would be absurd for us to deny the relevance of theory and method to political science, but the point is to apply the rich and diverse approaches and theories of political science to the 'real problems' of society. Political science that is relevant is not restricted to technical matters and short-term policy prescriptions. It may well be critical of existing practices and principles within society. It should be prepared to make its findings known in an accessible manner. It should not duck the challenge of policy prescription, although in seeking to engineer changes in the world it should recognise the severe limits to its knowledge and capacity. Above all, political science should address the big issues. A concern with big issues led us to develop Part 3 of our book, with its focus on issues of the state and the distribution of power in society.

## ■ Meeting the multi-theoretical challenge

This collection clearly indicates that there are a variety of approaches to political science. As we have seen, within the discipline there are authors utilising perspectives as diverse as rational choice theory and discourse analysis. The former operates from a positivist epistemological position and emphasises quantitative analysis; the latter operates from a relativist epistemological position and concentrates on qualitative analysis. In our view, such diversity is a strength; examining political phenomena from different conceptual and theoretical approaches can offer alternative explanations of, and insights into, these phenomena. However, such positive consequences of diversity are only likely if the proponents of a given position are sophisticated, not only in their exposition of their own position, but also in their treatment and critique of alternative positions.

### □ *Be fair to yourself*

If an author is operating within a particular theoretical perspective, then it is likely that s/he will develop a sophisticated reading of that position and, as we have seen, it is evident that each approach has become considerably more sophisticated over time. However, sometimes authors are insufficiently explicit about the version of a particular approach they are using. In particular, some authors fail to take account of the most sophisticated critiques of the approach they adopt. Hugh Ward, in Chapter 4 on rational choice, amply illustrates all these points. Some rational choice theory is insufficiently precise about the assumptions it is making with regard to preferences, the decision making scheme, or the nature of costs and benefits. In addition, many rational choice theorists ignore the sophisticated critiques of the position, particularly those developed by sociologists and other rational choice theorists; yet it is just such criticism which, as Ward shows, has led to improvements in the rational choice model. However, this does not mean that the rational choice approach has little or nothing to offer the political scientist. Rather, Ward shows, first, that a sophisticated version of rational choice theory can help to explain many political phenomena; but, second, that it should be more modest about its claims. This plea for modesty is one which all political scientists would do well to take to heart.

## □ Be fair to the enemy

One other point needs emphasising before we move on. If the way in which a particular researcher develops an approach involves a criticism of other perspectives in order to establish the superiority of the one adopted, then the treatment of that alternative approach should also be sophisticated. There is a tendency for researchers, when criticising an alternative perspective, to offer an unsophisticated reading of the 'opposition': to set up a 'straw man'. So, for example, many critics of Marxism still offer an economistic reading; they still suggest that Marxists see economic relations as determining social or class relations, which in turn determine the form and function of the state. Yet the history of Marxism since the 1940s can be characterised as a struggle with exactly that form of economism. Anyone criticising Marxism in order to develop his/her own perspective should at the very least engage with contemporary, more sophisticated, Marxist work, such as that discussed by Taylor in Chapter 13.

## □ Beware a cafeteria approach

Of course, some authors would suggest (see Dunleavy and O'Leary, 1987) that a fuller explanation inevitably involves the use of a number of different approaches or theoretical perspectives. We would endorse that claim, but with a major qualification. If one is utilising a number of approaches, it is imperative to ensure that they are articulated: to be clear and precise as to how the different approaches are being used and integrated into a fuller explanation. There is potential danger in using a cafeteria approach, in which particular concepts, operating within specific theoretical frameworks, are drawn on to attempt to explain aspects of a phenomenon with little concern about how they relate to other concepts, located within different theoretical frameworks, which are being utilised to explain different aspects of the same phenomenon. This point is of sufficient importance to justify an extended example of how the integration of different perspectives can work. The example is drawn from the work of David Marsh and Rod Rhodes on policy networks; a concept in which there has been a great deal of interest within political science (see Marsh and Rhodes, 1992).

# Integrating different theoretical perspectives and levels of analysis

Marsh and Rhodes utilise the policy network concept to provide a model of interest group intermediation; that is, of relations between interest groups and the government. In fact, they argue strongly that it is a model of interest group intermediation that is superior to either the pluralist or the corporatist model. Thus, they view the policy network as a meso-level concept.

Marsh and Rhodes are most concerned with how networks affect policy outcomes. However, they make modest claims for the policy network model. They do argue that the existence, membership and characteristics of policy networks influence policy outcomes. Essentially, networks involve relationships in which resources are exchanged and power dependence is a central feature of them. So Marsh and Rhodes suggest that the distribution and type of resources within a network explain the relative power of its members, whether individuals or organisations. In addition, they argue that the different patterns of resource-dependence explain some of the differences between policy networks. Most significantly, the differences between networks affect policy outcomes. For example, the outcome of a tight policy network: a 'policy community' in the terminology advocated by Marsh and Rhodes (see Marsh and Rhodes, 1992b, p. 251), is likely to be policy continuity – some would say inertia – because participants share a common ideology, and thus policy preferences, and all participants acknowledge that they are involved in a positive-sum game. Similarly, a policy network dominated by a particular interest, most probably a professional or an economic interest, is likely to advocate and push through policies favouring that interest.

However, Marsh and Rhodes also acknowledge that in order to explain the membership of networks, and the policy outcomes from them, it is also imperative to utilise both micro-level analysis, based on theories of individual/group behaviour, and macro-level analysis, dealing with models of the relationship between the state and civil society. It is this point that is crucial here. As Marsh and Rhodes emphasise, in order to explain the membership of networks, and the outcomes from them, the policy network model needs to integrate with both micro-level and macro-level analysis.

At the micro-level, a model of individual/group behaviour is needed in order to help explain how individuals in networks act, given the constraints which face them from both inside and outside the network. Dowding (1994), in criticising Marsh and Rhodes, has argued that only rational choice theory provides the tools to develop such an explanation. This is not the place to rehearse this argument (see Marsh, 1995). The key point here is that the meso-level analysis, utilising the policy network framework, needs to be integrated with a micro-level analysis of the exchanges within the network; these could, as Dowding suggests, be based upon rational choice theory.

While Dowding is right that in order to explain outcomes we need to integrate meso-level and micro-level analysis, he neglects what might be an even more important point. We also need to integrate meso-level and macro-level analysis. The key point is that if we are to use network analysis to explain policy outcomes, we need to go beyond exchanges in the network; beyond the narrow, if important, concerns of the rational choice theorist and into the realms of political sociology. We need to explain how the network came about and what factors lead to network change. Networks are political structures which constrain and facilitate, but do not determine, policy outcomes. To explain the origins, shape and outcomes of a network it is necessary to examine why some interests are privileged in a given network or, if no interests are privileged, why the network is open. As Marsh (1995) argues, it is not possible to explain either the membership or the outcomes of policy networks outside the context of a theory of power, of the relation between the state and civil society; networks are characterised by consistent structured privilege which needs to be explained to enable an understanding of policy outcomes. As Part 3 of this book indicates, this is exactly the problem that power theories address; although, of course, as we saw in Chapters 11 to 14, there are no easy answers to the questions raised.

To put it another way, policy network analysis addresses the first two of four questions any theory of the state should address: 'Who rules/makes policy?' and 'How do they rule/make policy?' Rational choice theory, more particularly, may help to answer the second question, which is the one on which it would focus. Network analysis does not directly, or necessarily, address the two more important questions: 'Why are certain actors in a privileged position in the policy-making process?' and 'In whose interest do they rule, and how does their rule result in that interest being served?' These last two questions are the key concern of political sociologists and state theorists.

As Marsh (1995) argues, policy network analysis needs to be integrated with state theory and the policy network concept can be, and has been, integrated with different models of state–civil society relations: pluralist,

Marxist and elitist. However, the main point for our purposes here is that Marsh and Rhodes' work emphasises both the need to utilise concepts derived from different theoretical traditions in explaining policy-making and outcomes, and the crucial importance of integrating such analysis so that the concepts are used in a complementary, rather than a contradictory, way.

# ■ Two key issues

## ▯ *A plea to take epistemological problems more seriously*

We emphasised the importance of epistemological questions in the Introduction, and many of the chapters in this book have borne out that judgement. The approaches considered in Part 1 of the book are underpinned by different epistemological positions; so behaviouralism and rational choice theory operate from a positivist position, while discourse analysis and much of the feminist approach operate from a relativist position. Similarly, as far as methodology is concerned, quantitative analysis is rooted in positivism, while qualitative analysis tends to derive from a relativist position. Finally, as far as state theory is concerned, Marxism is the classic realist position, while pluralism was associated historically with positivism. However, as we have seen, both perspectives have had to respond to relativist critiques. In our view, even this brief exposition indicates the centrality of these epistemological questions. It has not been our aim in this book to champion one position; indeed, the positions adopted by our authors are too diverse to allow such sleight of hand. Rather, we have two concerns. First, we wish to emphasise the importance of these issues and indeed to argue that authors should acknowledge their explicit, and more often implicit, epistemological positions. Second, we believe that these issues should be introduced to all politics students, and taught in the context of a course on the philosophy of the social sciences.

## ▯ *Globalisation*

There is no doubt that, given the processes of globalisation which are a crucial feature of the developing political environment, political science needs to take the international dimension more seriously. Certainly, political decision makers in individual countries are subject to a number of cross-national constraints which affect the conduct of politics in any given country. Of course, globalisation is not a single or a simple process. In fact, there are at least four distinct, yet clearly interrelated, dimensions or processes involved:

## The geopolitical dimension

Geopolitical and strategic considerations have always affected economic policy as much as foreign policy. However, the growing interdependencies in the world have accentuated these constraints. As one example, it is clear that Britain's economic problems owe something, some would say a great deal, to its high levels of expenditure on defence. Such high levels of expenditure reflect an exaggerated view of Britain's world role which harks back to the imperial past (see Taylor, 1989).

## Political integration

The influence of some supra-national organisations, such as the EU, is growing. As such, individual European governments have limited autonomy over economic policy and will obviously have less if there is full monetary union. This has clear consequences for political science. So, for example, no comparative study of industrial policy-making in two or more European countries could fail to examine both the way in which the EU affects industrial policy-making in each country or the way in which each country affects EU policy.

## The internationalisation of capital

The internationalisation of capital, the growth in the economic, and thus political, power of trans-national corporations and, perhaps particularly, the liberalisation, and thus increased flexibility, of the financial markets are three key aspects of globalisation which obviously constrain both individual governments and the EU. The changes in the international political economy, and in the particular location of a given country in it, have a very important influence on political decisions (see Taylor, 1989 and 1992, for an analysis of the affect these changes have had on British political developments).

## Global communications

Advances in telecommunications mean that, in the developed world at least, more information is available and the potential at least for scrutiny of government is greater. Of course, it would be wrong to see these developments as necessarily extending democracy. After all, certain groups within society have more access to this technology and much of the coverage of politics trivialises and personalises the process. However, these developments clearly do have political consequences. So, for example, they mean that both politicians and the electorate have more chance to observe the policy problems faced, and the solutions adopted, by other countries. This is reflected in the growing interest that politicians, and political scientists, have taken in policy transfer (see Dolowitz and Marsh, 1995). This aspect of globalisation may also be leading to increased cultural homogeneity and, perhaps, to the strengthening of American cultural hegemony. Equally, it could provide the opportunity for radical experiments to spread as social movements; for example, dealing with the environment or feminist concerns, learn from one another.

Our point here is that all these constraints need to be acknowledged by political scientists in both the development of theory and the choice of methodology. The theories need to take the international dimension more seriously, and we need more comparative analysis. We need to analyse in what ways, and to what extent, the globalisation processes affect political institutions, behaviour and policy in particular states; this is merely to re-emphasise, and to an extent recast, what Gourevitch (1978) called the 'international sources of domestic politics'. At the same time, however, we must study the way in which individual states contribute to the processes of globalisation.

Of course, although we need to take the international dimension seriously, we must also acknowledge difference; recognise the autonomy of individual states and, indeed, the role played by sub-national governments. Analysis needs to take into account the variety and diversity of reaction both between and within nation states. On issues such as transport policy or economic development, for example, different nation states are responding with a diverse range of strategies. What is more, within nation states, forces of regional or sub-national autonomy give a particular flavour, and a certain diversity, to seemingly common, developments.

Globalisation makes demands on analysis at all levels of political science. To study urban government, for example, requires not only an examination of the impact of globalisation as an economic and geopolitical force; it also means placing urban government in the context of the changing architecture of government and the rising practice of global communication. In the case of countries within the EU urban governments relate not only to their respective national governments but also to European-level institutions. The EU offers a range of cross-national programmes with associated funding and support. It consults with sub-national governments over policy initiatives and regulations. Urban governments bid for support from the EU, are subject to its regulations and seek to influence its policies, either on an individual basis or, increasingly, through trans-national networks of urban governments. Above and beyond their involvement in this complicated governmental architecture, urban governments place themselves within a global communication exchange. Lessons about policy initiatives in relation to economic development, cultural programmes and environmental schemes are drawn increasingly from cities and towns in other countries as well as from sources closer to home.

The challenge of globalisation is that it changes the terrain for political science. The neat division between a political science within nation states and a study of international relations between nation states breaks down. It becomes less acceptable to study in isolation the experience of particular countries. In a world in which political actors and interests are experiencing the impact of globalisation then political science cannot be immune from such forces. The challenge is to develop a political science which has a capacity to think globally but act with sufficient clarity and strength to tackle the particular 'local' forces and developments within each country.

# Bibliography

Abel, P. (1971) *Model Building in Sociology* (New York: Schocken).

Adorno, T. (1976) *The Positivist Dispute in German Sociology* (trans. Glyn Adey and David Frisby) (London: Heineman).

Aldrich, J. (1993) 'Rational Choice and Turnout', *American Journal of Political Science*, 37, pp. 246–78.

Alker, H. R. (1965) *Mathematics and Politics* (New York: Macmillan).

Alker, H. R. (1969) 'A Typology of Ecological Fallacies', in M. Dogan and S. Rokkan (eds), *Quantitative Ecological Analysis in the Social Sciences* (Cambridge, Mass: MIT Press), pp. 69–86.

Allison, G. T. (1971) *Essence of Decision: Explaining the Cuban Missile Crisis* (Boston, Mass.: Little, Brown).

Almond, G. A. (1980) 'The Intellectual History of the Civic Culture Concept', in G. Almond and S. Verba (eds), *The Civic Culture Revisited* (Boston: Little, Brown).

Almond, G. (1988) 'The Return of the State', *American Political Science Review*, 82, pp. 853–74.

Almond, G. and B. Powell (1960) *Comparative Politics* (Boston, Mass.: Little, Brown).

Almond, G. A. and S. Verba (1963) The Civic Culture: (Political Attitudes and Democracy in Five Nations (Princeton, NJ: Princeton University Press); reissued by Sage, 1989.

Almond, G. A. and S. Verba (eds) (1980) *The Civic Culture Revisited* (Boston: Little Brown).

Althusser, L. (1969) *For Marx* (London: Verso).

Althusser, L. (1971) 'Ideology and Ideological State Apparatuses', in L. *Althusser, Lenin and Philosophy and Other Essays* (London: New Left Books).

Althusser, L. and E. Balibar (1970) *Reading Capital* (London: New Left Books).

Anderson, C. (1977) *Statecraft: An Introduction to Political Choice and Judgement* (New York: John Wiley).

APSA, (American Political Science Association) (1950) *Toward A More Responsible Party System,* (A Report of the Committee on Political Parties), *American Political Science Review,* 44, Supplement.

APSA, (American Political Science Association) (1994) *Directory of Members* (Washington DC: American Political Science Association).

Arber, S. (1993) 'Designing Samples', in N. Gilbert (ed.), *Researching Social Life* (London: Sage).

Arblaster, A. (1993) 'The Proper Limits of Pluralism', in I. Hampshire Monk (ed.), *Defending Politics* (London: Academic Press).

Arrow, K. J. (1951) *Social Choice and Individual Values* (New York: John Wiley).

Atkinson, J. and J. Heritage (1984) *Structures of Social Action* (Cambridge: Cambridge University Press).

Atkinson, P. (1990) *The Ethnographic Imagination: Textual Constructions of Reality* (London: Routledge).

Axelrod, R. (1986) 'An Evolutionary Approach to Norms', *American Political Science Review*, 80, pp. 1095–111.

Ayer, A. J. (1971) *Language, Truth and Logic* (2nd edn.) (Harmondsworth: Penguin).

Bachrach, P. and M. Baratz (1962) 'Two Faces of Power', *American Political Science Review*, 56, pp. 947–52.

Baldwin, D. A. (ed.) (1993) *Neorealism and Neoliberalism: The Contemporary Debate* (Princeton N. J.: Princeton University Press).

Banks, A. and R. Textor (1963) *A Cross-Polity Survey* (Cambridge Mass.: MIT Press).

Banks, O. (1986) *Faces of Feminism; the Study of a Social Movement* (Oxford, Basil Blackwell).

Barnes, S. and M. Kaase *et al.* (1979) *Political Action* (London: Sage).

Barnett, A., C. Ellis and P. Hirst (eds) (1993) *Debating the Constitution: A New Perspective on Constitutional Reform* (Cambridge: Polity Press).

Barrett, M. (1988) *Women's Oppression Today: The Marxist–Feminist Encounter* (London, Verso).

Barrett, M. (1992) 'Womens' Oppression Today: Problems in Marxist–Feminist Analysis', in M. Humm, *Feminisms: A Reader* (Hemel Hempstead: Harvester-Wheatsheaf).

Barry, B. (1970) *Sociologists, Economists and Democracy* (London: Collier–Macmillan).

Barry, B. (1989) *Theories of Justice* (vol. 1) (Hemel Hempstead: Harvester-Wheatsheaf).

Barry, B. and R. Hardin (eds) (1982) *Rational Man and Irrational Society? An Introduction and a Sourcebook* (Beverley Hills, Calif.: Sage).

Barth, E. (1986) Keynote Address to the International Congress of Women, Gottingen.

Barzun J. M. and H. F. Graff (1992) *The Modern Researcher* (5th edn.) (New York: Harcourt Brace).

Bauman, Z. (1989) 'Hermeneutics and Modern Social Theory', in D. Held and J. B. Thompson (eds), *Social Theory and Modern Societies* (Cambridge: Cambridge University Press).

Bauman, Z. (1992) *Intimations of Postmodernity* (London: Routledge).

Beer, S. (1982) *Modern British Politics* (London: Faber).

Bellamy, R. (1993) 'Introduction: The Demise and Rise of Political Theory', in R. Bellamy (ed.), *Theories and Concepts of Politics: An Introduction* (Manchester University Press).

Bennington, G. (1993) *Jacques Derrida* (Chicago: University of Chicago Press).

Bentham, J. (1967) *An Introduction to the Principles of Morals and Legislation* (Oxford: Basil Blackwell).

Bentley, A. (1967) *The Process of Government* (Chicago: Chicago University Press).

Benton, T. (1977) *Philosophical Foundations of the Three Sociologies* (London: Routledge & Kegan Paul).

Benton, T. (1984) *The Rise and Fall of Structuralist Marxism* (London: Macmillan).

Berger, P. and T. Luckmann (1967) *The Social Construction of Reality* (Harmondsworth: Penguin).

Berlin, I. (1984) *Four Essays on Liberty* (Oxford: Oxford University Press).

Bernstein, R. (1979) *The Restructuring of Social and Political Theory* (London: Methuen).

Berrington, H. and P. Norris (1988) *Political Studies in the Eighties* (Newcastle upon Tyne: Political Studies Association).

Bertramsen, R., J. Thomsen and J. Torfing (1990) *State, Economy and Society* (London: Unwin Hyman).

Bhaskar, R. (1975) *A Realist Theory of Science* (Brighton: Harvester).

Bhaskar, R. (1979) *The Possibility of Naturalism* (Hemel Hempstead: Harvester-Wheatsheaf).

Bhaskar, R. (1986) *Scientific Realism and Human Emancipation* (London: Verso).

Bhaskar, R. (1989) *Reclaiming Reality* (London: Verso).

Billig, M. (1978) *Fascists: A Social–Psychological View of the National Front* (London: Academic Press).

Birch, A. H. (1964) *Representative and Responsible Government* (London: Allen & Unwin).

Birch, A. (1993) *The Concepts and Theories of Modern Democracy* (London: Routledge).

Birch, A. H. et al. (1959) *Small Town Politics: a Study of Political Life in Glossop* (Oxford: Oxford University Press).

Blalock, H. M. (1964) *Causal Inferences in Non-Experimental Research* (Chapel Hill, N.C.: University of North Carolina Press).

Blalock, H. M. (1969) *Theory Construction: From Verbal to Mathematical Formulations* (Englewood Cliffs, N.J.: Prentice-Hall).

Blalock, H. M. (1970) *An Introduction to Social Research* (Englewood Cliffs, N.J.: Prentice-Hall).

Blalock, H. M. (ed.) (1972) *Causal Models in the Social Sciences* (London: Macmillan).

Block, F. (1977) 'The Ruling Class Does Not Rule', *Socialist Revolution*, 3, pp. 6–28.

Block, F. (1980) 'Beyond Relative Autonomy: State Managers as Historical Subjects', in R. Miliband and J. Saville (eds), *Socialist Register* (London: Merlin Press).

Blondel, J. (1976) *Thinking Politically* (London: Wildwood House).

Bogdanor, V. (ed.) (1987) *The Blackwell Encyclopaedia of Political Institutions* (Oxford: Blackwell).

Bonefeld, W. (1987) 'Reformulation of State Theory', in *Capital and Class*, 33, pp. 96–127.

Boudon, R. (1981) 'Undesired Consequences and Types of System of Interaction', in P. Blau and R. Merton (eds) *Continuities in Structuralist Enquiry* (London: Sage).

Bourque, S. and J. Grossholtz (1974) 'Politics an Unnatural Practice: Political Science Looks at Female Participation', *Politics and Society*, 4 (2).

Brand, J. and T. Mackie (1995) 'The Elections: New Electoral System and New Party System', in P. Ignazi and R. Katz (eds), *Italian Politics: A Review*, Volume 10 (London: Pinter).

Braybrooke, D. and C. E. Lindblom (1963) *A Strategy of Decision: Policy Evaluation as a Social Process* (New York: Free Press).

Brenner, M., J. Brown and D. Canter (eds) (1985) *The Research Interview: Uses and Approaches* (London: Academic Press).

Brittan, S. (1975) 'The Economic Conseqeunces of Democracy', *British Journal of Political Science*, 5, pp. 129–59.

Brown, B. (1993) 'Feminism', in R. Bellamy (ed.) *Theories and Concepts of Politics: An Introduction* (Manchester: Manchester University Press).

Bryman, A. (1988) *Quantity and Quality in Social Research* (London: Unwin Hyman).

Brzezinski, Z. (1989) *The Grand Failure* (London: Macdonald).

Budge, I., I. Crewe and D. Fairlie (eds) (1976) *Party Identification and Beyond* (New York: John Wiley).

Budge, I. and D. Fairlie (1983) *Explaining and Predicting Elections: Issue Effects and Party Strategies in Twenty Three Democracies* (London: Allen & Unwin).

Budge, I., D. Robertson and D. Hearl (1987) *Ideology, Strategy and Party Change* (Cambridge: Cambridge University Press).

Budge, I. and M. Laver (1992) *Party Policy and Government Coalitions* (London: Macmillan).

Bulmer, M. (1984) 'Facts, Concepts, Theories and Problems', in M. Bulmer (ed.), *Sociological Research Methods: An Introduction* (2nd edn.) (London: Macmillan).

Bulmer, S. (1994) 'Institutions, Governance Regimes and the Single European Market: Analysing the Governance of the European Union'. Paper presented to the Conference of Europeanists panel on 'Contending Approaches to EC Governance', Chicago, 31 March–2 April.

Burgess, R. (1984) *In the Field: An Introduction to Field Research* (London: Allen & Unwin).

Burrell, G. and G. Morgan (1979) *Sociological Paradigms and Organizational Analysis* (London: Heinemann).

Butler, D. E. (1958) *The Study of Political Behaviour* (London: Hutchinson).

Butler, D. amd D. Stokes (1974) *Political Change in Britain* (London: Macmillan)

Callinicos, A. (1984) 'Marxism and Politics', in A. Leftwich (ed.) *What is Politics?* (Oxford: Basil Blackwell).

Campbell, A., P. E. Converse, W. E. Miller and D. Stokes (1960) *The American Voter* (New York: Wiley); reprinted by University of Chicago Press, 1980.

Campbell, A., P. Converse, W. Miller and D. Stokes (1960) *The American Voter* (New York: John Wiley).

Carlsnaes, W. (1992) 'The Agency-Structure Problem in Foreign Policy Analysis', *International Studies Quarterly*, 36, pp. 245–70.

Carnap, R. (1936) 'Testability and Meaning', *Philosophy of Science*, 3, pp. 420–71; 4, pp. 1–40.

Carnap, R. (1950) 'Empiricism, Semantics and Ontology', *Revue Internationale de Philosophe*, 4, pp. 20–40.

Carnoy, M. (1984) *The State and Political Theory* (Princeton, N.J.: Princeton University Press).

Carr, E. H. (1961) *The Twenty Years Crisis 1919–1939* (London: Macmillan).

Carrol, L. (1987) *Through the Looking-Glass, and What Alice Found There* (London: Treasure Press).

Carroll, S. J. and L. M. G. Zerilli (1993) 'Feminist Challenges to Political Science' in A. W. Finifter (ed.), *Political Science: The State of the Discipline II* (Washington DC, American Political Science Association, 1993) pp. 55–76.

Cawson, A. (1982) *Corporatism and Welfare* (London: Heinemann).

Cawson, A. (ed.) (1985) *Organised Interests and the State: Studies in Meso-Corporatism* (London: Sage).

Cerny, P. G. (1989) *The Changing Architecture of Politics* (London: Sage).

Chalmers, A. F. (1986) *What is This Thing Called Science?* (Milton Keynes: Open University Press).

Chalmers, A. F. (1990) *Science and its Fabrication* (Milton Keynes: Open University Press).

Chandler, A. D. (1969) *Strategy and Structure* (Cambridge, Mass.: MIT Press).

Chapman, B. (1959) *The Profession of Government* (London: Allen & Unwin).

Chapman, J. (1985) 'Marital Status, Sex and the Formation of Political Attitudes in Adult Life', *Political Studies*, 23, (4), pp. 592–609.

Chapman, Jenny (1987) 'Adult Socialization and Out-Group Politicization: An Empirical Study of Consciousness-Raising', *British Journal of Political Science*, 17, (3), pp. 315–40.

Chapman, J. (1991) 'The Political Versus the Personal: Participatory Democracy and Feminism', *Strathclyde Papers in Government and Politics*.

Chapman, J. (1993) *Politics, Feminism and the Reformation of Gender* (London: Routledge).

Chapman, J. (1994) *Democracy: Does it Pay? Slovak Political Development and Democratisation Theory*, Comenius Papers in Politics and Human Rights, No. 2 (Bratislava).

Chester, D. N. (1975) 'Political Studies in Britain: Recollections and Comments', *Political Studies*, XXIII, pp. 151–64.

Chodorow, N. (1978) *The Reproduction of Mothering: Psychoanalysis and the Sociology of Gender* (Berkeley, Cal.: University of California Press).

Christy, C. (1987) *Sex Differences in Political Participation: Processes of Change in Fourteen Nations* (New York: Praeger).

Clarke, S. (1988) 'Overaccumulation, Class Struggle and the Regulation Approach', *Capital and Class*, 38, pp. 59–92.

Clarke, H. D., M. C. Stewart and G. Zuk (1986) 'Politics, Economics and Party Popularity in Britain 1979–83', *Electoral Studies*, 5, pp. 123–41.

Coakley, J. and L. Harris (1983) *The City of Capital: London's Role as a Financial Centre* (Oxford: Basil Blackwell).

Coates, D. (1992) *Running the Country* (Milton Keynes: Open University Press).

Cohen, A. (1964) *Attitude Change and Social Influence* (New York: Basic Books).

Cohen, G. (1978) *Marx's Theory of History: A Defence* (Oxford: Clarendon Press).

Collard, D. (1978) *Altruism and the Economy* (Oxford: Robertson).

Collier, D. (1993) 'The Comparative Method', in A. Finifter (ed.) *Political Science: The State of the Discipline* (Washington DC: American Political Science Association).

Collier, R. and D. Collier (1991) *Shaping the Political Arena; Critical Junctures, the Labor Movement and Regime Dynamics in Latin America* (Princeton N.J.: Princeton University Press).

Commission of the European Communities (1993) *Eurobarometer: Public Opinion in the European Community, Trends 1974–1992* (Brussels: EC).

Comte, A. (1974) *Discourse on the Positive Spirit* (trans. Andreski Stanislav).

Converse, P. and R. Pierce (1986) *Representation in France* (Cambridge, Mass.: Harvard University Press).

Cook, A. and G. Kirk (1983) *Greenham Women Everywhere: Dreams, Ideas and Actions from the Women's Peace Movement* (London: Pluto).

Coole, D. (1994) 'Whither Feminisms?' *Political Studies*, 42, (1), pp. 128–34.

Coplin, W. D. (1968) *Simulation in the Study of Politics* (Chicago: Markham).

Cowling, M. (1963) *The Nature and Limits of Political Science* (Cambridge: Cambridge University Press).

Cox, A. (1988) 'The Old and New Testaments of Corporatism: Is it a Political Form or a Method of Policy-making?', *Political Studies*, 36, pp. 294–308.

Crewe, I. and M. Harrop (eds) (1986) *Political Communications: the General Election Campaign of 1983* (Cambridge: Cambridge University Press).

Crewe, I. and P. Norris (eds) (1992) *British Politics and Elections Yearbook 1991* (London: Simon & Shuster).

Crick, B. (1959) *The American Science of Politics: Its Origins and Conditions* (Berkeley, Calif.: University of California Press).

Crick, B. (1993) *In Defence of Politics* (4th edn) (Harmondsworth: Penguin).

Crouch, C. (1977) *Class Conflict and the Industrial Relations Crisis* (London: Heinemann).

Dahl, R. (1957) 'The Concept of Power', *Behavioural Sciences*, pp. 202–3.

Dahl, R. (1958) 'A Critique of the Ruling Elite Model', *American Political Science Review*, 52, 2 (June), pp. 463–9.

Dahl, R. (1961) *Who Governs?* (New Haven, Conn.: Yale University Press).

Dahl, R. A. (1967) *Pluralist Democracy in the United States* (Chicago: Rand McNally).

Dahl, R. (1971) *Polyarchy* (New Haven, Conn.: Yale University Press).

Dahl, R. (1982) *Dilemmas of Pluralist Democracy* (New Haven, Conn.: Yale University Press).

Dahl, R. and C. Lindblom (1976) *Politics, Economics and Welfare* (New York: Harper).

Dahl, T. S. and H. M. Hernes (1988) 'After Equality', *Scandinavian Polital Review* (Summer).

Dahlerup, D. (1984) 'Overcoming the Barriers: An Approach to How Women's Issues are Kept from the Political Agenda', in J. Stiehm (ed.), *Women's View of the Political World of Men* (New York: Transnational Publishers).

Dahlerup, D. (1986) *The New Women's Movement: Feminism and Political Power in Europe and the USA* (London: Sage).

Dahlerup, D. (1994) 'Learning to Live with the State: State, Market and Civil Society: Women's Need for State Intervention in East and West', *Women's Studies International Forum*, 17, (2/3), pp. 117–27.

Dallmayr, F. (1988) 'Hegemony and Democracy: On Laclau and Mouffe', *Strategies*, 1, pp. 29–49.

Dallmayr, F. and T. McCarthy (1977), 'The Crisis of Understanding', in F. Dallmayr and T. McCarthy *Understanding and Social Inquiry* (Notre Dame, Ind.: University of Notre Dame Press).

Dalton, R. (1988) *Citizen Politics in Western Democracies: Public Opinion and Political Parties in the United States, Great Britain, West Germany and France* (Chatham, N.J.: Chatham House).

Daly, M. (1978) *Gyn/Ecology: The Mathematics of Radical Feminism* (London: The Women's Press).

Daniels, N. (ed.) (1975) *Reading Rawls: Critical Studies on Rawls' 'A Theory of Justice'* (Oxford: Basil Blackwell).

de Beauvoir, S. (1972) *The Second Sex* (transl. and edited by H. M. Parshley) (Harmondsworth: Penguin).

de Vaus, D. A. (1991) *Surveys in Social Research* (2nd edn) (London: Unwin Hyman).

Dearlove, J. (1973) *The Politics of Policy in Local Government* (London: Cambridge University Press).

Dearlove, J. (1989) 'Bringing the Constitution Back In: Political Science and the State', *Political Studies*, XXXVII, pp. 521–39.

Dearlove, J. and P. Saunders (1984) *An Introduction to British Politics* (Cambridge: Polity Press).

Delphy, C. (1993) 'Rethinking Sex and Gender', *Women's Studies International Forum*, 16, (1), pp. 1–9.

Dennis, J. (ed.) (1973) *Socialisation to Politics* (New York: Wiley).

Derrida, J. (1981) *Positions* (Chicago: University of Chicago Press).

Dessler, D. (1989) 'What's at Stake in the Agent/Structure Debate?', *International Organization*, 41, 3.

Devine, F. (1992) *Affluent Workers Revisited: Privatism and the Working Class* (Edinburgh University Press).

Devine, F. (1995) 'Learning More about Mass Political Behaviour: Beyond Dunleavy', in D. Broughton *et al.* (eds) *British Elections and Parties Yearbook 1994* (London: Frank Cass).

Diamond, L. (1992) 'Economic Development and Democracy Reconsidered', *American Behavioral Scientist*, 35, pp. 450–86.

Dogan, M. (1994) 'Limits to Quantification in Comparative Politics: The Gap between Substance and Method', in M. Dogan and A. Kazancigil (eds) *Comparing Nations: Concepts, Strategies, Substance*. (Oxford: Basil Blackwell).

Dogan, M. and A. Kazancigil (eds) (1994) *Comparing Nations: Concepts, Strategies, Substance* (Oxford: Basil Blackwell).

Dogan, M. and D. Pelasy (eds) (1990) *How to Compare Nations: Strategies in Comparative Politics* (2nd edn) (Chatham, N.J.: Chatham House).

Dogan, M. and S. Rokkan (eds) (1969) *Quantitative Ecological Analysis in the Social Sciences* (Cambridge, Mass.: MIT Press).

Dolowitz, D. and D. Marsh (1995) 'Who Learns What from Whom. A Review of the Policy Transfer Literature', *Political Studies* (forthcoming).

Domhoff, G. W. (1967) *Who Rules America* (Englewood Cliffs, N.J.: Prentice Hall).
Domhoff, G. W. (1970) *The Higher Circles: The Governing Class in America* (New York: Random House).
Donaldson, L. (1985) *In Defence of Organisation Theory: A Reply to the Critics* (Cambridge: Cambridge University Press).
Douglas, J. (1989) 'The Changing Tide–Some Recent Studies of Thatcherism', *British Journal of Political Science*, 19, pp. 399–424.
Dowding, K. (1994), 'Policy Networks: Don't Stretch a Good Idea Too Far', in P. Dunleavy and J Stanyer, *Contemporary Political Studies, 1994* (Belfast: Political Studies Association), pp. 59–78.
Downs, A. (1957) *An Economic Theory of Democracy* (New York: Harper & Row).
Downs, A. (1967) *Inside Bureaucracy* (Boston, Mass.: Little, Brown).
Downs, A. (1991) 'Social Values and Democracy', in K. R. Monroe (ed.) *The Economic Approach Politics: A Critical Reassessment of the Theory of Rational Action* (New York: Harper Collins).
Drewry, G. (1995) 'Public Law', *Public Administration*, 73, forthcoming.
Drewry, G. and Butcher, T. (1988) *The Civil Service Today* (Oxford: Basil Blackwell).
Dryzek, J. (1990) *Discursive Democracy: Politics, Policy and Political Science* (Cambridge: Cambridge University Press).
Dunleavy, P. (1982) 'Is There a Radical Approach to Public Administration?', *Public Administration*, 60, pp. 215–33.
Dunleavy, P. (1987) 'Political Science', in V. Bogdanor (ed.) *The Blackwell Encyclopaedia of Political Institutions* (Oxford: Basil Blackwell) pp. 468–72.
Dunleavy, P. and B. O'Leary (1987) *Theories of the State* (London: Macmillan).
Dunleavy, P. (1990) 'Mass Political Behaviour: Is There More to Learn?' *Political Studies*, XXXVII, pp. 453–69.
Dunleavy, P., G. W. Jones and B. O'Leary (1990) 'Prime Ministers and the Commons: Patterns of Behaviour', *Public Administration*, 68, pp. 123–40.
Dunleavy, P. (1991) *Democracy, Bureaucracy and Public Choice: Economic Explanations in Political Science* (Hemel Hempstead: Harvester-Wheatsheaf).
Dunleavy, P. and G. Jones *et al.* (1993) 'Leaders, Politics and Institutional Change: The Decline of Prime Ministerial Accountability to the House of Commons, 1968–1990', *British Journal of Political Science*, 23, pp. 267–98.
Dunleavy, P. and H. Ward (1981) 'Exogenous Voter Preferences and Parties with State Power', *British Journal of Political Science*, 11, pp. 351–80.
Duverger, M. (1959) *Political Parties* (2nd revd edn) (London: Methuen).
Dworkin, R. (1977) *Taking Rights Seriously* (London: Duckworth).
Dworkin, R. (1984) 'Liberalism', in M. Sandel (ed.), *Liberalism and its Critics* (Oxford: Basil Blackwell).
Eagleton, T. (1991) *Ideology: An Introduction* (London: Verso).
Easton, D. (1971) [1967] [1953] *The Political System. An Inquiry into the State of Political Science* (New York: Alfred A Knopf, second edition).
Eckersley, R. (1992) *Environmentalism and Political Theory: Towards an Ecocentric Approach* (London: UCL Press).
Eckstein, H. (1963a) 'A Perspective on Comparative Politics, Past and Present', in H. Eckstein and D. E. Apter (eds), *Comparative Politics: A Reader* (London: Free Press of Glencoe), pp. 3–32.
Eckstein, H. (1963b) 'Group Theory and the Comparative Study of Pressure Groups', in H. Eckstein and D. Apter (eds), *Comparative Politics* (New York: Free Press).
Eckstein, H. (1975) 'Case Study and Theory in Political Science', in F. I. Greenstein and N. Polsby (eds) *Handbook of Political Science, vol. 7: Strategies of Inquiry* (Reading, Mass.: Addison-Wesley), pp. 79–137.
Eckstein, H. (1979) 'On the "Science" of the State', *Daedalus*, 108, 4, pp. 1–20.
Edelman, M. (1964) *The Symbolic Uses of Politics* (Urbana, Ill.: University of Illinois Press).
Einhorn, H. J. and R. M. Hogarth (1986) 'Decision Making Under Ambiguity', in R. M. Hogarth and M. W. Reder (eds) *Rational Choice: The Contrast Between Economics and Psychology* (Chicago: Chicago University Press) pp. 41–66.
Elshtain, J. B. (1987) *Women and War* (New York: Basic Books).
Elster, J. (1979) *Ulysses and the Sirens: Studies in Rationality and Irrationality* (Cambridge: Cambridge University Press).

Elster, J. (1982) 'Marxism, Functionalism and Game Theory', *Theory and Society*, 11, 4.
Elster, J. (1983) *Sour Grapes: Studies in the Subversion of Rationality* (Cambridge: Cambridge University Press).
Elster, J. (ed.) (1985) *The Multiple Self* (Cambridge: Cambridge University Press).
Elster, J. (ed.) (1986) *Rational Choice* (Oxford: Basil Blackwell).
Elster, J. (1989a) *The Cement of Society: A Study of Social Order* (Cambridge: Cambridge University Press).
Elster, J. (1989b) *Solomic Judgements: Studies in the Limitations of Rationality* (Cambridge: Cambridge University Press).
Elster, J. (1989c) *Nuts and Bolts for the Social Sciences* (Cambridge: Cambridge University Press).
Elster, J. (1991) *Making Sense of Marx* (Cambridge: Cambridge University Press).
Elster, J. (1993a) *Political Psychology* (Cambridge: Cambridge University Press).
Elster, J. (1993b) 'Constitution-making in Eastern Europe: Rebuilding the Boat in the Open Sea', *Public Administration*, 71, pp. 169–217.
Enelow, J. M. and M. J. Hinich (eds) (1990) *Advances in the Spatial Theory of Voting* (Cambridge: Cambridge University Press).
Etzioni, A. (1967) 'Mixed Scanning: A Third Approach to Decision Making', *Public Administration Review*, 27, pp. 385–92.
Etzioni, A. (1992) 'Normative–Affective Factors: Towards A New Decision Making Model', in Zey (ed.), *Decision Making*.
Etzioni, A. (1993) *The Spirit of Community. Rights, Responsibilities and the Communitarian Agenda* (Crown Publishing Group).
Etzioni-Halevy, E. (1993) *The Elite Connection* (Oxford: Polity Press).
Evans, M. (1975) *Karl Marx* (London: Allen & Unwin).
Eysenck, H. (1951) *The Psychology of Politics* (London: Routledge).
Fairclough, L. (1992) *Discourse and Social Change* (Oxford: Basil Blackwell).
Femia, J. (1987) *Gramsci's Political Thought* (Oxford: Clarendon).
Ferguson, K. (1984) *The Feminist Case against Bureaucracy* (Philadelphia: Temple University Press).
Fielding, N. (1993a) 'Ethnography', in N. Gilbert (ed.), *Researching Social Life* (London: Sage).
Fielding, N. (1993b) 'Qualitative Interviewing' in N. Gilbert (ed.), *Researching Social Life* (London: Sage).
Fiorina, M. (1977) 'An Outline of a Model of Party Choice', *American Journal of Political Science*, 21 pp. 601–25.
Fiorina, M. (1981) *Retrospective Voting in American National Elections* (London: Yale University Press).
Finch, J. (1984) 'It's Great to have Someone To Talk To: Ethics and Politics of Interviewing Women', in C. Bell and H. Roberts (eds), *Social Researching: Politics, Problems and Practice* (London: Routledge).
Finer, H. (1932) *The Theory and Practice of Modern Government* 2 vols (London: Methuen).
Finer, H. (1954) *The Theory and Practice of Modern Government* (abridged, 1 vol. edn.) (London: Methuen).
Finer, S. (1987), 'Thatcherism and British Political History', in K. Minogue and M. Biddiss (eds), *Thatcherism: Personality and Politics* (London: Macmillan) pp.127–140.
Finer, S. E. (1966) *Anonymous Empire* (London: Pall Mall).
Finer, S. E. (1987) 'Herman Finer', in V. Bogdanor (ed.), *The Blackwell Encyclopaedia of Political Institutions* (Oxford: Basil Blackwell).
Firestone, S. (1979) *The Dialectic of Sex* (London: Virago).
Fischer, E. (1970) *Marx in His Own Words* (London: Allen Lane).
Flora, C. and N. Lynn (1974) 'Women and Political Socialization: Considerations of the Impact of Motherhood' in J. Jaquette *Women in Politics* (New York: John Wiley).
Foucault, M. (1972) *The Archaeology of Knowledge* (London: Tavistock Publications).
Franklin, M., T. Mackie and H. Valen (1992) *Electoral Change* (Cambridge: Cambridge University Press).
Freccero, C. (1990) 'Notes of a Post-Sex Wars Theorizer' in M. Hirsch and E. F. Keller *Conflicts in Feminism* (New York: Routledge).
Freeman, J. (1984) 'The Women's Liberation Movement: Its Origins, Structure, Activities and Ideas', in J. Freeman (ed.), *Women: A Feminist Perspective* (Palo Alto, Cal.: Mayfield).

Friedman, M. (1953) 'The Methodology of Positive Economics', in M. Friedman *The Methodology of Positive Economics* (Chicago: University of Chicago Press).

Fudenberg, D. and E. Maskin (1986) 'The Folk-Theorem in Repeated Games With Discounting or With Imperfect Information', *Econometrica*, 54, pp. 533–56.

Fukuyama, F. (1992) *The End of History* (New York: Free Press).

Galbraith, J. K. (1963) *American Capitalism* (Harmondsworth: Penguin).

Gamble, A. (1988) *The Free Economy and the Strong State* (London: Macmillan).

Gamble, A. (1990a) 'Theories of British Politics', *Political Studies*, XXXVIII, 3, pp. 404–20.

Gamble, A. (1990b) *Britain in Decline* (3rd edn) (London: Macmillan).

Gasche, R. (1986) *The Train of the Mirror: Derrida and the Philosophy of Reflection* (Cambridge, Mass.: Harvard University Press).

Gauthier, D. (1986) *Morals by Agreement* (Oxford University Press).

Gavanta, J. (1980) *Power and Powerlessness* (Oxford: Clarendon Press).

Gelb, J. *Feminism and Politics: A Comparative Perspective* (Berkeley, Cal.: University of California Press).

Gelb, J. and M. Palley (1987) *Women and Public Policies* (Princeton, N.J.: Princeton University Press).

Geras, N. (1978) 'Althusser's Marxism: An Assessment', *Western Marxism: A Critical Reader* (London: Verso).

Geras, N. (1985) 'The Controversy about Marx and Justice', *New Left Review*, 150.

Geras, N. (1987) 'Post-Marxism?', *New Left Review*, 163, pp. 3–27.

Gewirth, A. (1978) *Reason and Morality* (Chicago: University of Chicago Press).

Gibbard, A. (1973) 'Manipulation of Voting Schemes: A General Result', *Econometrica*, 41, pp. 587–602.

Giddens, A. (1976) *New Rules of Sociological Method* (London: Hutchinson).

Giddens, A. (1979) *Central Problems in Social Theory* (London: Macmillan).

Giddens, A. (1981) *A Contemporary Critique of Historical Materialism* (London: Macmillan).

Giddens, A. (1984) *The Constitution of Society* (Cambridge: Polity Press).

Giddens, A. (1985) *The Nation-State and Violence* (Cambridge: Polity Press).

Giddens, A. (1990) *The Consequences of Modernity* (Cambridge: Polity Press).

Giddens, A. (1991) *Modernity and Self-Identity* (Cambridge: Polity Press).

Giddens, A. (1992) *The Transformation of Intimacy* (Cambridge: Polity Press).

Gilligan, C. (1982) *In a Different Voice* (Cambridge Mass.: Harvard University Press).

Githens, M., P. Norris and J. Lovenduski (1994) *Different Roles, Different Voices: Women and Politics in the United States and Europe* (New York: HarperCollins).

Goldthorpe, J. (1991) 'The Uses of History in Sociology: Reflections on Some Recent Tendencies', *British Journal of Sociology*, 42, pp. 211–30.

Goldthorpe, J. H. *et al.* (1968a) *The Affluent Worker: Industrial Attitudes and Behaviour* (Cambridge: Cambridge University Press).

Goldthorpe, J. H. *et al.* (1968b) *The Affluent Worker: Political Attitudes and Behaviour* (Cambridge: Cambridge University Press).

Goldthorpe, J. H. *et al.* (1969) *The Affluent Worker in the Class Structure* (Cambridge: Cambridge University Press).

Goodhart, C. A. E. and R. J. Bhansali (1970) 'Political Economy', *Political Studies*, 18, pp. 43–106.

Goodwin, B. and K. Taylor (1982) *The Politics of Utopia. A Study in Theory and Practice* (London: Hutchinson).

Goot, M. and E. Reid (1975) *Women and Voting Studies: Mindless Matrons or Sexless Scientists?* (London: Sage).

Gorz, A. (1980) *Ecology as Politics* (London: Pluto Press).

Gorz, A. (1982) *Farewell to the Working Class* (London: Pluto Press).

Gorz, A. (1989) 'The New Agenda', in R. Blackburn (ed.) *After the Fall* (London: New Left Books).

Gourevitch, P. (1978) 'The Second Image Revisited: The International Sources of Domestic Politics', *International Organization*, 32, pp. 881–912.

Gramsci, A. (1971) *Selections from the Prison Notebooks of Antonio Gramsci*, ed. Q. Hoare and G. Nowell-Smith (London: Lawrence & Wishart).

Grant, W. (1989) *Pressure Groups, Politics and Democracy in Britain* (Hemel Hempstead: Philip Allan).

Grant, W. and D. Marsh (1977) *The Confederation of British Industry* (Sevenoaks: Hodder & Stoughton).

Greenleaf, W. H. (1983) *The British Political Tradition. Vol. 1, The Rise of Collectivism* (London: Methuen).

Greenstein, F. (1965) *Children and Politics* (New Haven: Yale University Press).

Greenstein, F. I. and N. W. Polsby (1975) *Handbook of Political Science* (Reading, Mass.: Addison-Wesley).

Greenwood, R., K. Walsh, C. R. Hinings and S. Ranson (1980) *Patterns of Management in Local Government* (Oxford: Martin Robertson).

Gregory, D. (1990) 'Grand Maps of History: Structuration Theory and Social Change', in J. Clark, (ed.), *Anthony Giddens: Controversy and Critique* (London: Falmer).

Griffin, S. (1981) *Pornography and Silence: Culture's Revenge Against Nature* (New York: Harper & Row).

Gurr, Ted Robert (1968a) 'Psychological Factors in Civil Violence', *World Politics*, 20, pp. 245–78.

Gurr, T. R. (1968b) 'A Causal Model of Civil Strife', *American Political Science Review*, 62, pp. 1104–24.

Gurr, T. R. (1970) *Why Men Rebel* (Princeton, N.J.: Princeton University Press).

Gyford, J. *et al.* (1984) *The Changing Politics of Local Government* (London: Unwin Hyman).

Habermas, J. (1976) *Legitimation Crisis* (trans. Thomas McCarthy) (London: William Heineman).

Hague, R., M. Harrop and S. Breslin (1992) *Comparative Government and Politics* (London: Macmillan).

Halfpenny, P. (1982) *Positivism and Sociology: Explaining Social Life* (London: Allen & Unwin).

Hall, P. (1986) *Governing the Economy* (Cambridge: Polity Press).

Hall, S. (1983) 'The Great Moving Right Show', in S. Hall and M. Jacques (eds), *The Politics of Thatcherism* (London: Lawrence & Wishart).

Hall, S. (1988) *The Hard Road to Renewal* (London: Verso).

Hammersley, M. and P. Atkinson (1983) *Ethnography: Principles in Practice* (London: Tavistock).

Hanson, N. R. (1958) *Patterns of Discovery* (Cambridge: Cambridge University Press).

Harden, I. (1992) *The Contracting State* (Milton Keynes: Open University Press).

Hardin, G. (1969) 'The Tragedy of the Commons', *Science*, 162, pp. 1243–8.

Harding, S. (1987) 'Introduction: Is There a Feminist Method?', in S. Harding (ed.), *Feminism and Methodology* (Milton Keynes: Open University Press).

Hargreaves-Heap, S., M. Hollis, B. Lyons, R. Sugden and A. Weale (1992) *The Theory of Choice: A Critical Guide* (Oxford: Basil Blackwell).

Harrop, M. (1986) 'The Press and Post-war Elections', in Crewe and Harrop (eds).

Harrop, M. and W. L. Miller (1987) *Elections and Voters: A Comparative Introduction* (London: Macmillan).

Hartmann, H. (1992) 'The Unhappy Marriage of Marxism and Feminism: Towards a More Progressive Union', in M. Humm, *Feminisms: A Reader* (Hemel Hempstead: Harvester Wheatsheaf).

Harvey, L. (1990) *Critical Social Research* (London: Unwin Hyman).

Hay, C. (1993) 'The Political Economy of State Failure in Britain's Post-War Reconstruction'. A paper presented at the ECPR Conference on the Political Economy of Post-War Reconstruction, Leiden, Netherlands, April.

Hay, C. (1994a) 'Crisis and the Discursive Unification of the State', in P. Dunleavy and J. Stanyer (eds.) *Contemporary Political Studies 1994, Vol. 1* (The Political Studies Association of the United Kingdom), pp. 236–55.

Hay, C. (1994b) 'Structural and Ideological Contradiction in Britain's Post-War Reconstruction', *Capital and Class*, 54, pp. 25–60.

Hay, C. (1994c) 'Werner in Wunderland, or Notes on a Marxism Beyond, Pessimism and False Optimism', in F. Sebsi and C. Vercellone (eds), *École del la Régulation et Critique de la Raison* (Paris: Futur Anterieur, Editions L'Harmattan).

Hayward, J. E. S. (1986) 'The Political Science of Muddling Through: the defects paradigm', in J. Hayward and P. Norton (eds) *The Political Science of British Politics* (Brighton: Wheatsheaf) pp. 3–20.

Hayek, F. A. von (1960), *The Constitution of Liberty* (London: Routledge).

Headey, B. (1974) *British Cabinet Ministers* (London: George Allen & Unwin).

Heath, A., R. Jowell and J. Curtice (1985) *How Britain Votes* (Oxford: Pergamon Press).

Heath, A. *et al.* (1991) *Understanding Political Change: The British Voter 1964–1987* (Oxford: Pergamon Press).

Heath, A. *et al.* (eds) (1994) *Labour's Last Chance?: The 1992 General Election and Beyond* (Aldershot: Dartmouth).

Hekman, S. J. (1990) *Gender and Knowledge: Elements of Postmodernism* (London: Polity Press).

Heclo, H. and A. Wildavsky (1981) *The Private Government of Public Money* (2nd edn) (London: Macmillan).

Held, D. (1987) *Models of Democracy* (Cambridge: Polity Press).

Held, D. (1991) 'Democracy, the Nation-State and the Global System', in D. Held (ed.), *Political Theory Today* (Cambridge: Polity Press), pp. 197–235.

Held, D. and A. Leftwich (1984) 'A Discipline of Politics?' in A. Leftwich (ed.) *What is Politics?* (Oxford: Basil Blackwell).

Heller, A. (1991) 'The Concept of the Political Revisited', in D. Held (ed.) *Political Theory Today* (Cambridge: Polity Press).

Hellevik, G. (1984) *Introduction to Causal Analysis* (London: George Allen & Unwin).

Hempel, C. G. (1965) *Aspects of Scientific Explanation and Other Essays in the Philosophy of Science* (New York: Free Press).

Hempel, C. G. (1966) *Philosophy of Natural Science* (Englewood Cliffs, N.J.: Prentice Hall).

Henry, N. (1986) *Public Administration and Public Affairs* (3rd edn) (Englewood Cliffs, N.J.: Prentice Hall).

Henwood, K. L. and N. F. Pidgeon (1993) 'Qualitative Research and Psychological Theorising', in M. Hammersley (ed.), *Social Research: Philosophy, Politics and Practice* (London: Sage).

Hernes, H. M. (1988) *Welfare State and Woman Power* (Oxford University Press; Oslo University Press, 1987).

Hewitt, C. J. (1974) 'Elites and the Distribution of Power in British Society', in A. Giddens and P. Stanworth (eds), *Elites and Power in British Society* (Cambridge: Cambridge University Press).

Heywood, A. (1994) *Political Ideas and Concepts* (London: Macmillan).

Higley, J. *et al.* (1991) 'Elite Integration in Stable Democracies', *European Sociological Review*, 77, May, pp. 35–45.

Hill, S. and P. Rock (eds) (1994) '"The Uses of History in Sociology": a Debate' *British Journal of Sociology*, 45, pp. 1–77.

Hindess, B. (1980) 'Marxism and Parliamentary Democracy', in A. Hunt (ed.) *Marxism and Democracy* (London: Lawrence & Wishart).

Hindess, B. (1988) *Choice, Rationality and Social Theory* (London: Unwin Hyman).

Hindess, B. and P. Hirst (1977) *Pre-Capitalist Models of Production* (London: Routledge).

Hirsch, M. and E. F. Keller (eds) (1990) *Conflicts in Feminism* (London: Routledge).

Hirst, P. (1990) *Representative Democracy and its Limits* (Oxford: Polity Press).

Hoff, J. (1994) 'Gender as a Postmodern Category of Paralysis', *Women's Studies International Forum*, 17, (2/3), pp. 443–7.

Hollis, M. (1977) *Models of Man: Philosophical Thoughts on Social Action* (Cambridge: Cambridge University Press).

Hood, C. C. (1987) 'Public Administration', in V. Bogdanor (ed.), *The Blackwell Encyclopaedia of Political Institutions* (Oxford: Basil Blackwell), pp. 504–7.

Hood, C. C. (1990) 'Public Administration: Lost an Empire, Not Yet Found a Role?', in A. Leftwich (ed.), *New Developments in Political Science* (Aldershot: Edward Elgar), pp. 107–25.

Hood, C. C. (1991) 'A Public Management for All Season?', *Public Administration*, 69, pp. 3–19.

Humm, M. (1992) *Feminism: A Reader* (Hemel Hempstead: Harvester-Wheatsheaf).

Hunter, F. (1953) *Community Power Structure* (Chapel Hill, N.C.: University of North Carolina Press).

Iglitsin, L. (1974) 'The Making of the Apolitical Woman: Femininity and Sex-Stereotyping in Girls', in J. Jaquette (ed.) *Women in Politics* (New York: John Wiley).

Iyengar, S. and D. R. Kinder (1987) *News that Matters* (London: University of Chicago Press).

Jackson, P. (1982) *The Political Economy of Bureaucracy* (Oxford: Philip Allan).

Janis, I. L. (1972) *Victims of Groupthink* (Boston, Mass.: Houghton Mifflin).

Janis, I. L. and L. Mann (1977) *Decision Making: A Psychological Analysis of Conflict, Choice and Commitment* (New York: Free Press).

Jennings, M. K. and R. Niemi (1979) 'Another Look at the Life-Cycle and Political Participation', *American Journal of Political Science*, 73, pp. 755–71.

Jervis, R. (1976) *Perception and Misperception in International Politics* (Princeton: Princeton University Press).

Jessop, B. (1982) *The Capitalist State* (Oxford: Martin Robertson).

Jessop, B. (1983) 'The Democratic State and the National Interest' in D. Coates and G. Johnston (eds) *Socialist Arguments* (Oxford: Martin Robertson).

Jessop, B. (1985) *Nicos Poulantzas: Marxist Theory and Political Strategy* (London: Macmillan).

Jessop, B. (1989) *Thatcherism: the British Road to Post-Fordism*, Essex Working Papers in Politics and Government.

Jessop, B. (1990) *State Theory: Putting the Capitalist State in Its Place* (Cambridge: Polity Press).

Jessop, B. (1992) *Towards the Schumpeterian Workfare State*, Lancaster Regionalism Group Working Paper.

Jessop, B. *et al.* (1988) *Thatcherism: A Tale of Two Nations* (Cambridge: Polity Press).

Johnson, N. (1973) *Government in the Federal Republic of Germany: The Executive at Work* (Oxford: Pergamon Press).

Johnson, J. (1993) 'Is Talk Really Cheap? Prompting Conversation Between Critical Theory and Rational Choice', *American Political Science Review*, 87, pp. 74–85.

Johnson, J. B. and R. A. Joslyn (1991) *Political Science Research Methods* (Washington, DC: Congressional Quarterly).

Johnson, N. (1975) 'The Place of Institutions in the Study of Politics', *Political Studies*, XXIII, pp. 271–83.

Johnson, N. (1980) *In Search of the Constitution* (London: Methuen University Paperback).

Johnson, N. (1989) *The Limits of Political Science* (Oxford: Clarendon Press).

Jones, K. B. (1993) *Compassionate Authority; Democracy and the Representation of Women* (New York: Routledge).

Jones, B. and Bachelor, L. (1986) *The Sustaining Hand: Community Leadership and Corporate Power* (Lawrence: University Press of Kansas).

Jones, G. W. and J. Stewart (1983) *The Case for Local Government* (London: George Allen & Unwin).

Jordan, A. G. (1981) 'Iron Triangles, Woolly Corporatism and Elastic Nets: Images of the Policy Process', *The Journal of Public Policy*, 1, pp. 95–123.

Jordan, A. G. (1990a) 'Policy Community Realism Versus "New" Institutionalist Ambiguity', *Political Studies*, XXXVIII, pp. 470–84.

Jordan, A. G. (1990b) 'The Pluralism of Pluralism: An Anti-Theory', *Political Studies*, 38, pp. 286–301.

Jordan, A. G., W. A. Maloney and A. M McLaughlin (1994) 'Characterising Agriculture Policy Making', *Public Administration*, 72, 4, pp. 502–26.

Jordan, A. G. and J. J. Richardson (1987a) *Government and Pressure Groups in Britain* (Oxford: Clarendon).

Jordan, A. G. and J. J. Richardson (1987b) *British Politics and the Policy Process* (London: Unwin Hyman).

Jowell, J. and D. Oliver (eds) (1989) *The Changing Constitution* (2nd edn) (Oxford: Clarendon Press).

Judge, D. (1993) *The Parliamentary State* (London: Sage).

Judge, D, G. Stoker and H. Wolman (eds) (1995) *Theories of Urban Politics* (London: Sage).

Kavanagh, D. (1991) 'Why Political Science Needs History', *Political Studies*, XXXIX, pp. 479–95.

Keat, R. and J. Urry (1975) *Social Theory as Science* (London: Routledge & Kegan Paul).

Keohane, R. O. (1984) *After Hegemony: Cooperation and Discord in the International Political Economy* (Princeton, N.J.: Princeton University Press).

Keohane, R. and J. Nye (1977) *Power and Interdependence* (Boston: Little, Brown).

King, A. (1975), 'Overload: Problems of Governing in the 1970s', *Political Studies*, 23, pp. 283–96.

King, A. (ed.) (1985) *The British Prime Minister* (2nd edn) (London: Macmillan).

King, G. (1989) *Unifying Political Methodology* (Cambridge: Cambridge University Press).

King, G., R. O. Keohane and S. Verba (1994) *Designing Social Enquiry: Scientific Inference in Qualitative Research* (Princeton, N.J.: Princeton University Press).

Kirkpatrick, J. J. (1979) 'Politics and the New Class', in B. Bruce-Briggs (ed.), *The New Class* (New Brunswick, N.J.: Transaction Books).

Kolakowski, L. (1972) *Positivist Philosophy* (Harmondsworth: Penguin).

Kollman, K., J. H. Miller and S. E. Page (1992) 'Adaptive Parties in Spatial Elections', *American Political Science Review*, 86, pp. 929–37.

Kontopoulos, K. (1993) *The Logics of Social Structure* (Cambridge: Cambridge University Press).

Kuhn, T. (1970) *The Structure of Scientific Revolutions* (Chicago: University of Chicago Press).

Lacey, A. R. (1976) *A Dictionary of Philosophy* (London: Routledge & Keegan Paul).

Laclau, E. (1988) 'Building a New Left: An Interview with Ernsto Laclau', *Strategies*, 1, pp. 10–28.

Laclau, E. (1990) *New Reflections on the Revolution of Our Time* (London: Verso).

Laclau, E. (1991) 'Community and Its Paradoxes: Richard Rorty's "Liberal Utopia"', in Miami Theory Collective (ed.) *Community at Loose Ends*, (Minneapolis: Minnesota University Press).

Laclau, E. (ed.) (1994) *The Making of Political Identities* (London: Verso).

Laclau, E. and C. Mouffe (1985) *Hegemony and Socialist Strategy* (London: Verso).

Laclau, E. and C. Mouffe (1987) 'Post-Marxism without Apologies', *New Left Review*, 166, pp. 79–106.

Lakatos, I. (1974) 'Falsification and the Methodology of Scientific Research Programmes', in I. Lakatos and A. E. Musgrave (eds), *Criticism and the Growth of Knowledge* (Cambridge: Cambridge University Press), pp. 132–5.

Landau, M. (1979) *Political Theory and Political Science: Studies in the Methodology of Political Inquiry* (Brighton: Harvester Press).

Lansing, M. (1974) 'The American Woman: Voter and Activist', in J. Jaquette, *Women in Politics* (New York: John Wiley).

Laski, H. J. (1939) *The Danger of Being a Gentleman and Other Essays* (London: George Allen & Unwin).

Laumann, E. O. and D. Knoke (1987) *The Organizational State*, (Madison, Wis.: University of Wisconsin Press).

Laumann, F. *et al.* (1977) 'Community-Elite Influence Structures: Extension of a Network Approach', *American Journal of Sociology*, 83, pp. 594–631.

Laver, M. and N. Schofield (1990) *Multiparty Government: The Politics of Coalition in Europe* (Cambridge: Cambridge University Press).

Layder, D. (1994) *Understanding Social Theory* (London: Sage).

Lee, R. M. (1993) *Doing Research on Sensitive Topics* (London: Sage).

Leftwich, A. (ed.) (1984a) *What is Politics?* (Oxford: Basil Blackwell).

Leftwich, A. (1984b) 'On the Politics of Politics', in A. Leftwich (ed.) *What is Politics?* (Oxford: Basil Blackwell), pp. 1–18.

Levi, I. (1986) *Hard Choices: Decision Making Under Unresolved Conflict* (Cambridge: Cambridge University Press).

Lewin, L. (1991) *Self-Interest and Public Interest in Western Politics* (Oxford University Press).

Lewis, N. and I. Harden (1986) *The Noble Lie* (London: Hutchinson).

Lewis-Beck, M. (1990) *Economics and Elections: The Major Western Democracies* (Ann Arbor, Mich.: University of Michigan Press).

Lijphart, A. (1968) *The Politics of Accommodation* (Berkeley, Calif.: University of California Press).

Lijphart, A. (1971) 'Comparative Politics and the Comparative Method', *American Political Science Review*, 65, pp 652–93.

Lijphart, A. (1977) *Democracy in Plural Societies: A Comparative Exploration* (New Haven CT: Yale University Press).

Lijphart, A. (1994) *Electoral Systems and Party Systems* (Oxford: Oxford University Press).

Lindblom, C. E. (1977) *Politics and Markets* (New York: Basic Books).

Lindblom, C. (1982) 'The Market As Prison', *The Journal of Politics*, 44, pp. 324–36.

Lipset, S. M. (1994) 'The Social Requisites of Democracy Revisited', *American Sociological Review*, 59, pp. 1–22.

Lofland, J. and L. Lofland (1984) *Analyzing Social Settings: A Guide to Qualitative Observation and Analysis* (2nd edn) (Belmont: Wadsworth).

Longstreth, F. (1979), 'The City, Industry and the State', in C. Crouch (ed.), *State, Economy in Contemporary Capitalism* (London: Croom Helm), pp.157–90.

Lovenduski, J. and J. Outshoorn (eds) (1986) *The New Politics of Abortion* (London, Sage).

Lovenduski, J. and V. Randall (1993) *Contemporary Feminist Politics: Women and Power in Britain* (Oxford University Press).

Lowi, T. (1969) *The End of Liberalism* (New York: Norton).

Lowndes, V. and Stoker, G. (1992) 'An Evaluation of Neighbourhood Decentralisation', *Policy and Politics*, 20, pp. 47–71.

Luce, R. D. and H. Raiffa (1989) *Games and Decisions: Introduction and Critical Survey* (New York: Dover).

Lukács, G. (1971) *History and Class Consciousness* (London: Merlin).

Lukes, S. (1974) *Power: A Radical View* (London: Macmillan).

Lukes, S. (1977) 'Methodological Individualism Reconsidered', reprinted in S. Lukes, *Essays in Social Theory* (London: Macmillan).

Lyotard, J. F. (1984) *The Postmodern Condition* (Manchester: Manchester University Press).

Machiavelli, N. (1961) *The Prince* (Harmondsworth: Penguin).

MacIntyre, A. (1981) *After Virtue* (Notre Dame, Ind.: University of Notre Dame Press).

Mackenzie, W. (1967) *Politics and Social Science* (Harmondsworth: Penguin).

Mackinnon, C. (1992) 'Feminism, Marxism, Method and the State: An Agenda for Theory', in M. Humm, *Feminisms: A Reader* (Hemel Hempstead: Harvester).

MacPherson, C. B. (1970) *The Political Theory of Possessive Individualism* (Oxford University Press).

Macridis, R. C. (1963) 'A Survey of the Field of Comparative Government', in H. Eckstein and D. E. Apter (eds), *Comparative Politics: A Reader* (London: Collier-Macmillan), pp. 43–52.

Manheim, J. B. and R. C. Rich (1991) *Empirical Political Analysis. Research Methods in Political Science* (3rd edn) (White Plains, N.Y.: Longman).

Mann, M. (1986) *The Sources of Social Power, Vol. I: A History of Power from the Beginning to 1760* (Cambridge: Cambridge University Press).

Mann, M. (1988) *States, War and Capitalism* (New York: Basil Blackwell).

Mann, M. (1993) *The Sources of Social Power, Vol. II: The Rise of Classes and Nation-States 1760–1914* (Cambridge: Cambridge University Press).

Mann, P. H. (1985) *Methods of Social Investigation* (Oxford: Basil Blackwell).

Mansbridge, J. (1980) *Beyond Adversary Democracy* (New York: Basic Books).

Mansbridge, J. J. (ed.) (1990a) *Beyond Self-Interest* (Chicago: University of Chicago Press).

Mansbridge, J. J. (1990b) 'The Rise and Fall of Self-Interest in the Explanation of Political Life', in J. Mansbridge (ed.), *Beyond Self Interest* (Chicago: University of Chicago Press).

Mansbridge, J. J. (1990c) 'Expanding the Range of Formal Modelling', in J. Mansbridge (ed.), *Beyond Self Interest* (Chicago: University of Chicago Press).

March, J. G. and J. P. Olsen (1984) 'The New Institutionalism: Organisational Factors in Political Life', *American Political Science Review*, 78, pp. 734–49.

March, J. G. and J. P. Olsen (1989) *Rediscovering Institutions: The Organizational Basis of Politics* (New York: The Free Press).

March, J. G. and H. A. Simon (1958) *Organisations* (New York: John Wiley).

Margolis, H. (1990) 'Dual Utilities and Rational Choice', in J. Mansbridge (ed.), *Beyond Self Interest* (Chicago: University of Chicago Press).

Mark-Lawson, J. and A. Witz (1990) 'Familial Control or Patriarchal Domination? The Case of the Family System of Labour in 19th-Century Coal Mining', in H. Corr and L. Jamieson (eds), *The Politics of Everyday Life: Continuity and Change in Work and the Family* (London: Macmillan).

Markus, G. and P. Converse (1979) 'A Dynamic Simultaneous Equation Model of Electoral Choice', *American Political Science Review*, 76, pp. 1055–70.

Marsh, A. (1977) *Protest and Political Consciousness* (London: Sage).

Marsh, C. (1982) *The Survey Method* (London: Allen & Unwin).

Marsh, C. (1984) 'Problems with Surveys: Method or Epistemology?', in M. Bulmer (ed.), *Sociological Research Methods: An Introduction* (2nd edn) (London: Macmillan).

Marsh, D. (1983) 'Interest Group Activity and Structural Power: Lindblom's *Politics and Markets', West European Politics*, 6, pp. 3–13.

Marsh, D. (1986), 'The Politics of Private Investment', in A. Blais (ed.), *Industrial Policy* (Toronto: University of Toronto Press) pp. 83–117.

Marsh, D. (1994) 'Coming of Age But Not Learning by the Experience: One Cheer for Rational Choice Theory', Paper delivered at the European Consortium for Political Research Workshops, Madrid, April 1994.

Marsh, D. (1995) *State Theory and the Policy Networks Model*, Strathclyde Papers on Government and Politics, No. 102..

Marsh, D. and G. Locksley (1983), 'Capital in Britain: Its Structural Power and Influence over Policy', in D. Marsh (ed.), *Capital and Politics in Western Europe* (London: Frank Cass), pp. 36–60.

Marsh, D. and R. A. W. Rhodes (eds) (1992a) *Implementing Thatcherite Policies: Audit of an Era* (Milton Keynes: Open University Press).

Marsh, D. and R. A. W. Rhodes (eds) (1992b), *Policy Networks in British Government* (Oxford: Oxford University Press).

Marsh, D., H. Ward and D. Sanders (1992) 'Modelling Government Popularity in Britain, 1979–87: A Disaggregated Approach', in Crewe and Norris (eds).

Marshall, G. (1984) *Constitutional Conventions: The Rules and Forms of Political Accountability* (Oxford: Clarendon Press).

Marshall, G. *et al.* (1988) *Social Class in Modern Britain* (London: Hutchinson).

Marx, K. (1843/1975) 'On the Jewish Question', in L. Colletti (ed.), *Marx's Early Writings* (London: Penguin).

Marx, K. (1844/1975) 'Economic and Philosophical Manuscripts', in L. Colletti (ed.) *Marx's Early Writings* (Harmondsworth: Penguin).

Marx, K. (1845/1976) 'The German Ideology' in C. J. Arthur (ed.), *The German Ideology* (London: Lawrence & Wishart).

Marx, K. (1846/1976) *The Poverty of Philosophy* in *Marx and Engels, Collected Works* (London: Lawrence & Wishart).

Marx, K. (1847/1976) 'Wage Labour and Capital', in *Marx and Engels, Collected Works* (London: Lawrence & Wishart).

Marx, K. and F. Engels (1848/1976) 'The Communist Manifesto', in *Marx and Engels, Collected Works* (London: Lawrence & Wishart).

Marx, K. (1850/1976) 'The Class Struggle in France', in *Marx and Engels, Collected Works* (London: Lawrence & Wishart).

Marx, K. (1852/1976) 'The 18th Brumaire of Louis Bonaparte', in *Marx and Engels, Collected Works* (London: Lawrence & Wishart).

Marx, K. (1859/1975) '*A Preface to a Contribution to a Critique of Political Economy*', in L. Colletti (ed.) *Marx's Early Writings* (Harmondsworth: Penguin).

McClure, K. (1992) 'On the Subject of Rights: Pluralism, Plurality and Political Identity', in C. Mouffe (ed.), *Dimensions of Radical Democracy* (London: Verso).

McClosky, H. and A. Brill (1983) *Dimensions of Tolerance: What Americans Believe About Civil Liberties* (New York: Russell Sage).

McConnell, G. (1953) *The Decline of American Democracy* (New York: Atheneum).

McConnell, G. (1966) *Private Power and American Democracy* (New York: Alfred A. Knopf).

McFarland, A. (1987) 'Interest Groups and Theories of Power in America', *British Journal of Political Science*, 17, pp.129–47.

McIntosh, M. (1978) 'The State and the Oppression of Women' in A. Kuhn and A. M. Wolpe (eds), *Feminism and Materialism* (London: Routledge & Kegan Paul).

McLean, I. (1987) *Public Choice: An Introduction* (Oxford: Basil Blackwell).

McLennan, G. (1989) *Marxism, Pluralism and Beyond* (Cambridge: Polity Press)

Mead, M. (1949/1972) *Male and Female* (London: Pelican).

Meehan, E. and S. Sevenhuisen (eds) (1991) *Equality, Politics and Gender* (London, Sage).

Meisel, J. (ed.) (1965) *Pareto and Mosca* (Englewood Cliffs, N.J.: Prentice Hall).

Merrington, J. (1978) 'Theory and Practice in Gramsci's Marxism', in *New Left Review*, Editorial Collective, *Western Marxism: A Critical Reader* (London: Verso).

Meszaros, I. (1970) *Marx's Theory of Alienation* (London: Merlin).
Michels, R. (1911/1962) *Political Parties* (New York: Free Press).
Middlemas, K. (1979) *Politics in Industrial Society* (London: André Deutsch).
Miliband, R. (1968) *The State in Capitalist Society* (London: Weidenfeld & Nicolson).
Miliband, R. (1970) 'The Capitalist State: Reply to Poulantzas', *New Left Review*, 59, pp. 53–60.
Miliband, R. (1973) 'Poulantzas and the Capitalist State', *New Left Review*, 82, pp. 83–92.
Mill, J. S. (1978) *Utilitarianism* (Glasgow: Collins/Fontana).
Miller, A. H., W. M. Reisinger and V. L. Hesli (eds) (1993) *Public Opinion and Regime Change: The New Politics of Post-Soviet Societies* (Boulder, Col.: Westview).
Miller, D. (1990) 'The Resurgence of Political Theory', *Political Studies*, XXXVIII, 3, pp. 421–37.
Miller, W. L. (1977) *Electoral Dynamics in Britain Since 1918* (London: Macmillan).
Miller, W. L. (1978) 'Social Choice and Party Choice in England', *British Journal of Political Science*, vol. 8, pp. 257–84.
Miller, W. L. (1983) *The Survey Method* (London: Pinter).
Miller, W. L. (1988) *Irrelevant Elections? The Quality of Local Democracy in Britain* (Oxford University Press).
Miller, W. L. (1991) *Media and Voters* (Oxford: Oxford University Press).
Miller, W. L., H. D. Clarke, M. Harrop and P. F. Whiteley (1990) *How Voters Change* (Oxford University Press).
Miller, W. L., A. M. Timpson and M. Lessnoff (forthcoming) *The Political Culture of People and Politicians in Britain* (Oxford University Press).
Miller, W. L., S. White, P. Heywood and M. Wyman (1994) *Democratic, Market and Nationalist Values in Russia and East Europe: December 1993*, Paper to Annual Conference of Political Studies Association, Swansea, 1994).
Miller, W. L. *et al.* (1995) *Alternative to Freedom: Arguments and Opinions* (London: Longman).
Mills, C. W. (1956) *The Power Elite* (New York: Oxford University Press).
Mills, M. (1993) *The Politics of Dietary Change* (Aldershot: Dartmouth).
Moe, T. M. (1979) 'On the Scientific Status of Rational Models', *American Journal of Political Science*, 23, pp. 215–43.
Mommsen, W. J. (1974) *The Age of Bureaucracy* (Oxford: Basil Blackwell).
Monroe, K. R. (ed.) (1991) *The Economic Approach to Politics: A Critical Reassessment of the Theory of Rational Action* (New York: HarperCollins).
Moodie, G. C. (1984) 'Politics is About Government', in A. Leftwich (ed.), *What is Politics?* (Oxford: Basil Blackwell) pp. 19–32.
Moon, J. (1994) 'Evaluating Thatcher: Sceptical versus Synthetic Approaches', *Politics*, 14, pp. 43–49.
Moore, B. (1966) *The Social Origins of Dictatorship and Democracy: Lord and Peasant in the Making of the Modern World* (Boston, Mass.: Beacon Press).
Moore, G. (1979) 'The Structure of a National Elite Network', *American Sociological Review*, 44 (October), pp. 673–92.
Moran, M. (1981) 'Finance Capital and Pressure Group Politics', *British Journal of Political Science*, 11, pp. 381–404.
Morgenthau, H. J. (1946) *Power Politics vs Scientific Man* (Chicago: Chicago University Press).
Mosca, G. (1939) *The Ruling Class* (New York: McGraw Hill).
Moseley, P. (1976) 'Towards a Satisficing Theory of Economic Policy', *Economic Journal*, 86, pp. 59–72.
Mossuz-Lavau, J. (1991) *Women and Men of Europe Today: Attitudes Towards Europe and Politics*, Commission of the European Communities, Women of Europe Supplements, 35.
Mouffe, C. (1993) *The Return of the Political* (London: Verso).
Mount, F. (1993) *The British Constitution Now: Recovery or Decline?* (London: Mandarin).
Mouzelis, N. (1988) 'Marxism or Post-Marxism?', *New Left Review*, 167, pp 107–23.
Mueller, D. C. (1989) *Public Choice II* (Cambridge: Cambridge University Press).
Muller, E. N. (1979) *Aggressive Political Participation* (Princeton, N.J.: Princeton University Press).
Nagel, J. (1993) 'Populism, Heresthetics and Political Stability', *British Journal of Political Science*, 23, pp. 139–75.

Nain, G. T. (1994) 'Black Women, Sexism and Racism: Black or Anti-Racist Feminism?', in M. Githens, P. Norris and J. Lovenduski *Different Roles, Different Voices: Women and Politics in the United States and Europe* (New York, HarperCollins).

Newell, R. (1993) 'Questionnaires', in N. Gilbert (1993), *Researching Social Life* (London: Sage).

Nicholson, M. (1989) *Formal Theories in International Relations* (Cambridge: Cambridge University Press).

Niemi, R. G. (1973) 'Collecting Information about the Family: A Problem in Survey Methodology', in J. Dennis (ed.), *Socialisation to Politics* (New York: John Wiley).

Niskanen, W. A. (1971) *Bureaucracy and Representative Government* (Chicago: Aldine-Atherton).

Nordhaus, W. D. (1975) 'The Political Business Cycle', *Review of Economic Studies*, 42, pp. 1969–90.

Nordlinger, E. (1981) *On the Autonomy of the Democratic State* (Cambridge, Mass.: Harvard University Press).

Norris. P. and J. Lovenduski (1983) '"If Only More Candidates Came Forward": Supply-Side Explanations of Candidate Selection in Britain', *British Journal of Political Science*, 23, pp. 373–408.

North, D. C. (1986) 'The New Institutional Economics', *Journal of Institutional and Theoretical Economics*, 142, pp. 230–37.

Norton, P. (1982) *The Constitution in Flux* (Oxford: Martin Robertson).

Norton, P. (1991a) *New Directions in British Politics? Essays on the Evolving Constitution* (Aldershot: Edward Elgar).

Norton, P. (1991b) 'In Defence of the Constitution: A Riposte to the Radicals', in P. Norton (ed.), *New Directions in British Politics? Essays on the Evolving Constitution* (Aldershot: Edward Elgar) pp. 145–72.

Norval, A. (1994) 'Social Ambiguity and the Crisis of Apartheid', in E. Laclau (ed.), *The Making of Political Identities* (London: Verso).

Norval, A. (1995) *Accounting for Apartheid* (London: Verso).

Nozick, R. (1974) *Anarchy, State and Utopia* (Oxford: Basil Blackwell).

Oakeshott, M. (1967) *Rationalism in Politics and Other Essays* (London: Methuen).

Oakeshott, M. (1984) 'Michael Oakeshott: Political Education', in M. Sandel (ed.), *Liberalism and its Critics* (Oxford: Basil Blackwell).

Okin, S. M. (1979) *Women in Western Political Thought* (Princeton, N.J.: Princeton University Press).

Oliver, D. (1991) *Government in the United Kingdom: The Search for Accountability, Effectiveness and Citizenship* (Milton Keynes: Open University Press).

Ollman, B. (1971) *Alienation: Marx's Concept of Man in Capitalist Society*. (Cambridge: Cambridge University Press).

Ollman, B. (1993) *Dialectical Investigations* (London: Routledge).

Olsen, J. (1988) 'Political Science and Organisation Theory', University of Bergen, Norwegian Research Centre in Organisation and Management (mimeo).

Olsen, M. and M. Marger (1993) *Power in Modern Societies* (Oxford: Westview Press).

Olson, M. (1965) *The Logic of Collective Action: Public Goods and the Theory of Groups* (Cambridge Mass.: Harvard University Press).

Olson, M. (1982) *The Rise and Decline of Nations: Economic Growth, Stagflation and Social Rigidities* (New Haven, Conn.: Yale University Press).

Ordeshook, P. C. (1986) *Game Theory and Political Theory* (Cambridge: Cambridge University Press).

Ortner, S. (1974) 'Is Female to Male as Culture is to Nature?', in M. Rosaldo and L. Lamphere (eds), *Woman Culture and Society* (Stanford: Stanford University Press).

Outhwaite, W. (1987) *New Philosophies of Social Science* (London: Macmillan).

Outhwaite, W. (1990) 'Agency and Structure', in J. Clark (ed.) *Anthony Giddens: Controversy and Critique* (London: Falmer).

Page, E. (1990) 'British Political Science and Comparative Politics', *Political Studies*, 38, pp. 275–305.

Pareto, V. (1935) *The Mind and Society* (London: Jonathan Cape).

Pareto, V. (1966) *Sociological Writings* (London: Pall Mall).

Parry, G., G. Moyser and N. Day (1992) *Political Participation and Democracy in Britain* (Cambridge: Cambridge University Press).

Pateman, C. (1987) 'Feminism and Democracy', in G. Duncan (ed.), *Democratic Theory and Practice* (Cambridge: Cambridge University Press).

Pateman, C. (1988) *The Sexual Contract* (London: Polity Press).

Pateman, C. (1989) *The Disorder of Women: Democracy, Feminism and Political Theory* (London: Polity Press).

Paul, J. (ed.) (1981) *Reading Nozick. Essays on Anarchy, State and Utopia* (Oxford: Basil Blackwell).

Perrow, C. (1986) *Complex Organisations: A Critical Essay* (New York: Random House).

Phillips, A. (1993) *Democracy and Difference* (London: Polity Press).

Plant, R. (1993) *Modern Political Thought* (Oxford: Basil Blackwell).

Plumwood, V. (1993) *Feminism and the Mastery of Nature* (London: Routledge).

Polsby, N. (1960) 'How to Study Community Power: The Pluralist Alternative', *Journal of Politics*, 22, pp. 474–84.

Polsby, N. (1963) *Community Power and Democratic Theory* (New Haven, Conn.: Yale University Press).

Polsby, N. (1980) *Community Power and Political Theory* (New Haven, Conn.: Yale University Press).

Popkin, S. (1979) *The Rational Peasant: The Political Economy of Rural Society in Vietnam* (Berkeley, Calif.: University of California Press).

Popper, K. R. (1959) *The Logic of Scientific Discovery* (London: Hutchinson).

Potter, C. *et al.* (1967) *Social Science and Society* (Milton Keynes: Open University Press).

Powell, G. B. (1982) *Contemporary Democracies: Participation, Stability and Violence* (London: Harvard University Press).

Poulantzas, N. (1969), 'The Problem of the Capitalist State', *New Left Review*, 58, pp. 63–83.

Poulantzas, N. (1974) *Political Power and Social Classes* (London: New Left Books).

Poulantzas, N. (1976) *Classes in Contemporary Capitalism* (London: Verso).Poulantzas, N. (1978) *State Power and Socialism* (London: Verso).

Powdermaker, H. (1966) *Stranger and Friend: The Way of an Anthropologist* (New York: W. W. Norton and Co.).

Prewitt, K. and A. Stone (1973) *The Ruling Elites: Elite Theory, Power and American Democracy* (New York: Harper & Row).

Price, S. and D. Sanders (1993) 'Modelling Government Popularity in Post-war Britain: A Methodological Example', *American Journal of Political Science*, 37, pp. 317–34.

Przeworski, A. (1985) 'Marxism and Rational Choice', *Politics and Society*, 14, 4.

Przeworski, A. and G. A. D. Soares (1971) 'Theories in Search of a Curve', *American Political Science Review*, 65, pp. 51–68.

Przeworski, A. and H. Teune (1970) *The Logic of Comparative Social Inquiry* (New York: John Wiley).

Przeworski, A. and M. Wallerstein (1982) 'The Structure of Class Conflict in Democratic Capitalist Societies', *American Political Science Review*, 76, pp. 215–38.

Putmam, R. D. (1988) 'Diplomacy and Domestic Politics: The Logic of Two-Level Games', *International Organisation*, 37, pp. 270–316.

Quattrone, G. A. and A. Tversky (1988) 'Contrasting Rational and Psychological Analyses of Political Choice', *American Political Science Review*, 82, pp. 719–36.

Rachels, J. (1986) *The Elements of Moral Philosophy* (New York: McGraw Hill).

Radice, G. and S. Pollard (1993) *More Southern Discomfort: A Year On: Taxing and Spending* (London: Fabian Society).

Rae, D. (1967) *The Political Consequences of Electoral Laws* (London: Yale University Press).

Ragin, C. (1987) *The Comparative Method: Moving Beyond Qualitative and Quantitative Strategies* (Berkeley, Calif.: University of California Press).

Randall, V. (1987) *Women and Politics* (Rev edn) (London: Macmillan).

Randall, V. (1994) 'Feminism and Political Analysis' in Githens, Norris and Lovenduski (eds), *Different Roles, Different Voices*.

Rasmusen, E. (1989) *Games and Information: An Introduction to Game Theory* (Oxford: Basil Blackwell).

Rawls, J. (1972) *A Theory of Justice* (Oxford: The Clarendon Press).

Rendell, J. (1985) *The Origins of Modern Feminism: Women in Britain, France and the United States, 1780–1860* (London: Macmillan).

Rhodes, R. A. W. (1979) *Public Administration and Policy Analysis* (Farnborough: Saxon House).

Rhodes, R. A. W. (1991) 'Theory and Methods in British Public Administration: The View from Political Science', *Political Studies*, XXXIX, pp. 533–54.

Rhodes, R. A. W. (1994) 'State-Building without a Bureaucracy: The Case of the United Kingdom', in I. Budge and D. Mckay (eds) *Developing Democracy* (London: Sage), pp. 165–88.

Rhodes, R. A. W. (1995) 'From Prime Ministerial Power to Core Executive', in R. A. W. Rhodes and P. Dunleavy (eds) *Prime Minister, Cabinet and Core Executive* (London: Macmillan).

Rich, A. (1977) *Of Woman Born: Motherhood as Experience and Institution* (London: Virago).

Richardson, J. J. and A. G. Jordan (1979) *Governing Under Pressure* (Oxford: Martin Robertson).

Ridley, F. F. (1975) *The Study of Politics: Political Science and Public Administration* (London: George Allen & Unwin).

Rigby, S. H. (1987) *Marxism and History* (Manchester University Press).

Riker, W. (1982) *Liberalism Against Populism* (San Francisco: Freeman).

Riker, W. and P. C. Ordeshook (1973) *Introduction to Positive Political Theory* (Englewood Cliffs, N.J.: Prentice Hall).

Robinson, W. S. (1950) 'Ecological Correlation and the Behaviour of Individuals', *American Sociological Review*, 15, pp. 351–71.

Robson, W. A. (1975) 'The Study of Public Administration Then and Now', *Political Studies*, XXIII, pp. 193–201.

Roemer, J. (ed.) (1987) *Analytical Marxism* (Cambridge: Cambridge University Press).

Rorty, R. (1980) *Philosophy and the Mirror of Nature* (Oxford: Basil Blackwell).

Rorty, R. (1982) *Consequences of Pragmatism* (Hemel Hempstead: Harvester-Wheatsheaf).

Rorty, R. (1989) *Contingency, Irony and Solidarity* (Cambridge: Cambridge University Press).

Rorty, R. (1991) *Essays on Heidegger and Others* (Cambridge: Cambridge University Press).

Rose, G. (1982) *Deciphering Sociological Research* (London: Macmillan).

Rose, R. (1991) 'Comparing Forms of Comparative Analysis', *Political Studies*, 39, pp. 446–62.

Rose, R. and I. McAllister (1986) *Voters Begin to Choose* (London: Sage).

Rosenau, J. N. (1969) *International Politics and Foreign Policy: A Reader in Research and Theory* (New York: Free Press).

Ross, A. (1989) *No Respect: Intellectuals and Popular Culture* (New York, Routledge).

Roth, G. (1978) *Introduction to Max Weber, Economy and Society*, 2 vols (Berkeley, Calif.: University of California Press).

Roth, G. and C. Wittich (1978) *Max Weber: Economy and Society: An Outline of Interpretative Sociology* (Berkeley: University of California Press).

Rowbotham, S. (1986) 'Feminism and Democracy', in D. Held and C. Pollitt (eds), *New Forms of Democracy* (Milton Keynes: Open University Press).

Rowbotham, S. (1992) *Women in Movement: Feminism and Social Action* (London: Routledge).

Rowbotham, S., L. Segal and H. Wainwright (1980) *Beyond the Fragments: Feminism and the Making of Socialism* (London: Merlin).

Rudner, R. (1966) *Philosophy of Social Science* (Englewood Cliffs, N.J.: Prentice Hall).

Runciman, W. (ed.) (1978) *Max Weber: Selections in Translation* (Cambridge: Cambridge University Press).

Ryan, M, (1978) *The Acceptable Pressure Group* (Farnborough: Saxon House).

Sahlins, M. (1972) *Stone-Age Economics* (Chicago: Aldine-Atherton).

Sait, E. M. (1938) *Political Institutions: A Preface* (New York: D. Appleton-Century).

Saled, R. (1994) 'The Crisis of Identity and the Struggle for New Hegemony in the Former Yugoslavia', in E. Laclau (ed.) *The Making of Political Identities* (London: Verso), pp. 205–32.

Sampson, A. (1982) *The Changing Anatomy of Britain* (London: Hodder & Stoughton).

Sandel, M. (1984) 'Introduction' and 'Justice and the Good', in M. Sandel (ed.) *Liberalism and its Critics* (Oxford: Basil Blackwell).

Sanders, D. (1990) *Losing an Empire, Finding a Role: British Foreign Policy Since 1945* (London, Macmillan).

Sanders, D. and S. Price (1992) *Economic Expectations and Voting Intentions in the UK, 1979–87: A Pooled Cross-Section Study*, Essex Papers in Politics and Government, No. 93.

Sarlvik, B. and I. Crewe (1983) *Decade of Dealignment* (Cambridge: Cambridge University Press).

Sartori, G. (1970) 'Concept Misformation in Comparative Politics', *American Political Science Review*, 64, pp. 1033–53.

Sartori, G. (1984) *Social Science Concepts: A Systematic Analysis* (Beverly Hills, Calif.: Sage).

Sartori, G. (1994) 'Compare Why and How: Comparing, Miscomparing and the Comparative Method', in M. Dogan and A. Kazancigil (eds), *Comparing Nations: Concepts, Strategies, Substance* (London: Basil Blackwell).

Saunders, P. (1981) *Urban Politics: A Sociological Interpretation* (London: Hutchinson).

Saussure, F. (1983) *Course in General Linguistics* (London: Gerald Duckworth).

Saward, M. (1992) 'The Civil Nuclear Network in Britain' in D. Marsh and R. A. W. Rhodes (eds), *Policy Networks in British Government* (Oxford: Oxford University Press).

Saxonhouse, A. (1985) *Women in the History of Political Thought: Ancient Greece to Machiavelli* (New York: Praeger).

Sayer, A? (1992) *Method in Social Science: A Realist Approach* (London: Routledge).

Schelling, T. C. (1960) *The Strategy of Conflict* (Cambridge Mass.: Harvard University Press).

Schlick, M. (1974) *General Theory of Knowledge* (trans. A. E. Blumberg), (New York: Springer Verlag).

Schmitter, P. (1974) 'Still the Century of Corporatism', *Review of Politics*, 36, pp. 85–131.

Schmitter, P. C. and G. Lehmbruch (eds) (1979) *Trends Towards Corporatist Intermediation* (Beverly Hills, Calif.: Sage).

Schumpeter, J. A. (1976) *Capitalism, Socialism and Democracy* (London: George Allen & Unwin).

Schwarzmentel, J. (1994) *The State in Contemporary Society* (London: Harvester-Wheatsheaf).

Scott, J. (1979) *Corporations, Classes and Capitalism* (London: Hutchinson).

Scott, J. (1991) *Who Rules Britain?* (Cambridge: Polity Press).

Segal, L. (1987) *Is the Future Female? Troubled Thoughts on Contemporary Feminism* (London: Virago).

Segal, L. (1989) 'Slow Change or No Change: Feminism, Socialism and the Problem of Men', in *The Past Before Us: Twenty Years of Feminism, Feminist Review*, 31.

Segal, L. (1991) 'Whose Left? Socialism, Feminism and the Future', in R. Blackburn (ed.), *After the Fall* (London: Verso).

Segal, L. (1994) *Straight Sex: The Politics of Pleasure* (London: Verso).

Selecl, R. (1994) 'The Crisis of Identity and the Struggle for New Hegemony in the Former Yugoslavia', in E. Laclau (ed.) *The Making of Political Identities* (London: Verso).

Self, P. (1993) *Government by the Market: The Politics of Public Choice* (London: Macmillan).

Sen, A. K. (1977) 'Rational Fools: A Critique of the Behaviouralist Foundations of Economic Theory', *Philosophy and Public Affairs*, 6, 4, pp. 317–44.

Sen, A. and B. Williams (eds) (1982) *Utilitarianism and Beyond* (Cambridge: Cambridge University Press).

Seyd, P. (1987) *The Rise and Fall of the Labour Left* (London: Macmillan).

Shively, W. P. (1969) 'The Development of Party Identification Among Adults: Exploration of a Functional Model', *American Political Science Review*, 73, pp. 1039–54.

Showstack-Sassoon, A. (1987) *Gramsci's Politics*. (London: Hutchinson).

Sigelman, L. and G. Gadbois (1983) 'Contemporary Comparative Politics: An Inventory and Assessment', *Comparative Political Studies*, 16, pp. 275–305.

Siim, B. (1991) 'Welfare State, Gender Politics and Equality Policies: Women's Citizenship in the Scandinavian Welfare States' in E. Meehan and S. Sevenhuisen (eds), *Equality Politics and Gender* (London: Sage).

Silverman, D. (1985) *Qualitative Methods and Sociology* (Aldershot: Gower).

Simon, H. A. (1982) *Models of Bounded Rationality*, Vol. 2 (Cambridge, Mass.: MIT Press).

Simon, H. A. (1986) 'Rationality in Psychology and Economics', in Hogarth and Reder (eds), *Rational Choice: The Contrast Between Economics and Psychology* (Chicago: Chicago University Press), pp. 25–40.

Skocpol, T. (1979) *States and Social Revolutions* (Cambridge: Cambridge University Press).

Skocpol, T. (1985) 'Bringing the State Back In: Strategies of Analysis in Current Research', in P. B. Evans, D. Rieschemeyer and T. Skocpol, *Bringing the State Back In* (Cambridge: Cambridge University Press).

Smith, A. M. (1994) *New Right Discourse on Race and Sexuality* (Cambridge: Cambridge University Press).

Smith, M. J. (1990a) *The Politics of Agricultural Support in Britain* (Aldershot: Dartmouth).

Smith, M. J. (1990b) 'Pluralism, Reformed Pluralism and Neo-Pluralism', *Political Studies*, 38, pp. 302–22.

Smith, M. J. (1993) *Pressure, Power and Policy: State Autonomy and Policy Networks in Britain and the United States* (Hemel Hempstead: Harvester-Wheatsheaf).

Smith, M. J., D. Marsh and D. Richards (1993) 'Central Government, Departments and the Policy Process', *Public Administration*, 71, 4, pp. 567–94.

Smith, R. B. (1987) 'Linking Quantity and Quality; Part One: Understanding and Explanation', *Quantity and Quality*, 21, pp. 291–311.

Smith, R. B. (1988) 'Linking Quantity and Quality; Part Two: Surveys as Formulations', *Quantity and Quality*, 22, pp. 3–30.

Sniderman, P. M., R. A. Brody and P. E. Tetlock (1991) *Reasoning and Choice* (Cambridge: Cambridge University Press).

Snitow, A. (1990) 'A Gender Diary' in Hirsch and Keller (eds) *Conflicts in Feminism*.

Spradley, J. P. (1980) *Participant Observation* (New York: Holt, Rinehart & Winston).

Stanley, L. and S Wise (1993) *Breaking Out: Feminist Consciousness and Feminist Research* (rev edn) (London: Routledge).

Stanworth, M. (1990) 'Birth Pangs: Contraceptive Technologies and the Threat to Motherhood', in Hirsch and Keller (eds), *Conflicts in Feminism*.

Stedward, G. (1987) 'Entry to the System; A Case-Study of Women's Aid in Scotland', in Jordan and Richardson (eds), *Government and Pressure Groups in Britain*.

Steedman, I. and U. Krause (1985) 'Goethe's Faust, Arrow's Possibility Theorem and the Individual Decision Maker', in Elster (ed.), *The Multiple Self*, pp. 197–233.

Steinfel, P. (1979) *The Neo-Conservatives: The Men Who Are Changing America's Politics* (New York: Simon & Schuster).

Stinchcombe, A. L. (1968) *Constructing Social Theories* (New York: Harcourt, Brace & World).

Stone, C. (1989) *Regime Politics: Governing Atlanta 1946–1988* (Lawrence: University Press of Kansas).

Stones, R. (1991) 'Strategic Conduct Analysis: A New Research Strategy for Structuration Theory', *Sociology*, 25, 4.

Storper, M. (1985) 'The Spatial and Temporal Constititution of Social Action', *Environment and Planning Society and Space*, 3, 4.

Sylvester, C. (1994) *Feminist Theory and International Relations in the Post-Modern Era* (Cambridge: Cambridge University Press).

Sztompka, P. (1993) *The Sociology of Social Change* (Oxford: Basil Blackwell).

Tant, T. (1993) *British Government: The Triumph of Elitism* (Aldershot: Dartmouth).

Taylor, B. (1984) *Eve and the New Jerusalem* (London: Virago).

Taylor, C. (1975) *Hegel* (Cambridge: Cambridge University Press).

Taylor, C. and D. Jodice (1983) World Handbook of Political and Social Indicators.

Taylor, G. (1994) 'From Marx to Block: An Analysis of Contemporary Marxist State Theory', Working Paper, Centre for Public Policy Studies, University College, Galway.

Taylor, M. (1987) *The Possibility of Cooperation* (Cambridge: Cambridge University Press).

Taylor, M. (1989) 'Structure, Culture and Action in the Explanation of Social Change', *Politics and Society*, 17, pp. 115–62.

Taylor, P. (1989) 'Britain's Changing Role in the World Economy', in J. Mohan (ed.), *The Political Geography of Contemporary Britain* (London: Macmillan), pp. 18–34.

Taylor, P. (1992), 'Changing Political Relations', in P. Cloke (ed.), *Policy and Change in Thatcher's Britain* (Oxford: Pergamon Press), pp. 33–54.

Teer, F. and J. D. Spence (1973) *Political Opinion Polls* (London: Hutchinson).

Thomas, D. (1979) *Naturalism and Social Science: A Post-Empiricist Philosophy of Social Science* (Cambridge: Cambridge University Press).

Thompson, J. B. (1989) 'The Theory of Structuration', in D. Held and J. B.Thompson (eds), *Social Theory and Modern Societies*. (Cambridge: Cambridge University Press).

Thrift, N. (1985) 'Bear and Mouse or Tree and Bear? A. Giddens's Reconstruction of Social Theory', *Sociology*, 19.

Torfing, J. (1991) 'A Hegemony Approach to Capitalist Regulation', in R. Bertramsen, J. Thomsen and J. Torfing (eds), *State, Economy and Society* (London: Unwin Hyman), pp. 35–93.

Torfing, J. (1994) 'Politics, Regulation and the Modern Welfare State', PhD (University of Essex).

Truman, D. (1951) *The Governmental Process* (New York: Alfred A. Knopf).

Tufte, E. R. (1983) *The Visual Display of Quantitative Information* (Cheshire, Conn.: Graphics Press).

Tversky, A. and D. Kahneman (1982) 'Judgement Under Uncertainty: Heuristics and Biases', in Kahneman *et al.* (eds), *Judgement Under Uncertainty: Heuristics and Biases* (Cambridge: Cambridge University Press).

Tversky, A. and D. Kahneman (1986) 'Rational Choice and the Framing of Decisions', in Hogarth and Reder (eds) *Rational Choice* (Chicago: Chicago University Press).

Vanhanen, T. (1990) *The Process of Democratization: A Study of 147 States 1980–1988* (New York: Crane Russak).

Verba, S. and N. Nie (1972) *Participation in America: Political Democracy and Social Equality* (New York: Harper & Row).

Verba, S., N. Nie and J. O. Kim (1978) *Participation and Political Equality: A Seven Nation Study* (Cambridge: Cambridge University Press).

Vogel, D. (1987) 'Political Science and the Study of Corporate Power: A Dissent from the New Conventional Wisdom', *British Journal of Political Science*, 17, pp. 385–408.

Vogel, D. (1989) *Fluctuating Fortunes* (New York: Basic Books).

Wainwright, H. (1993) *Arguments for a New Left* (Oxford: Basil Blackwell).

Walby, S. (1990) *Theorising Patriarchy* (Oxford: Basil Blackwell).

Waldo, D. (1975) 'Political Science: Tradition, Discipline, Profession, Science, Enterprise', in F. I. Greenstein and N. Polsby (eds), *Handbook of Political Science. Vol. 1. Political Science: Scope and Theory* (Reading, Mass.: Addison-Wesley), pp. 1–130.

Wallas, G. (1908/1948) *Human Nature in Politics* (London: Constable).

Walzer, M. (1985) *Spheres of Justice: A Defence of Pluralism and Equality* (Oxford: Basil Blackwell).

Ward, H. (1989) '*Beyond Fred Block's Theory of the Structural Power of Capital*', Essex Papers in Politics and Government, No. 63.

Ward, H. (1993) 'State Exploitation, Capital Accumulation and the Evolution of Modes of Regulation: A Defence of "Bottom Line Economism"', Paper presented to the PSA Annual Conference, Leicester, April 1993.

Ward Schofield, J. (1993) 'Increasing the Generalisability of Qualitative Research', in M. Hammersley (ed.), *Social Research: Philosophy, Politics and Practice* (London: Sage).

Watson, S. (ed.) (1990) *Playing the State: Australian Feminist Interventions* (London: Verso).

Wax, R. H. (1971) *Doing Fieldwork: Warnings and Advice* (Chicago: University of Chicago Press).

Weber, M. (1950) *Max Weber: ein Lebensbild* (Heidelberg).

Weber, M. (1947) *The Theory of Social and Economic Organisation*, trans. and ed. A. M. Henderson and T. Parsons (New York: Free Press) pp. 328–40.

Weber, M. (1961) *General Economic History* (trans. F. H. Knight) (New York: Collier).

Welch, S. (1977) 'Women as Political Animals? A Test for Some Explanations for Male-Female Political Participation Differences', *American Journal of Political Science* , 21, (4), pp. 711–30.

Welch, S. (1980) 'Sex Differences in Political Activity in Britain', *Women and Politics*, 1, (2), pp. 29-46.

Wendt, A. (1987) 'The Agent/Structure Problem in International Relations', *International Organization*, 41, 3.

Wharton, A. S. (1991) 'Structure and Agency in Socialist-Feminist Theory', *Gender and Society*, 5, 3.

Wheare, K. C. (1946) *Federal Government* (4th edn) (London: Oxford University Press).

Whiteley, P. (1983) *The Labour Party in Crisis* (London: Methuen).
Wildavsky, A. (1978) 'Changing Forward Versus Changing Back', *Yale Law Journal*, 88, 1 (November).
Williamson, P. (1985) *Varieties of Corporatism* (Cambridge: Cambridge University Press)
Wilson, G. (1977) *Special Interests and Policy Making* (Chilchester: John Wiley).
Wilson, G. (1990) *Interest Groups* (Oxford: Basil Blackwell).
Wilson, G. (1994) 'The Westminster Model in Comparative Perspective', in I. Budge and D. McKay (eds) *Developing Democracy* (London: Sage), pp. 189–201.
Wilson, J. Q. (1973) *Political Organisations* (New York: Basic Books).
Wilson, W. (1899) *The State: Elements of Historical and Practical Politics* (London: Isbister & Co.).
Winch, P. (1958) *The Idea of a Social Science and its Relation to Philosophy* (London: Routledge & Keegan Paul).
Winchester, S. (1981) *Their Noble Lordships* (London: Faber & Faber).
Wittgenstein, L. (1961) *Tractatus Logico-Philosophicus* (London: Routledge).
Wittman, D. (1983) 'Candidate Motivation: A Synthesis of Alternative Theories', *American Political Science Review*, 77, pp. 142–57.
Wittman, D. (1991) 'An Economist's Perspective on Why Cognitive Psychology Does Not Explain Democratic Politics', in Monroe (ed.), *The Economic Approach to Politics*, pp. 405–32.
Wolf-Philips, L. (1972) *Comparative Constitutions* (London: Macmillan).
Wolin, S. (1960) *Politics and Vision* (Boston, Mass.: Little, Brown).
Woodhouse, M. B. (1994) *A Preface to Philosophy* (Cal.: Wadsworth).
Woodiwiss, A. (1990) *Social Theory after Postmodernism* (London: Pluto).
Yin, R. K. (1984) *Case Study Research: Design and Methods* (London: Sage).
Young, I. M. (1984) 'Is Male Gender Identity the Cause of Male Domination?', in J. Trebilcot (ed.), *Mothering: Essays in Feminist Theory* (Ottowa: Rowman & Allanheld).
Young, I. M. (1989) 'Polity and Group Difference: A Critique of the Ideal of Universal Citizenship', *Ethics*, 99, (2), pp. 250–74.
Young, O. (1989) *International Cooperation: Building Regimes for Natural Resources and the Environment* (Ithaca, N.Y.: Cornell University Press).
Zizek, S. (1989) *The Sublime Object of Ideology* (London: Verso).
Zuckerman, A. (1991) *Doing Political Science* (Boulder, Col.: Westview).

# Index

320